May We Quote You?

Be a part of
ZAGATSURVEY®

To join in any of our Surveys, please fill out and return this card.

☐ Mr. ☐ Mrs. ☐ Ms.
_____
Your Name

_____
Street Address   Apt. #

_____
City   State   Zip

_____
E-mail Address

_____
Occupation

I'd like to be a surveyor for the following city:

_____

or a surveyor for Hotels, Resorts & Spas ☐

To order our guides as gift copies or spares, go to
zagat.com/shop.

More to say? Join our special squad of savvy consumers to share
your opinions in all kinds of compelling polls. To sign up,
check the box below.

☐ YES, I want to participate in special Zagat polls
   throughout the year.

*   *   *

☐ This book was a gift   ☐ Bought by me   ☐ Surveyor copy

U.S. HOTEL

BUSINESS REPLY MAIL
FIRST-CLASS MAIL PERMIT NO 4064 NEW YORK, NY

POSTAGE WILL BE PAID BY ADDRESSEE

ZAGATSURVEY®
4 COLUMBUS CIRCLE FL 5
NEW YORK NY 10102-1374

ZAGAT SURVEY®

2001

TOP U.S. HOTELS, RESORTS & SPAS

Edited by David Jefferys
with Nancy Hawley

Published and distributed by
ZAGAT SURVEY, LLC
4 Columbus Circle
New York, New York 10019
Tel: 212 977 6000
E-mail: travel@zagat.com
Web site: www.zagat.com

Acknowledgments

Besides the nearly 20,000 travelers who shared their experiences with us, we are grateful to Nichole Bernier, Olga Boikess, Mark Boyden, Nikki Buchanan, Andrea Clurfeld, Amy Conway, Eric Crites, Elizabeth Curry, Bonnie Davidson, Jeanette Foster, Randy Fuller, Jennifer Hinkle, Mike Klein, Alison Leigh-Guerin, Tracy Mallozzi, Radha McLean, Ben Morse, Amy Nebens, Susan Safronoff, Shelley Sawyer, Denise Shoukas, Helen Sillett, Ron Tanner and Stephen Whitlock.

This guide would not have been possible without the following members of our staff: Al Cadalzo, Phil Cardone, Douglas Choi, Erica Curtis, Liz Daleske, Jessica Fields, Jeff Freier, Michelle Gallagher, Gail Horwood, Katie Hottinger, Yohei Igarashi, Sarah Kagan, Julia Korda, Hope LaDue, Robert Lazo, Natalie Lebert, Charles Levine, Mike Liao, Dave Makulec, Jefferson Martin, Lorraine Mead, Andrew O'Neill, Matthew Pereira, Benjamin Schmerler, Robert Seixas, Zamira Skalkottas, LaShana Smith, Sal Terillo, Danny Vera and Gail Hall Zarr.

We are especially grateful to the American Society of Travel Agents, thanks to whose cooperation we have had the professional input of over 900 travel agents and meeting planners.

Contents

About This Survey

Here are the results of our sixth travel survey since 1987, with over 1,900 hotels, resorts, spas and chains. Over 800 favorites have been elected as the "best in America."

This *Survey* is based on voting by nearly 20,000 people like you, up more than 7,000 from our last outing, in 1998. Since the average participant stayed at hotels upward of 30 nights per year, the *Survey* is based on roughly 600,000 nights at hotels per year – or viewed another way, 1,630 visits per night. For the top properties listed in this book, there were, on average, 265 surveyors per hotel and resort, 125 per spa and 1,670 per chain. Most of these people spent several nights at the properties on which they voted, thus it is safe to say that there were one or more of our surveyors staying in every place, every night of the year.

Our surveyors are roughly equally divided between men and women, with 12% in their 20s; 24%, 30s; 23%, 40s; 26%, 50s; and 15% in their 60s or older. We are especially grateful to the American Society of Travel Agents, who helped us gain the participation of more than 900 travel professionals. Their in-depth knowledge and expertise gives this guide an extra dimension – next time you call your travel agent, think of this book, in which a metaphoric 900 experts are answering your call. Knowing that the quality of this *Survey* is the direct result of the thoughtful voting and commentary of all our surveyors, we sincerely thank each and every one of them. This book is dedicated to them; they are its real authors.

On the assumption that most people are eager for quick information about the places at which they are considering staying, we have tried to keep all reviews as concise as possible, and we've created a number of "best" lists and handy indexes throughout the book.

Though all ratings and reviews come from our surveyors, all factual information in this *Survey* was gathered directly from the hotels, resorts and spas themselves, and we have made every effort to be as up-to-date as possible. Because the travel industry changes so fast, we have added new properties right up to our publication date.

We invite you to be a reviewer in our future travel surveys. Simply send a SASE marked "Travel" to ZAGAT SURVEY, 4 Columbus Circle, New York, NY 10019, or e-mail us at travel@zagat.com. Each participant will receive a free copy of the next *Survey* when it is published.

Your suggestions on this guidebook are also solicited. There is always room for improvement with your help.

New York, New York
November 17, 2000

Nina and Tim

Nina and Tim Zagat

What's New

The travel industry has gone through a revolution in the last decade: the buying, selling, renaming and reinventing of hotel and resort chains has become a new form of Monopoly. In the process, stalwart brands like Hilton, Fairmont and Inter-Continental, whose reputations had been hard-won over decades, have been diluted, and new brands such as St. Regis and W Hotels have evolved into leaders for the consumer. All these changes leave travelers, at least for the moment, with fewer road markers for their voyages across the country. Fortunately, there are some beacons.

Top Performers: The top two hotel chains from this *Survey,* Four Seasons and Ritz-Carlton, have maintained their standards of excellence with extraordinary flair, service and fine dining. Both chains are renowned for their urban locations but increasingly for resort destinations as well, with such properties as the new Four Seasons Scottsdale at Troon North and the slated opening of the Ritz-Carlton Lodge, Reynolds Plantation outside of Atlanta. At either chain, one picks up the phone and is addressed by name and it's hard to walk down the hall without getting a smile or a kind word from each and every hotel employee – we're talking real hospitality. If the Ritz-Carlton has a single fault, it's that all of its hotels tend to look like an English club – which may work in Boston but doesn't necessarily work on the beach in Hawaii. The Four Seasons hotels tend to be more individualistic, reflecting their surroundings, with one common denominator: luxury.

All Roads Lead East: High-end hotel chains from the Far East (you'll be reading more about them in our forthcoming survey of *Top International Hotels, Resorts & Spas*) are consistently applauded for quality and service by our surveyors and have begun to expand vigorously here in the U.S. The Peninsula Group manages three properties stateside and is set to open in Chicago in 2001. The Mandarin Oriental Group has four properties, is opening (as we go to press) in Miami and plans to crown the corner of New York City's Central Park at Columbus Circle by 2003. Amanresorts, famed for its small luxury hideaways in Asia, has recently launched its first U.S. outpost, Amangani in Wyoming.

The *Wallpaper** Effect: Smaller lodgings infused with quirky character and designer touches – known as boutique hotels – have burgeoned in the U.S. during the last several years. These unique properties are often fashioned from vintage buildings and managed and marketed in collections, like Ian Schrager's Royalton and Hudson (NYC), Delano (Miami) and Mondrian (LA); likewise Bill Kimpton's Prescott (SF) and Alexis (Seattle). The success of these hotels, which emphasize style and price, has resulted in a niche appealing to a young, hip, good-looking clientele (visit a lobby of Schrager's and you'll see what we mean). Boutique hotels have not gone unnoticed by the large American brands, which are diversifying their presence to capture this younger, trendy market. The proliferation of Starwood's W brand is but one example of this.

The Business Traveler and the Internet Effect: The need to stay connected – whether with home or the home office – has been embraced by the hotel industry, making things like voicemail, multiple phones with multiple lines, in-room fax machines and high-speed Internet connections (see our Index) de rigueur. Hilton's Embassy Suites feature two-room configurations, allowing enough space for meetings and making extended stays more comfortable. Rooms at any Courtyard by Marriott location have sitting areas and large desks designed with the business traveler in mind.

Personal Touches: Our surveyors were struck by a new focus on the quality of things like bed linens, lighting, signature toiletries and creative room-service and mini-bar choices. As the number of women business travelers continues to grow, hotels have responded with more secure room and floor avail-ability, comfortable single-dining venues and appropriate amenities. The ability via technology to track and log repeat guests not only allows hotels to provide frequent-stay privileges but also enables them to provide higher levels of customer service – frequent guests at the Peninsula Beverly Hills even enjoy monogrammed pillowcases.

Relaxation Techniques: With the average trip away from home getting shorter and shorter and often combining busi-ness with pleasure, there's less time these days for an indulgent stay at a destination spa. Our health-conscious surveyors voted enthusiastically on what has become an industry trend: the full-service resort or hotel with first-rate spa facilities. Check out our "Top Spas" lists and Spas section to see the winners – in both categories.

High Occupancy/Higher Rates: In the last decade we have seen the hotel industry move from a buyer's market – where discounts proliferated – to a seller's market. The strong economy has led to a predictable increase in room rates. Thus it's harder to negotiate deep discounts these days, especially at the top properties, but there are plenty of deals to be had. Remember: Don't be shy – negotiate, or at least try (see "Travel Tips").

Value: Since our last full *Survey* two years ago, average room rates of Top Hotels (our surveys focus on the better hotels in most cities, not all hotels) have climbed 25% in Los Angeles and 22% in Chicago. New York City still has the most expensive room rates in the country, climbing 27% since 1998 to an average of $377.80. However, New York City is a good value when compared with other world capitals, as you will see in our forthcoming *Top International Hotels, Resorts & Spas*. This may also explain why you hear so many foreign accents in leading hotels across the country.

New York, New York   David Jefferys
November 17, 2000

Travel Tips

Remember this motto: "Ask and you will receive." Inquire about services you need, anticipate problems and don't hesitate to negotiate for the lowest rate available or request upgrades – if you don't, you won't get them.

Get the Best Rates: Check into discounts obtained via corporate affiliations, club and society memberships, senior citizen qualifications, even frequent-flyer specials. When a rate is quoted, always ask: "Is this the lowest price you have?"

Know Whom to Call: If you want to secure the best deal, you must talk to the people on the scene. Many hotels' toll-free numbers are answered by national operators with limited flexibility for bargaining. Alternatively, try one of the hotel brokers who reserve blocks of rooms in major cities in advance and sell them at savings of up to 60% off published room rates (see "Important Web Sites & Toll-Free Numbers"). Of course, if you have a travel agent you know and trust, this may be the way to go.

Research Online: These days, browsing the Internet for property descriptions, photos and maps is simply good sense. For your convenience we have included Web site addresses for places listed throughout this guide. You can often find great deals, including city hotel weekend packages, midweek resort specials and off-season discounts, just about everywhere.

Check the Facts: You should always ask specific questions about the room you are reserving. Does it have a view, balcony, interconnecting doors, kitchenette, bathtub or shower, disabled access, etc.? If possible, have the hotel confirm these facts in writing.

Look for More Details: Ask if there are renovations, conventions or major parties during your stay. With resorts, make sure you are aware of hidden costs; many add a "resort fee" to room rates. The same attention applies to hotel taxes (as much as 15%) and phone/fax charges (a major profit center for many hotels and a major pain in the neck for customers). To the extent it is relevant, ask about special features: business/concierge floors, high-speed computer connections, multi-line phones, voicemail, nonsmoking rooms or childcare.

Don't Be Afraid to Complain: If you've been given an unsatisfactory room, call the front desk and ask for the manager. Calmly explain the problem, and be firm in your request to change rooms. If something needs repair, ask when it will be fixed. Assume that any decent hotel will want to please you, however, should you be treated poorly you have some recourse: Send a letter to the hotel's general manager and parent company stating your case clearly and concisely, indicating that copies have been sent to Zagat Survey and the local newspaper editor (a wonderful way of getting the hotel's attention).

Key to Ratings/Symbols

Name, Address, Phone Numbers, Fax, Web Site, Rooms

Zagat Ratings

	R	S	D	P	$
TIM & NINA'S INN	▽ 16	5	4	22	$150

4 Columbus Circle; 212-977-6000; fax 212-977-9760;
800-977-9000; www.zagat.com; 20 rooms (2 suites)

☑ Despite "dazzling views" of Central Park and "lovely public spaces", surveyors are split over this "miniscule" "mini-priced" Midtown boutique hotel; fans tout its "handy location", but critics knock "rooms too small to change your mind", dining at Chez Z that's "outshone by the corner hot dog stand" and a staff that "makes Attica guards seem agreeable."

Review, with surveyors' comments in quotes

• Properties with top ratings are shown in **CAPITAL LETTERS**.

• The total number of rooms per property is followed by the number of suites, etc. as a subset, e.g. 20 rooms (2 suites).

• **Ratings:** Rooms, Service, Dining and Public Spaces/Facilities of Hotels and Resorts are rated on a scale of **0** to **30** as follows:

R	Rooms	S	Service	D	Dining	P	Public Spaces/Facilities
16		5		4		22	

• In the Spas section **T** = Treatments/Facilities

10–15 fair to good	**20–25** very good to excellent
16–19 good to very good	**26–30** extraordinary to perfection
▽ low voting/less reliable	

• The Cost ($) column reflects surveyors' recollected estimated price for a double room for one night and *should be used only as a benchmark,* since rates vary by season and even time of week. They may also be affected by special discounts, packages and number of guests in the party.

• A property listed without ratings/comments is a write-in or an important newcomer. In these cases, as well as for Hotel Chains and Spas, cost is indicated by the following symbols:

I	Inexpensive, below $150	**E**	Expensive, $250–$349
M	Moderate, $150–$249	**VE**	Very Expensive, $350 & up

• The following symbols indicate whether comments were uniform ■ or mixed ☑.

• For "top" and "best" lists throughout, the numerical score is the overall average rating, and the letter abbreviations are defined as follows: **H** = Hotel; **R** = Resort; **SR** = Small Resort; **SI** = Small Inn; **SL** = Small Lodge.

Important Web Sites & Toll-Free Numbers

HOTEL CHAIN	WEB SITE	PHONE
Adam's Mark	adamsmark.com	800-444-2326
Amanresorts	amanresorts.com	877-734-7333
Best Western	bestwestern.com	800-528-1234
Caesars	caesars.com	800-223-7277
Clarion	clarionhotel.com	800-252-7466
Courtyard by Marriott	courtyard.com	800-321-2211
Crowne Plaza	crowneplaza.com	800-227-6963
Days Inn	daysinn.com	800-325-2525
DoubleTree	doubletree.com	800-222-8733
Embassy Suites	embassy-suites.com	800-362-2779
Fairfield Inns	fairfieldinn.com	800-228-2800
Fairmont	fairmont.com	800-527-4727
Four Seasons	fourseasons.com	800-332-3442
Hampton Inn	hamptoninn.com	800-426-4329
Harrah's	harrahs.com	800-427-7247
Hilton	hilton.com	800-774-1500
Hilton Garden Inn	hilton.com	800-774-1500
Holiday Inn	holiday-inn.com	800-465-4329
Homewood Suites	homewood-suites.com	800-225-5466
Hyatt	hyatt.com	800-233-1234
Inter-Continental	interconti.com	800-327-0200
La Quinta Inns	laquinta.com	800-531-5900
Leading Hotels	lhw.com	800-223-6800
Le Meridien	lemeridien.com	800-543-4300
Loews Hotels	loewshotels.com	800-235-6397
Luxury Collection	luxurycollection.com	800-325-3589
MainStay Suites	mainstaysuites.com	800-660-6246
Mandarin Oriental	mandarinoriental.com	800-526-6566
Marriott	marriott.com	800-228-9290
Nikko	nikkohotels.com	800-645-5687
Omni	omnihotels.com	800-843-6664
Pan Pacific	panpac.com	800-327-8585
Park Hyatt	parkhyatt.com	800-633-7313
Peninsula	peninsula.com	800-262-9467
Preferred Hotels	preferredhotels.com	800-323-7500
Radisson	radisson.com	800-333-3333
Ramada	ramada.com	800-272-6232
Red Lion	redlion.com	800-733-5466
Regent	regenthotels.com	800-545-4000
Relais & Châteaux	relaischateaux.com	800-735-2478
Renaissance	marriotthotels.com	800-468-3571
Residence Inn	residenceinn.com	800-331-3131
Ritz-Carlton	ritzcarlton.com	800-241-3333
Rosewood	rosewood-hotels.com	888-767-3966
Sheraton	sheraton.com	800-325-3535

HOTEL CHAIN	WEB SITE	PHONE
Small Luxury Hotels	slh.com	800-525-4800
Sonesta	sonesta.com	800-766-3782
St. Regis	stregis.com	800-759-7550
Swissôtel	swissotel.com	888-737-9477
Westin	westin.com	800-228-3000
W Hotels	whotels.com	877-946-8357
Wyndham	wyndham.com	800-822-4200

AIRLINE

AirTran	airtran.com	800-247-8726
Alaska Airlines	alaskaair.com	800-426-0333
Aloha Airlines	alohaair.com	800-367-5250
American	aa.com	800-433-7300
America West	americawest.com	800-235-9292
Continental	continental.com	800-525-0280
Delta	delta-air.com	800-221-1212
Frontier	frontierairlines.com	800-432-1359
Hawaiian Airlines	hawaiianair.com	800-367-5320
JetBlue	jetblue.com	800-538-2583
Legend	legendairlines.com	877-359-5343
Midway	midwayair.com	800-446-4392
Midwest Express	midwestexpress.com	800-452-2022
Northwest	nwa.com	800-225-2525
Southwest	iflyswa.com	800-435-9792
Sun Country	suncountry.com	800-359-6786
TWA	twa.com	800-221-2000
United	united.com	800-241-6522
US Airways	usairways.com	800-428-4322

CAR RENTAL

Alamo	goalamo.com	800-327-9633
Avis	avis.com	800-331-1212
Budget	budget.com	800-527-0700
Dollar	dollarcar.com	800-800-4000
Enterprise	pickenterprise.com	800-325-8007
Hertz	hertz.com	800-654-3131
National	nationalcar.com	800-227-7368
Payless	paylesscar.com	800-729-5377
Thrifty	thrifty.com	800-367-2277

RAILROAD

Amtrak	amtrak.com	800-872-7245

BUS

Greyhound	greyhound.com	800-231-2222

HOTEL BROKER

Accom. Express	accommodationsexpress.com	800-444-7666
Hotel Res. Network	hoteldiscounts.com	800-964-6835
Priceline	priceline.com	866-925-5373
Quikbook	quikbook.com	800-789-9887
USA Hotels	1800usahotels.com	800-872-4683

OTHER

AAA		800-222-4357
Western Union		800-325-6000

Top Ratings[†]

Top 20 Hotel Chains

29 Four Seasons (29)
28 Ritz-Carlton (23)
26 Park/Grand Hyatt (12)
25 Fairmont (10)
24 W Hotels (20)
   Hyatt Regency (81)
   Inter-Continental (12)
23 Loews (13)
   Westin (59)
   Renaissance (44)
22 Marriott (263)
   Hyatt (120)
   Omni (36)
21 Harrah's (21)
   Wyndham (150)
   Residence Inn (335)
   Embassy Suites (151)
   Hilton (227)
20 Sheraton (192)
   Homewood Suites (92)

The number to the left of each chain's name is its Overall Rating, the average of its scores for Rooms, Service and Public Facilities. The number in parenthesis after the chain's name reflects the number of U.S. properties in its chain.

The above list is made up of hotel chains with a minimum of 10 properties in the United States and does not include marketing companies that represent collections of hotels and resorts (such as Leading Hotels of the World, Preferred Hotels, Relais & Châteaux and Small Luxury Hotels). To be represented by any of these marketing groups, especially Leading Hotels or the Relais, a hotel or resort must meet rigorous standards. Thus, the traveler who makes a reservation through any of these companies can be assured of staying in a hotel of quality. Surveyor reviews for these marketing companies and other noteworthy hotel chains can be found in the Hotel Chains section.

---

† Excluding hotels, resorts & spas with low voting.

Top 50 Hotels

28 Four Seasons, *New York City*
Four Seasons, *Chicago*
Mansion on Turtle Creek, *Dallas*
Peninsula, *Los Angeles*
Four Seasons, *Las Vegas*
Windsor Court, *New Orleans*
Ritz-Carlton (A Four Seasons Hotel), *Chicago*
Ritz-Carlton, *San Francisco*
Four Seasons, *Boston*
Four Seasons Beverly Hills, *Los Angeles*
Four Seasons, *Philadelphia*

27 Ritz-Carlton Buckhead, *Atlanta*
Ritz-Carlton Huntington, *Los Angeles*
Four Seasons, *Washington, DC*
Four Seasons, *Newport Beach, CA*
St. Regis, *New York City*
Four Seasons, *Austin*
Four Seasons, *Atlanta*
L'Ermitage, *Los Angeles*
Ritz-Carlton, *St. Louis*
Four Seasons, *Houston*
Shutters on the Beach, *Los Angeles*
Four Seasons Olympic, *Seattle*
Sherman House, *San Francisco*
Regent Beverly Wilshire, *Los Angeles*

26 Mandarin Oriental, *San Francisco*
St. Regis, *Aspen**
Ritz-Carlton Pentagon City, *Arlington, VA*
Ritz-Carlton, *Phoenix*
Ritz-Carlton Tyson's Corner, *McLean, VA*
Pierre, *New York City*
Peninsula, *New York City*
Mark, *New York City*
Carlyle, *New York City*
Crescent Court, *Dallas*
Ritz-Carlton Marina del Rey, *Los Angeles**
Beverly Hills Hotel, *Los Angeles*
Ritz-Carlton, *Boston*
Ritz-Carlton, *Cleveland*
Ritz-Carlton, *Atlanta*
Casa Del Mar, *Los Angeles*
Boston Harbor, *Boston*
Willard Inter-Continental, *Washington, DC*
du Pont, *Wilmington, DE*
Hilton at Short Hills, *NJ*
Plaza Athénée, *New York City*

25 Wyndham Grand Bay, *Miami*
Campton Place, *San Francisco*
St. Regis, *Washington, DC*
New York Palace, *New York City*

---

* Tied with the hotel listed directly above it.

Top 50 Resorts*

29 Four Seasons Hualalai, *Big Island, HI*
Lodge at Koele, *Lanai, HI*
Four Seasons Wailea, *Maui, HI*
28 Ritz-Carlton, *Naples, FL*
Halekulani, *Oahu, HI*
Four Seasons Aviara, *San Diego*
Manele Bay, *Lanai, HI*
Boulders, *Carefree, AZ*
Phoenician, *Scottsdale*
Ritz-Carlton Laguna Niguel, *Dana Point, CA*
Ritz-Carlton Rancho Mirage, *Rancho Mirage, CA*
Bellagio, *Las Vegas*
Ritz-Carlton, *Palm Beach, FL*
Greenbrier, *White Sulphur Springs, WV*
27 Mauna Lani Bay, *Big Island, HI*
Ritz-Carlton Kapalua, *Maui, HI*
Kahala Mandarin Oriental, *Oahu, HI*
Inn at Spanish Bay, *Carmel, CA*
Ritz-Carlton, *Amelia Island, FL*
Four Seasons, *Palm Beach, FL*
Four Seasons at Troon North, *Scottsdale*
Princeville, *Kauai, HI***
Kea Lani, *Maui, HI*
Grand Wailea, *Maui, HI*
Hyatt Regency, *Kauai, HI*
Cloister, *Sea Island, GA*
Four Seasons at Las Colinas, *Irving, TX*
Orchid at Mauna Lani, *Big Island, HI*
Royal Palms, *Phoenix***
Four Seasons Biltmore, *Santa Barbara, CA*
Lodge at Pebble Beach, *Pebble Beach, CA*
Stein Eriksen Lodge, *Park City, UT*
Caneel Bay, *St. John, USVI*
Broadmoor, *Colorado Springs*
26 Ritz-Carlton, *St. Thomas, USVI*
Enchantment, *Sedona, AZ*
American Club, *Kohler, WI*
Arizona Biltmore, *Phoenix*
Kona Village, *Big Island, HI*
Peaks, *Telluride, CO*
Turnberry Isle, *Miami***
Homestead, *Hot Springs, VA*
Disney's Grand Floridian, *Orlando*
JW Marriott Ihilani, *Oahu, HI*
Breakers, *Palm Beach, FL*
Loews Ventana Canyon, *Tucson*
Westin Mauna Kea, *Big Island, HI*
Fairmont Scottsdale Princess, *Scottsdale*
Villas of Grand Cypress, *Orlando*
Ritz-Carlton, *San Juan, PR*

---

* Resorts with 100 or more rooms.
** Tied with the resort listed directly above it.

Top 50 Small Resorts, Inns & Lodges*

29 Twin Farms, *Barnard, VT*
   Point, *Saranac Lake, NY*
28 Inn at Little Washington, *Washington, VA*
   Blackberry Farm, *Walland, TN*
   Bel-Air, *Los Angeles*
   Chateau du Sureau, *Oakhurst, CA*
   Post Ranch Inn, *Big Sur, CA*
   Rancho Valencia, *Rancho Santa Fe, CA*
   Auberge du Soleil, *Napa, CA*
   Little Nell, *Aspen*
27 Lodge & Spa at Cordillera, *Edwards, CO*
   Blantyre, *Lenox, MA*
   Marquesa, *Keys, FL*
   Amangani, *Jackson, WY*
   Richmond Hill Inn, *Asheville, NC*
   Las Casitas, *Fajardo, PR*
   Horned Dorset Primavera, *Rincon, PR*
   Mayflower Inn, *Washington, CT*
   Meadowood, *Napa, CA*
   Inn at Perry Cabin, *St. Michaels, MD*
   Lake Placid Lodge, *Lake Placid, NY*
   Ventana Inn, *Big Sur, CA*
   Fearrington House, *Pittsboro, NC*
   Sherman House, *San Francisco*
   Little Palm Island, *Keys, FL*
   San Ysidro Ranch, *Santa Barbara, CA*
26 Inn at National Hall, *Westport, CT*
   Inn at Shelburne Farms, *Shelburne, VT*
   White Barn Inn, *Kennebunkport, ME*
   Charlotte Inn, *Martha's Vineyard, MA*
   Fisher Island Club, *Miami*
   Keswick Hall, *Charlottesville, VA*
   Bernardus Lodge, *Carmel, CA*
   Wauwinet, *Nantucket, MA*
   Inn at Sawmill Farm, *West Dover, VT*
   Inn of the Anasazi, *Santa Fe*
   Morrison House, *Alexandria, VA*
   Soniat House, *New Orleans*
   Sonnenalp, *Vail*
   Hana-Maui, *Maui, HI*
   Lodge & Club, *Ponte Vedra, FL*
   L'Auberge de Sedona, *Sedona, AZ*
   Bellevue Club, *Seattle*
25 Salish Lodge, *Snoqualmie, WA*
   Kenwood Inn, *Sonoma, CA*
   Inn at Irving Place, *New York City*
   Rusty Parrot Lodge, *Jackson, WY*
   Lodge at Ventana, *Tucson*
   Castle at Tarrytown, *Tarrytown, NY*
   Arizona Inn, *Tucson*

---

* Resorts, inns and lodges with fewer than 100 rooms.

Top Places by Region

California
28 Bel-Air, *Los Angeles*/SR
    Peninsula Beverly Hills, *Los Angeles*/H
    Chateau du Sureau, *Oakhurst*/SI
    Four Seasons Aviara, *San Diego*/R
    Ritz-Carlton, *San Francisco*/H
    Post Ranch Inn, *Big Sur*/SR
    Four Seasons Beverly Hills, *Los Angeles*/H
    Rancho Valencia Resort, *San Diego*/SR

Florida
28 Ritz-Carlton, *Naples*/R
    Ritz-Carlton, *Palm Beach*/R
27 Ritz-Carlton, *Amelia Island*/R
    Four Seasons, *Palm Beach*/R
    Marquesa, *Keys*/SR
    Little Palm Island, *Keys*/SR
26 Turnberry Isle, *Miami*/R
    Disney's Grand Floridian, *Orlando*/R

Hawaii
29 Four Seasons Hualalai, *Big Island*/R
    Lodge at Koele, *Lanai*/R
    Four Seasons Wailea, *Maui*/R
28 Halekulani, *Oahu*/R
    Manele Bay, *Lanai*/R
27 Mauna Lani Bay, *Big Island*/R
    Ritz-Carlton Kapalua, *Maui*/R
    Kahala Mandarin Oriental, *Oahu*/R

Mid-Atlantic (DC, DE, MD, PA, VA, WV)
28 Inn at Little Washington, *Washington, VA*/SI
    Four Seasons, *Philadelphia*/H
    Greenbrier, *White Sulphur Springs, WV*/R
27 Four Seasons, *Washington, DC*/H
    Inn at Perry Cabin, *St. Michaels, MD*/SI
26 Ritz-Carlton Pentagon City, *Arlington, VA*/H
    Homestead, *Hot Springs, VA*/R
    Ritz-Carlton Tyson's Corner, *McLean, VA*/H

Midwest (IL, IN, MI, MN, MO, OH, OK, WI)
28 Four Seasons, *Chicago*/H
    Ritz-Carlton, *Chicago*/H
27 Ritz-Carlton, *St. Louis*/H
26 American Club, *Kohler, WI*/R
    Ritz-Carlton, *Cleveland*/H
25 Ritz-Carlton, *Dearborn, MI*/H
    Townsend, *Birmingham, MI*/H
    Grand, *Mackinac Island, MI*/R

New England (MA, ME, NH, RI, VT)
29 Twin Farms, *Barnard, VT*/SI
28 Four Seasons, *Boston*/H
27 Blantyre, *Lenox, MA*/SR
26 Inn at Shelburne Farms, *Shelburne, VT*/SI
White Barn Inn, *Kennebunkport, ME*/SI
Charlotte Inn, *Martha's Vineyard, MA*/SI
Wauwinet, *Nantucket, MA*/SI
Inn at Sawmill Farm, *West Dover, VT*/SI

Pacific Northwest (OR, WA)
27 Four Seasons Olympic, *Seattle*/H
26 Bellevue Club, *Seattle*/H
25 Salish Lodge, *Snoqualmie, WA*/SL
W, *Seattle*/H
Monaco, *Seattle*/H
Inn at Langley, *Whidbey Island, WA*/SI
Inn at the Market, *Seattle*/SI
24 Heathman, *Portland, OR*/H

Rocky Mountains (CO, ID, MT, NV, UT, WY)
28 Four Seasons, *Las Vegas*/H
Bellagio, *Las Vegas*/H
Little Nell, *Aspen*/H
27 Lodge & Spa at Cordillera, *Edwards, CO*/SL
Amangani, *Jackson, WY*/SR
Stein Eriksen Lodge, *Park City, UT*/SL
Broadmoor, *Colorado Springs*/R
26 St. Regis, *Aspen*/H

Southeast (AL, AR, GA, KY, LA, MS, NC, SC, TN)
28 Windsor Court, *New Orleans*/H
27 Ritz-Carlton Buckhead, *Atlanta*/H
Richmond Hill Inn, *Asheville, NC*/SI
Cloister, *Sea Island, GA*/R
Four Seasons, *Atlanta*/H
Fearrington House Country Inn, *Pittsboro, NC*/SI
26 Pinehurst Resort, *Pinehurst, NC*/R
Ritz-Carlton, *Atlanta*/H

Southwest (AZ, NM)
28 Boulders, *Carefree, AZ*/R
Phoenician, *Scottsdale*/R
27 Four Seasons Troon North, *Scottsdale*/R
Royal Palms, *Phoenix*/R
26 Enchantment Resort, *Sedona, AZ*/R
Arizona Biltmore, *Phoenix*/R
Ritz-Carlton, *Phoenix*/H
Loews Ventana Canyon, *Tucson*/R

Texas

28 Mansion on Turtle Creek, *Dallas*/H
27 Four Seasons Las Colinas, *Dallas*/R
Four Seasons, *Austin*/H
Four Season, *Houston*/H
26 Crescent Court, *Dallas*/H
25 Westin La Cantera, *San Antonio*/R
Lancaster, *Houston*/H
Houstonian, *Houston*/H
Hyatt Regency Hill Country, *San Antonio*/R

Tri-State (CT, NJ, NY)

29 Point, *Saranac Lake, NY*/SL
28 Four Seasons, *New York City*/H
27 St. Regis, *New York City*/H
Mayflower, *Washington, CT*/SI
Lake Placid Lodge, *Lake Placid, NY*/SL
26 Inn at National Hall, *Westport, CT*/SI
Pierre, *New York City*/H
Peninsula, *New York City*/H

U.S. Caribbean

27 Horned Dorset, *Rincon, Puerto Rico*/SR
Caneel Bay, *St. John, U.S. Virgin Islands*/R
26 Ritz-Carlton, *St. Thomas, U.S. Virgin Islands*/R
Ritz-Carlton, *San Juan, Puerto Rico*/R
25 Wyndham El Conquistador, *Fajardo, Puerto Rico*/R
24 Westin, *St. John, U.S. Virgin Islands*/R
Carambola Beach, *St. Croix, U.S. Virgin Islands*/R
Wyndham El San Juan, *San Juan, Puerto Rico*/H

Top 10 Stand-Alone Spas

29 Miraval, *Catalina, AZ*
28 Golden Door, *Escondido, CA*
Greenhouse, *Arlington, TX*
Canyon Ranch, *Tucson*
27 Cal-a-Vie, *Vista, CA*
Canyon Ranch, *Lenox, MA*
25 Ten Thousand Waves, *Santa Fe*
24 Two Bunch Palms, *Desert Hot Springs, CA*
Green Mountain at Fox Run, *Ludlow, VT*

Top 10 Hotel Spas

29 Four Seasons Hualalai, *Big Island, HI*
Four Seasons Wailea, *Maui, HI*
28 Boulders, *Carefree, AZ*
Post Ranch Inn, *Big Sur, CA*
Hyatt Regency, *Kauai, HI*
Four Seasons, *New York City*
Phoenician, *Scottsdale*
Four Seasons Aviara, *San Diego*
Ritz-Carlton, *Naples, FL*
27 Four Seasons, *Palm Beach, FL*

Hotel Chains

Clarion
17 | 16 | 15 | I

800-252-7466; www.clarionhotel.com

☑ While this "basic" chain may be "inconsistent" (critics carp that some of the 124 lodgings are "low end" and "can be shabby around the edges"), fans say they're a "good buy" – "clean and safe, which is sometimes just what you need."

Courtyard by Marriott
20 | 19 | 17 | I

800-321-2211; www.courtyard.com

■ "Modern and well maintained", the 462 locations of this Marriott sub-brand may be "a bit boring" but make "a good standby: always clean, with good service and a reasonable price"; fans like that "you know up front what you're getting", including rooms in a "cookie-cutter layout", with a desk and dataport for business travelers, and "fitness centers that place it above the competition."

Crowne Plaza
21 | 20 | 19 | M

800-227-6963; www.crowneplaza.com

■ A "reliable mid-to-upscale chain", these "best hotels in the Holiday Inn family" (with some 75 nationwide) are "clean and efficient for business stays", and surveyors say they're also a "good choice when not on an expense account"; while some think they're "dull and safe", most agree they're "quite comfortable, sometimes even elegant" and "not bad for the money."

DoubleTree
21 | 20 | 19 | I

800-222-8733; www.doubletree.com

■ Part of the Hilton group since 1999, these "mid-level hotels" (159 among its standard Hotels, roomier Guest Suites and businesslike Club Hotels) win loyalty with "cookies at check-in", "roomy rooms" that are "good for business travel" or "for kids sharing quarters with parents" and locations that are often "near airports."

EMBASSY SUITES HOTELS
23 | 20 | 20 | I

800-362-2779; www.embassy-suites.com

☑ These "fair deal" hotels (there are 151 nationwide) are "often the best available in odd places" – "the name to look for when on the road for business" or traveling with the kids; all-suite, two-room layouts are "well set up for computers" and come with "free breakfast" and "complimentary evening cocktails"; surveyors like that the chain is "now a part of HHonors program" but wish this "leader of the pack" weren't such a "zoo."

Fairfield Inns by Marriott
18 | 17 | 15 | I

800-228-2800; www.fairfieldinn.com

■ "One of the best of the low-cost, no-frills motels", this "clean and cheap" chain of 430 properties is a "good value on the road", with "all you need for a night or two", such as "comfy rooms", "safety-minded management" and complimentary breakfast.

FAIRMONT
25 | 25 | 25 | M

800-527-4727; www.fairmont.com

☑ "Class without condescension" is the word on the 10 outstanding grande dames that are "an experience in luxury and stateliness"; a minority grouses about "inconsistency", however loyalists love the "glamorous" public spaces at the chain's nine hotels and one resort in the U.S. and tout them as "always a good bet – especially if you are unfamiliar with the destination."

FOUR SEASONS HOTELS & RESORTS　　　| 29 | 29 | 29 | E |
800-332-3442; www.fourseasons.com

■ As the top-rated chain in this *Survey* – with seven of 11 top-ranked hotels and two of the three top-rated resorts – it's not surprising that this group gets "extravagant" praise: the gold standard", "impeccable service", "wonderful rooms", "superb food", "staff who always smiles and knows your name" and "fabulous gym facilities"; "you get what you pay for" in life, but these 29, 29-rated American city and resort locations don't seem that expensive given all they offer, including "without a doubt the most comfortable beds in the hotel industry"; P.S. its three Regent hotels, in NY, LA and Vegas, are no slouches either.

Hampton Inn　　　　　　　　| 19 | 18 | 16 | I |
800-426-4329; www.hamptoninn.com

■ "On a budget" business road trip and need a "one-nighter"?; you can't do much better than this "no-nonsense" chain's "dependably" "clean", "quiet" and "safe" rooms in more than 1,040 locations, which come with "complimentary Continental breakfast"; for a big bed bang-for-the-buck, bounce on in.

HARRAH'S　　　　　　　　　| 21 | 21 | 21 | I |
800-427-7247; www.harrahs.com

■ "If you like casinos in the lobby" of your hotel, then it's a good bet you'll feel like a winner at this "very player-friendly", "garish" gambling outfit's convenient "comfortable" lodgings (there are 21 casino hotels in all), "which serve a purpose" in between marathon blackjack and buffet sessions.

HILTON　　　　　　　　　　| 21 | 20 | 20 | M |
800-774-1500; www.hilton.com

☑ "In a strange place, seeing a Hilton is like a beacon at sea" is most surveyors' view of the "no-nonsense" hotels and resorts of this "dependable" chain "priced just right" with "a great rewards system" and "weekend Internet specials"; considered better "for conferences than individuals", the chain maintains "decent rooms" at more than 227 "convenient locations"; however, "some are impressive while others are surprisingly outdated", so "do your homework before you book."

Hilton Garden Inn　　　　　| 20 | 18 | 18 | I |
800-774-1500; www.hilton.com

■ "Business travelers" find themselves "pleasantly surprised" with the accommodations and amenities ("I like the broadband connections") at these relatively new "upscale value chain" outlets (79 properties nationwide), which some insist are even "better than a lot of the traditional Hiltons."

Holiday Inn　　　　　　　　| 16 | 16 | 15 | I |
800-465-4329; www.holiday-inn.com

☑ "What would we do without them?" ask surveyors about this "no-frills" chain that offers guests "a good, clean place to sleep" (especially for "unplanned highway stops"), where "the best surprise is no surprise" in "basic accommodations at budget prices"; though "competent" in almost all respects, the 1,147 properties vary from "shopworn" to "attractive", with the Sunspree and Express brands winning favor over "tin standard" flagships.

HOMEWOOD SUITES
800-225-5466; www.homewood-suites.com

22 | 19 | 18 | I

■ "Roomy rooms" that feel "like a home away from home" and come complete with full kitchens are the hallmark of this "value chain for families" and business travelers on "extended stays"; don't be surprised if a visit "exceeds your expectations" and makes you reassess your tiny, big-city apartment after a night in one of the 92 locations.

HYATT
800-233-1234; www.hyatt.com

22 | 22 | 22 | M

■ "Respectable" and "dignified" are apt words to describe this "efficiently run" chain of business-oriented "upscale, large-city hotels", which often feature "lovely public spaces", if not the big atriums of the Grand Hyatts; a clear "cut above" the budget places, they also impress with perks like a frequent-guest program honored at all 120 hotels and resorts.

HYATT REGENCY
800-233-1234; www.hyatt.com

24 | 24 | 24 | M

■ "A distinct step up from regular Hyatts", these hotels may turn out "cookie-cutter rooms, but you know what to expect" from this "trustworthy" name: "solid value" for "nice rooms", "always-accommodating" service and "well-maintained" public spaces ("big atriums, lots of plants"), if "lacking a certain flair"; considering there are more than 80 of them, this chain rates well "in terms of overall satisfaction."

INTER-CONTINENTAL HOTELS & RESORTS
800-327-0200; www.interconti.com

25 | 24 | 24 | M

☑ "Very businesslike (too much so for a pleasure stay)", the 12 American locations are reportedly "very uneven from hotel to hotel, city to city"; the "very good" ones please guests with "interesting architecture and individual personalities", but the "nothing-special" sorts appear to be "slipping badly"; although "some are hit-or-miss, generally they're outstanding", and world travelers assert that the "chain operates better internationally."

Kimpton Group
800-546-7866; www.kimptongroup.com

– | – | – | M

With a diverse and affordable collection of 27 city hotels in the West and now expanding eastward, the Kimpton Group injects a playful style into its design and management of small and mid-sized properties (all renovated, older buildings – most with a signature lobby fireplace) that appeal to travelers looking for a more colorful experience, personalized service and offbeat charm.

La Quinta
800-531-5900; www.laquinta.com

18 | 17 | 16 | I

■ Road warriors on "long trips" in the South appreciate this chain's "easy freeway locations" (301 of them), "cheap" prices, "clean" "beds to crash on" and (in most cases) pet-friendly regulations; while some surveyors stress that it's safe to stay at only the "newer ones", which are called La Quinta Inns *and* Suites (the "older facilities are very motor lodge-ish"), either way the experience is generally "better than you think it's going to be."

Leading Hotels of the World

| – | – | – | VE |

800-223-6800; www.lhw.com

The 41 domestic properties of this marketing and reservations consortium of independents run from top-notch city hotels (such as a number of Ritz-Carltons) to out-of-the-way spots that are destinations unto themselves, like The Greenbrier in West Virginia; when it comes to the myriad international locations, it'd be justified to add the word "Guaranteed" to its name.

LOEWS

| 24 | 23 | 23 | M |

800-235-6397; www.loewshotels.com

■ Given the variety of the 13 properties in this group, not everyone even realizes they're a chain, however they typically offer solid management, good value and service that "gets an A for effort"; it's likely to "become a great chain", especially if its current expansion meets the standards of its new Miami hotel.

Luxury Collection

| 28 | 27 | 27 | E |

800-325-3589; www.luxurycollection.com

■ The "name says it all" about the 15 U.S. properties that are "fast becoming favorites" for "splurging"; "excellent rooms" and "well-trained staff" "make you feel pampered", and "the generous Starwood points program" helps to make it a "good value."

MainStay Suites

| ▽ 22 | 19 | 18 | I |

800-660-6246; www.mainstaysuites.com

◪ The public "facilities are a mixed" bag and some aspects are "do-it-yourself", but "at least there's plenty of space" in the "nice" rooms of this 59-link chain, which serves as a mainstay ("I will return") of wallet-watchers on long trips.

MARRIOTT

| 22 | 22 | 21 | M |

800-228-9290; www.marriott.com

■ "Neat and nice" sums up this meticulously managed mega-chain of hotels and resorts with 263 properties across the country that is "a safe bet" (the company is "growing rapidly, but maintaining quality"); "good for corporate travel" (with "bargain weekend rates" for vacationers), most find accommodations "utilitarian" but reliably good with a "well-trained staff."

OMNI HOTELS

| 23 | 22 | 21 | M |

800-843-6664; www.omnihotels.com

◪ With "a nice mix of new and historic properties" (some are "real stars"), this "classy" chain of 36 properties provides "medium-priced good value" for rooms that are both "innovative" and "traditional"; a "hospitable" staff makes staying at these mostly large hotels and resorts "worth every penny", but many call the "mismatched" roster "inconsistent" for overall quality.

PARK HYATT & GRAND HYATT

| 26 | 26 | 26 | M |

800-633-7313; www.parkhyatt.com

◪ Hyatt extends its brand further up the travel chain with Park and Grand designations; the seven Park Hyatts land just "one step below excellent" for business travelers, with "good conference rooms", event managers and "always comfortable" rooms; the four Grand Hyatts "aspire to luxe", but most consider them "a notch above the typical chain", offering "good but not great" rooms, "decent" food and overall "good value."

Preferred Hotels & Resorts Worldwide
_ | _ | _ | VE

800-323-7500; www.preferredhotels.com
With 68 U.S. affiliates, this international marketing group includes independent lodgings ranging from the traditional (The Broadmoor in Colorado Springs) to the tropical (Honolulu's Halekulani); flavors and characters may vary, but one thing remains consistent: each property must meet the association's famously finicky standards.

Radisson Hotels & Resorts
19 | 18 | 18 | I

800-333-3333; www.radisson.com
☑ Surveyors observe that this chain of 233 hotels is "working to improve" itself and "change its reputation" from "middle of the road" by adding the "occasional classy touch" in what are generally regarded as "reasonable" properties (the suites are especially "good values"); service is usually "friendly", but quality "varies widely", so it's "hard to generalize."

Red Lion Hotels & Inns
18 | 17 | 16 | I

800-733-5466; www.redlion.com
☑ Since it scaled back to 33 locations in 10 western states, this "local chain" (it became a division of Hilton in 1999) has some surveyors wondering "do they still exist?"; those in the know praise these "very good, basic accommodations" as a "great business and senior value" and "usually clean" with "fast" service, but "some are better than others."

Relais & Châteaux
29 | 29 | 28 | E

800-735-2478; www.relaischateaux.com
■ "You can count on a superb stay" at this exquisitely run "haute chain" of "eclectic" small properties; there are 31 U.S. locations in this alliance of 426 independently owned petit hotels worldwide, "all different and charming", with "personal attention" and "consistently outstanding" food; P.S. the affiliated Relais Gourmandes restaurants (e.g. NY's Daniel, Jean Georges and Le Bernardin) are among the best in the U.S.

RENAISSANCE
24 | 23 | 22 | M

800-468-3571; www.renaissancehotels.com
☑ "Part of the Marriott chain", these 44 "middle-upper-class" American properties "in good locations" are a "first choice" for many who appreciate a "dependable", "comfortable" "value"; despite "consistent service" that's "accommodating to special requests" and often-"excellent" restaurant choices, critics sigh "you've seen one, you've seen them all."

RESIDENCE INN BY MARRIOTT
23 | 20 | 19 | I

800-331-3131; www.residenceinn.com
☑ Though the "lovely little apartments" of this 335-link chain may be "advertised to business travelers" for their "great extended-stay option", they're also "a good place for the family" since the rooms' "full kitchens reduce the number of meals eaten out"; most agree "you can always count on them", though some carp they "do not feel at all like home."

RITZ-CARLTON, THE   29 | 29 | 28 | E
800-241-3333; www.ritzcarlton.com
■ "Old-world style and luxury" is no cliché when applied to this "classic, classy" chain that supplies "consistently excellent service", "plush accommodations" and "sumptuous food"; however, some protest that the 23 American hotels and resorts (9 more opening in 2001) "can be a bit stuffy", and the "predictable" English club–style patina is "inappropriate in some locales" ("e.g. Hawaii"); still, most concur "you can't go wrong" when "only the best will do."

SHERATON   20 | 20 | 20 | M
800-325-3535; www.sheraton.com
◪ Among the 192 properties in this chain, "quality varies greatly", ranging from "lovely" ("they're best in big cities") to "lowly" ("avoid small-town Sheratons"); most agree these "business-friendly" but "bland" hotels "usually have good service" and "membership in frequent-guest programs helps immeasurably with checkout and upgrades."

Small Luxury Hotels of the World   – | – | – | VE
800-525-4800; www.slh.com
The 37 U.S. members truly define the name of this reservations-and-marketing alliance that includes only independently owned lodgings that deliver some of the most refined accommodations around; offerings range from urban favorites (NY's The Inn at Irving Place and Bellevue Club Hotel outside Seattle) to lesser-known, but equally fine, places throughout the country.

WESTIN   24 | 23 | 23 | M
800-228-3000; www.westin.com
◪ Sure, there are "some clunkers" among 59 U.S. hotels, but this chain nonetheless garners solid reviews: "always comfortable", "friendly" and "the best value for the road warrior"; "heavenly beds" (a Westin trademark) win raves as "the best unifying element of the chain", while "customer-oriented, pro service" and "grand public spaces" also help keep clients happy.

W HOTELS   25 | 23 | 25 | M
877-946-8357; www.whotels.com
◪ "Wear Prada" and expect "small rooms" and "ultra-hip bars" at this "swank, stylish" chain that will comprise 20 American hotels by year's end (new openings include two Chicago locations, San Diego, Philadelphia and Miami's South Beach); "service needs some work" (staff suffers from "a bit of attitude"), but for visitors wanting "happening, see-and-be-seen spots" and "great interior decor", the W stands for "wonderful."

WYNDHAM   22 | 21 | 21 | M
800-996-3426; www.wyndham.com
◪ Among the 150 of the chain's U.S. properties are some "almost-luxury", "newer hotels with fine amenities" ("Dallas' Wyndham Anatole is amazing"); fans of the "clean, stylish rooms" and "friendly service" claim "it's always a pleasure to stay" at these resorts and "business traveler" hotels, while foes point out that "many are old and badly in need of renovation."

Hotels & Resorts

27

Alabama

Birmingham

Tutwiler   21 | 20 | 19 | 20 | $142
2021 Park Pl. N.; 205-322-2100; fax 205-325-1183; 800-996-3426;
www.wyndham.com; 147 rooms (52 suites)
☑ Redolent with "Southern hospitality", this "old-timer" (built in
1914) offers "lots of character", "convenience to Downtown" and
relief from chains; on the downside, critics are irked by "confused
service" and "slightly dowdy" rooms, but few beef at these prices.

Point Clear

Marriott's Grand Hotel   22 | 24 | 22 | 25 | $163
1 Grand Blvd.; 334-928-9201; fax 334-990-6349; 800-544-9933;
www.marriott.com; 278 rooms (21 suites)
☑ A "dear old treasure", this "low-adrenaline" "Southern-style"
resort (think "Spanish moss hanging from trees") is a "super mint-
julep spot" for "watching ships go in and out of Mobile Bay"; sure,
some rooms "need to be redecorated", but "helpful employees"
and all the resort facilities at reasonable prices balance the scales.

Alaska

Anchorage

Captain Cook   21 | 21 | 20 | 20 | $166
939 W. Fifth Ave.; 907-276-6000; fax 907-343-2298; 800-843-1950;
www.captaincook.com; 547 rooms (96 suites)
☑ Downtown's "sophisticated outpost" has "dynamite views",
"clean, not fancy" rooms and a "friendly staff" to "get you into
the Alaskan spirit"; despite being filled with "tour bus types" and
"stuck-in-the-'70s" decor, it's "a great place to recover from the
wilderness", especially in the Crow's Nest bar.

Regal Alaskan Hotel   20 | 20 | 18 | 19 | $163
4800 Spenard Rd.; 907-243-2300; fax 907-243-8815; 800-544-0553;
248 rooms (6 suites)
■ "Comfortable beds" and "above-average service" are assets at
this "bold" lakeside hotel close to the airport; for a "great Alaska
experience", request a "cozy" room with a view of float planes
landing and the northern lights at night, and "relax in the lobby"
"dominated by stuffed wildlife", e.g. a huge Kodiak bear.

Denali

Mt. McKinley Princess   21 | 21 | 20 | 22 | $151
Wilderness Lodge
MM 133, Denali National Park; 907-733-2900; fax 907-733-2922;
800-426-0500; www.princessalaskalodges.com; 238 rooms (6 suites)
☑ "Gorgeous scenery" in the middle of nowhere surrounds this
series of "rustic lodges" "overlooking a roaring river", with Mt.
McKinley in the distance; catering to families and "grown-ups
reliving scout camp", the lodge has "helpful" staff and "adequate"
dining; fans insist "the big outdoors" makes up for "spartan"
rooms, while less woodsy types yowl "there's nothing to do."

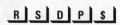
Girdwood

Westin Alyeska Prince | 26 | 24 | 24 | 26 | $188
*1000 Arlberg Ave.; 907-754-1111; fax 907-754-2200; 800-880-3880;
www.westin.com; 307 rooms (11 suites)*
☑ "Smart rooms" and "amazing views" thrill travelers at this
"stately" resort in the Chugach Range 40 miles south of Anchorage;
skiers love the mountain tram into the lobby, hikers like the "helpful
naturalist on call" to locate wild berries and all are enthralled by
vistas and "awesome food" at the mountaintop Seven Glaciers
restaurant; if a few gripe the staff is "too young to handle problems",
most enjoy that the place is so "serene" and "beautiful even on
a rainy day."

Glacier Bay

Glacier Bay Lodge | 20 | 22 | 21 | 22 | $161
*199 Bartlett Cove Rd.; 907-697-2226; fax 907-697-2408;
800-451-5952; www.glacierbaytours.com; 56 rooms (2 suites)*
■ "Incomparable views" of the national park that cradles this
"rustic" wilderness retreat lead some to imagine they're in
"another world" where the "seafood menu is so fresh you
might even get to meet the fisherman" ("salmon dinners are a
must" but "pricey"); "sparsely furnished" "rooms are fit for
practicality", "considering where you are"; N.B. open mid-May
through mid-September only.

Arizona

★ **Best in State**
28 Boulders, *Carefree*/R
   Phoenician, *Scottsdale*/R
27 Four Seasons Troon North, *Scottsdale*/R
   Royal Palms, *Phoenix*/R
26 Enchantment, *Sedona*/R
   Arizona Biltmore, *Phoenix*/R
   Ritz-Carlton, *Phoenix*/H
   Loews Ventana Canyon, *Tucson*/R
   Fairmont Princess, *Scottsdale*/R
   L'Auberge de Sedona, *Sedona*/SR

Grand Canyon

El Tovar | 19 | 21 | 21 | 24 | $164
*South Rim; 303-297-2757; fax 303-297-3175; www.amfac.com;
78 rooms (4 suites)*
☑ "A helluva way to rough it", this "grande dame of lodges"
is only steps from the canyon edge, where guests hear coyotes
at night and watch the sunrise over a cup of coffee; some
guestrooms come with balconies, but "don't expect anything
fancy", even in the four suites with views for which you must "book
years in advance"; service ranges from "warm" to "indifferent",
so "get friendly with the hostess to score a window table" for
a "lovely meal."

Phoenix/Scottsdale

ARIZONA BILTMORE
| 26 | 26 | 25 | 27 | $263 |

Missouri & 24th Sts., Phoenix; 602-955-6600; fax 602-381-7600;
800-950-0086; www.arizonabiltmore.com; 730 rooms (80 suites)
■ "Frank Lloyd Wright lives" under the stars and mountains at this
"grand" old resort designed by one of his former students; "darkly
sumptuous" rooms, "beautifully landscaped grounds", golf, pools
("try the water slide – it's a hoot") and first-rate New American
food persuade guests there's "no need to leave" the "art deco
oasis"; for more, see Spa section.

BOULDERS, THE
| 28 | 28 | 27 | 28 | $361 |

34631 N. Tom Darlington Dr., Carefree; 480-488-9009;
fax 480-488-4118; 800-553-1717; www.wyndham.com; 210 rooms
(160 casitas, 50 villas)
■ If you're looking for "lazy days" and "solitude", then this top-
rated "sexy" resort built into age-old rocks ("Fred Flintstone would
be amused") delivers "bliss" with fireplace-furnished casitas,
"unsurpassed service" and "exquisite food"; golfers and others
"can't wait to go back" for jeep tours, ballooning and rock climbing
as well as "fresh air and freedom"; for more, see Spa section.

FAIRMONT
SCOTTSDALE PRINCESS
| 27 | 25 | 25 | 27 | $267 |

7575 E. Princess Dr., Scottsdale; 480-585-4848; fax 480-585-9895;
800-344-4758; www.fairmont.com; 650 rooms (208 suites)
■ There's "lots to do" for all types at this pink adobe-style resort
with "gargantuan" rooms (all with terraces) and "amazing"
casitas alongside "beautiful" outdoor fireplaces; some say "golf
is the raison d'être" (there are two championship courses),
others argue that the squash, tai chi, bike tours and spa make
it a "family getaway", while couples insist "the bathtubs will
reinvigorate your marriage"; no matter your purpose, "put on
your walking shoes, since everything is spread out" here.

FOUR SEASONS
AT TROON NORTH
| 28 | 27 | 26 | 27 | $273 |

10600 E. Crescent Moon Dr., Scottsdale; 480-515-5700; fax 480-513-5055;
888-207-9696; www.fourseasons.com; 210 rooms (22 suites, 7 villas)
■ It's almost too soon to tell how this relative newcomer will do, but
it "holds promise" for golfers and vacationers at the base of
Pinnacle Peak (some say "way out in nowhere", others "nicely
removed"); "beautifully decorated rooms" (many suites have
garden showers and plunge pools), "friendly service", spa and
dining should "only get better"; for more, see Spa section.

Hermosa Inn
| 24 | 23 | 26 | 23 | $231 |

(fka Phoenix Plaza)
5532 N. Palo Cristi Rd., Paradise Valley; 602-955-8614; fax 602-955-8299;
800-241-1210; www.hermosainn.com; 35 rooms (3 haciendas, 4 villas)
■ Those craving a "break from chains" head to this hacienda built
around the adobe studio of a 1930s cowboy artist for "fantastic"
Southwestern food served at "romantic" Lon's restaurant and
outdoor patio; more about "great ambiance" than amenities (no
room service outside of restaurant hours), the "comfy" inn treats
guests to "luxurious" quarters (some with beehive fireplaces),
"peaceful" gardens and "backdrop views" of Camelback Mountain.

Hyatt Regency Gainey Ranch   25   25   24   27 $251
7500 E. Doubletree Ranch Rd., Scottsdale; 480-991-3388;
fax 480-483-5540; 800-554-9288; www.hyatt.com; 493 rooms
(25 suites, 7 casitas)
■ Where else can you "take a gondola ride next to cacti", swim
interconnected pools so "large you think you're in the ocean" and
bask in the warmth of a "romantic" outdoor fireplace?; in sum,
this "complete resort" with "terrific staff" and "incredible views"
across the Sonoran Desert provides "total pleasure" for both kids
and adults (who forgive "nondescript" rooms, "average" dining
and "corporate functions that can take over the place").

Marriott's Camelback Inn   24   24   23   24 $219
5402 E. Lincoln Dr., Scottsdale; 480-948-1700; fax 480-951-5452;
800-242-2635; www.marriott.com; 453 rooms (27 suites)
■ "How the West was won" – or should have been – this
"calm" "New Age"-esque resort (like a "valium pill") lets you pick
grapefruits from the patio of your own adobe-style casita or "spend
days staring off" into the distance as the "incredible masseuses"
administer relaxation at the spa; a "SW motif" imbues the "rustic
lobby" and grounds, while "prompt, courteous staff" earns it the
moniker "Old Faithful."

PHOENICIAN, THE   28   27   27   28 $308
6000 E. Camelback Rd., Scottsdale; 480-941-8200; fax 480-947-4311;
800-888-8234; www.thephoenician.com; 654 rooms (66 suites, 7 villas)
■ "Ask for caviar by the pool and candy on the greens" and "bring
your diamonds" advise veterans of this "shrine to '80s excess"
"designed to wow the senses" with a "masterful blend of desert
ambiance and urban opulence"; rooms (with marble "baths you
could live in") give way to a mother-of-pearl pool, golf course,
"state-of-the-art" "center for well-being" and "culinary odyssey"
at Mary Elaine's restaurant; what's more, the resort staff "gives
you what you want before you want it"; of course, it's "pricey",
but what would you expect for all this "indulgence"?; for more,
see Spa section.

Pointe Hilton Tapatio Cliffs   23   23   22   24 $201
11111 N. Seventh St., Phoenix; 602-866-7500; fax 602-870-2783;
800-876-4683; www.hilton.com; 585 suites
■ "Beautiful vistas" make it "easy to spend a lot of time here", but
"you need to be a mountain goat to get around" the hilly topography
of this mountainside resort; romantics marvel at the "breathtaking
views" from the restaurant perched 1,800 feet above the city, while
"kids love the water slide" and duffers go for golf; most cheer
the loss of "'70s room decor" (in favor of tonal purples) at this
"practical-more-than-luxury" getaway.

Renaissance   23   23   21   23 $171
6160 N. Scottsdale Rd., Scottsdale; 480-991-1414; fax 480-951-3350;
800-228-9290; www.renaissancehotels.com; 171 rooms (106 suites)
■ "This is what a vacation should be": "low-key elegance" at
a "quiet retreat" with "excellent staff" and casita-style rooms
decorated in traditional Southwestern motifs and connected by
flower-lined walkways; the "24-hour pool is great for night owls",
and private, outdoor hot tubs are "a luxury for the price" of a suite;
it's also popular with families looking for "good value."

RITZ-CARLTON, THE   27 | 27 | 26 | 25 |$245

2401 E. Camelback Rd., Phoenix; 602-468-0700; fax 602-468-0793; 800-241-3333; www.ritzcarlton.com; 281 rooms (14 suites)
■ Finding "olde England" in the desert confirms that this "Ritz is a Ritz"; enthusiasts tout the "as expected" "luxurious", "consistently comfy" "clublike" rooms, seamless service and tea in the afternoon as well as "very good food" at the restaurant; it's also convenient for upscale shopping at Biltmore Fashion Park.

ROYAL PALMS HOTEL & CASITAS   27 | 27 | 27 | 26 |$255

5200 E. Camelback Rd., Phoenix; 602-840-3610; fax 602-840-0233; 800-672-6011; www.royalpalmshotel.com; 116 rooms (35 suites)
■ This "A-one" Spanish hacienda "feels like a private estate" at the base of Camelback Mountain; Mediterranean dining ("out-of-this-world") at T. Cook's and service that "bends over backward" are topped by "stupendous casita" rooms and landscaping for the "ultimate getaway" that "wows" guests with its recent renovations.

Tempe Mission Palms   ▽ 23 | 22 | 19 | 23 |$137

60 E. Fifth St., Tempe; 480-894-1400; fax 480-968-7677; 800-547-8705; www.missionpalms.com; 303 rooms (6 suites)
■ Within walking distance of ASU, this "spacious, modern" property is close to all the action "yet peaceful within its walls"; a "lovely courtyard", rooftop pool (too bad it's "under a flight path"), "friendly staff" and "great decor" (heavy on "cacti and stucco") remind surveyors of a "Hollywood set."

Wigwam Resort, The   25 | 24 | 23 | 24 |$223

300 Wigwam Blvd., Litchfield Park; 623-935-3811; fax 623-856-1081; 800-327-0396; www.wigwamresort.com; 331 rooms (72 suites)
☑ "Palatial", "well-designed rooms", three golf courses, tennis, riding and meals at the Arizona Kitchen are the highlights of this "palm-tree-lined" suburban estate; skeptics say it may be "off-the-beaten-track" (some say "in the boondocks") and "difficult to navigate" due to its scattered "motel-like parking lots."

Wyndham Buttes Resort   24 | 24 | 23 | 25 |$183

2000 W. Court Way, Tempe; 602-225-9000; fax 602-438-8622; 800-843-1986; www.wyndham.com; 353 rooms (7 suites)
☑ "Carved" into its namesake land formation, this "true SW" resort has "great views" of the Phoenix Valley (and an audible hum from a "too-close" freeway); strong points include "impeccable service" ("even the geckos are friendly"), diversions like golf, hiking and horseback riding, "imaginative food" and dramatic panoramas in the circular Top of the Rock restaurant.

Sedona

ENCHANTMENT RESORT   27 | 26 | 25 | 27 |$276

525 Boynton Canyon Rd.; 520-282-2900; fax 520-282-9249; 800-826-4180; www.enchantmentresort.com; 222 rooms (115 suites)
■ "Aptly named", this "hidden treasure" built into the red rocks of Boynton Canyon exudes a "magical" quality; spiritual pursuits in the spa are paired with down-to-earth comforts like "huge bathrooms", fresh-squeezed o.j. and newspapers at the door each morning; there's hiking, tennis and swimming, but this "bit of paradise" also offers the chance to do nothing all day, sip cocktails at sunset and scan a sky "cloudy with stars" at night; for more, see Spa section.

L'AUBERGE DE SEDONA   26 | 25 | 26 | 25 | $249

301 L'Auberge Ln.; 520-282-1661; fax 520-282-2885; 800-272-6777; www.lauberge.com; 100 rooms (3 suites, 37 cottages)

☑ "Nature and spirits collide" amid "gorgeous rock and babbling brook" at this country inn on Oak Creek; reviewers call rooms with a view on the hillside "okay", but the "pricier" cottages down by the water are "lovely and romantic"; while some consider the resort and its jacket-required restaurant "stuffy", others call it "the best in the West"; P.S. don't miss the summertime Sunday brunch by the creek.

Los Abrigados   23 | 22 | 21 | 22 | $205

160 Portal Ln.; 520-282-1777; fax 520-282-6913; 800-521-3131; 181 rooms (173 suites)

■ Adjacent to "great shopping" at the Tlaquepaque marketplace, this "resort among the red rocks" but close to Downtown wins praise for "neat cooking classes", wine-tasting seminars and "great cigars and scotch", though most concede the "large, clean rooms" "lack character"; nevertheless, the place is "great for families", who appreciate an outdoor hot tub, night swimming (until 10 PM) and the Christmas-season light display.

Tucson

Arizona Inn   25 | 26 | 24 | 26 | $197

2200 E. Elm St.; 520-325-1541; fax 520-881-5830; 800-933-1093; www.arizonainn.com; 86 rooms (16 suites, 2 private houses)

■ The smitten "could live forever" amid the "old-fashioned adobe charm" of this hotel with its "tasteful marriage of antiques, sun and sky" that's a "throwback to the 1930s"; clay tennis courts and pool, "beautiful gardens" ("go when the cacti are blooming"), "distinctive", casita-style rooms with private patios and "people-scaled public areas" all score points, as does the "English high tea served in front of wood fires" in winter months.

Hacienda del Sol   23 | 24 | 25 | 23 | $172

5601 N. Hacienda del Sol Rd.; 520-299-1501; fax 520-299-5554; 800-728-6514; www.haciendadelsol.com; 30 rooms (7 suites, 3 casitas)

■ "For a totally authentic Southwestern stay", this "funky" lodge in the Santa Catalina foothills (once a hideaway for stars like Tracy and Hepburn) "fills its surroundings perfectly" and also offers "breathtaking sunsets and sunrises"; guests savor "wonderful" breakfasts and sophisticated dinners in the "spectacular" dining room before returning to "delightful" individually decorated rooms.

Lodge at Ventana Canyon, The   26 | 26 | 24 | 25 | $244

6200 N. Clubhouse Ln.; 520-577-1400; fax 520-577-4065; 800-828-5701; www.wyndham.com; 50 suites

☑ "Everyone's so friendly" at this small resort surrounded by a 600-acre nature preserve; besides "enormous suites" (800 to 1,500 sq. ft.) with views of city and mountains, there are two Fazio-designed courses, "good food" and "unbeatable service"; about the only negative is that the "pool is awkwardly located across a parking lot."

LOEWS VENTANA CANYON   27 | 26 | 25 | 27 | $243
7000 N. Resort Dr.; 520-299-2020; fax 520-299-6832; 800-234-5117;
www.loewshotels.com; 398 rooms (27 suites)
■ This "resplendent" resort reflects the "pastels and quietude" of
the surrounding Santa Catalina mountains with "serene" rooms
and "immense bathtubs"; a "favorite" with both families and
conventioneers, it offers two pools, "fabulous golf courses", live
music and dancing and "food as superb as the views" – all with
"personalized service"; one caveat: "don't leave terrace screens
open", as "critters come in at night"; for more, see Spa section.

Omni Tucson National Golf Resort   22 | 21 | 21 | 23 | $182
2727 W. Club Dr.; 520-297-2271; fax 520-877-2360; 800-528-4856;
www.omnihotels.com; 167 rooms (133 suites)
■ Host to the PGA Tucson Open, this "established" resort north
of the city "feels appropriately desert-y" and is obviously "great
for golfers" as well as a "good place for small conventions";
"comfortable" rooms are "tastefully decorated", and a spa offers
"relaxation" for golf widows and others who like scenic views.

Sheraton El Conquistador   23 | 23 | 21 | 24 | $184
10000 N. Oracle Rd.; 520-544-5000; fax 520-544-1222; 800-325-8131;
www.sheraton.com; 428 rooms (100 suites)
☑ "Good service and no pretensions" mark this low-key resort
with "golf and tennis aplenty" (45 holes and 31 lighted courts),
"majestic views", sunset rides on horseback and a "wonderful
pool" at the base of the mountains; naysayers balk at "kitschy"
Southwestern decor, "mediocre rooms" and "pedestrian food"
("dry, like the weather"), but all agree that "attentive staff makes
this a friendly place to stay" for families and business travelers.

Tanque Verde Guest Ranch   21 | 24 | 21 | 24 | $230
14301 E. Speedway; 520-296-6275; fax 520-721-9426; 800-234-3833;
www.tanqueverderanch.com; 74 rooms (23 suites, 3 private houses)
■ "Great if you're a horse lover", this historic resort (founded as
a cattle ranch in 1868) is just the sort of "relaxed" place to bring
the whole family for a "taste of the West in luxury"; a "great staff"
shows "patience with beginners", but first-timers should wear "old
boots or get a lot of ribbing"; "comfortable" rooms, "entertaining
nature programs" and "down-home cooking" keep 'em comin'.

Westin La Paloma   25 | 25 | 23 | 26 | $221
3800 E. Sunrise Dr.; 520-742-6000; fax 520-577-5878; 888-625-5144;
www.westin.com; 487 rooms (32 suites)
☑ "Waking up" in the Santa Catalina foothills with "desert wildlife
everywhere" makes this resort feel like "a Georgia O'Keeffe
painting"; add oversized rooms, an "awesome water slide", "pools
for all ages", a "challenging" Nicklaus-designed golf course and
food from local star chef Janos Wilder and it's no surprise that
there are lots of regulars; the one drawback: "convention central."

Westward Look   22 | 22 | 23 | 23 | $179
245 E. Ina Rd.; 520-297-1151; fax 520-297-9023; 800-722-2500;
www.westwardlook.com; 244 rooms (8 suites)
■ Fans who like the "expansive", "moderately priced" rooms and
"down-to-earth" atmosphere at this "vintage" resort (built in 1912)
report that this "golden oldie" still pleases with "awesome" tennis,
a spa, "knowledgeable" staff and "beautifully landscaped" grounds.

Wickenburg

Merv Griffin's Wickenburg Inn   ▽ 25 | 26 | 23 | 24 | $234
34801 N. US Hwy. 89; 520-684-7811; fax 520-684-2981; 800-942-5362;
www.merv.com; 63 rooms (31 suites)
■ "All dude ranches should be so enjoyable" assert enthusiasts
who've seen "cowboys made out of city dwellers in less than a
week" at this refreshingly "unfancy" family favorite in the "dusty
desert"; "wonderful staff" supervises trail rides, cattle drives and
evening cookouts on a "gorgeous" private preserve; two "great
pools" keep the layabouts happy as well.

Arkansas

Little Rock

Capital Hotel   22 | 21 | 21 | 21 | $140
111 W. Markham St.; 501-374-7474; fax 501-370-7091;
800-766-7666; www.thecapitalhotel.com; 126 rooms (5 suites)
☑ The "antebellum splendor" of this "hoity-toity" Downtown
"classic" truly stands out in its "great elevator" (it's made for hoop
skirts) and size of the rooms ("could barely see the TV from the
bed"); a few critics don't feel the staff is "up for the challenge",
especially when the first family and entourage are in town, and
"breakfast buffets" lead some to believe "it would be easier to
just inject all that cholesterol."

California

★ **Best in State**
28 Bel-Air, *Los Angeles*/SR
  Peninsula Beverly Hills, *Los Angeles*/H
  Chateau du Sureau, *Oakhurst*/SI
  Four Seasons Aviara, *Carlsbad*/R
  Ritz-Carlton, *San Francisco*/H
  Post Ranch Inn, *Big Sur*/SI
  Four Seasons Beverly Hills, *Los Angeles*/H
  Rancho Valencia, *Rancho Santa Fe*/SR
  Ritz-Carlton Laguna Niguel, *Dana Point*/R
  Ritz-Carlton Rancho Mirage, *Rancho Mirage*/R

Albion

Albion River Inn   24 | 24 | 26 | 22 | $207
3790 Hwy. 1 N.; 707-937-1919; fax 707-937-2604; 800-479-7944;
www.albionriverinn.com; 20 rooms
■ Romantics "can't say enough" about this inn, possibly "the
best place south of Mendocino", but "whether or not you stay
here, make sure you eat" at the "top-quality restaurant", which
serves coastal Californian cuisine as well as "great wine"; rooms
come with fireplaces (some with spa tubs) and incredible ocean
views, so you probably won't notice the lack of TV, but surveyors
say "take earplugs" to drown out the foghorn.

Berkeley

Claremont Resort
22 | 23 | 21 | 24 | $225

41 Tunnel Rd.; 510-843-3000; fax 510-842-6239; 800-551-7266;
www.claremontresort.com; 279 rooms (32 suites)
☑ This "sprawling" "princess dowager" resort nestled in a
residential area high in the Berkeley hills has recently been
renovated to retain its original 1915 "elegance" and add all the
modern business services and conveniences; a spa and fitness
center, two outdoor pools, 10 hard tennis courts and "reliable
service", plus a view of the Golden Gate Bridge, Bay and SF skyline,
make up for slightly "uneven room quality."

Big Sur

POST RANCH INN
29 | 28 | 28 | 27 | $437

Hwy. 1; 831-667-2200; fax 831-667-2824; 800-527-2200;
www.postranchinn.com; 30 cottages
■ The "perfect" "combo of luxury and eco-friendliness" at this
"woodsy" resort is like "camp for millionaires"; the rooms – some
actual tree houses – are "spiritual cocoons" with "plush beds",
"house-size" bathrooms and no TV, while the food at Sierra Mar
Restaurant "gives new meaning to the word 'upscale'"; in-room
massages, "stargazing" (both celebrities and real ones) and an
"extraordinary" staff add to the "magic"; for more, see Spa section.

VENTANA INN
27 | 27 | 26 | 27 | $330

Hwy. 1; 831-667-2331; fax 831-667-2419; 800-628-6500;
www.ventanainn.com; 62 rooms (30 suites, 2 private houses)
■ "Only a corkscrew couldn't unwind" at this "woodsy" lodge built
in 1975 amid "sweeping" vistas; Japanese baths for "au naturel"
soaking, massages, walking trails and an adults-only policy inspire
plenty of renewed romance ("leave the kids at home and bring the
birth control"); though some aren't so keen on the "spare" room
decor despite many amenities, the majority is willing to pay a
pretty price for "paradise on earth"; for more, see Spa section.

Carmel Area

BERNARDUS LODGE
27 | 25 | 27 | 25 | $311

415 Carmel Valley Rd., Carmel; 831-658-3400; fax 831-659-3529;
888-648-9463; www.bernardus.com; 58 rooms (1 suite)
■ Privacy-seeking, price-insensitive couples hail this Carmel Valley
hideaway as "a lovely place to play" amid "luxury" mixed with
"rustic charm"; cheers go to "huge bathrooms", "the best linens",
fireplaces, private decks, the "spectacular" setting and "food and
wine pairings" in the "excellent" Californian-French dining room,
but the real star here is the "great vineyard" and eponymous winery.

Carmel Valley Ranch
26 | 25 | 23 | 25 | $272

1 Old Ranch Rd., Carmel; 831-625-9500; fax 831-624-2858;
800-422-7635; www.wyndham.com; 144 suites
■ "Deer peer though ground-floor windows" at this "luxury ranch"
with a "homey feel", Pete Dye–designed championship golf course,
tennis courts and sweeping vistas of the Carmel Valley and Santa
Lucia mountains; "spacious" suites with wood-burning fireplaces
are highly "romantic" and a trio of Californian-cuisine restaurants
overlook the "stunning" 1,700-acre landscape.

Highlands Inn | 26 | 25 | 26 | 25 | $292 |
120 Highlands Dr., Carmel; 831-620-1234; fax 831-626-8105;
800-682-4811; www.highlands-inn.com; 142 rooms (100 suites)
☑ Like "Carmel candy", you "can't get enough" of this "romance-
oozing" inn set on a pine-covered bluff looking out over the Pacific;
binocular-equipped rooms and picture windows in the Pacific's
Edge restaurant let you "see, feel and breathe the pounding surf";
although ratings are high across the board, a few hairsplitters
pooh-pooh "musty-smelling rooms."

INN AT SPANISH BAY, THE | 28 | 27 | 27 | 27 | $323 |
2700 17 Mile Dr., Pebble Beach; 831-647-7500; fax 831-644-7955;
800-654-9300; www.pebblebeach.com; 269 rooms (17 suites)
■ Duffers think they've "gone to heaven" at this "golf Nirvana",
"one of the finest luxury resorts in the world" on the shores of the
Pacific; off the links, loyalists laud "fantastic" rooms, service, ocean
views, gardens and outdoor cocktails while a bagpiper plays down
the sun; the Euro-Asian fare at Roy's restaurant is "sure to please."

John Gardiner's Tennis Ranch | 23 | 25 | 26 | 26 | $291 |
114 Carmel Valley Rd., Carmel Valley; 831-659-2207;
fax 831-659-2492; 800-453-6225; www.jgtr.com; 16 rooms
☑ Tennis is the racket and the real "reason to stay" at this "sunny",
"beautiful spot" that claims almost as many courts as "very dated
rooms"; some visitor-players deem the property "expensive", but
given that some rates include lessons and three meals each day,
most maintain it's "great for couples" and "well worth the cost."

La Playa Hotel | 23 | 24 | 22 | 23 | $197 |
Camino Real & Eighth Ave., Carmel; 831-624-6476; fax 831-624-7966;
800-582-8900; www.laplayacarmel.com; 80 rooms (5 private cottages)
☑ Despite its name, there's no on-site beach (it's two blocks away),
only a "feeling of comfort and solitude" at this 1904 hotel ("it's not a
B&B, which is rare for this area") centrally located within "easy
walking distance of Downtown"; respondents praise the gardens
and "warm service", though some gripe about "small" rooms that
"need to enter the 21st century" and "geriatric" clientele.

LODGE AT PEBBLE BEACH, THE | 27 | 27 | 26 | 27 | $332 |
17 Mile Dr., Pebble Beach; 831-624-3811; fax 831-625-8598;
800-654-9300; www.pebblebeach.com; 185 rooms (11 suites)
■ At "ground zero for golfers", duffers are in their glory playing
upon these "legendary links" ("the course is even prettier in
person") and "relaxing" post-game at this "world-class" resort; the
"classic" main building and cottage-style rooms exude a sense of
"old elegance", while the service, food and oceanfront location
prompt the über-praise "staying here is a religious experience."

Quail Lodge | 25 | 25 | 25 | 25 | $271 |
8205 Valley Greens Dr., Carmel; 831-624-2888; fax 831-624-3726;
888-828-8787; www.quail-lodge-resort.com; 97 rooms (18 suites)
☑ For "tranquility without compare" try this golf, tennis and wildlife
resort set in the "warm valley" of the Santa Lucia Mountains; it's
a "refuge for lovers" among the "country-club set", but business
travelers also flock here for the "corporate facilities" and the lake
or garden views from every room; "rustic elegance" carries over to
The Covey restaurant (jacket required) and service wins applause,
but a few protest "being treated like a peasant at those prices."

Seven Gables Inn   26 | 26 | 24 | 24 | $212
555 Ocean View Blvd., Pacific Grove; 831-372-4341; 14 rooms (1 suite, 2 cottages)
■ With some of "the best views in America", this Victorian mansion (circa 1886) on Monterey Bay is the place to "hear and see waves crashing against the shore" from "Laura Ashley-ish" rooms (some call them "quaint", others "tiny"); "tasty breakfasts and a constant supply of snacks through the day" fortify guests as they explore the nearby Aquarium, Cannery Row and Carmel.

Stonepine   25 | 25 | 24 | 26 | $397
150 E. Carmel Valley Rd., Carmel; 831-659-2245; fax 831-659-5160; www.stonepinecalifornia.com; 16 rooms (8 suites, 2 private cottages)
◪ "If only I were rich enough to stay forever" declare fans of the "secluded" grounds, "joyous gardens" and "excellent" horseback riding at this 330-acre Relais & Châteaux resort; "butler-type service" caters to an "exclusive" crowd at this European-style estate whose "big rooms" some find "charming" and others call "aggressively over-the-top" and "in need of renovation" despite a 1998 spruce-up.

Tickle Pink Inn   25 | 27 | 17 | 21 | $188
155 Highland Dr., Carmel; 831-624-1244; fax 831-626-9516; 800-635-4774; www.ticklepinkinn.com; 34 rooms (11 suites, 1 cottage)
■ "Fabulous rooms" (some with wood-burning fireplaces) treat travelers to "spectacular ocean and cove views" from this small cliff-top inn that also affords "privacy" and "peace" to nature-lovers escaping bustling Downtown Carmel; "personal service" "goes the extra mile", especially during complimentary afternoon wine-and-cheese get-togethers on the Terrace Lounge.

Dana Point

RITZ-CARLTON LAGUNA NIGUEL   28 | 27 | 27 | 29 | $276
1 Ritz-Carlton Dr.; 949-240-2000; fax 949-240-1061; 800-241-3333; www.ritzcarlton.com; 393 rooms (31 suites)
■ Fans can't rave enough about the "jewel in the crown" of the Ritz chain (rated tops for Public Spaces); "high on a bluff above [the Pacific's] crashing waves", it's blessed with "the most astounding views in Southern California"; "rooms are spacious and beautifully laid out", all with balconies, and the "staff prides itself on service" that goes "hand over glove" to "pamper"; the dining here is an "overindulgence not to be skipped", but "don't forget your blazer", as this is "ground zero" for Republicans.

Gualala

St. Orres   22 | 22 | 26 | 22 | $174
36601 S. Hwy. 1; 707-884-3303; fax 707-884-1840; www.saintorres.com; 20 rooms (12 cottages)
■ On a stretch of coast about three hours north of San Francisco, this "back-to-the-'70s" getaway features "Russian architecture" (weathered wood and onion domes) and outstanding Californian cuisine on 50 acres, where you can watch for "wild turkeys roaming the property"; guests stay at the "quirky" eight-room inn or one of a dozen "very private cottages in the woods", all "loaded with charm" (but not phones or TV) at this "affordable" original.

Lafayette

Lafayette Park Hotel   25 | 24 | 23 | 23 | $188
3287 Mt. Diablo Blvd.; 925-283-3700; fax 925-284-1621;
800-368-2468; www.lafayetteparkhotel.com; 139 rooms (10 suites)
☑ Loyalists maintain a "sweet spot" for this "classy hotel in the 'burbs" that offers the "best of the East Bay"; most agree this "lovely nouveau chateau in the hills" of hot-and-dry Contra Costa County "surprises" with a swimming "pool that makes you feel like you're in Italy", but others deem the "Laura Ashley" look "a bit surreal" and "too fancy for the area."

Laguna Beach

Surf & Sand Resort   25 | 24 | 24 | 24 | $257
1555 S. Coast Hwy.; 949-497-4477; fax 949-494-2897;
800-837-9230; www.surfandsandresort.com; 165 rooms
(13 suites)
■ "True to its name", this "great little romantic getaway" has "tranquil", "elegant rooms" right on the beach ("any closer and you'd sleep in a wet suit") that embody a "California-casual, beach-y atmosphere" that extends throughout the "spectacular setting" with "unparalleled views"; guests also tout the "pro staff" and "love" Splashes' Cal-Med fare; in other words, this is a "perfect place to relax or play."

Los Angeles

★ **Best in City**
28 Bel-Air/SR   L'Ermitage/H
    Peninsula/H   Shutters on the Beach/H
    Four Seasons/H   Regent Beverly Wilshire/H
27 Ritz-Carlton Huntington/H **26** Ritz-Carlton Marina del Rey/H

Argyle, The   24 | 23 | 24 | 23 | $230
8358 Sunset Blvd., West Hollywood; 323-654-7100;
fax 323-654-9287; 800-225-2637; www.argylehotel.com; 64 rooms
(44 suites)
■ "Feel like a movie star" at this newly renovated "old-Hollywood" boutique hotel, an "art deco gem" that's "trendy but unpretentious" in "style-drenched LA"; rooms are "small but charming", the pool has been featured in lots of movies and an "oh-so-cool" lobby bar attracts a "young, hip" crowd; restaurant Fenix fills up for terrace dining with a view of the skyline.

Avalon Hotel   ▽ 23 | 21 | 20 | 20 | $186
9400 W. Olympic Blvd., Beverly Hills; 310-277-5221;
fax 310-277-4928; 800-535-4715; www.avalonlosangeleshotel.com;
88 rooms (14 suites)
☑ With its "hipper-than-thou", "Jetsonian" decor this "cool, funky hotel" is considered by those few in the know to be "the place to stay in LA"; formerly the Beverly Carlton, it's a "re-creation of glamorous 1950s Beverly Hills" ("love the bar and enclosed pool") tucked away from hubbub on a remote residential block that nonfans dismiss as being in a "dumpy part of town"; if service is "sometimes flaky", there's no question that the "vibe" is "fab."

Barnabey's

19 | 20 | 19 | 18 | $149

3501 Sepulveda Blvd., Manhattan Beach; 310-545-8466;
fax 310-545-8621; 800-552-5285; 122 rooms

☑ An "antiques-laden" "cross between a Victorian inn and a
Marriott", this hotel's "reasonable" prices and handy suburban
location – a mile from the beach and two from LAX – qualify it as a
"best value"; gardens and a "secluded pool area" are "ideal for an
intimate rendezvous", but the "surprisingly large" rooms are "dark"
and "a little musty" in a "shabby" 19th-century English way.

BEL-AIR, HOTEL

28 | 28 | 28 | 28 | $359

701 Stone Canyon Rd.; 310-472-1211; fax 310-909-1606;
800-648-4097; www.hotelbelair.com; 92 rooms (40 suites)

■ "Indecently good" sings a chorus who've experienced this
legendary Mission-meets-Mediterranean-style garden hotel that
ranks No. 1 in the city and state for small properties; 11 acres of
"lush", "serene" grounds create a "sanctuary" where you're
"greeted by white swans", while "secluded super-romantic
bungalow" rooms offer "ultimate privacy"; guests are cosseted
by the staff, and the Cal-French restaurant has a "delectable
menu"; to put it succinctly, this is "one of the world's greatest."

BEVERLY HILLS HOTEL & BUNGALOWS, THE

26 | 26 | 25 | 26 | $313

9641 Sunset Blvd., Beverly Hills; 310-276-2251; fax 310-887-2887;
www.thebeverlyhillshotel.com; 203 rooms
(37 suites, 44 bungalows)

■ "They make everyone feel like a star" at this pink palace,
recently rehabbed but still dripping with "history"; it's the "place
to be seen" – "bring your shades" to the cabana-encircled pool
for "great people-watching"; ditto the Polo Lounge, "where all LA
gathers"; "quiet" rooms are "beautifully restored" but maintain
their "old-Hollywood" feel, however the bungalows are still *the*
spot to stay.

Beverly Hilton

21 | 22 | 20 | 21 | $232

9876 Wilshire Blvd.; 310-274-7777; fax 310-285-1308; 800-445-8667;
www.hilton.com; 581 rooms (96 suites)

☑ Fanciers of this "nuts-and-bolts mega-hotel" claim its "splendid
location" near Rodeo Drive and "fair" price make it the "best value
for the area"; with a ballroom and banquet facilities, the home of
the Golden Globes is big on black-tie events and award dinners,
giving it "good stargazing" status, but reviewers concede the
"comfortable" rooms are "boring", and a smattering snipe "Beverly
Hills deserves better."

Beverly Plaza

23 | 23 | 21 | 19 | $178

8384 W. Third St.; 323-658-6600; fax 323-653-3464; 800-624-6835;
www.beverlyplazahotel.com; 98 rooms

☑ "Conveniently located for business travel", museums and Rodeo
Drive, this boutique hotel is "a wonderful find" on the cusp of
Beverly Hills and West Hollywood; the staff is "helpful", the
Spanish/Caribbean food at Cava "recommended", and despite a
"tiny" lobby and "smallish rooms", cost-conscious cheerleaders
chant it's "an excellent bargain."

Biltmore, The   21 | 22 | 22 | 25 | $195
(fka Regal Biltmore)
506 S. Grand Ave.; 213-624-1011; fax 213-612-1545; 800-245-8673;
www.thebiltmore.com; 683 rooms (43 suites)
▧ The "doyenne of Downtown is aging gracefully", report guests of
this historic hotel that's handy for business travelers but "borders
on a terrible end of the city"; the Renaissance lobby and public
spaces are graced with soaring hand-painted ceilings ("almost a
museum"), however many warn that the "regal splendor" "begins
and ends there", referring to rooms that may be "ready for rehab."

CASA DEL MAR, HOTEL   26 | 26 | 24 | 27 | $286
1910 Ocean Way, Santa Monica; 310-581-5533; fax 310-581-5503;
800-334-9000; www.hotelcasadelmar.com; 129 rooms (17 suites)
▮ It's easy to be awed by the mosaic and Italian tiles and "stylish
yet comfortable" Neo-classical decor in the entry rotunda of this
"beautifully restored" 1920s revival boutique hotel, Shutters' next
door offspring; visitors commend the beachfront location, a staff
that's "ready to please" and rooms with views, marble bathrooms
and whirlpool tubs; in short, this newcomer is "off to a great start."

Century Plaza   23 | 22 | 21 | 22 | $233
2025 Ave. of the Stars; 310-277-2000; fax 310-551-3355;
800-228-3000; www.centuryplazala.com; 727 rooms (44 suites)
▧ "Convenient to theater, shopping, West Side and Beverly Hills",
this "dependable" Westin is popular for business, weddings and
"political fund-raisers" thanks to extensive banquet and meeting
facilities; overnight guests report "heavenly beds" and "efficient"
service, and those who stay in the tower (upgraded in August 2000
to parent company Starwood's St. Regis brand) say the "superior"
quarters are "worth the difference" in price; only a few complain
about the "hustle and bustle" and "somewhat sterile" quality in the
main part of the hotel; for more, see St. Regis Los Angeles review.

Chateau Marmont   23 | 22 | 21 | 23 | $288
8221 Sunset Blvd., West Hollywood; 323-656-1010; fax 323-655-5311;
800-242-8328; 63 rooms (39 suites, 4 bungalows, 9 cottages)
▧ LA's version of "la vie boheme" – where Garbo slept and Belushi
died – is set on a hill above the jumping Sunset Strip, "secluded,
yet in the center of everything"; the "creepy" main building, built
in 1929 but frequently face-lifted, "defines shabby chic" and is
"crawling" with "independent film directors", "movie stars and
producers in sunglasses"; rooms range from "small" to "massive",
but all are "homey"; P.S. expect a "so-hip-it-hurts" crowd at the
"cool bar" and "at least four photo shoots during your stay."

Fairmont Hotel   23 | 22 | 21 | 23 | $226
(fka Miramar Sheraton)
101 Wilshire Blvd., Santa Monica; 310-576-7777; fax 310-458-7912;
800-866-5577; www.fairmont.com; 302 rooms (62 suites, 32 bungalows)
▧ "What a place for a daydream" aptly describes this "low-key"
former Sheraton's "sunny", off-the-beaten-path perch on the bluffs
above the beach; those who can take their eyes off the view are
within easy walking distance of the pier and bike and blading paths;
but most prefer to laze about in the "tropical-garden" bungalows
or the "wonderful" historic wing; however, some say "the new
tower is nothing special", and "if you aren't famous, forget it."

FOUR SEASONS BEVERLY HILLS   28 | 28 | 28 | 27 | $327

300 S. Doheny Dr., Beverly Hills; 310-273-2222; fax 310-859-3824;
800-819-5053; www.fourseasons.com; 285 rooms (105 suites)

■ "These folks wrote the book on doing things right" claim fans of this "tranquil", "radiant" hotel in a residential area "far from the fast lane"; staff "better dressed" than most guests "go that extra mile" to make you "feel like you own the world" (don't be surprised if the "doorman is waiting with a towel and Evian after your jog"); praiseworthy pursuits include lazing in "fluffy beds", lounging by the "flower-banked pool", relishing "gastronomic delights" at Gardens restaurant and "movie-star gazing."

Hollywood Roosevelt   17 | 18 | 16 | 18 | $152

7000 Hollywood Blvd.; 323-466-7000; fax 323-462-8056; 800-950-7667;
www.hollywoodroosevelt.com; 335 rooms (20 suites, 68 cabana rooms)

☑ "A glimpse of Hollywood's Golden Age", "this historic hotel across the street from Mann's Chinese Theater" draws raves from guests who love to "sit in the eagle-claw bathtub and feel like I'm in an old movie" or "wear a bright swimsuit by the pool and live the life of Lucy and Desi"; those who prefer not to play-act can't get past the "terrible neighborhood" and "fleabag rooms" (some of which have recently been renovated).

Hyatt Regency   22 | 21 | 19 | 20 | $185

711 S. Hope St.; 213-683-1234; fax 213-629-3230; 800-233-1234;
www.hyatt.com; 485 rooms (41 suites)

☑ It's "pretty standard for a chain", but the coffee in the lobby is a "bonus" and rooms are "surprisingly creatively decorated" say business travelers; the majority is mildly disappointed and recommends staying here "only if you have to be Downtown", since its "not in the greatest location – just like all of LA, you have to drive to anything you want to do."

Le Meridien Beverly Hills   25 | 24 | 23 | 23 | $236
(fka Nikko Beverly Hills)

465 S. La Cienega Blvd., Beverly Hills; 310-247-0400; fax 310-247-0315;
800-645-5624; www.lemeridien.com; 297 rooms (58 suites)

■ Retaining some "Japanese touches" from its Nikko days, this "sleek" re-flagged hotel treats guests to "spacious rooms" ("love the bedside controls" and loaded CD player) and "huge bathrooms" with deep-soak tubs; service "couldn't be more friendly" amid a "chic" "elegance" that promotes a "most peaceful" ambiance; in-the-know guests relish the "secret of a central location with self-parking", while nervous out-of-towners can relax knowing that the "building's on rollers" in case of "earthquakes."

Le Merigot   ▽ 25 | 25 | 22 | 25 | $257
Santa Monica Beach Hotel

1740 Ocean Ave., Santa Monica; 310-395-9700; fax 310-395-9200;
800-926-9524; www.lemerigotbeachhotel.com; 175 rooms (15 suites)

☑ Bringing the "beachy yet glam" ambiance of the Riviera to Southern California, this "very private hotel" is directly across the street from sand and surf; satisfied surveyors salute the "first-rate pool", "good gym", beds with "quality sheets", "great service" and spa, and though some feel the young property is experiencing a few "growing pains", they predict "it will catch on", since staying here is already a "wonderful experience."

L'ERMITAGE   28 | 27 | 26 | 25 | $326
9291 Burton Way, Beverly Hills; 310-278-3344; fax 310-278-8247;
800-800-2113; www.lermitagehotel.com; 123 rooms (12 suites)
■ "Excessively good" – if that's possible – this "heavenly" boutique
hotel has "Zen-like" room decor that belies "state-of-the-art"
"techno-gadget" amenities, such as multiline phones, big-screen
TV and fax/printer/copier machines; bonus comforts for business
travelers include complimentary limo service, cell phone rentals
and personalized business cards, but most guests choose to
watch the "pretty people" lounging poolside or simply relax in the
"lavish" rooftop garden.

Loews Santa Monica Beach Hotel   22 | 22 | 21 | 23 | $237
1700 Ocean Ave., Santa Monica; 310-458-6700;
fax 310-458-6761; 800-235-6397; www.loewshotels.com;
343 rooms (25 suites)
☑ Most travelers cheer this hotel's "grand ocean views" and "very
accommodating" staff, but others jeer a split personality ("can't
decide if it's a convention or leisure hotel"); current construction
should lead to improvement.

Maison 140   – | – | – | – | I
140 S. Lasky Dr., Beverly Hills; 310-281-4000; fax 310-281-4001;
45 rooms
Take black-lacquer furniture, zebra-print upholstery and Lucite
fixtures, arrange well on patterned carpets within walls that
change color on every floor and you'll get the feel of one of
Beverly Hills' latest boutique offerings; opened in August 2000,
this follow-up to Avalon Hotel may also be one of the West Side's
best hip bargains.

Malibu Beach Inn   22 | 21 | 17 | 19 | $202
22878 Pacific Coast Hwy., Malibu; 310-456-6444;
fax 310-456-1499; 800-462-5428; www.malibubeachinn.com;
47 rooms (3 suites)
☑ "Location, location, location" chant devotees of this "low-key"
little hideaway perched on its own stretch of sandy shoreline;
"bright" rooms have fireplaces and balconies that overhang the
sea, but some grumble the hotel "needs a restaurant" (fortunately,
nearby eateries deliver) and "better paint colors"; still, when you
"can hear the pounding surf and watch the sun set" in privacy,
it's all perfectly "idyllic."

Mondrian   23 | 21 | 23 | 25 | $267
8440 Sunset Blvd., West Hollywood; 323-650-8999;
fax 323-650-9241; 800-525-8029; www.mondrianhotel.com;
238 rooms (187 suites)
☑ "Stay here if you love a scene" "teeming with ultra-thin
starlets and Hollywood playboys" exclaim both fans and foes
of this "über-hip" Ian Schrager–owned hot spot; rooms with
white-on-white minimalist furnishings are "clean and comfy,
but snug", and though the "bellmen are too busy trying to get
themselves 'discovered' to carry your bags", most guests are
awestruck by the "chichi" pool, Asia de Cuba restaurant and
"buzz" in the Skybar; those who are left unimpressed protest "get
over yourselves already."

New Otani Hotel & Gardens   21 | 22 | 22 | 21 | $183

120 S. Los Angeles St.; 213-629-1200; fax 213-473-1416;
800-421-8795; www.newotani.com; 434 rooms (20 suites)
☑ The location of this heart-of-Downtown high-rise is both a blessing and a curse: it's full of "high-strung businesspeople" who appreciate the proximity to the Civic Center, major corporations and courthouse, but it's "not a great neighborhood at night"; most find the decor "upscale yet sterile", except in the "authentic" Japanese garden, which "emanates tranquility."

Oceana Hotel   25 | 21 | 19 | 20 | $231

849 Ocean Ave., Santa Monica; 310-393-0486; fax 310-458-1182;
800-777-0758; www.hoteloceana.com; 63 suites
■ "Serene" and "Mediterranean-esque", this "hidden gem" across from Palisades Park – and just a hop, skip and jump from the beach and Third Street shopping district – wins applause for its "comfortable and solid" suites with kitchenettes (many have patios or lanais and Pacific views); the staff makes you "feel like you're not a tourist" and room service comes from the Wolfgang Puck Café, so it should be clear why this small hotel is considered "as cool as the ocean breeze."

Omni Hotel   – | – | – | – | E

251 S. Olive St.; 213-617-3300; fax 213-617-3399; 800-843-6664;
www.omnihotels.com; 439 rooms (18 suites)
Formerly an Inter-Continental, in May 2000 this Bunker Hill high-rise reopened as the chain's first Golden State foothold, close to the Museum of Contemporary Art; there's lots here for business and leisure travelers, with plenty of meeting space (including a War Room for attorneys arguing at the nearby courthouse) and greeting space, like a heated outdoor lap pool and the Angels Flight Lounge, named after the funicular just outside.

Park Hyatt   25 | 25 | 22 | 23 | $240

2151 Ave. of the Stars; 310-277-1234; fax 310-785-9240;
800-233-1234; www.hyatt.com; 367 rooms (167 suites)
■ Compensating for a "marginal location" in Century City, this "top-notch" high-rise attracts "industry folk" and visitors with "airy, bright rooms", "warm, cordial" service that "meets the most unusual request" and free limos to Rodeo Drive; the majority agrees that even "without spectacular grounds" the hotel's "beautiful" indoor and outdoor pools and "professional" yet "low-key" standards make a stay "outstanding."

PENINSULA BEVERLY HILLS   29 | 28 | 28 | 27 | $343

9882 Little Santa Monica Blvd., Beverly Hills; 310-551-2888;
fax 310-788-2319; 800-462-7899; www.peninsula.com; 196 rooms
(32 suites, 16 villas)
■ At this No. 1–ranking large hotel in the city and state, you can expect a "guaranteed feeling of luxury" with service so personal that some frequent guests get monogrammed pillowcases in plush rooms and "heavenly" villa suites; "impeccably civilized (is this LA?)", in fact, the star-studded hotel will "constantly delight" with extras like spa treatments, tea service and fine food; all agree you'll be thoroughly "pampered"; for more, see Spa section.

REGENT BEVERLY WILSHIRE   27 | 27 | 26 | 26 | $321
9500 Wilshire Blvd., Beverly Hills; 310-275-5200; fax 310-274-2851;
800-427-4354; www.regenthotels.com; 395 rooms (120 suites)
■ "Everything you saw in *Pretty Woman* was true", and you can't
go wrong if you book the "more modern" rooms in the new tower
and use the fleet of Bentleys to whisk you down nearby Rodeo
Drive (just a short stroll away); fans applaud service ("they almost
sent a search party when I didn't answer my wake-up call") but
keep hoping to run into Julia Roberts or Richard Gere.

Renaissance Beverly Hills   24 | 22 | 21 | 19 | $195
(fka Beverly Prescott)
1224 S. Beverwil Dr., Beverly Hills; 310-277-2800; fax 310-203-9537;
800-421-3212; www.renaissancehotels.com; 137 rooms (8 suites)
☑ The "California-style" "floral decor" feels "homey" to guests
who stay in the "modern but comfortable" rooms of this "well-run"
boutique hotel on the edge of Beverly Hills; balconies afford
"great views", but street noise penetrates "poor soundproofing";
still, most agree that "the price seems a bargain for the luxury."

RITZ-CARLTON HUNTINGTON   27 | 28 | 26 | 28 | $278
1401 S. Oak Knoll Ave., Pasadena; 626-568-3900; fax 626-585-6420;
800-241-3333; www.ritzcarlton.com; 392 rooms (26 suites)
■ "High-end clientele" discovers "Eden in Pasadena" at this
Mediterranean-style hotel and spa set below the San Gabriel
Mountains, surrounded by "sweeping views" of Downtown LA
and "lovely gardens" in a "quiet", residential area; "it's a hard
place in which to work" with so much "to enjoy", and its formality
may "make you want to study your etiquette book."

RITZ-CARLTON MARINA DEL REY   27 | 27 | 25 | 26 | $282
4375 Admiralty Way, Marina del rey; 310-823-1700; fax 310-823-2403;
800-241-3333; www.ritzcarlton.com; 304 rooms (12 suites)
☑ This waterfront hotel with "million-dollar views" of "yachts you
can't afford" and a spa provides a "perfect weekend getaway"
within walking (or cycling) distance of Venice Beach; while many
call it "extremely romantic", especially in the superbly served club-
level rooms, a few consider the formal Ritz-style ambiance too
"haute couture for a dress-down location."

Shangri-La   19 | 16 | 13 | 16 | $169
1301 Ocean Ave., Santa Monica; 310-394-2791; fax 310-451-3351;
800-345-7829; www.shangrila-hotel.com; 55 rooms (33 suites)
☑ Though most agree "it's no Shangri-la (what a dump)", some
look past this art deco getaway's "tattered" decor, "rude and surly
staff" and "noise" from buses and cars to deem it "the best value
in LA", particularly for its kitchen-equipped studios and suites and
"fabulous location" that's "perched over the Pacific."

SHUTTERS ON THE BEACH   28 | 26 | 26 | 27 | $311
1 Pico Blvd., Santa Monica; 310-458-0030; fax 310-458-4589;
800-334-9000; www.shuttersonthebeach.com; 198 rooms (12 suites)
■ "The toy whale and candle in the bath did it for me" exclaim
devotees of this "superbly situated" beachfront hotel; it's one of
America's best thanks to "airy rooms" big enough for "sunbathing
or stargazing", "exceptional dining" at One Pico, service "without
stuffiness" and ocean views that are "worth the premium"; go for
a "glorious" "escape" that "feels more Cape Cod" than California.

Sofitel | 22 | 22 | 20 | 20 | $191 |
8555 Beverly Blvd.; 310-278-5444; fax 310-657-2816; 800-763-4835; www.sofitel.com; 311 rooms (11 suites)
☑ "An island of French service and simplicity", this hotel is an alternative in an "ignoble area" across from Beverly Center that offers "quality for a reasonable price"; many love touches like "fresh apples in the workout room" and "great croissants", and most enjoy the sizable rooms (surveyors recommend "a north view"), even if they are "a little run down."

Standard, The | – | – | – | – | I |
8300 Sunset Blvd., West Hollywood; 323-650-9090; fax 323-650-2820; www.standardhotel.com; 139 rooms (2 suites)
Over-the-top details like electric-blue AstroTurf carpeting on the pool deck and minimalist rooms outfitted with inflatable sofas and T1 lines grab attention, but a down-to-earth price tag makes this transformed 1960s motel (the latest effort of hotelier Andre Balazs, owner of the legendary Chateau Marmont) a haven for heat-seekers with Gucci tastes and Gap budgets; investors include Leonardo DiCaprio and Cameron Diaz, so celeb sightings are almost, well, standard.

St. Regis | – | – | – | – | VE |
2055 Ave. of the Stars; 310-277-6111; fax 310-277-3711; 800-759-7550; www.stregis.com; 297 rooms (40 suites)
Occupying the former tower of the Century Plaza since August 2000, this first West Coast location of the luxury hotel group puts the world (at least the part that can be seen from higher floors: Downtown, Santa Monica, Bel-Air and the Hollywood Hills) at well-heeled guests' feet; along with subdued furnishings, all rooms and suites come with balconies to maximize the views and, should you need to reach someone outside of shouting distance, three phone lines, a fax machine and high-speed Internet access.

Sunset Marquis Hotel & Villas | 22 | 24 | 21 | 22 | $246 |
1200 N. Alta Loma Rd.; 310-657-1333; fax 310-652-5300; 800-858-9758; www.srs.worldwide.com; 114 rooms (102 suites, 12 villas)
☑ "A good alternative to the more 'boogie-ing' spots" nearby, this "little paradise in West Hollywood" satisfies its clients with "comfortable, fairly standard rooms" and solid service, but really turns them on with villas where the backyard gardens "feel as if they were your own"; peace-seekers take note – "the Whiskey Bar can be too fabulous" with a "very high" "heavy-metal quotient."

W | 24 | 23 | 22 | 22 | $246 |
(fka Westwood Marquis)
930 Hilgard Ave.; 310-208-8765; fax 310-824-0355; 877-946-8357; www.whotels.com; 258 suites
☑ Neon-lit steps lead "young professionals who work all day and rock all night" to this "ultra-hip" all-suite "contemporary mecca" next to UCLA; most love the new "minimalist" look that's "like living in a Pottery Barn catalog", but "thin walls" may make your stay a shared experience; with the "chic" Mojo restaurant and "super-cruisy" Mojito bar scene, expect weekend crowds heavy on "trendy Westsiders and Valley wanna-bes."

Wyndham Bel Age   22 | 22 | 21 | 21 | $200
1020 N. San Vicente Blvd., West Hollywood; 310-854-1111;
fax 310-854-0926; 800-996-3426; www.wyndham.com; 200 suites
◪ Large, all-suite rooms with balconies and a "great location in
the heart of things" (you can walk to Spago Hollywood and Tower
Records) keep surveyors coming back to this "wonderfully run"
midsize hotel frequented by music celebs; though most praise its
"cool rooftop pool" and "friendly staff", dissenters say it's "a little
threadbare" and "needs a face-lift."

Wyndham Checkers   24 | 25 | 25 | 23 | $211
535 S. Grand Ave.; 213-624-0000; fax 213-626-9906; 800-996-3426;
www.wyndham.com; 188 rooms (17 suites)
■ "Very private and quiet", this European-style hotel offers
business travelers and weekenders a "civilized oasis in scruffy
Downtown" that's close to theater, opera and museums; "public
areas get more attention" than the "small, comfortable rooms",
but with a lobby that's "great for cocktails", rooftop fitness center
and "Continental cuisine (with Asian overtones) at its best" from
Checkers Restaurant, no one is complaining.

Mendocino

Stanford Inn by the Sea   25 | 24 | 23 | 23 | $220
Hwy. 1 & Comptche-Ukiah Rd.; 707-937-5615; fax 707-937-0305;
800-331-8884; www.stanfordinn.com; 33 rooms (10 suites)
■ A "vegetarian's utopia" (the garden's bounty appears on the
restaurant's meat-free menu), this "nature-oriented", "upscale" but
"unpretentious" inn sits on a working organic farm in the center
of this "artsy community"; the "caring hosts" are dog lovers who
provide welcome biscuits for Skippy and let his masters pet the
llamas and relax in rooms with fireplaces and balconies overlooking
an "exquisite lawn of flowers."

Menlo Park

Stanford Park Hotel   22 | 22 | 21 | 21 | $215
100 El Camino Real; 650-322-1234; fax 650-330-2796; 800-368-2468;
163 rooms (9 suites)
◪ "Perfect when visiting Stanford University" or for Silicon Valley
folks to "live after a divorce", this hotel is "as good as [the area]
gets", with "cheerful rooms", pleasing pool area, "fast laundry
service" and a popular restaurant downstairs; still, a few complain
of the "4 AM wake-up call from the train rattling by" and wish that
there were fewer supplicants to Sand Hill Road.

Monterey

Monterey Plaza Hotel   24 | 23 | 22 | 24 | $206
400 Cannery Row; 831-646-1700; fax 831-646-0439; 800-334-3999;
www.montereyplazahotel.com; 290 rooms (10 suites)
■ "A room facing the water is a must" at this "well-appointed",
fairly priced hotel where you can "sleep with your balcony doors
open" and let "barking sea lions be your alarm clock", then "spend
breakfast watching otters do the backstroke"; when not distracted
by these goings-on, surveyors are also impressed by the "caring
staff" and "Spanish-style" architecture.

Pacific, Hotel   25 | 24 | 20 | 21 | $207
300 Pacific St.; 831-373-5700; fax 831-373-6921; 800-554-5542; 105 suites
☑ With "Spanish decor in the best of taste" and niceties like down comforters, four-poster feather beds and gas fireplaces in every room, surveyors dub this "pretty" all-suite hotel in Old Monterey "an undiscovered delight"; "tranquility" reigns at what regulars consider "the best deal in the area", but a handful complain about "no dining facilities" (only room service).

Spindrift Inn   25 | 24 | 21 | 21 | $220
652 Cannery Row; 831-646-8900; fax 831-646-5342; 800-841-1879; www.spindriftinn.com; 42 rooms
■ Guests "fall asleep to waves breaking" and "awaken to seals yelping" at this historic Cannery Row inn that wins praise for "unbeatable views" from oceanfront rooms and for its "extremely helpful staff"; all rooms have goose-down beds, fireplaces and marble baths, and fans insist "don't miss the lovely rooftop garden."

Napa

AUBERGE DU SOLEIL   28 | 27 | 28 | 27 | $377
180 Rutherford Hill Rd., Rutherford; 707-963-1211; fax 707-963-8764; 800-348-5406; www.aubergedusoleil.com; 50 rooms (19 suites, 2 cottages)
■ "Go with someone you love" to this "splurge" that has surveyors hoping "heaven is this nice"; it may "empty your wallet", but "all the senses are satisfied" by the Franco-Mediterranean fare, "unbelievable wine list", rooms that "resemble luxurious bachelor pads" with oversize tubs and "breathtaking" views of the valley; the only split decision among guests is whether the "difficult-to-leave" "paradise" is more like going to Tuscany or Provence.

Harvest Inn   23 | 21 | 19 | 21 | $219
1 Main St., St. Helena; 707-963-9463; fax 707-963-4402; 800-950-8466; www.harvestinn.com; 54 rooms (3 suites)
☑ "Spacious rooms" fitted with feather beds and fireplaces mark this English Tudor–style inn on the edge of a working vineyard; "handy after a day of wine tasting", it's also "good for families", especially with the "great buffet breakfasts"; some bristle at nearby traffic, but most find this a "great value" run by "people who care."

MEADOWOOD NAPA VALLEY   27 | 27 | 26 | 27 | $354
900 Meadowood Ln., St. Helena; 707-963-3646; fax 707-963-5863; 800-458-8080; www.meadowood.com; 85 rooms (45 suites)
☑ Like a "camp for adults", this "fine retreat for business or pleasure" in 250 acres of woodlands creates "a world unto itself" with "romantic" cottage clusters on "lush grounds" that sport tennis courts, croquet fields and a "challenging" nine-hole golf course; "spoil yourself" insist the smitten, who tout the "great spa" and "unbeatable" wine-country meals; for more, see Spa section.

Silverado   21 | 22 | 21 | 23 | $245
1600 Atlas Peak Rd., Napa; 707-257-0200; fax 707-257-2867; 800-532-0500; www.silveradoresort.com; 280 suites
☑ Accessible to the wine country but decidedly "golf-focused", this 1,500-acre resort can feel like "a factory" but is "saved by its beautiful location", "condo-like" cottages and 1870 mansion house; still, some conclude that it's "better" "for meetings than leisure."

Villagio Inn & Spa   26 | 23 | 21 | 23 | $289
6481 Washington St., Yountville; 707-944-8877; fax 707-944-8855;
800-351-1133; www.villagio.com; 112 rooms (26 suites)
■ "A great place to go back to after a day of wine tasting" in
the Valley concur guests at this "beautiful addition to the area
hotel scene" (opened in 1998); the "charming" Tuscan-inspired
villa situated on 23 acres houses "gorgeous" guestrooms and a
spa as well; there may not be a restaurant on-site, but a "huge"
daily champagne breakfast and afternoon tea are included in the
price of the room; for more, see Spa section.

Vintage Inn   24 | 22 | 19 | 21 | $216
6541 Washington St., Yountville; 707-944-1112; fax 707-944-1617;
800-351-1133; www.vintageinn.com; 80 rooms (12 suites)
■ "Snuggle with a loved one by the fireplace" at this inn, where the
"airy" rooms (some with beamed ceilings) make "a great home
base for exploring the wine country"; located a half block from
the French Laundry restaurant, this surveyors' "choice for peace
and quiet" shares 23 acres with its sibling, Villagio Inn & Spa, and
boasts a "top-notch concierge."

Newark

W Suites   – | – | – | – | M
8200 Gateway Blvd.; 510-494-8800; fax 510-494-8809; 877-946-8357;
www.whotels.com; 174 suites
'Silicon Valley style' may mean Palm Pilots and promotional
Polartec to some, but with the July 2000 opening of its first
all-suite property, next to the Sun Microsystems/JAVA campus,
this boutique chain hopes to kill that stereotype; high-tech
features like wireless Internet access and secure printing are
as expected; less predictable are bold colors and clean lines
in the guestrooms, the bar's buzzing crowd and the cafe's
light Californian fare.

Newport Beach

FOUR SEASONS   28 | 28 | 27 | 27 | $275
690 Newport Ctr. Dr.; 949-759-0808; fax 949-720-1718;
800-332-3442; www.fourseasons.com; 285 rooms (93 suites)
■ "If you're staying in Orange County, stay here" insist fans
of this "sophisticated retreat" in the heart of Newport Center
shopping, where guests get "excellent" personal service, "great
people-watching", views of the Pacific and "divine food" at not
just one, but three restaurants; "breathtaking decor" extends
from the "plush lobby" to the "airy", "well-appointed" rooms
and "huge bathrooms."

Sutton Place   22 | 22 | 22 | 21 | $192
4500 MacArthur Blvd.; 949-476-2001; fax 949-250-7191;
800-243-4141; www.suttonplace.com; 435 rooms (29 suites)
■ "Convenient to the airport", this "surprise" may be "the best
buy in Orange County"; regulars "like the suites" with huge
terraces, pool with cabanas, "accommodating" service and
"high-end" decor that is good enough "for a wedding."

Oakhurst

CHATEAU DU SUREAU   28 | 29 | 28 | 27 | $376

48688 Victoria Ln.; 559-683-6860; fax 559-683-0800;
www.chateausureau.com; 10 rooms (1 villa)
■ "If only every national park had a luxury 'trip to Europe' nearby"
like this "magical" "gateway to Yosemite" yearn surveyors; the
"charming" inn's rooms are each named for a different flower or
herb, and the staff "actually ties bows in your sneakers while you
are out and brings you fresh-baked cookies and cocoa upon your
return"; as for food, its restaurant, Erna's Elderberry House, sets
one of "the best tables west of Chicago."

Ojai

Ojai Valley Inn   24 | 25 | 25 | 26 | $258

905 Country Club Rd.; 805-646-5511; fax 805-646-7969;
800-422-6524; www.ojairesort.com; 206 rooms (15 suites)
■ "It's really Shangri-la!" marvel families, who find "enough
sophistication for adults" plus an "awesome kids' program" at this
resort overlooking the Ojai Mountains; acres of "lush landscaping"
with walking paths surround a golf course and spa that achieves
"the perfect balance between relaxation and practical therapy";
during downtime, guests relax in rooms with a Spanish motif.

Palm Springs Area

★ **Best in Area**
28 Ritz-Carlton Rancho Mirage/R
25 Renaissance Esmeralda/R
    Marriott's Desert Springs/R
    La Quinta/R
24 Hyatt Grand Champions/R

Hyatt Grand Champions   25 | 24 | 22 | 26 | $226

44-600 Indian Wells Ln., Indian Wells; 760-341-1000; fax 760-568-2236;
800-233-1234; www.hyatt.com; 338 rooms (319 suites, 19 villas)
☑ Surrounded by the Santa Rosa mountains, this "sportsman's
paradise in the sun" yields views in all directions; the energetic
report having "a fine time in the desert" at this sprawling golf-and-
tennis resort with its "huge", "lovely" villas and private pools; most
are pleased with the spa facilities and service too, but dissenters
suggest a "face-lift" is overdue.

La Quinta Resort & Club   25 | 24 | 23 | 26 | $253

49-499 Eisenhower Dr., La Quinta; 760-564-4111; fax 760-564-7625;
800-598-3828; www.laquintaresort.com; 851 rooms (26 suites,
193 casitas)
☑ For a large resort, "it doesn't feel that way", with perpetual
springtime flowers around Spanish-style bungalows and oodles of
pools; the staff "tries to please and succeeds", even though the
resort has expanded enormously in recent years; regulars tout
older rooms for the '40s-era style that drew the likes of Garbo and
Gable and the "superior" new spa facilities; critics mourn the
triumph of sprawl over charm; for more, see Spa section.

Marriott's Desert Springs
24 | 24 | 24 | 26 | $227

74855 Country Club Dr., Palm Desert; 760-341-2211;
fax 760-341-1872; 800-228-9290; www.marriott.com; 884 rooms
(51 suites)

◪ For an "over-the-top" desert escape, gondolas will transport you
from the lobby lake to the five restaurants and your room at this
resort that "tries to be upscale" while catering to everyone from
conventioneers to families and golfers; though the vistas, spa and
setting are "fabulous", many feel that they don't compensate for
the "citylike" size, "overcrowded pools" and "plain" rooms; for
more, see Spa section.

Marriott's Rancho Las Palmas
21 | 23 | 21 | 23 | $197

41000 Bob Hope Dr., Rancho Mirage; 760-568-2727;
fax 760-568-5845; 800-228-9290; www.marriott.com; 450 rooms
(22 suites)

◪ Sprawled over 240 acres with "tranquil lakes, gardens and
swaying palms", this Hacienda-style desert resort stands out from
the Marriott crowd for its "older charm" and "lovely landscaping"
that makes you think of "a lush oasis"; most guests give thumbs-
up to "spacious" rooms (where kids are welcome) and to golf
and tennis facilities, but others say though "it's perfectly nice,
it's nothing special."

Merv Griffin's Resort Hotel & Givenchy Spa
24 | 22 | 22 | 24 | $253

4200 E. Palm Canyon Dr., Palm Springs; 760-770-5000; fax 760-324-6104;
800-276-5000; www.merv.com; 103 rooms (34 suites)

◪ Surveyors advise "don't bring kids" to this classic French–style
desert resort, where guests savor "gorgeous gardens", "friendly
staff" and the occasional Merv sighting; most relish the spa
(with its seaweed treatments) and "peaceful" ambiance, but a
few liken the all-white property to a "ghost town" and suggest
the rooms get "a nip and tuck."

Miramonte
▽ 23 | 24 | 22 | 21 | $176

4500 Indian Wells Ln., Indian Wells; 760-341-2200;
fax 760-568-0541; 800-237-2926; www.miramonte-resort.com;
222 rooms (23 suites, 3 villas)

■ Surveyors discover "hidden treasure" in an area dominated
by huge resorts; "Tuscan atmosphere" pervades this "intimate",
"wonderfully uncrowded" getaway with "affable service" that
caters more to golfers and spa visitors than conventioneers;
given its relatively modest prices, more people should get to
know this sleeper.

Renaissance Esmeralda
25 | 24 | 23 | 26 | $199

44-400 Indian Wells Ln., Indian Wells; 760-773-4444; fax 760-773-9250;
800-468-3571; www.renaissancehotels.com; 560 rooms (22 suites)

■ We hear "no complaints" about this "luxurious" resort with its
"perfect layout" of "spectacular grounds", two golf courses, pool
and "architecture that's grand yet intimate"; to make the most of
its "lovely, quiet atmosphere", regulars like to go when it's not
crowded (especially since it's "cheap off-season") and families
savor "friendly" service and "roomy" accommodations, all with
balconies or patios.

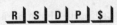
RITZ-CARLTON RANCHO MIRAGE `28 28 27 28 $277`
68-900 Frank Sinatra Dr., Rancho Mirage; 760-321-8282;
fax 760-321-6928; 800-241-3333; www.ritzcarlton.com; 240 rooms
(21 suites)
■ "Oasis defined", this "beautiful hotel in the middle of the desert"
faces the "best views in the valley" from its hilltop vantage; English
"clubby" interiors "could be more Western", and there's no golf on
premises, but most relish the "excellent food", "chilled swimming
pool" (it "hits 120 degrees" here in summer) and the "best staff"
that leaves the well-heeled crowd feeling "very pampered"; for
more, see Spa section.

Westin Mission Hills `23 23 21 25 $215`
71333 Dinah Shore Dr., Rancho Mirage; 760-328-5955; fax 760-770-2199;
888-625-5144; www.westin.com; 512 rooms (40 suites)
☑ It's "no strain to have a good time" at the "superb" pools, tennis
courts and two golf courses at this resort imbued with the spirit
of an old Spanish villa amid "outstanding floral grounds" and
mountains; "spacious rooms" (a few call the decor "so-so"),
"speedy room service" and an "accommodating staff" add to the
ambiance, while "unbelievably affordable" summer specials make
this big convention resort a year-round "favorite."

Palo Alto

Garden Court Hotel `24 23 21 21 $236`
520 Cowper St.; 650-322-2194; fax 650-324-3609; 800-824-9028;
www.gardencourt.com; 62 rooms (13 suites)
■ Serving those who need to be in Downtown Palo Alto (or near
Stanford University), this hotel, "well-outfitted for business", holds
a "virtual monopoly" on the Silicon Valley VC community and the
PowerPoint, cell phone and laptop types who come to California to
get financing; besides its handy location, "clean" and comfortable
rooms and a branch of Il Fornaio restaurant are pluses causing
fans to treat it as their "home away from home."

Riverside

Mission Inn `22 22 22 22 $160`
3649 Mission Inn Ave.; 909-784-0300; fax 909-683-1342;
800-843-7755; www.missioninn.com; 283 rooms (32 suites)
■ Staying at this "architectural wonder" tucked away in the
middle of nowhere "is an event" in itself; courtyards "mix history
and elegance", while the "quirky rooms", many with wall niches
and wrought-iron balconies, are studies in "unique shapes and
furniture"; guests appreciate the "good" service as they dine on
steak at Duane's restaurant or belly up to the Presidential Lounge
("best bar in Riverside").

San Diego Area

★ **Best in Area**
28 Four Seasons Aviara/R   La Valencia Hotel/H
    Rancho Valencia/SR   **24** del Coronado/H
25 L'Auberge Del Mar/R   Loews Coronado Bay/R
    Rancho Bernardo/R   Marriott Coronado Island/R

del Coronado, Hotel | 23 | 24 | 24 | 26 | $240 |
1500 Orange Ave., Coronado; 619-435-6611; fax 619-522-8262;
800-468-3533; www.hoteldel.com; 681 rooms (22 suites,
1 beach house)
☑ An "old favorite" that has hosted presidents and prime ministers
(not to mention Marilyn Monroe, Jack Lemmon and Tony Curtis
when *Some Like It Hot* filmed here), this 1888 "classic" comes with
"cool ocean breezes" (and much-needed a/c in every room when
ongoing renovations are finally complete); "gracious" public spaces
("lunch on the veranda is a joy") add to the appeal of this turreted,
red-roofed Victorian landmark that a few deem an "overpriced
behemoth" with a "circus" for a lobby.

FOUR SEASONS AVIARA | 28 | 28 | 27 | 28 | $315 |
7100 Four Seasons Point, Carlsbad; 760-603-6800;
fax 760-603-6878; 800-332-3442; www.fourseasons.com;
331 rooms (44 suites)
■ This top-rated "island of serenity" on a bluff above Batiquitos
Lagoon may be in the middle of nowhere, but guests who go for
the "gorgeous golf course", "beguiling buffets" and poolside
strawberries and Evian spritzes aren't complaining; "large, well-
appointed rooms" and "kind staff" that caters to families with small
children "make you feel right at home"; for more, see Spa section.

Hilton La Jolla Torrey Pines | 23 | 23 | 21 | 23 | $205 |
(fka Sheraton Grand Torrey Pines)
10950 N. Torrey Pines Rd., La Jolla; 858-558-1500;
fax 858-450-4584; 800-762-6160; www.hilton.com; 394 rooms
(17 suites)
☑ The "views of the golf course and grounds are gorgeous" at this
Palisades resort frequented by business travelers who stay in
"spacious and seemingly soundproof" rooms (scheduled for a
little updating soon); though some complain that the hotel is "not
convenient to town" and "could be closer to the beach", those who
appreciate the walk to Del Mar Race Track and drinks next to the
pool consider this "well-maintained property" an "old friend."

Hyatt Regency | 22 | 22 | 21 | 22 | $197 |
1 Market Pl., San Diego; 619-232-1234; fax 619-233-6464;
800-233-1234; www.hyatt.com; 875 rooms (61 suites)
☑ "Lots of hustle and bustle" and "incredible views of San Diego
harbor" are de rigueur at this "basic businessman's" high-rise
close to prime shopping and the convention center; light sleepers
protest the location "right under the flight path to the airport", but
most appreciate the "clean rooms."

Hyatt Regency La Jolla at Aventine | 23 | 23 | 22 | 23 | $199 |
3777 La Jolla Village Dr., San Diego; 858-552-1234;
fax 858-552-6066; 800-233-1234; www.hyatt.com; 419 rooms
(25 suites)
☑ "Michael Graves' Tuscan-inspired architecture makes this not
just another Hyatt" claim fans of the "hip" high-rise that's part of a
popular commercial complex; its "most spectacular health club,
large pool and outdoor Jacuzzi" attract fitness freaks, while Pacific
Rim fare lures the hungry to Cafe Japengo; cognoscenti, however,
warn "be careful of the cost of parking."

Inn at Rancho Santa Fe, The   24 | 24 | 23 | 23 | $213

5951 Linea Del Cielo, Rancho Santa Fe; 858-756-1131; fax 858-759-1604; 800-843-4661; www.theinnatranchosantafe.com; 89 rooms (8 suites, 6 cottages)

■ Set amid rolling hills and 20 "charming", old-"California-style" cottages, this country inn is a "dignified nostalgia trip", popular with the "geriatric" crowd, who enjoy "formal lunches" in the Vintage Room, "wonderful landscaping", "lovely pool" and "lots of space to walk" at this eucalyptus plantation turned "sedate getaway."

La Casa Del Zorro Desert Resort   24 | 24 | 22 | 25 | $198

3845 Yaqui Pass Rd., Borrego Springs; 760-767-5323; fax 760-767-5963; 800-824-1884; www.lacasadelzorro.com; 77 rooms (6 suites, 19 casitas)

■ This "oasis" may "not be as flashy and new" as some chic urban hotels, but it's an "absolute delight" (and "tremendous value") for those who know how "wonderful wildflower time" is in the Anza Borrego Desert; a couple of hours from the Pacific, the small resort offers rooms and casitas (including two bi-level suites with pianos), plus five pools to cool the "killer" heat – or the sweat worked up on the walking paths and tennis courts; jazz weekends throughout the year are "great for family reunions."

La Costa   22 | 24 | 22 | 24 | $283

2100 Costa Del Mar Rd., Carlsbad; 760-438-9111; fax 760-438-3758; 800-854-5000; www.lacosta.com; 479 rooms (76 suites)

☑ "Golf, golf, golf" chant longtime fans of this "classic" spa resort's two PGA championship courses, while tennis players swat balls on 21 courts and sybarites sigh "ahhh" on massage tables; but one reviewer's "great retreat" is another's "weary" "has-been": rooms that "look like they were decorated by Nancy Reagan" and "pedestrian food" draw barbs from those unimpressed with the package deals offered at this "old-school" resort.

L'Auberge Del Mar   25 | 25 | 24 | 25 | $240

1540 Camino Del Mar, Del Mar; 858-259-1515; fax 858-755-4940; 800-553-1336; www.laubergedelmar.com; 120 rooms (8 suites)

■ "A true sleeper" in a "quaint" San Diego suburb, this Tudor-style "destination resort for those who want to get away but still be near the city" wins praise for its "exquisite setting" overlooking an almost-private town beach; it "feels very European" to some, perhaps because you can leave your car at the hotel and walk to shopping and restaurants before retreating to the "most comfortable beds in the world."

La Valencia Hotel   23 | 25 | 25 | 25 | $278

1132 Prospect St., La Jolla; 858-454-0771; fax 858-551-3751; 800-451-0772; www.lavalenciahotel.com; 117 rooms (17 suites)

■ "Reminiscent of the '20s", this Spanish-style period hotel and "anchor of La Jolla" earns kudos for its "great lobby bar" (try the Whaler Drink) and bougainvillea trailing the wrought-iron banisters on the patio; pink-stucco exteriors house "small but absolutely charming" rooms and more spacious villas, while an "attentive staff" that "respects privacy" helps make this "a perfect place" for a "romantic getaway with great views."

Loews Coronado Bay Resort   25 | 23 | 23 | 24 | $222
4000 Coronado Bay Rd., Coronado; 619-424-4000; fax 619-424-4400;
800-815-6397; www.loewshotels.com; 4,348 rooms (37 suites)
■ Blessed with a "lovely setting" on a private peninsula, this
Mediterannean-style resort dishes up a slice of "heaven by the
sea", where guests watch the sunset over San Diego Bay, dive into
the water sports, indulge in "incredible gluttony" at the champagne
brunch or relax in large rooms with "fabulous" bathrooms; though
a few bemoan an off-the-beaten-path locale, vacationers and
conventioneers dub this a "must-stay" "secluded getaway."

Marriott Coronado Island Resort   24 | 24 | 23 | 25 | $214
2000 Second St., Coronado; 619-435-3000; fax 619-435-4183;
800-228-9290; www.marriott.com; 300 rooms (28 suites)
☑ Vacationers and conference-goers alike are attracted to the
resort's "great bayside location", views and "lovely grounds" –
the waterfall and ponds are "like being in the middle of a nature
preserve"; while room size varies "tremendously" from "little" to
"very large" and some call dining "spotty", most agree this retreat
remains a "good value."

Rancho Bernardo Inn   24 | 25 | 25 | 25 | $226
17550 Bernardo Oaks Dr., San Diego; 858-675-8500; fax 858-675-8501;
800-542-6096; www.ranchobernardoinn.com; 287 rooms (12 suites)
■ Tucked away in a suburban area north of San Diego, this
California Mission–style resort for "sports enthusiasts" edges a
"gorgeous golf course" visible from most of its rooms, all of which
come with patio or "peaceful balcony"; the "exquisitely manicured
yet casual grounds" and French restaurant El Bizcocho ("I didn't
want to leave the table") make this "lovely older inn" "great for
corporate retreats" yet "perfect for kids too: I taught my eight-
year-old chess in the cozy lobby" says one surveyor.

RANCHO VALENCIA RESORT   29 | 28 | 27 | 28 | $351
5921 Valencia Circle, Rancho Santa Fe; 858-756-1123; fax 858-756-0165;
800-548-3664; www.ranchovalencia.com; 43 suites
■ This "glorious colony" of "fabulous" casita suites attracts more
than tennis buffs to its 18 hard courts – seekers of "tranquil bliss"
can contentedly pick oranges or stroll among the "trees and
incredible flowers" growing in tiered grounds at this "great
hideaway for the rich and famous"; whether it's serving fresh o.j.
every morning or "excellent food" in the Cal-Pacific dining room,
"they do what they do stupendously" agree surveyors, who add
that this "expensive" "well-kept secret" is "worth every penny."

San Diego Marriott   23 | 22 | 20 | 22 | $182
333 W. Harbor Dr.; 619-234-1500; fax 619-234-8678; 800-228-9290
www.marriott.com; 1,354 rooms (54 suites)
☑ A "regular Marriott in a great place" (it's "connected to the
convention center", " near Seaport Village", " close to the
Gaslamp Quarter" and "on a marina"), its "clean rooms with no
clutter", "excellent meeting facilities" and "attentive service"
keep this "impressive building" "always busy" with business folk;
those seeking chic say "there are better places to stay in San
Diego", since "nothing really stands out" here.

Westgate Hotel, The | 25 | 23 | 22 | 23 | $205 |
1055 Second Ave., San Diego; 619-238-1818; fax 619-557-3737;
800-221-3802; www.westgatehotel.com; 223 rooms (10 suites)
☑ A "good" "pick for business or pleasure", this "old-fashioned"
hotel, "conveniently" located Downtown, accommodates guests in
"immense rooms" with antiques, "marble bathrooms" and "plush
bathrobes"; fans savor the "yummy breakfast" and "afternoon tea"
served in an "old-world" setting that achieves "quaint without the
kitsch", but critics fault the "Versailles style for the blue-hair set."

San Francisco

★ **Best in City**
28 Ritz-Carlton/H   Pan Pacific/H
27 Sherman House/H   24 Palace/H
26 Mandarin Oriental/H   W San Francisco/H
25 Campton Place/H   Park Hyatt/H

Archbishop's Mansion | 26 | 23 | 21 | 23 | $223 |
1000 Fulton St.; 415-563-7872; fax 415-885-3193; 800-543-5820;
www.archbishopsmansion.com; 15 rooms (5 suites)
☑ "For Victorian flashbacks", surveyors tout this converted
mansion built for the archbishop of San Francisco in 1904; rooms
reside "one step from heaven", but the Alamo Square location (with
"classic view of the city" in a "cruddy neighborhood") makes it "too
far to walk to anything"; "accommodating service", free breakfast
and evening wine and cheese give this "treat" a "European" feel.

Argent Hotel | 22 | 21 | 19 | 20 | $207 |
(fka ANA)
50 Third St.; 415-974-6400; fax 415-543-8268; 877-222-6699;
www.argenthotel.com; 667 rooms (26 suites)
☑ Ambivalence abounds about this newly renovated Financial
District convention hotel: boosters are "pleasantly surprised" by
rooms with "great views" and "dynamite" design, but bashers
begrudge them as "shoebox-size"; similarly, supporters label the
staff "friendly" and "attentive", while disparagers prefer the word
"sleazy"; still, when it comes to location, all concur: "convenient."

Best Western Tuscan Inn | 22 | 22 | 22 | 20 | $150 |
425 North Point St.; 415-561-1100; fax 415-561-1199; 800-648-4626;
www.tuscaninn.com; 221 rooms (12 suites)
☑ "A late-afternoon wine guzzle" and tea and biscotti in the lobby
are two perks at this "modest" Fisherman's Wharf–side hotel; in
spite of "basic lodgings" and "too much pastel", loyalists like its
"sweet European feel": "who'da guessed it's a Best Western?"

CAMPTON PLACE HOTEL | 25 | 26 | 27 | 23 | $294 |
340 Stockton St.; 415-781-5555; fax 415-955-5536; 800-235-4300;
www.camptonplace.com; 110 rooms (9 suites)
■ "Class shows" at this "European-style hotel" with "peachy"
rooms that are surprisingly "quiet, considering it's on Union
Square"; the staff lavishes "personalized service" – "doormen
know your name", concierges "give you umbrellas" and "even
return your rental cars" – and the "excellent" restaurant serves
French Country cuisine and "the best breakfast in the cosmos"
(must-haves: French toast, oatmeal and "sinful hot chocolate").

Clift Hotel
23 | 24 | 23 | 22 | $251

495 Geary St.; 415-775-4700; fax 415-441-4621; 800-652-5438;
www.clifthotel.com; 326 rooms (103 suites)

☑ Although the famed Redwood Room bar and restaurant (a "hangout for aging rock stars") will be closed for a yearlong rehab, this 1915 "grande dame" still embodies "vintage luxury", including "dignified service" that compensates for rooms deemed "a little tired"; some call the hotel's edge-of-the-Tenderloin location somewhat "seedy", but others are grateful that there are "no hills to climb."

Donatello
22 | 22 | 22 | 19 | $207

501 Post St.; 415-441-7100; fax 415-885-8842; 800-227-3184; 94 rooms

■ "Huge rooms", "cheerful" staff ("even late night"), "exceptional, although viewless" rooftop bar and Union Square location put this Italianate boutique hotel high on the value-meter; "unpretentious" Northern cuisine and "jazz at night by the bar" further add to this "charming" "bargain."

Fairmont
23 | 24 | 23 | 24 | $249

950 Mason St.; 415-772-5000; fax 415-391-4833; 800-866-5577;
www.fairmont.com; 591 rooms (65 suites)

☑ The tippy-top of Nob Hill marks the "peerless location" of this "opulent" hotel – a "perennial favorite" among businessmen, presidents and sightseers – with "stunning views and service to match"; ongoing renovations to the 1906 building should make a "dramatic difference" in "dated" rooms, while the newly restored lobby and restaurants are "sparkling" and "palatial" once again.

Huntington Hotel
25 | 25 | 24 | 22 | $272

1075 California St.; 415-474-5400; fax 415-474-6227; 800-227-4683;
www.huntingtonhotel.com; 135 rooms (35 suites)

☑ Fans of this "clubby" Nob Hill hotel endorse its "stunning views", "innovative" restaurant and "gracious staff" (the concierge "can obtain any hot ticket"); some say rooms in the 1924 structure display "understated elegance", but a few feel they're "shabby" and "in need of updating"; still, a stay here is "divine" and should be enhanced by a brand-new spa.

Hyatt Regency
22 | 22 | 20 | 22 | $209

5 Embarcadero Ctr.; 415-788-1234; fax 415-291-6538; 800-233-1234;
www.hyatt.com; 823 rooms (45 suites)

☑ The "dramatic" atrium provides a "typical Hyatt" feel at this "convenient" Embarcadero Center and Financial District "monster" (it's "big enough to get lost in – and you will") that tends to draw a convention crowd; "helpful" service and rooms with "a harbor view from balconies are worth" the price of admission, but gourmets take note: dinner in the revolving rooftop restaurant is "so-so."

Laurel Inn, The
– | – | – | – | I

444 Presidio Ave.; 415-567-8467; fax 415-928-1866; 800-552-8735;
www.thelaurelinn.com; 49 rooms (18 suites)

Part of the stylish Joie de Vivre Hospitality group, this revamped Pacific Heights 1960s motor inn delivers a dose of design to an otherwise staid neighborhood; rooms set up like studio apartments come kitted out with Midcentury Modern touches (think club chairs and Matisse-print carpets), complimentary coffee and tea is poured in the lobby 24/7 and pets are welcome.

Majestic
25 │ 23 │ 24 │ 21 │ $201

1500 Sutter St.; 415-441-1100; fax 415-673-7331; 800-869-8966;
www.thehotelmajestic.com; 58 rooms (9 suites)
■ "Colorful, one-of-a-kind" rooms with antiques and "low noise
level" – plus a manager who "really takes care of his guests" –
inform this "well-maintained" 1902 property; seasonal American
fare in the new Perlot restaurant gets a thumbs-up, while an off-
the-beaten-path location near Japantown and Pacific Heights
makes this "value" an "attractive alternative" to big, glitzy hotels.

MANDARIN ORIENTAL
28 │ 27 │ 26 │ 24 │ $321

222 Sansome St.; 415-276-9888; fax 415-433-0289; 800-622-0404;
www.mandarinoriental.com; 154 rooms (4 suites)
■ Guests at this "swanky" Asian-inspired Downtowner have
a "tough call": "see San Francisco or stay in the hotel", which
occupies the top 11 floors of the city's third-tallest building; luckily,
you can do both, since every room comes with binoculars and a
"million-dollar view", even from tubs in some of the "apartment-
size" marble bathrooms; cuisine at top-rated Silks is "beautifully
presented", and "impeccable service" includes "slippers by the
bed", "cookies on your pillow at night" and 24-hour room service
that "retrieves the dirty dishes without being asked."

Mark Hopkins Inter-Continental
23 │ 24 │ 23 │ 24 │ $257

1 Nob Hill; 415-392-3434; fax 415-421-3302; 800-327-0200;
www.markhopkins.com; 380 rooms (38 suites)
■ "Don't miss drinks at Top of the Mark" remains the mantra for
this recently renovated Nob Hill landmark, built in 1926, that
reviewers characterize as a "quiet", "smooth operation", "except
for the sound of cable-car bells"; standard rooms can be "small",
but the legendary "grandeur" of the chateaulike building and the
"caring service" prompt frequent returnees to concede that they
"can't break the habit."

Monaco, Hotel
24 │ 23 │ 23 │ 23 │ $215

501 Geary St.; 415-292-0100; fax 415-292-0149; 800-214-4220;
www.hotelmonaco.com; 201 rooms (34 suites)
☑ "You have to like stripes and bold colors" to appreciate the
"*Alice in Wonderland*" decor that "feels like you're in a fairy tale" –
even though you're "in the heart of Downtown and shopping";
"small" rooms ("you need a shoehorn to get in") are "cool", and
"trendy" extras include a pet goldfish for your room, hot-stone
massages and tarot card readings each night in the spa parlor;
like the hotel itself, the "hip" restaurant goes beyond "standard
hotel fare", and "with-it" service resists "being condescending."

Nikko, Hotel
23 │ 24 │ 22 │ 22 │ $248

222 Mason St.; 415-394-1111; fax 415-394-1106; 800-645-5687;
www.nikkohotels.com; 532 rooms (22 suites)
■ "Minimalist ambiance" and "Japanese efficiency in everything"
they do make the Nikko seem "sleek and elegant" to proponents,
"austere" to detractors; white marble and silk wallpaper decorate
public areas of this business hotel, and guestrooms come with
"high-tech, comfortable furnishings"; though guests like the
restaurant's "stunning" sushi arrangements, and the "expert"
staff demonstrates a "kowtow courtesy", this is "not a place for
a romantic weekend."

Palace Hotel
24 | 24 | 24 | 26 | $242

2 New Montgomery St.; 415-512-1111; fax 415-543-0671; 800-325-3535; www.sfpalace.com; 553 rooms (34 suites)

■ It "feels like San Francisco 100 years ago" at this 1875 "grand old lady" that maintains the "majestic" aura and "jaw-dropping" architectural flourishes that earned its historic landmark status; a "magnificent stained-glass ceiling" in the Garden Court restaurant makes dining a "special event", and the original Maxfield Parrish mural in the Pied Piper lounge tops off a flute of local bubbly – it's just "too bad" the "well-appointed" rooms "have no view."

Palomar, Hotel
24 | 24 | 25 | 22 | $275

12 Fourth St.; 415-348-1111; fax 415-344-3312; 877-294-9711; www.hotelpalomar.com; 198 rooms (16 suites)

■ Even with "funky decor" in the art deco lobby and "racy leopard carpet" running through the "chic, cool rooms", this "phenomenal" "of-the-moment" hotel musters up substance amid all that style: tourists appreciate the "convenient" SoMa locale close to shopping and sight-seeing, and insiders know that "not-to-be-missed" "designer" French cuisine at its Fifth Floor restaurant is "one of the best secrets in the city."

Pan Pacific Hotel, The
26 | 25 | 24 | 24 | $253

500 Post St.; 415-771-8600; fax 415-398-0267; 800-533-6465; www.panpac.com; 329 rooms (33 suites)

■ The "bathrooms rock" with "more marble than a quarry" – not to mention Jacuzzis, TVs and "the fluffiest bathrobes" – at this high-rise hotel that feels "a bit '80s" (glass elevators zoom up a central atrium) but manages its "slickness" "without losing grace or comfort"; even if your timing isn't right for "personal birthday greetings from the staff", you can still "take the hotel's Rolls Royce to dinner"– that is, if you're not walking across the street to Wolfgang Puck's Postrio.

Park Hyatt
26 | 25 | 23 | 23 | $259

333 Battery St.; 415-392-1234; fax 415-421-4233; 800-233-1234; www.hyatt.com; 360 rooms (37 suites)

■ "More intimate than other Hyatts", this "solid convention hotel" near the Embarcadero affords "breathtaking" views of the Bay and the city "if you get the right room"; "chain elegance" is no insult here, because the company "knows how to treat the business traveler": guests praise "know-your-name" service ("housekeeping got flowers to my room almost before I made it upstairs"), "lovely" accommodations and lots of "personal touches."

Prescott Hotel, The
22 | 24 | 27 | 21 | $216

545 Post St.; 415-563-0303; fax 415-563-6831; 800-283-7322; www.prescotthotel.com; 164 rooms (35 suites)

☑ "Booking a room can be hard", since some Wolfgang Puck fans believe "staying here may be the only way to get a table" at his adjacent Postrio restaurant; try to land "on the concierge floor" for complimentary "breakfast and cocktails" (with "great hors d'oeuvres" from Puck's kitchen) or "ask for a room that's not at ground level", because busy Post Street keeps buzzing after midnight; quibblers note that these "small" quarters offer "no real scenery" – just "a view of a naked guy across the way."

Renaissance Stanford Court Hotel | 24 | 25 | 24 | 23 | $253 |
905 California St.; 415-989-3500; fax 415-391-0513; 800-468-3571;
www.renaissancehotels.com; 393 rooms (22 suites)
☑ Three-quarters of the way up Nob Hill, this "find" – with beaux
arts murals and a huge stained-glass dome in the lobby – displays
"grand hotel style" and "a sense of the past" (even though it was
built in 1972); an "agreeable staff" "takes courtesy to new heights",
"rooms are comfortable but small", Mediterranean-inspired
Californian cuisine in Fournou's Ovens is "unbeatable" and the
location allows easy access to "cable-car lines" and Union Square
shops; while some fear it "has slipped a bit", most rate this both a
"class act and good value."

RITZ-CARLTON, THE | 28 | 28 | 28 | 27 | $318 |
600 Stockton St.; 415-296-7465; fax 415-291-0147; 800-241-3333;
www.ritzcarlton.com; 336 rooms (44 suites)
■ Nob Hill's former Temple of Commerce (near Chinatown and
within walking distance of Union Square) gets 48-carat gold stars
for being "all-around fabulous" (and ranking No. 1 in the city);
expect white gloves at the door, "old money" on the concierge
floor, an indoor pool and "excellent everything" throughout an
"antiques-filled" hotel that "defines class and service"; thanks to
chefs Dubray and Portay (formerly of NYC's Le Cirque), The Dining
Room's "gourmet" cuisine is "exquisite"; in short, this place "is
a big 'wow'!"

Serrano Hotel | ▽ | 23 | 23 | 21 | 22 | $180 |
405 Taylor St.; 415-885-2500; fax 415-474-4879; 877-294-9709;
www.serranohotel.com; 235 rooms (16 suites)
■ "Where am I – Morocco?" you may wonder while ogling the
"bold color schemes" and "funky decor" at this "eye-opening",
"playful" hotel; restaurant Ponzu serves a "spicy" fusion of Thai,
Vietnamese, Japanese and Californian dishes, rooms are "small
but well appointed" and town-car rides to the Financial District
are on the house; devotees declare "you're never bored here."

SHERMAN HOUSE, THE | 28 | 27 | 26 | 25 | $391 |
2160 Green St.; 415-563-3600; fax 415-563-1882; 800-424-5777;
www.theshermanhouse.com; 8 rooms (6 suites)
■ It's so "charming" at this 1876 Pacific Heights mansion that you
may think you're staying at "a very rich friend's house" – complete
with an "accommodating" staff, "intimate" Empire-style rooms
with Biedermeier furniture and canopy beds (all but one have
fireplaces); in addition, there's a "romantic rooftop suite" that
showcases a "great view of the Golden Gate Bridge" and a chef
who serves in a guests-only dining room.

Triton, Hotel | 21 | 21 | 18 | 20 | $186 |
342 Grant Ave.; 415-394-0500; fax 415-394-0555; 800-433-6611;
www.hotel-tritonsf.com; 140 rooms (7 suites)
☑ "If you're willing to sacrifice personal space for a hip" ambiance,
this hotel located at the gates to Chinatown is the spot; the "artsy"
rooms designed by such music celebs as Jerry Garcia, Carlos
Santana and Graham Nash are "over the top" (like "staying in
Pee-Wee's Playhouse"), and the newsstand cafe is dubbed a
"fave", but guests yearning to "become cool just by walking in the
door" soon learn they "shouldn't expect too much from the staff."

Westin St. Francis Hotel, The   23 | 23 | 22 | 24 | $228
335 Powell St.; 415-397-7000; fax 415-774-0124; 800-228-3000;
www.westin.com; 1,194 rooms (84 suites)
■ You can choose between a "small, charming old room" in
the main section and "a big new room with a view in the tower
units" – either way, "drinks in the Compass Rose restaurant
are a must" at what some claim is a "tour-group-oriented" hotel
that's "too big"; fans praise "breathtaking" public spaces, "good
concierge services" and a history of visiting dignitaries like Queen
Elizabeth II; after all, staying at this "landmark on Union Square"
is a "great tradition."

White Swan Inn   25 | 25 | 22 | 23 | $180
845 Bush St.; 415-775-1755; fax 415-775-5717; 800-999-9570;
www.foursisters.com; 26 rooms (3 suites)
■ A curious cross between "Oxford" and "Pooh Corner", this
"country inn in the heart of the city" is close to Union Square, Nob
Hill and Chinatown but feels "tucked away", especially when staff
serves complimentary champagne at 5 PM and "a sumptuous
breakfast" every morning; though most guests delight in all the
"Victorian charm" (canopied beds with "fluffy" feather pillows), a
few wince over "teddy bears everywhere": "too cute for words."

W San Francisco   26 | 23 | 23 | 24 | $264
181 Third St.; 415-777-5300; fax 415-817-7823; 877-946-8357;
www.whotels.com; 423 rooms (5 suites)
☑ Brace for an "always-happening lobby scene" warn visitors to
SoMa's "hip" hotel next to the Museum of Modern Art and across
from the Moscone Center; "minimalist" rooms with high-speed
modems, CD players and Aveda bath products make surveyors
feel "like I died and woke up in a Banana Republic ad"; the "trendy"
XYZ Bar is "jammed with beautiful people", and though the
headset-clad staff seems to "have an attitude problem", they're
quick to "smile and anticipate your needs."

San Jose

De Anza, Hotel   ▽ 24 | 24 | 23 | 21 | $181
233 W. Santa Clara St.; 408-286-1000; fax 408-286-0500;
800-843-3700; www.hoteldeanza.com; 101 rooms (9 suites)
■ Guests gush over the open-pantry policy ("no joke – at 2 AM you
can make yourself a sandwich") at this "cool, funky and almost
trendy" art deco landmark on the outskirts of Downtown; the
"sleek, comfortable" rooms may be "small", but it's the "attention
to detail that makes all the difference" at this "find" where the
"personal service" helps make it the "classiest place in town."

Fairmont Hotel   24 | 22 | 22 | 23 | $195
170 S. Market St.; 408-998-1900; fax 408-280-6072; 800-866-5577;
www.fairmont.com; 541 rooms (41 suites)
■ Those looking for a "good alternative to San Francisco" find
their way to San Jose's "business travelers' mecca" in the reborn
Downtown area; most agree "reasonable prices" belie the
"understated elegance" of the rooms and lobby as well as the
"fantastic Sunday buffet" and "attentive personnel", though a
few snipe that this "upscale" high-rise is a "Silicon Valley joke"
with "a dot-com attitude."

San Luis Obispo

Apple Farm   24 │ 23 │ 21 │ 22 │ $148
2015 Monterey St.; 805-544-2040; fax 805-546-9495; 800-255-2040;
www.applefarm.com; 104 rooms (69 suites)
■ Guests "wake up to the smell of apple pies" baking at the
Central Coast's "ultimate country home", a "dependable" "rest
stop between SF and LA"; couples and families check in for the
"wholesome" comfort food, "cozy rooms" with fireplaces, carriage
rides and "congenial" staff ("they must be trained by Disney"),
while sourpusses cry "so cute it makes your teeth hurt."

Madonna Inn   22 │ 18 │ 16 │ 20 │ $165
100 Madonna Rd.; 805-543-3000; fax 805-543-1800; 800-543-9666;
www.madonnainn.com; 109 rooms (32 suites)
☑ "No trip through Central California is complete" without a visit
to this "mondo bizarro" "showplace" that "looks like a motor inn"
outside and "the Mad Hatter's fantasy" inside; "zany", individually
themed chambers – from American Beauty to Yosemite Rock
("nothing beats the Cave Man room: ugh!") – strike some as
"hilarious", others as "tourist kitsch", but on two points most
agree: "inattentiveness" is the norm among the staff, and the inn
serves "food my friends with no taste buds would love."

Santa Barbara

Bacara Resort & Spa, The   – │ – │ – │ – │ VE
8301 Hollister Ave.; 805-968-0100; fax 805-968-1800; 877-422-4245;
www.bacararesort.com; 360 rooms (49 suites)
A collection of Spanish Colonial casitas that look out onto Santa
Ynez peaks or a stretch of Pacific, this resort (opened in September
2000) fosters relaxation in rooms outfitted with plush robes and
balconies; inside its spa, you can get the kinks out in 41 treatment
rooms, 3,500 sq. ft. fitness center and a heated lap pool; once done
with pampering, guests can fill up in any of three restaurants (one
serves spa cuisine) or go into re-tox at the four bars and lounges.

El Encanto Hotel   22 │ 23 │ 23 │ 24 │ $236
1900 Lasuen Rd.; 805-687-5000; fax 805-687-3903; 800-346-7039;
83 rooms (27 suites)
☑ Perched on a "serene" hilltop overlooking town, this historic
hotel next to the Mission occupies 10 acres of "lush gardens" with
private bungalows that "make a romantic getaway feel like an
illicit rendezvous"; the smitten rave about the lily pond and terrace
dining with "the best vistas in the city", but the less enthralled think
the setting is "wasted" on "dowdy" facilities that are crying out
for "an overhaul – fast"; N.B. renovations are set to start in 2001.

FOUR SEASONS BILTMORE   26 │ 27 │ 26 │ 27 │ $312
1260 Channel Dr.; 805-969-2261; fax 805-565-8323; 800-819-5053;
www.fourseasons.com; 215 rooms (17 suites)
■ "You expect to see Gatsby" at this Spanish-style villa resort
where the smitten savor coastal romance with a "movie-star feel";
"flowers add an enchanting aroma" throughout the "beautifully
kept grounds", and "brunch galore on Sunday" is served by a
"best-of-the-best" (and "kid-friendly") staff, but to guarantee a
good night's sleep, splurge on a cottage facing the gardens (and
away from the train tracks); for more, see Spa section.

SAN YSIDRO RANCH　　　27 | 27 | 27 | 25 | $380
900 San Ysidro Ln.; 805-969-5046; fax 805-565-1995; 800-368-6788;
www.sanysidroranch.com; 38 rooms (25 suites)
■ There's an "intimate, dreamy" quality of "casual luxury" that makes this resort a favorite venue for weddings and honeymoons; perhaps it's the "plush" and "rustic" environs, the "exclusivity" of cottages in the foothills or "personal service" and "superb dining" at the Stonehouse Restaurant; regardless, "you'll hate to leave."

Upham Hotel　　　21 | 23 | 23 | 21 | $168
1404 De La Vina St.; 805-962-0058; fax 805-963-2825; 800-727-0876;
www.uphamhotel.com; 50 rooms (8 cottages)
☑ The "unpretentious" ambiance at this Victorian hotel (circa 1871) gets guests ready for "romance" – the evening wine and cheese doesn't hurt either; "if you like antique stuff", this "cozy place" with a "friendly staff" that serves late-night cookies and Continental breakfast offers "great value" in a "quiet neighborhood", but beware "sagging beds" in "old-fashioned rooms" in the main house.

Santa Rosa

Vintners Inn　　　25 | 23 | 25 | 22 | $206
4350 Barnes Rd.; 707-575-7350; fax 707-575-1426; 800-421-2584;
www.vintnersinn.com; 44 rooms (5 suites)
■ "You can almost pick the grapes" from your room at this small Sonoma "beauty" that's right in the middle of a working vineyard (like "a tiny Camelot set"); guests praise the "comfortable" New French Country rooms ("great views" from private balcony or patio) and savor the "excellent" food and "extensive wine list" at John Ash & Co. restaurant; the "hearty" breakfast and "friendly" service contribute to the "wonderful value", but a few veterans claim that with rising prices, it's "not as good a deal as it used to be."

Sausalito

Casa Madrona Hotel　　　25 | 23 | 24 | 20 | $223
801 Bridgeway; 415-332-0502; fax 415-332-2537; 800-567-9524;
www.casamadrona.com; 35 rooms (6 suites, 5 cottages)
■ A cluster of "comfortable" hillside cottages plus a circa-1885 main building afford "smashing views" of Sausalito Harbor and SF Bay at this "low-key" Marin County "charmer"; for "romance", paramours favor the Artist's Loft or Renoir Room, while foodies plug the "funky", "fun" Cal-Thai cuisine at Mikayla and hard-core enthusiasts plead "please keep this place a secret."

Solvang

Alisal Guest Ranch & Resort　　　21 | 25 | 23 | 24 | $261
1054 Alisal Rd.; 805-688-6411; fax 805-688-2510; 800-425-4725;
www.alisal.com; 73 rooms
☑ This resort ranch and "great family-reunion spot" in the Santa Ynez Valley doesn't cotton to air-conditioning, TVs or phones in its "simple, comfortable rooms", but it's "a heavenly retreat" for horseback riding, tennis, golf, fishing and wildlife watching (spend "a morning at the lake, complete with deer and heron"); most cowpokes rave about the staff, but recalcitrant city slickers rant that the "dreary" place is "tolerable only if you eat hay."

Fess Parker's Wine Country Inn 25 | 23 | 23 | 22 | $215
(fka Los Olivos Grand)
2860 Grand Ave.; 805-688-7788; fax 805-688-1942; 800-446-2455;
www.fessparker.com; 21 rooms (1 suite)
☑ "A lovely way to while away the weekend" in wineland purr
guests of this "restful" country inn; "charming", "well-appointed
rooms", all with fireplaces, come at "reasonable" "escape-from-
LA" prices, so even though some urbanites snub the "precious",
new-"Victorian" look of this "one-horse-town hotel", they admit
there's "no other decent choice" in the Santa Ynez Valley.

Sonoma

KENWOOD INN 26 | 26 | 25 | 25 | $250
10400 Sonoma Hwy., Kenwood; 707-833-1293; fax 707-833-1247;
800-353-6966; www.kenwoodinn.com; 12 rooms (2 suites)
■ "Hummingbirds hover as you feast on an incredible breakfast" at
this inn near the town of Sonoma that feels "like stepping into a
private villa in Tuscany" surrounded by herb bushes and olive and
fig trees; feather beds and fireplaces adorn a dozen "beautifully
decorated" suites, which maintain the "romantic" mood with no
TVs or phones (or children under 16); "you will not be treated
better anywhere" assert surveyors – "if you can get in."

Madrona Manor 23 | 23 | 24 | 23 | $216
1001 Westside Rd., Healdsburg; 707-433-4231; fax 707-433-0703;
800-258-4003; www.madronamanor.com; 22 rooms (5 suites)
☑ Set in an "opulent" mansion that "looks like it belongs to the
Munster family" (in a good way), this small inn exudes "Victorian
charm" throughout its antiques-furnished rooms that overlook
landscaped and wooded grounds; while some find service "uppity
(the wine must go to their heads)", most focus on the restaurant,
where dishes are prepared with ingredients from the gardens.

Sonoma Mission Inn 23 | 24 | 24 | 24 | $258
18140 Hwy. 12, Boyes Hot Springs; 707-938-9000; fax 707-935-1205;
800-862-4945; www.sonomamissioninn.com; 230 rooms (60 suites)
☑ "There are so many people in robes it feels like a monastery"
say veterans of this classic California Mission–style spa, who
tout "comfortable rooms" in the new wing; "bubbly, warm spring
water" supplies "decadence for the soul", while the staff ministers
to "the dot-com crowd" and celebs as they take thermal mineral
baths that are "so relaxing you may forget to visit the vineyards"
nearby; still, a few deem the location "so-so" given its "proximity
to a loud thoroughfare" and a "water tower marring the view";
for more, see Spa section.

Squaw Valley

PlumpJack Squaw Valley Inn ▽ 22 | 23 | 27 | 22 | $242
1920 Squaw Valley Rd.; 530-583-1576; fax 530-583-1734;
800-323-7666; www.plumpjack.com; 61 rooms (5 suites)
■ "The cool San Fran set" travels to this "ski lodge with an edge"
"located at the bottom of the gondola"; while some find the "small
rooms" "spartan", others say quarters at the "overflow lodge are
roomy"; après-ski hangouts include the "fun bar" and PlumpJack
Cafe – both pour vintages from the owners' Napa winery.

Resort at Squaw Creek   24 | 22 | 21 | 25 | $247
400 Squaw Creek Rd.; 530-583-6300; fax 530-581-5407;
800-327-3353; www.squawcreek.com; 403 rooms (200 suites)
☑ "Ski right from your door" at this "great place to be marooned during a blizzard" (also a fine escape for golfers, thanks to the Robert Trent Jones Jr. links); most praise the "luxury" and mountain views, but a few squawk that rooms are "pricey and a bit frayed" ("reminiscent of an airport hotel"); still, the "convenience to the slopes" and amenities are "unbeatable" – just "beware the ice and snow as you make a mad dash to the outdoor hot tubs."

Yosemite

Ahwahnee   23 | 23 | 23 | 27 | $240
Yosemite Nat'l Park; 559-252-4848; fax 559-456-0542;
www.yosemitepark.com; 127 rooms (5 suites, 2 cottages)
☑ "God is the landscape architect", so it's "worth making year-in-advance reservations" to stay at this "grand old lady" poised in the middle of Yosemite National Park; public areas in the 1927 landmark lodge display "museum-quality Native American rugs and baskets", stone "fireplaces big enough to stand in" and panoramic views of "natural splendor"; guestrooms, on the other hand, are "small" and "spartan", but dinner in an "amazing" beamed dining room satisfies creatures of comfort – and "a window table at Sunday brunch is a must!"

Colorado

★ **Best in State**
28 Little Nell, *Aspen*/SR
27 Lodge/Cordillera, *Edwards*/SL   Peaks, *Telluride*/R
    Broadmoor, *Co. Springs*/R   Sonnenalp, *Vail*/SL
26 St. Regis, *Aspen*/H   **25** Hyatt, *Beaver Cr.*/R
                   Monaco, *Denver*/H

Aspen

Jerome   25 | 25 | 24 | 24 | $264
330 E. Main St.; 970-920-1000; fax 970-925-2784; 800-331-7213;
www.hoteljerome.com; 93 rooms (16 suites)
■ A relic of the silver-boom era, this "old Wild West" hotel hums "perfectly in tune with local tradition"; "ghosts of cowboys and miners are good company" in "luxurious rooms" tended to by "helpful staff"; guests can walk to everything in town, but many like to belly up to the Library Bar for the view or shuttle to the Aspen Club spa's eucalyptus steam room; the restaurant keeps the frontier spirit alive with "breakfast to die for, dinner to kill for."

L'Auberge   ∇ 26 | 24 | 24 | 23 | $224
435 E. Main St.; 970-925-8297; fax 970-925-4164; 16 cabins
■ "Affectionately known as the huts of Aspen", these mountain cottages impress surveyors as "funky" yet "charming" with their peaked ceilings, fireplaces, kitchenettes and antler chandeliers; "great rates" and the "convenient" location on Main Street (six blocks from the mall) are topped off by fine service; bonus: an outdoor Jacuzzi and free skier shuttle.

LITTLE NELL, THE   28 | 28 | 28 | 27 | $345
675 E. Durant Ave.; 970-920-4600; fax 970-920-6328; 888-843-6355;
www.thelittlenell.com; 92 rooms (15 suites)

■ "Hobnob with the rich and famous" at this top-ranked "jewel"
right at the slopes; "unabashedly hedonistic rooms" come with
gas fireplaces, "big marble tubs to loll in", plus "spectacular views"
and service so good that "someone even got my skis and put them
on me"; an après-ski scene at the bar is followed by the "best
tortilla soup ever" from the restaurant's "innovative chef."

ST. REGIS   27 | 26 | 26 | 27 | $330
315 E. Dean St.; 970-920-3300; fax 970-925-8998; 888-454-9005;
www.stregis.com; 257 rooms (24 suites)

☑ It's "as gorgeous as its guests" observe fans of the "European
charm" at this "perfect location" that treats travelers to the
"most comfortable beds and comforters ever" in "regal rooms";
fans "love the food" from Boston's star chef Todd English in his
new Olives restaurant and stay "hip" at the Whiskey Rock bar,
but nitpickers say the decor is "over-the-top for the mountains",
with "one bronze elk too many."

Beaver Creek

Beaver Creek Lodge   25 | 25 | 24 | 24 | $257
26 Avondale Ln.; 970-845-9800; fax 970-845-7800; 800-525-7280;
www.beavercreeklodge.net; 76 suites

■ "Like a small mountain village", this "quiet" resort west of
Denver employs a staff "that couldn't be a bit nicer"; "tasteful"
furnishings in each suite and homestyle dining make this a "fine
facility" for "families or catching up with friends" – of course it's
also "a great place for skiing", and "don't forget summer vacations."

Charter at Beaver Creek, The   25 | 23 | 22 | 24 | $249
120 Offerson Rd.; 970-949-6660; fax 970-949-4489; 800-525-6660;
www.thecharter.com; 150 rooms

☑ "Convenience to the slopes" is a strong suit at this "sprawling",
"family-centered" ski-in/ski-out resort; "comfy" rooms in condos
come with a "great view of the mountains", while the spa, indoor/
outdoor pool and game room offer respite from the slopes; N.B. a
few get lost in the large resort's "rabbit warren" of hallways.

Hyatt Regency   25 | 25 | 24 | 27 | $280
50 W. Thomas Pl.; 970-949-1234; fax 970-949-4164; 800-554-9288;
www.hyatt.com; 275 rooms (26 suites)

☑ "The closest you can get to heaven in the Rockies", this ski-in/
ski-out resort at the foot of the mountains has "excellent service"
("they help you take your skis off"), a lobby for sitting by the fire to
drink cider and a "fabulous spa"; one drawback: "the chairlifts
have more space" than the guestrooms; for more, see Spa section.

Inn at Beaver Creek   24 | 23 | 23 | 23 | $238
10 Elk Track Ln.; 970-845-7800; fax 970-845-5279; 800-859-8242;
46 rooms (1 suite)

■ A "cozy" European-style lodge, this "rustic" inn at the base of
Strawberry Park lift has easy access to "a moving stairway to the
slopes"; "spacious" rooms "accommodate all your ski gear", and
nonwinter activities include golf, tennis and rafting (this is "where
the rich go to play"); year-round, "nothing beats the scenery."

Boulder

Boulderado, Hotel 22 | 23 | 22 | 22 | $177

2115 13th St.; 303-442-4344; fax 303-442-4378; 800-433-4344;
www.boulderado.com; 160 rooms (21 suites)

☑ "Ghosts of the Old West" thrill visitors at this historic hotel in the "vibrant" Downtown area near shopping, the arts, university and mountains; from a stained-glass lobby canopy to cherrywood staircase, "Victorian ambiance" abounds, but sticklers say rooms suffer from "inconsistent quality" (some "huge", others "cramped").

Colorado Springs

BROADMOOR, THE 26 | 27 | 26 | 27 | $255

1 Lake Ave.; 719-634-7711; fax 719-577-5700; 800-634-7711;
www.broadmoor.com; 700 rooms (107 suites)

■ A "queen of the Rockies" (built in 1918), this resort fills more than 3,000 acres with "everything athletes and hedonists could desire" – golf courses with views, pools, tennis courts, boating, shopping and dining; for calmer moments, the spa, outdoor fireplaces and rocking chairs inspire happy contemplation; for more, see Spa section.

Denver

Brown Palace Hotel 23 | 24 | 24 | 25 | $209

321 17th St.; 303-297-3111; fax 303-312-5900; 800-321-2599;
www.brownpalace.com; 241 rooms (51 suites)

☑ "You expect to see silver barons" in the lobby beneath the Tiffany stained-glass atrium at this "unsinkable" hotel; "it's worth fudging on your expense account" to dine at the Palace Arms, but "quirky rooms" in the triangular building are "not as impressive" despite antiques and faux-"19th-century plumbing."

Inverness Hotel 22 | 22 | 22 | 23 | $178

200 Inverness Dr. W., Englewood; 303-799-5800; fax 303-799-5874;
800-346-4891; www.invernesshotel.com; 302 rooms (19 suites)

☑ Twenty minutes south of Denver, this suburban hotel ranks high for conferences with a "great golf course" and nearby shopping; "panoramic views" of the Rockies make it like "a Scandinavian resort" to some, but the rooms are "nothing to write home about."

Loews Giorgio Hotel 23 | 23 | 22 | 21 | $178

4150 E. Mississippi Ave.; 303-782-9300; fax 303-758-6542;
800-345-9172; www.loewshotels.com; 183 rooms (19 suites)

■ "What a surprise: Tuscany in Denver" say fans of this "jewel" in upscale Cherry Creek with its "beautifully appointed" rooms, "art-museum-like lobby" and meals served by a grand fireplace in the "romantic" dining room; the "European feel", though, doesn't work for critics who say the Force is not with the "Star Wars exterior."

Monaco, Hotel 27 | 24 | 24 | 24 | $180

1717 Champa St.; 303-296-1717; fax 303-296-1818; 800-397-5380;
www.hotelmonaco.com; 189 rooms (32 suites)

■ "The hip and young" stay at this "whimsical" place in the Central Business District for the "funky rooms" – top-rated in Denver – adorned in "playful color"; "cute" touches include "a fish to keep you company", free morning coffee in a "cool" lobby and "wine [or other gift] with a thank-you note" that's sent to all return guests.

Oxford Hotel   22 | 23 | 21 | 22 | $159
1600 17th St.; 303-628-5400; fax 303-628-5553; 800-228-5838;
www.theoxfordhotel.com; 80 rooms (9 suites)
☑ "An excellent renovation in LoDo", this Gilded Age "classic" lets
guests "relive history" amid antiques; the spa and proximity to
Coors Field are pluses, and veterans advise "don't miss the Cruise
Room, a pink-and-chrome art deco martini bar", however, a few
find the "too-quaint rooms" "puny" with "paper-thin walls."

Teatro   – | – | – | – | M
1100 14th St.; 303-228-1100; fax 303-228-1101; 888-727-1200;
www.hotelteatro.com; 116 rooms (6 suites)
In its first act, this dramatic Downtown landmark played a role as
a garage and office space for a tram company; act two saw it as
the temporary CU Denver campus; when curtains rose on early
1999, this newly independent boutique property was starring as
one of the Mile High City's latest happening hotels; with its cushy,
modern rooms, Aveda amenities, two restaurants and proximity
to trendy LoDo, expect guests here to make encore appearances.

Westin Tabor Center   23 | 22 | 21 | 21 | $178
1672 Lawrence Street; 303-572-9100; fax 303-572-7288;
888-625-5144; www.westin.com; 430 rooms (13 suites)
☑ "A solid choice for the business traveler", with "an excellent
location to meet daily needs" (it's "at ground zero on the 16th Street
Mall" and blocks from the Performing Arts Complex), this hotel and
conference center is "classy and comfortable"; surveyors love the
"helpful staff", on-site Palm Restaurant and "diving into those
beds" in "tech-ready" rooms; the less-impressed, however, sigh
there's "nothing fancy" about this "plain-vanilla Westin."

Durango

Sheraton Tamarron Resort   23 | 22 | 20 | 24 | $181
40292 US Hwy. 550 N.; 970-259-2000; fax 970-382-7822;
800-678-1000; www.tamarron.com; 412 rooms (44 suites)
■ In the "middle of nowhere" (in the San Juan Mountains), this
Wild West–town resort's main winter draw is nearby Purgatory
ski area; in summer, the "gorgeous location" quiets down, although
golf, tennis, rafting, fly fishing, hiking and mountain biking – not to
mention "comfortable" rooms and "the cleanest air" around –
keep families (and conference attendees) coming back all year.

Edwards

LODGE & SPA   27 | 26 | 28 | 27 | $296
AT CORDILLERA, THE
2205 Cordillera Way; 970-926-2200; fax 970-926-6419; 800-877-3529;
www.cordillera-vail.com; 56 rooms (11 suites, 10 houses)
■ At the top of the world (elevation: 8,150 feet), this "small luxury
hotel" offers "secluded respite"; "breathtaking views" are par for
the course (as are off-season golf, tennis and hiking), but the real
standouts – and what keeps rooms filled with lots of luminaries –
are the "wonderful" spa and Restaurant Picasso, where "superb
meals" are served among real Picasso lithographs and silk screens;
for more, see Spa section.

Keystone

Keystone Lodge   23 | 23 | 21 | 24 | $181
22101 Hwy. 6; 970-496-2316; fax 970-496-4215; 888-222-9354;
www.keystoneresort.com; 152 rooms (14 suites)
■ "Close to the slopes", this bargain skiers' haven is "less
pretentious than other resorts in Colorado", making guests "feel
comfortable" after a "messy" day of skiing; with "affordable"
rooms, "friendly" staff, in-room fridges, shuttle to the lifts, even
apres-ski "cookies and cider in the lobby" at Christmas, fans
declare this accommodating lodge "fantastic for families."

Telluride

PEAKS   27 | 26 | 25 | 28 | $322
136 Country Club Dr.; 970-728-6800; fax 970-728-6175;
800-789-2220; www.wyndham.com; 174 rooms (34 suites)
■ Amid the San Juan Mountains, this "Shangri-la" just a gondola
away from tony Telluride is "the pinnacle of rustic elegance" with
its Southwestern decor, many balconied rooms and "top-notch"
Golden Door Spa; when not skiing, golfing, mountain biking, fly-
fishing or playing tennis, guests partake of "refreshments for the
body and soul", including "good food" at Appaloosa restaurant
and one of "the most magnificent views of any resort"; for more,
see Spa section.

Vail

Lodge at Vail, The   23 | 23 | 23 | 23 | $261
174 E. Gore Creek Dr.; 970-476-5011; fax 970-477-3742;
800-331-5634; www.lodgeatvail.com; 123 rooms (44 suites)
■ This "snug" lodge near a main lift and "steps from the Village"
maintains "alpine-accented" rooms and suites – some with
"awesome views of the mountain from bed"; a number praise
the sommelier at Wildflower Restaurant, and most agree that
Mickey's Lounge ("the ultimate piano bar") is a great post-slope
"ski bunny's warren."

SONNENALP   26 | 26 | 25 | 25 | $304
20 Vail Rd.; 970-476-5656; fax 970-476-1639; 800-654-8312;
www.sonnenalp.com; 90 rooms (88 suites)
■ A "little bit of Bavaria", this ski chalet (owned by a "hospitable"
German family) has guestrooms in various sizes – some are "cozy",
others "like staying in a castle" – but all come with amenities like
"divine pillows" and "heated bathroom floors"; old-world fare
includes "wonderful hot chocolate" and nightly fondue at the
"romantic" Swiss Chalet restaurant; for more, see Spa section.

Vail Cascade Resort   23 | 23 | 20 | 24 | $233
(fka Hotel & Club)
1300 Westhaven Dr.; 970-476-7111; fax 970-479-7020; 800-282-4183;
www.vailcascade.com; 291 rooms (26 suites)
☑ At the base of a mountain yet "off to itself", this ski-in/ski-out
resort, only 10 feet from a chairlift, features a "lobby that's great for
people-watching" and a number of rooms "right on a picturesque
babbling brook"; most reviewers spout compliments like "warm
and homey", "our favorite family roost" and "great value in an
unbeatable location", though a few sulk about "poor food."

Connecticut

Greenwich

Hyatt Regency   22 | 21 | 20 | 22 | $190
1800 E. Putnam Ave.; 203-637-1234; fax 203-637-2940;
800-233-1234; www.hyatt.com; 373 rooms (12 suites)

■ "A notch above the norm", this "immaculately maintained" hotel with its atrium lobby is "perfect for a business stay" or "weekend away"; guests like the "pleasant ambiance" in the "large", "clean" rooms and applaud "prompt" service, but be warned: many "feel poor" amid all the well-to-do "house hunters" from New York City.

Ledyard

Foxwoods Resort   23 | 22 | 20 | 22 | $176
Rte. 2; 860-312-3000; fax 860-312-5044; 800-369-9663;
www.foxwoods.com; 1,416 rooms (200 suites)

☑ "Vegas off I-95" buzz champions of this "glitzy" "gamblers' paradise", a trio of properties that strikes surveyors as a cross between "a cruise ship on land" and a "huge mall hotel"; "spacious rooms" and the New England scenery "take the sting out of a bad night" at the tables, but even winners growl about "so-so food."

New Preston

Boulders Inn, The   22 | 23 | 24 | 23 | $244
E. Shore Rd.; 860-868-0541; fax 860-868-1925; 800-552-6853;
www.bouldersinn.com; 17 rooms (3 suites)

■ "Rough it à la Ralph Lauren" at this inn on Lake Waramaug where "pampered" guests boat, hike, ski, antique and go to the theater; those who didn't "go up just for dinner" advise booking the "carriage house" for "newer rooms"; "killer" views make it a "wonderful Christmas gift", even if "the service charge is too high."

Norwich

Norwich Inn, The   22 | 22 | 21 | 22 | $230
607 W. Thames St.; 860-886-2401; fax 860-886-9299; 800-275-4772;
www.thespaatnorwichinn.com; 103 rooms (4 suites, 54 villas)

☑ For a "great girls' pampering weekend", respondents head for this "spa that's superb for the money", set in a "romantic" inn on 40 acres of Connecticut countryside; once you've been buffed, there's lots to do nearby (golf, gambling and the seashore), which takes the focus off rooms that "need a spa treatment of their own."

Washington

MAYFLOWER INN   28 | 27 | 26 | 26 | $355
118 Woodbury Rd.; 860-868-9466; fax 860-868-1497;
www.mayflowerinn.com; 25 rooms (8 suites)

■ In the heart of swish Litchfield Hills sits this "country manor hotel" that's "everything a bucolic Relais & Châteaux property should be", with "spectacular" gardens, sports facilities and a spa as well as "elegant" rooms ("feather beds", "needlepoint rugs"), "superb food" and "pampering" staff; price-sensitive fans swear "two days here is as rejuvenating as a week anywhere else."

Westport

INN AT NATIONAL HALL, THE 28 | 27 | 26 | 25 | $309

2 Post Rd. W.; 203-221-1351; fax 203-221-0276; 800-628-4255;
www.innatnationalhall.com; 15 rooms (7 suites)

■ "Creatively themed rooms", "first-rate" Mediterranean fare and
a "high level of service" make this circa-1872 Relais & Châteaux
Italianate gem in "the land of Martha Stewart" (actually, it's on the
banks of the Saugatuck River) a "fabulous" choice for "any VIP
looking for the best"; even if it is a "bit la-di-da", it earns nods as
"one of the most tasteful hotels in the country."

Delaware

Montchanin

Inn at Montchanin, The ▽ 28 | 25 | 27 | 22 | $205

Kirk Rd. & Rte. 100; 302-888-2133; fax 302-888-0389; 800-269-2473;
www.montchanin.com; 27 rooms (5 suites)

■ "Come play with the du Ponts" in "chateau country" midway
between New York and DC and a quick skip from the Winterthur
Museum and Longwood Gardens in the heart of the Brandywine
River Valley; "charming rooms" please folks who love to poke
around this village listed on the National Register of Historic Places
before dining at the inn's "totally delicious" Krazy Kat restaurant.

Wilmington

DU PONT, HOTEL 26 | 26 | 25 | 25 | $207

11th & Market Sts.; 302-594-3100; fax 302-594-3108; 800-441-9019;
www.hoteldupont.com; 217 rooms (12 suites)

■ "The staff caters to every demand" at this "aristocratic" haunt in
the "run-down" Downtown district; a "gorgeous marble lobby",
ballroom and "old-guard dining room" are "a fraction of big-city
prices", and rooms with "original art" are appreciated by a staid
business and legal clientele, even if it is "the only game in town."

District of Columbia

Washington

★ **Best in District**
27 Four Seasons/H   Hay-Adams/H
26 Willard Inter-Continental/H   Jefferson/H
25 St. Regis/H   24 Monarch/H
   Park Hyatt/H   Morrison-Clark Inn/SI

FOUR SEASONS 28 | 28 | 27 | 26 | $302

2800 Pennsylvania Ave., NW; 202-342-0444; fax 202-944-2076;
800-332-3442; www.fourseasons.com; 260 rooms (55 suites)

■ "Discreet and tasteful", this Georgetown hotel (No. 1 in the city)
offers an "interlude from power plays" despite "lots of dignitaries"
on the guest roster; the staff "takes pride" in "perfect service"
("they treated my Maltese dog like a princess") and rooms are
"cocoons" of "pure delight", with feather duvets and TV headsets;
foodies find the dining "superb", especially the Sunday brunch.

George, Hotel
25 | 23 | 25 | 21 | $202

15 E St., NW; 202-347-4200; fax 202-347-4213; 800-576-8331;
www.hotelgeorge.com; 139 rooms (3 suites)

■ "How hip can you be?" ask admirers of this "clean-as-a-whistle" Capitol Hill hotel where "romantic bedrooms" have "minimal decor" (and "minimal prices" to match); the "eclectic" menu and "wonderful wine list" at Bis restaurant and a staff that seems "like family" make this place "more fun than most", though proximity to Union Station means guests should "be careful at night."

Hay-Adams Hotel, The
25 | 26 | 25 | 25 | $277

1 Lafayette Sq.; 202-638-6600; fax 202-638-2716; 800-424-5054;
www.hayadams.com; 143 rooms (19 suites)

☑ "As close as you'll get to spending the night in the White House without sleeping in the Lincoln bedroom", this "oldie but goodie" provides "discreet service" geared to bipartisan "ambassadors", "bigwigs" and other "power-lunchers"; guests praise the "free fruit and cookies in the lobby" and rooms (some with a view of 1600 Pennsylvania Avenue) – if only they weren't "phone-booth size."

Henley Park
22 | 23 | 22 | 21 | $168

926 Massachusetts Ave., NW; 202-638-5200; fax 202-414-0513;
800-222-8474; www.henleypark.com; 96 rooms (10 suites)

■ This "friendly" "European"-style hotel off the beaten path but "convenient to the Convention Center" provides an "affordable option" to conference-goers and families; besides "comfortable" rooms and a period-piece lounge, weekend dancing gives it a "small-town feel."

Jefferson Hotel, The
25 | 26 | 24 | 24 | $260

1200 16th St., NW; 202-347-2200; fax 202-331-7982; 800-555-8000;
www.thejeffersonhotel.com; 100 rooms (35 suites)

■ "As stately as its namesake", this 1922 "clubby" Downtown hotel is frequented by business travelers, sightseers and members of the politerati (is this "the second seat of government?"); guestrooms have antiques, canopied four-poster beds and computer hookups, while staff provides "friendly" service; the city's bigwigs are often spied clinking glasses in the "lovely library bar", but the "underrated" Jefferson Restaurant is where they clinch deals.

JW Marriott Hotel
22 | 22 | 20 | 22 | $195

1331 Pennsylvania Ave., NW; 202-393-2000; fax 202-626-6991;
800-228-9290; www.marriott.com; 772 rooms (22 suites)

■ "A city within a city", this centrally located Downtown "icon" (read: flagship) accommodates tourists and conferences at "fair" prices; with "comfortable" albeit "bland" rooms, "polite service", large meeting spaces and many restaurants, the only thing guests lack is "a trail of bread crumbs to find your way out" of the complex.

Latham Hotel Georgetown
20 | 21 | 24 | 19 | $183

3000 M St., NW; 202-726-5000; fax 202-337-4250; 800-368-5922;
www.meristar.com; 143 rooms (23 suites)

☑ "Excellent value for the money", this "charming small hotel" has an even bigger draw than its "great location in funky Georgetown": onsite restaurant Citronelle, "one of the best spots in DC", is alone "worth the stay"; while optimists call rooms "small but good", some maintain "man cannot live on bread alone: the restaurant is terrific, the hotel is disappointing."

Madison Hotel, The   24 | 24 | 23 | 22 | $247

*15th & M Sts., NW; 202-862-1600; fax 202-785-1255; 800-424-8577;
www.themadisonhotel.net; 341 rooms (30 suites)*

◪ Favored by a "foreign clientele" of movers and shakers, this "old-style" hotel is definitely "not a tourist mecca", what with a lobby full of "art and antiques", "luxurious rooms", "superb location" and "quality service" from "a staff that has been there forever"; the majority finds this a "good value" for the area, but some complain of "third-class treatment unless you're in the political arena."

Mayflower   23 | 24 | 22 | 24 | $217

*1127 Connecticut Ave., NW; 202-347-3000; fax 202-776-9182;
800-228-9290; www.renaissancehotels.com; 660 rooms (76 suites)*

■ "They don't build 'em like this anymore" marvel admirers of this "still perky" 1925 "grand old lady" next to the White House; a "power scene" generates "good energy" in the "celebrity-spotting lobby" and lounge, and "a diligent" staff doesn't allow "conventions and large gatherings" to "overwhelm" nonparticipants.

Monarch Hotel   25 | 24 | 22 | 25 | $221
(fka ANA)

*2401 M St., NW; 202-429-2400; fax 202-457-5010; 877-222-2266;
www.washingtonmonarch.com; 415 rooms (28 suites)*

■ "On the fringe of Georgetown", this "upscale" "weekender" for locals and "convenient" home base for business travelers may be the "most underrated hotel in DC"; its "garden courtyard lobby" makes you "forget you're in a major city", and the exercise facility pleases, as do "richly appointed" rooms and "kind service"; ongoing renovations should further enhance an aura of "prestige."

Morrison-Clark Inn   23 | 24 | 26 | 22 | $188

*1015 L St., NW; 202-898-1200; fax 202-289-8576; 800-332-7898;
www.morrisonclark.com; 54 rooms (13 suites)*

◪ An "alternative to big hotels", this renovated Soldiers and Sailors Club (circa 1864) maintains a "guest-house feeling with modern amenities" and "respectful staff"; "stunning" "American cuisine with regional twists" earns high praise, but a few find the rooms "too tiny for heavy hitters" and all agree the "so-so" nabe can be downright "dangerous."

Park Hyatt   26 | 26 | 25 | 25 | $238

*M & 24th Sts., NW; 202-789-1234; fax 202-457-8823; 800-233-1234;
www.hyatt.com; 224 rooms (130 suites)*

◪ There's "always a friendly welcome" at this West End flagship; hearty cheers for "spacious rooms", "comfortable beds", Melrose restaurant's seafood, business services, "top-of-the-line" staff and location close to Georgetown and Foggy Bottom usually drown out the few grumbles about the "boring", "cookie-cutter formula."

Ritz-Carlton, The   – | – | – | – | VE

*1150 22nd St., NW; 202-835-0500; fax 202-835-1588; 800-241-3333;
www.ritzcarlton.com; 300 rooms (33 suites)*

Opened in October 2000, this third Ritz-y property in and around the Beltway mixes hotel guests with long-term residents on one-and-a-half acres in the West End, close to Georgetown; along with the opulent ballrooms, meeting spaces and restaurants that the chain's fans have come to expect, the structure's upper reaches grant views of the Potomac and nearby monuments.

ST. REGIS
26 │ 26 │ 25 │ 25 │ $283

923 16th St., NW; 202-638-2626; fax 202-347-4758; 800-562-5661;
www.stregis.com; 194 rooms (14 suites)

☑ After numerous refurbishments to the 1926 Italian Renaissance
building, this newly "fashionable" hotel ("within walking distance of
the President") runs "like a well-oiled machine"; guests welcome
the dining room change from formal Lespinasse to "contemporary"
Timothy Dean (its namesake hometown chef) and also appreciate
the guestrooms "filled with antiques", Bose radios and "great
toiletries", though some skeptics still scowl about "small" and
"stuffy" accommodations.

Swissôtel, The Watergate
24 │ 23 │ 23 │ 22 │ $241

2650 Virginia Ave., NW; 202-965-2300; fax 202-337-7915;
800-424-2736; www.swissotel.com; 250 rooms (142 suites)

■ "A taste of Europe" run with "Swiss efficiency", the hotel famous
for scandal has "wonderful views of the Potomac" from "spacious
rooms" and no more "Nixon-era decor" (although some sense a
"ghost lingers"); also noteworthy are a "nice pool and exercise
room", "lovely lobby", and "personal service", making this a
"decent" home base close to the monuments, museums and
the Kennedy Center.

Westin Fairfax, The
25 │ 24 │ 23 │ 22 │ $213

2100 Massachusetts Ave., NW; 202-293-2100; fax 202-293-0641;
800-937-8461; www.westin.com; 206 rooms (49 suites)

☑ "Hoorah for the beds" and "luxurious baths" cheer fans of this
former Ritz-Carlton near Dupont Circle; "still elegant", the hotel
offers "great weekend values", a staff that's a "delight from
reception to departure" and dining at the Jockey Club; rooms that
"were good enough for Al Gore" (who grew up here) strike some as
"tiny", and fans worry that if the property "keeps changing owners"
it may "forget its luxury roots."

WILLARD INTER-CONTINENTAL
26 │ 26 │ 25 │ 26 │ $274

1401 Pennsylvania Ave., NW; 202-628-9100; fax 202-637-7326;
800-327-0200; www.interconti.com; 341 rooms (39 suites)

■ Legend says "the term 'lobbying' was coined" a century ago in
this beaux arts hotel that still "drips with power and opulence";
"elaborate and expensive" rooms (Godiva chocolates at turndown),
"elegant dining" among an "international clientele" and a "well-
trained staff" make guests want to linger in the "grandeur" ("I was
not overdressed in my wedding gown").

Florida

★ **Best in State**

28 Ritz-Carlton, *Naples*/R	Breakers, *Palm Beach*/R
Ritz-Carlton, *Palm Beach*/R	Villas Gr. Cyp., *Orlando*/R
27 Ritz-Carlton, *Amelia Island*/R	Ren. Vinoy, *St. Pete*/H
Four Seasons, *Palm Beach*/R	Lodge, *Ponte Vedra*/SR
Marquesa, *Key West*/H	Loews Portofino, *Orlando*/R
Little Palm, *Little Torch*/SR	**25** Wyndham Gr. Bay, *Miami*/H
26 Turnberry Isle, *Miami*/R	Disney's, *Vero Beach*/R
Disney's Gr. Flor., *Orlando*/R	Delano, *Miami*/H
Fisher Island Club, *Miami*/SR	Hyatt Gr. Cyp., *Orlando*/R

Amelia Island

Amelia Island Plantation   24 | 23 | 22 | 24 | $218
3000 First Coast Hwy.; 904-261-6161; fax 904-277-5945; 800-874-6878;
www.aipfl.com; 667 rooms (380 suites)
☑ "Beautiful surroundings" keep loyalists coming back, as do clay
tennis courts, bike trails, three golf courses and "comfortable
quarters" with "views" at this resort on oceanside marshlands;
guests enjoy the "secluded beach" but are lukewarm about
service and dining that "try hard with mixed results."

RITZ-CARLTON, THE   28 | 27 | 27 | 27 | $268
4750 Amelia Island Pkwy.; 904-277-1100; fax 904-277-1145;
800-241-3333; www.ritzcarlton.com; 449 rooms (45 suites)
☑ "Plush beach digs" amid historical surrounds and "windswept"
scenery are "superb", but expect "familiar Ritz clubbiness" inside
rooms and suites with water views; the staff "aims to please" and
food at The Grill is "divine" (especially the 10-course tasting menu);
best of all, it's "as beautiful as Hawaii without the jet lag"; for more,
see Spa section.

Boca Raton

Boca Raton Resort & Club   25 | 25 | 24 | 26 | $279
501 E. Camino Real; 561-447-3000; fax 561-447-3185; 800-327-0101;
www.bocaresort.com; 963 rooms (117 suites)
☑ This "lovely old dame at the beach" (renovated in 2000) spreads
over "tropical gardens" that surround the 1920s Cloister complex;
families insist the waterside "Beach Club is the place to be", while
others say "stay in the pink tower" for the views; there's plenty of
tennis, golf and boating, but reviewers complain about the long trek
by boat to the beach; others aren't thrilled with "dated" quarters in
older buildings and "faulty" service during the mid-winter season.

Captiva Island

South Seas Resort   23 | 23 | 22 | 25 | $241
5400 Captiva Rd.; 941-472-5111; fax 941-481-4947; 800-965-7772;
www.southseas.com; 683 rooms (273 condos, 19 houses,
43 townhouses)
☑ This resort stretches over 330 acres, so "even when it's fully
booked there's a sense of solitude"; fans call it a "great family
vacation spot" with miles of beach, seashells, a nine-hole golf
course, 18 tennis courts, boat rentals, fishing excursions and
every water sport imaginable; rooms "vary greatly in quality and
price", and a few gripe about "spotty" service and "mediocre" food.

Fort Lauderdale

Lago Mar Resort & Club   23 | 23 | 20 | 23 | $209
1700 S. Ocean Ln.; 954-523-6511; fax 954-524-6627; 800-524-6627;
www.lagomar.com; 212 rooms (160 suites)
☑ Thanks to a "relaxed" ambiance and location on Harbor Beach's
largest private stretch of sand, "old snowbirds and young families"
deem this "perfectly modest" spot their "best-kept secret"; suites
have balconies with ocean views and service is "congenial",
though skeptics squirm over a dearth of dining options.

Marriott's Harbor Beach Resort   23 | 23 | 22 | 24 | $215
3030 Holiday Dr.; 954-525-4000; fax 954-766-6152; 800-222-6543;
www.marriott.com; 624 rooms (35 suites)
☑ Beach views draw families – and businesses – to this high-rise
resort on 16 acres of sand, where a "fantastic" kids' program
"keeps children busy and parents happy"; a pool with waterfalls
and plants tops the list, followed by an "upbeat" staff; critics say
some rooms "don't live up to the rest of the resort" (which will
add a spa soon) and weekend crowds of locals can be "a drag."

Keys

Cheeca Lodge   23 | 24 | 23 | 24 | $238
US Hwy. 1 (MM 82), Islamadora; 305-664-4651; fax 305-664-2893;
800-327-2888; www.rockresorts.com; 203 rooms (64 suites)
☑ Expect "barefoot luxury" at this "quiet hideaway", known as a
bonefishing mecca; "beautiful" grounds and "laid-back" ambiance
win praise from nonfishers and families, and all say the "food is
fresh", whether it's "your catch or theirs"; two complaints: lobby
and rooms "are a little worn" and there isn't "great swimming."

Gardens Hotel   ∇ 27 | 26 | 23 | 27 | $226
526 Angela St., Key West; 305-294-2661; fax 305-292-1007;
800-526-2664; www.gardenshotel.com; 17 rooms (2 suites)
■ "An oasis in a ticky-tacky town" note fans of this collection of
19th-century Conch houses in private gardens; guestrooms contain
"an interesting blend of old and new" with yew and mahogany
furnishings, brass beds, hardwood floors and marble baths – some
with Jacuzzis; breakfast is served in the solarium, and the "best-
ever bartender" holds court at a poolside bar.

Hawk's Cay Resort   21 | 22 | 21 | 23 | $209
61 Hawk's Cay Blvd., Duck Key; 305-743-7000; fax 305-743-0641;
800-432-2242; www.hawkscay.com; 341 rooms (16 suites, 165 villas)
☑ "Swim with dolphins" in a saltwater lagoon at this 60-acre island
resort; families find vacations "thoroughly enjoyable" with kids'
programs that focus on marine life, "friendly staff" and "affordable
dining options", but it's "too noisy if you're looking for a romantic
respite" and room quality ranges from "comfortable" to "tired."

Hilton Key West   23 | 21 | 20 | 22 | $214
245 Front St., Key West; 305-294-4000; fax 305-294-4086;
800-445-8667; www.hilton.com; 178 rooms (31 suites, 37 cottages
on Sunset Key)
☑ This "standard name-brand" resort is "close to everything" yet
"it's totally quiet at night", so most say it's safe to "get a room with a
view" overlooking Mallory Square and street life; "too bad you have
to take a boat to get to the beach" grumble some, adding that
though "rooms are roomy", "service can be chaotic."

Hyatt Key West   23 | 22 | 21 | 22 | $227
601 Front St., Key West; 305-296-9900; fax 305-292-1038;
800-554-9288; www.hyatt.com; 120 rooms (10 suites)
☑ In the heart of Old Town, this resort with a "Cape Cod feel"
offers "calm in the craziness" of an increasingly "commercialized"
spot; guests enjoy "views of the sunset" (rooms on the Gulf side
have "the best vantage point"); a "nice" (if "sandbox"-size) beach
and "friendly staff" "outweigh" "cramped" quarters and pool.

LITTLE PALM ISLAND   28 | 27 | 26 | 25 | $453

28500 Overseas Hwy., Little Torch Key; 305-872-2524; fax 305-872-4843; 800-343-8567; www.littlepalmisland.com; 30 bungalows

■ "Be prepared for total relaxation" at this "hideaway" where the staff "can't do enough for you"; thatch-roofed bungalows give a "South Pacific feel" to a five-acre swath of sand and palms reached by launch from Little Torch Key; there's little to do "but sun or dine" on "extraordinary Floribbean" cuisine (the resort bans phones, TV and children under 16), so "don't miss flats fishing for bonefish" if you're feeling energetic, or try the spa if you're not.

MARQUESA HOTEL, THE   28 | 27 | 28 | 26 | $238

600 Fleming St., Key West; 305-292-1919; fax 305-294-2121; 800-869-4631; www.marquesa.com; 27 rooms (13 suites)

■ "Everything's first-rate" rave reviewers of this "chic oasis" comprising four 19th-century houses "in a tropical setting" just a block from Duval Street; guestrooms are decorated with antiques, custom fabrics and marble baths, and if you "get a suite" you'll have a private porch overlooking two shaded pools and a flower-filled courtyard; Café Marquesa serves contemporary American cuisine that's "quite simply the best" in town, and a "helpful staff" will "make you feel like family."

Ocean Reef Club   23 | 23 | 22 | 23 | $261

31 Ocean Reef Dr., Key Largo; 305-367-2611; fax 305-367-2224; 800-741-7333; www.oceanreef.com; 413 rooms (156 suites, 1 villa, 70 condos, 38 homes)

☑ This family vacation spot on 4,000 acres provides a "relaxing" atmosphere – and golf carts for transport from accommodations, which range from an oceanfront inn to villas, condos and private residences; "good meeting sites" (conference center, ballroom and banquet facilities) lend an "almost institutional" air to the resort, but two 18-hole golf courses, tennis courts, marina and 10 restaurants make it a "pleasant", "self-sufficient community", though naysayers insist that too many rooms "need refurbishing."

Pier House Resort   22 | 23 | 23 | 23 | $230

1 Duval St., Key West; 305-296-4600; fax 305-296-9085; 800-327-8340; www.pierhouse.com; 142 rooms (16 suites)

■ Guests like to "chill out at sunset" at this Gulfside resort close to "the heart of a happening town" or soak up "great vibes" at the "cool bar"; service is "friendly" and accommodations "comfortable but not special" unless you request a room in the spa section for "expensive" treatments at this "fun property" that's "clean and quiet (even during Spring Break)."

Sheraton Suites Key West   23 | 21 | 21 | 21 | $189

2001 Roosevelt Blvd., Key West; 305-292-9800; fax 305-294-6009; 800-452-3224; www.sheraton.com; 180 suites

☑ It's "a gold mine away from the crowds" say vacationers not troubled by the "isolated location" of this "family-oriented" resort across from a "true beach"; suites accommodate "early risers and late sleepers" with "room dividers" before they head to a "buffet breakfast" or free shuttle to Mallory Square and airport; the only drawback surveyors find is "marginal" service.

Wyndham Casa Marina Resort   23 | 22 | 22 | 22 | $205 |
(fka Marriott)
1500 Reynolds St., Key West; 305-296-3535; fax 305-296-4633;
800-626-0777; www.wyndham.com; 311 rooms (71 suites)
☑ With an enviable position on the largest private beach, this resort
is "far enough from crowds to feel secluded" yet blocks from the
Atlantic end of Duval Street; the facility is "great for kids and
families" with two oceanfront pools and watersports from sailing
to scuba; guests call the staff "very friendly" and dub the conch
fritters and piña coladas "surprisingly good", but also point out that
rooms at this "not particularly elegant" property "could use an
update" (so "stay in the new wing" and "ask for an ocean view").

Lake Wales

Chalet Suzanne Inn   ▽ 22 | 24 | 26 | 22 | $188 |
3800 Chalet Suzanne Dr.; 863-676-6011; fax 863-676-1814;
800-433-6011; www.chaletsuzanne.com; 30 rooms (4 suites)
■ "Your cholesterol count rises as soon as you hit the parking lot"
of this "European-style" "miniature fairy-tale" inn with "eclectic"
meals ("nothing prepares you for chicken liver on grapefruit" or
"to-die-for Moon Soup") on a 100-acre estate in the "central
boonies"; inside, guests marvel at "funky" rooms (each designed
differently), while outdoor diversions include a swimming pool,
lake and even a small grass airstrip if you prefer to fly in to this
"truly unique property."

Marco Island

Hilton Beach Resort   23 | 22 | 20 | 22 | $206 |
560 S. Collier Blvd.; 941-394-5000; fax 941-394-8410; 800-445-8667;
www.hilton.com; 297 rooms (26 suites)
☑ "Sleep to the sound of the waves" at this "secluded" Gulf Coast
resort; "large rooms" are "clean and comfy" (all with water views),
and guests swoon over the sunset view from the beachfront bar
and restaurant; most agree this is a "good value" even if the "food's
not great" and the "town's dead after 8 PM."

Marriott   23 | 23 | 21 | 24 | $201 |
400 S. Collier Blvd.; 941-394-2511; fax 941-642-2672; 800-438-4373;
www.marriott.com; 735 rooms (62 suites)
☑ On a strand of sand lined with high-rises, this "huge", "friendly"
hotel is "not for the hip set"; "lots of water activities" and seashells
galore are "a dream for beachaholics", the staff really "aims
to please", and guests in Gulf-front rooms enjoy "spectacular
views", but accommodations could use "updating" and the food
is only "so-so."

Miami

★ **Best in City**
26 Turnberry Isle/R   Tides/H
     Fisher Island Club/SR   Biltmore/H
25 Wyndham Grand Bay/H   **23** Mayfair House/H
     Delano/H   Loews Miami Beach/H

Astor, The

23 | 23 | 25 | 21 | $220

956 Washington Ave., Miami Beach; 305-531-8081;
fax 305-531-3193; 800-270-4981; www.hotelastor.com; 40 rooms
(22 suites)

☑ At the epicenter of "hip" South Beach sits this "deco beauty" where "low-key" rooms are outfitted with "beige tone-on-tone minimalist" decor, built-in stereo systems and soundproofing; groupies delight in a "happening bar scene" and New World fusion cuisine at two restaurants, while critics bristle over "tiny quarters", service with "lots of attitude" and "no view" unless you reserve a "pricey suite overlooking the pool."

Beach House Bal Harbour

▽ 23 | 24 | 23 | 24 | $221

9449 Collins Ave., Bal Harbour; 305-535-8600; fax 305-535-8603;
877-782-3557; www.rubellhotels.com; 170 rooms (5 suites)

■ "Very Nantucket" say admirers of this beachfront hotel near an "upscale tanning and shopping" mecca that seems "a thousand miles from South Beach"; rooms are Polo Ralph Lauren–designed with high-tech conveniences (CD player, portable phone, Sony Playstation, Internet access), and The Atlantic restaurant menu was developed by *Silver Palate Cookbook* author Sheila Lukins; throw in the poolside spa and "you never need to leave" this "kid-friendly" spot.

Biltmore Hotel, The

23 | 24 | 24 | 27 | $221

1200 Anastasia Ave., Coral Gables; 305-445-1926;
fax 305-913-3159; 800-727-1926; www.biltmorehotel.com;
280 rooms (35 suites)

☑ This landmark born in the 1920s bowls over reviewers with its "fairy-tale" tower and "drop-dead-impressive" lobby – 45-foot ceilings, massive wrought-iron fixtures and stone colonnades; guests keep busy at the fitness center, spa, golf course and "mammoth pool" that makes swimmers "feel like Esther Williams"; still, this happy ending comes with a caveat about "small" rooms that "need freshening."

Delano Hotel

25 | 24 | 26 | 27 | $305

1685 Collins Ave., Miami Beach; 305-672-2000; fax 305-532-0099;
800-555-5001; 208 rooms (24 suites)

■ "If it isn't white, it's yours" assert guests in rooms so "serenely" "Starck" that "all that's missing are straitjackets" in this "surreal" hotel; a "dark, sexy lobby" with "flowing drapes" and "models blowing through on ocean breezes" is "theater" for "the fashion-forward" crowd that comes for dining at the Blue Door, "service with a smile (and an attitude)" and preening "buff bodies" by the infinity pool – leading most "mere mortals" to cry "I'm not worthy!"

Doral, The

21 | 22 | 20 | 23 | $238

4400 NW 87th Ave., Miami; 305-592-2000; fax 305-594-4682;
800-713-6725; www.doralgolf.com; 693 rooms (48 suites)

☑ The infamous "Blue Monster" and four other courses beckon at this "serious golfer's" haven that sports an Arthur Ashe Tennis Center and cascading waterfalls to boot; Camp Doral for kids lets parents indulge in the spa or lounge in recently renovated rooms that have replaced their "tired" look with an "airy feel"; dining, however, fares as strictly "average."

FISHER ISLAND CLUB | 27 | 26 | 25 | 27 | $357 |
1 Fisher Island Dr., Fisher Island; 305-535-6026; fax 305-535-6003;
800-537-3708; www.fisherisland-florida.com; 60 rooms (44 suites,
7 villas, 3 cottages)
■ "Exceptional" say reviewers of the "splendid isolation" at this
resort in Biscayne Bay, "seven minutes from South Beach", with
imported Bahamian sand, manicured golf greens, "super food"
and a "fantastic staff" that "treats you like Mr. and Mrs. Howell";
add the "spa and Jeb Bush" for a "touch of unreality" and "what
more could you want" on this veritable "Gilligan's Island"?

Grove Isle Club & Resort | ▽ | 25 | 24 | 25 | 24 | $253 |
4 Grove Isle Dr., Coconut Grove; 305-858-8300; fax 305-858-5908;
800-884-7683; 49 rooms (9 suites)
■ Proximity to South Beach but "without the noise" wins loyalty
from guests at this "private" resort "on its own island"; Baleen
offers "everything a Miami restaurant should" – "fab menu", "great
service" and waterside views of Biscayne Bay – while a pool and
tennis courts tempt fans to stay mum about this "best-kept secret."

Hotel, The | ▽ | 25 | 24 | 26 | 25 | $230 |
801 Collins Ave., Miami Beach; 305-531-2222; fax 305-532-6310;
877-843-4683; www.thehotelofsouthbeach.com; 53 rooms (5 suites)
▣ "Love what he did!" declare the fashion-conscious of designer
Todd Oldham's rehab of the once-derelict Tiffany Hotel, now
sporting "fantastical" colors and fabric throughout; "you'll spend
your vacation" by the rooftop pool with cabanas and an ocean view
and at the "absolutely fabulous" indoor/outdoor Wish restaurant,
which is just as well given the "small" rooms and "cramped" loos.

Hyatt Regency Coral Gables | 24 | 23 | 22 | 22 | $196 |
50 Alhambra Plaza, Coral Gables; 305-441-1234; fax 305-441-0520;
800-233-1234; www.hyatt.com; 242 rooms (50 suites)
■ "A real business-class hotel" with a "charming Spanish facade
and decor", this "class act" may be "off the beaten path" in
Downtown Coral Gables, but most agree its "gracious service
(though it's probably better if you speak Spanish)" and "clean
and spacious rooms" make this suburban spot "a favorite."

Loews Miami Beach Hotel | 24 | 22 | 23 | 24 | $245 |
1601 Collins Ave., Miami Beach; 305-604-1600; fax 305-604-3999;
800-235-6397; www.loewshotels.com; 800 rooms (50 suites)
▣ This "sexy newcomer to the beach" emits art deco "glamour" in
an "industrial-size" high-rise convention hotel that some tout as a
"much-needed" addition to the area; "design sense" extends from
the public areas to "palm-lined walkways" to the pool; most hope
the "hip" ambiance and celeb clientele will help make it all "great
in the future", despite "boxy rooms" and "inconsistent service."

Mandarin Oriental | – | – | – | – | VE |
500 Brickell Key Dr.; 305-373-0141; fax 305-913-8300; 800-526-6566;
www.mandarinoriental.com; 329 rooms (31 suites)
Set to open in late 2000, the curvy high-rise of this Asian chain hotel
looms on the skyline near Downtown; expect this resort to attract
guests looking for luxurious details, such as the latest massage
techniques and bay views at the spa, an infinity pool that seems
to pour into Biscayne Bay, bamboo-accented rooms with marble
baths and Internet access – and, of course, a pampering staff.

Mayfair House Hotel　　25 | 23 | 23 | 22 |$233
3000 Florida Ave., Coconut Grove; 305-441-0000;
fax 305-447-9173; 800-433-4555; www.mayfairhousehotel.com;
179 suites
■ A "bold hotel" with a twist (it's in a mall), this "eclectic"
"favorite" feels "surprisingly secluded" yet is obviously close to
shops and "tons of nightlife"; "attentive service" and "sexy"
suites furnished in mahogany and stained glass (plus hot tubs on
the balconies) set the scene for "romantic weekends" that feel
like "first-class" fun at a "coach fare."

Nash, Hotel　　– | – | – | – | M
1120 Collins Ave., Miami Beach; 305-674-7800; fax 305-538-8288;
www.hotelnash.com; 53 rooms (18 suites)
French-influenced art deco design harkens back to the 1940s
Riviera at this landmark lodging, opened in December 1999 as
hotelier Gregg Lurie's follow-up to Hotel Astor; soothing touches
abound, such as the linen, sage, and blond-wood color scheme in
guestrooms, black-and-white floral photography in public spaces
and three courtyard swimming pools filled with fresh-, salt- or
mineral water; come mealtime, fashionistas graze on a light menu
that's heavy on seafood at Mark's South Beach.

Raleigh, The　　18 | 18 | 20 | 21 |$230
1775 Collins Ave., Miami Beach; 305-534-6300;
fax 305-538-8140; 800-848-1775; www.raleighhotel.com;
107 rooms (14 suites)
☑ It's SoBe "for the low-key" at this "art deco" hotel; an "Esther
Williams pool" lined with Moroccan Majul palms makes "a lovely
setting for a party", and the "music crowd" and "model clientele"
like to sip "killer Raleigh Martinis" at this "alternative spot",
despite "spare" guestrooms ("the bathroom felt like my
grandparents' in Brooklyn").

Sonesta Beach Resort　　22 | 22 | 20 | 23 |$230
Key Biscayne
350 Ocean Dr., Key Biscayne; 305-361-2021; fax 305-361-3096;
800-766-3782; www.sonesta.com; 292 rooms (12 suites,
3 vacation homes)
☑ Set on one of the "best beachfront properties in the city" (10
minutes from Downtown), this family resort provides "so much
fun" in the sea and sand ("great kids' program") that "well-kept"
rooms, some with water views, are disappointing ("not as top-class
as expected"); still, a "friendly staff" helps make this vacation spot
a "real pleasure."

Tides Hotel　　26 | 24 | 24 | 25 |$318
1220 Ocean Dr., Miami Beach; 305-604-5070;
fax 305-604-5180; 800-688-7678; www.islandoutpost.com;
45 rooms (45 suites)
☑ "Enormous rooms with unbelievable views" (all ocean-facing
with telescopes) claim this "hip" address in the heart of South
Beach; the small suite hotel embodies "minimalism at its best"
with an all-white decor, and you won't find "a mob scene",
even at the "classy Terrace restaurant"; cynics snub a "terrible
pool" overlooking an alley (in all fairness, it overlooks the beach
too) and snipe "overpriced."

R | S | D | P | $

TURNBERRY ISLE RESORT & CLUB 28 | 26 | 25 | 27 | $295
19999 W. Country Club Dr., Aventura; 305-932-6200;
fax 305-933-6560; 800-327-7028; www.turnberryisle.com;
395 rooms (41 suites)
■ A pocket of "gated serenity", this resort proves "there's still
some class left" in South Florida (it ranked No. 1 in the city);
"lush grounds" surround four wings that house guestrooms
with terraces and marble baths that are "a destination unto
themselves"; dining at Veranda, "gracious service", a "terrific
spa" and "A-one" golf, tennis and marina complete the "treat"
(too bad "you need to take a shuttle to get to the beach"); for
more, see Spa section.

WYNDHAM GRAND BAY HOTEL 26 | 26 | 25 | 25 | $271
(fka Grand Bay Hotel)
2669 S. Bayshore Dr., Coconut Grove; 305-858-9600; fax 305-859-2026;
800-327-2788; www.wyndham.com; 177 rooms (49 suites)
☑ "Quietly distinguished" coo fans of this "first-class" hotel in
the "trendy Grove" close to Cocowalk shops; rooms sport "luxury
linens and robes", balconies ("not much of a view") and "fabulous"
bathrooms; Northern Italian cuisine at Bice is "excellent", as is
service; in general, things "keep getting better" under the new
management, though some frown upon the "pathetic gym."

Naples

Registry Resort, The 25 | 24 | 23 | 25 | $252
475 Seagate Dr.; 941-597-3232; fax 941-597-9151; 800-247-9810;
www.registryhotels.com; 474 rooms (78 suites)
■ From its lobby to "Gulf-view" rooms and villas, all is "casual
elegance" at this "well-run resort"; the secluded beach is "worth
the tram ride" or half-mile walk through a mangrove forest, while
a "solid kids' program", "good choice of restaurants", staff that
"fawns all over you" and "good buffet breakfast" add up to
a "wonderful" place.

RITZ-CARLTON, THE 28 | 28 | 28 | 28 | $303
280 Vanderbilt Beach Rd.; 941-598-3300; fax 941-598-6690;
800-241-3333; www.ritzcarlton.com; 463 rooms (36 suites)
■ "Eden on earth" exclaim reviewers about the "heavenly"
antiques-filled lobby and pure-white-sand beach of this resort
that ranks No. 1 in the state; the staff really knows how to
"pamper" – "you just think of something and they're right there
with it" – and the food is "superb", from breakfast on your room
balcony to high tea to dinner in The Dining Room ("a must"); for
more, see Spa section.

Orlando

★ **Best in City**
26 Disney's Grand Floridian/R
   Villas of Grand Cypress/R
   Loews Portofino Bay/R
25 Hyatt Regency Grand Cypress/R

24 Disney's Wilderness Lodge/R
   Disney's Boardwalk/R
   Peabody Orlando/H
   Disney's Yacht Club/R

Disney Institute
22 | 23 | 20 | 24 | $218

1960 Magnolia Way, Lake Buena Vista; 407-827-1100; fax 407-827-4102;
www.disneyworld.com; 585 rooms (316 bungalows, 141 townhouses,
60 treehouses, 64 villas, 4 vista homes)

☑ For "adults who don't want to deal with out-of-control kids"
Disney hosts this "vacation of exploration", where guests learn
new skills, such as cooking or rock climbing (and yes, there's
golf, swimming and tennis); to some, the "comfortable" "campus
setting" along Lake Buena Vista's north shore embodies an "unreal
feel not unlike a 1960s TV series", while others just call the decor
"boring" and the food "average."

Disney's Beach Club
24 | 24 | 22 | 25 | $226

1800 Epcot Resorts Blvd., Lake Buena Vista; 407-934-3827;
fax 407-934-8000; 800-647-7900; www.disneyworld.com;
572 rooms (21 suites)

☑ Epcot's an "easy walk" from this "fine place" that recalls a turn-
of-the-century Cape Cod resort; the circular current pool and 150-
foot water slide are "more fun than the rides at Disney World",
though kids still squeal when characters drop by ("Goofy tried to
eat my breakfast"); families also savor "clambake dinner for huge
appetites", but some find the guestrooms "disappointing."

Disney's Boardwalk
25 | 25 | 22 | 26 | $238

2101 N. Epcot Resorts Blvd., Lake Buena Vista; 407-939-5100;
fax 407-939-5150; www.disneyworld.com; 892 rooms (520 villas)

■ Like "classic Coney Island" or pre-gambling Atlantic City, this
pseudo-seaside resort on Lake Crescent is perpetually "bustling",
thanks to the adjacent dining, shopping and entertainment complex;
guestrooms are "spacious", and "immense condolike" villas give
even "a family of 10 room to spare"; eateries offer everything
"from pizza to bagels to blackened salmon", and there's access
to obvious attractions, but "you won't be moused to death" here.

DISNEY'S GRAND FLORIDIAN
27 | 26 | 25 | 27 | $287

4401 Floridian Way, Lake Buena Vista; 407-824-3000;
fax 407-824-3186; www.disneyworld.com; 867 rooms (61 suites)

■ "The grandest of them all" extol fans of this faux-Victorian
Disney "crown jewel" that's "logistically perfect" for touring the
Magic Kingdom (or combing the hotel's lagoon-front fake beach);
accommodations provide "more than enough room for the seven
dwarfs", and the staff gives the "best nightly turndown service
ever" ("they folded my child's blanket into a flower") – yes, "it's
hard to believe Mickey's behind this one"; for more, see Spa section.

Disney's Polynesian
22 | 23 | 21 | 24 | $222

1600 Seven Seas Dr., Lake Buena Vista; 407-824-2000;
fax 407-824-3174; www.disneyworld.com; 847 rooms (6 suites)

☑ "The Brady Bunch goes Hawaiian" at this "delightfully corny"
re-creation of a South Seas island, where tropical gardens
surround longhouses and individual huts; admirers enjoy the
"good, cheesy fun" like an "authentic Polynesian luau" and
"entertaining hula shows", but critics note that the resort (among
Disney's oldest) "needs an overhaul badly."

Disney's Wilderness Lodge   23 24 23 27 $211
901 Timberline Dr., Lake Buena Vista; 407-824-3200;
fax 407-824-3232; www.disneyworld.com; 728 rooms (27 suites)
◪ "Echoes of Yosemite" fill this "rustic" National Park Service–
style lodge, "transporting guests from tropical Florida to the
Pacific Northwest"; most visitors are thrilled by the atrium lobby
(with teepee chandeliers, totem poles, trickling stream and
"massive" fireplace), "neat geyser out back" and wild game on
some menus, but a vocal minority is reluctant to "rough it" in
"small rooms" and rates the re-creation "too contrived."

Disney's Yacht Club   24 24 22 25 $237
1700 Epcot Resorts Blvd., Lake Buena Vista; 407-934-7000;
fax 407-934-3450; www.disneyworld.com; 621 rooms (11 suites)
◪ "Ahoy, matey" – a "taste of New England" awaits all who dock
at this "nautical-theme resort" that's "convention oriented" but
"perfect for families" too; habitués shout hooray for the hotel's
pool, proximity to Epcot and "efficient" service; saltier sorts,
however, sniff "the yacht-club pedigree is only skin deep."

Hyatt Regency Grand Cypress   25 25 24 27 $232
1 Grand Cypress Blvd., Orlando; 407-239-1234; fax 407-239-3800;
800-554-9288; www.hyatt.com; 750 rooms (74 suites)
■ "Eat your heart out, Mickey" say fans of this resort on 1,500
acres that's a "respite from theme parks" (barring exotic birds in
the hotel atrium); an "outrageous pool area" features a water
slide, cascades and a grotto with caves, while five restaurants
please; most are eager to "come back", but a few reluctant
vacationers admit it's "okay if there are no conventions."

Loews Portofino Bay   28 24 24 27 $244
5601 Universal Blvd., Orlando; 407-503-1000; fax 407-503-1010;
800-837-2273; www.loewshotels.com; 750 rooms (48 suites)
■ "Que bella!" exclaim those transported by this "new resort" – a
"rendition of Italy" with "inviting" rooms, "plush beds" and "great
big bathrooms"; three swimming pools, bocce ball courts and a
health spa add to the "wonderland" close to Universal Studios, and
dining at regional Italian restaurants and service that's "getting
better" could "put Disney in the shade" for "the best vacation ever."

Marriott's Orlando World Center   22 22 21 24 $184
8701 World Ctr. Dr., Orlando; 407-239-4200; fax 407-238-8777;
800-621-0638; www.marriott.com; 2,003 rooms (111 suites)
■ It's "an entire world" so big "you exercise just walking from
lobby to room" at this skyscraper resort with "everything for
everybody"; guests keep busy with golf, two tropical lagoon areas
with five pools and a "water slide that's a delight for kids", and, of
course, Disney is just a five-minute stroll from the hotel.

Peabody Orlando, The   24 24 24 24 $206
9801 Int'l Dr., Orlando; 407-352-4000; fax 407-351-0073;
800-732-2639; www.peabodyorlando.com; 891 rooms (58 suites)
■ Everyone "loves the duck parade" through the lobby of this large,
hotel "convenient to the Convention Center"; guests relax in "crisp
rooms" with "lots of space" and "first-class amenities", enhanced
by "Southern hospitality throughout"; dining at the "somewhat
formal" Dux restaurant earns praise from business travelers,
who warn that "there is not much entertainment for vacationers."

VILLAS OF GRAND CYPRESS, THE   28 | 26 | 24 | 26 | $276
1 N. Jacaranda St., Orlando; 407-239-4700; fax 407-239-7219;
800-835-7377; www.grandcypress.com; 146 suites
■ "If Mickey Mouse could golf, he'd stay here", where there's
"putting luxury" on 45 Jack Nicklaus–designed holes set on 1,500
acres; the resort also lays claim to one of "the best equestrian
centers in the U.S.", a dozen clay tennis courts and two pools, but
the highest kudos go to the "spacious" quarters (dining room, living
room, full kitchen, porches) and the "fantastic service."

Walt Disney World Dolphin   21 | 21 | 20 | 23 | $212
1500 Epcot Resorts Blvd., Lake Buena Vista; 407-934-4000;
fax 407-934-4710; 800-227-1500; www.swandolphin.com;
1,509 rooms (136 suites)
☑ "Eek! Mickey's everywhere" at this Michael Graves–designed
"convention hotel" near Epcot, where two 50 ft. dolphin sculptures
adorn the roof; "business transpires in spite of it" thanks to "great
conference facilities", and during off-time reviewers who stay in
the "clean" but "ordinary" rooms enjoy watching fireworks; some
find it all "too cute", while other critics say the property is "just
too corporate for vacationers."

Walt Disney World Swan   21 | 21 | 20 | 23 | $214
1200 Epcot Resorts Blvd., Lake Buena Vista; 407-934-4000;
fax 407-934-4710; 800-227-1500; www.swandolphin.com;
758 rooms (55 suites)
■ Sister to Disney's World Dolphin, this "twin with great appeal"
has a Michael Graves design and decor that may be "aging", but
those who don't mind the "crowds of people and long waits for
elevators" at this "convention venue" appreciate the "clean,
convenient rooms", pool area and "fun" touches like "room-service
delivery of delicious Belgian waffles shaped like Mickey."

Wyndham Palace Resort   22 | 22 | 21 | 22 | $188
1900 Buena Vista Dr., Lake Buena Vista; 407-827-2727;
fax 407-827-3364; 800-327-2906; www.wyndham.com; 1,014 rooms
(124 suites)
☑ This "busy convention hotel" has a "perfect location" in
Downtown Disney that's "convenient" to Pleasure Island's bars
and discos; guests welcome a "refreshing lack" of the mouse in
"civilized", "decently sized" rooms with "views of Lake Buena
Vista" from balconies, but even with a spa and nine restaurants,
most say it's a "no-frills" place with "reasonable" prices – so
what does "'palace' imply?"

Palm Beach

Brazilian Court   22 | 23 | 23 | 23 | $239
301 Australian Ave.; 561-655-7740; fax 561-655-0801; 800-552-0335;
www.braziliancourt.com; 108 rooms (43 suites)
☑ "Super-convenient" to the beach and glamorous Worth Avenue,
this "laid-back" hideaway with "considerate" service, flowered
courtyard and "spacious" rooms was renovated in 1997, but
cynics already say the large resort's accommodations are a little
"tired" and the style a bit "campy."

R S D P $

BREAKERS, THE
25 | 26 | 25 | 27 | $300

1 S. County Rd.; 561-655-6611; fax 561-655-3577; 888-273-2537; www.thebreakers.com; 569 rooms (45 suites)

■ This throwback to the halcyon days of the Gold Coast makes well-heeled patrons (blue bloods and conventioneers) "feel like Rockefellers"; a three-year, $120 million renovation has "restored the magic" of "beautifully appointed rooms", "lavish grounds" and a health club, which are a bit marred by "pretentious attitudes" from "some guests"; for more, see Spa section.

Chesterfield
22 | 24 | 22 | 23 | $257

363 Cocoanut Row; 561-659-5800; fax 561-659-6707; 800-243-7871; www.redcarnationhotels.com; 55 rooms (11 suites)

■ With its mix of "English motifs and animal prints", this boutique hotel near Worth Avenue and the shore tries to scale the "height of charm" with "highly decorated" – but "tiny" – rooms; the bar is a "celeb-sighters'" dream and the staff gives "outstanding" service.

FOUR SEASONS
28 | 27 | 27 | 27 | $310

2800 S. Ocean Blvd.; 561-582-2800; fax 561-547-1374; 800-432-2335; www.fourseasons.com; 210 rooms (12 suites)

■ The staff "remembers you from trip to trip" at this seaside resort that bowls guests over with its lobby decor and room terraces that overlook the pool and private beach; food wins bravos from both man and beast – there's an unusual room service menu for Fido – and a kids' club keeps little ones busy while parents are "treated like kings and queens" in the spa; for more, see Spa section.

RITZ-CARLTON, THE
28 | 28 | 27 | 27 | $309

100 S. Ocean Blvd.; 561-533-6000; fax 561-588-4202; 800-241-3333; www.ritzcarlton.com; 270 rooms (56 suites)

■ "Service, service, service!" is the mantra at this English-antiques-adorned resort on the beach in Manalapan; just "what you would expect" guests exclaim over the rooms (most with views, some with balconies) that sport marble loos and "perfect water pressure"; with "dancing in the lobby" and "fabulous Sunday brunch", most wonder "who could ever be in a bad mood" here?

Ponte Vedra

LODGE & CLUB, THE
26 | 26 | 25 | 26 | $222

607 Ponte Vedra Blvd.; 904-273-9500; fax 904-273-0210; 800-243-4304; www.pvresorts.com; 66 rooms (24 suites)

☑ It "feels like old money" at this "relaxing" Mediterranean-style resort "on the sea"; "everything is first-class", from "oceanfront rooms" with balcony "views to die for" to on-site amenities like two pools, beachside cabanas and a spa; "great" food is matched by "attentive" service, but some find the place "a bit old-fashioned."

Ponte Vedra Inn & Club
26 | 26 | 23 | 25 | $225

200 Ponte Vedra Blvd.; 904-285-1111; fax 904-285-2111; 800-234-7842; www.pvresorts.com; 200 rooms (40 suites)

☑ Rooms 50 feet from the ocean plus 36 holes of Trent Jones–designed golf equal a "great value" ("go for one of the sports packages") at this "casual but elegant" resort; folks who have "known and loved this spot for 50 years" (it opened in 1928) applaud the "simple, comfortable" accommodations, service and spa (the largest in northern Florida) but aren't so keen on "bland" hotel fare.

Sanibel Island

Casa Ybel Resort   24 | 22 | 21 | 24 | $215
2255 W. Gulf Dr.; 941-472-3145; fax 941-472-2109; 800-276-4753;
www.casaybelresort.com; 114 suites
☑ With the "Gulf of Mexico out your back door", "you're always
close to the beach" at this condo resort featuring "large units" with
kitchenettes; gentle surf and a "good kids' program" make it a
"great family vacation spot" where guests search for seashells,
unwind with "tasty drinks by the pool" or play tennis; however,
critics chide the restaurant for food that's barely "average."

Sanibel Harbour Resort   23 | 22 | 21 | 23 | $206
17260 Harbour Pointe Dr.; 941-466-4000; fax 941-466-2150;
800-767-7777; www.sanibel-resort.com; 417 rooms (66 suites,
65 condos)
☑ This "low-key" group of rooms and condos on a private
peninsula offers clay tennis courts, six pools, a "lovely" but
"small" beach and spa ("you leave smelling like a mango") that
have most surveyors calling this a prime "place to relax" with
the "sunset", in spite of strictly "decent" rooms.

Sarasota

Resort at Longboat Key Club, The   26 | 24 | 23 | 24 | $275
301 Gulf of Mexico Dr., Longboat Key; 941-383-8821;
fax 941-383-0359; 800-237-8821; www.longboatkeyclub.com;
232 rooms (208 suites)
☑ For "true relaxation", this high-rise resort with "a gorgeous
island setting" is "perfect for families" (two-bedroom, two-bath
suites come equipped with kitchen, washer/dryer and "balconies
as big as swimming pools"); most like the "calm, caring service",
"stunning beach" and "tennis", but the "decor is so-so."

Tampa/St. Petersburg

Belleview Biltmore   20 | 22 | 21 | 24 | $162
25 Belleview Blvd., Clearwater; 727-442-6171; fax 727-441-4173;
800-237-8947; www.belleviewbiltmore.com; 244 rooms
(16 suites)
☑ This "amazing wooden structure" (built in 1897) houses a "nicely
kept up" resort (on the exterior at least – some say "*The Shining*
could have been filmed in the run-down halls"); guests like the
porches, meals on the terrace, pools, "beautiful grounds" and
shuttle bus to Clearwater Beach; in fact, the "kind staff" reminds
many of "what hotels used to be about."

Colony Beach & Tennis Resort, The   23 | 24 | 24 | 22 | $262
1620 Gulf of Mexico Dr., Long Boat Key; 941-383-6464;
fax 941-383-7549; 800-426-5669; www.colonybeachresort.com;
234 rooms (208 suites)
■ It's "tennis till you drop", with 21 hard and clay courts and 10
professional instructors at this sporty resort set on a white-sand
beach; "friendly" service ministers to "fitness" needs (let's hope
it's not tennis elbow), while "huge" apartment-style suites (some
with ocean views) are "great for families" to rest up in before
heading to the Dining Room.

Don CeSar, The
23 | 24 | 23 | 25 | $211

3400 Gulf Blvd., St. Pete Beach; 727-360-1881; fax 727-367-7597;
800-282-1116; www.don-cesar.com; 275 rooms (45 suites)

☑ "Romantics" are drawn to the "Gulf sunsets" at this 1920s ocean resort with "solid" service and "funky, fun food" at Uncle Andy's Ice Cream Parlor and the aquarium-decorated Maritana Grill; others cite "rooms that vary from grand to horrendous", "too many conventions" and "not much to do when you leave the grounds" of this pink "castle in the midst of nursing homes."

Hyatt Regency Westshore
23 | 22 | 22 | 22 | $183

6200 Courtney Campbell Cswy., Tampa; 813-874-1234; fax 813-281-9168;
800-233-1234; www.hyatt.com; 445 rooms (23 suites)

■ Incongruously "convenient to the airport" and "perfect for nature lovers", this business-oriented hotel surprises some with "bay views of dolphins" from "basic" rooms ("who knew Tampa had such vistas?"); between e-mails, catch a glimpse of ibis on the grounds and along a wildlife trail or dine on food served by a "spirited staff" at Armani's rooftop restaurant, where "people still dress for dinner."

Renaissance Vinoy
26 | 26 | 25 | 26 | $218

501 Fifth Ave. NE, St. Petersburg; 727-894-1000; fax 727-822-2785;
800-468-3571; www.renaissancehotels.com; 360 rooms (20 suites)

☑ "Everything is well cared for – including guests" – at this "restored" Downtown hotel (in a "good walking neighborhood") that invites relaxation on the front porch; there's "a wide variety of rooms" in the original building or tower ("get one with a marina-view balcony" or Jacuzzi), and the "high style" carries over to a "gracious staff" and meals at Marchand's or the Clubhouse (which overlooks the golf club on "pretty Snell Island"); the "only problem" at this "paradise in pink": "no beach."

Saddlebrook Resort
22 | 22 | 20 | 24 | $209

5700 Saddlebrook Way, Wesley Chapel; 813-973-1111;
fax 813-973-4504; 800-729-8383; www.saddlebrookresort.com;
800 rooms (278 suites)

☑ Travelers "come for the golf" (and brush up at Arnold Palmer Golf Academy), tennis or "good conference" facilities at this "quality" resort; the "great walking paths" keep most outdoors, even those seeking just "rest and relaxation"; "typical" condo rooms may sport "outdated" tropical decor, so "for quaintness, look elsewhere", and brace yourself for dining that "needs work."

Vero Beach

Disney's Vero Beach Resort
26 | 25 | 24 | 26 | $216

9250 Island Grove Terrace; 561-234-2000; fax 407-354-1944;
800-359-8000; www.disneyworld.com; 204 rooms (58 suites,
6 cottages)

☑ Disney's first oceanfront resort is a surprisingly "romantic experience" with a "very quiet, turn-of-the-century laid-back" feel; "cheery rooms" have beach views, "an activity pool and slide are great for all ages", and miniature golf, nature trails and a sandlot make this a "fun" place (for real kids) with "friendly service" despite "no fine dining."

Georgia

★ Best in State

27 Ritz Buckhead, *Atlanta*/H
   Cloister, *Sea Island*/R
   Four Seasons, *Atlanta*/H
26 Ritz, *Atlanta*/H

25 Ballastone, *Savannah*/SI
24 Jekyll Is. Club, *J. Is.*/H
23 Swissôtel, *Atlanta*/H
   Chât. Elan, *Braselton*/R

Atlanta

★ Best in City

27 Ritz-Carlton Buckhead/H
   Four Seasons/H
26 Ritz-Carlton/H
23 Swissôtel/H

FOUR SEASONS   27 | 27 | 26 | 26 |$252
(fka Occidental Grand)
*75 14th St.; 404-881-9898; fax 404-873-4692; 800-332-3442;
www.fourseasons.com; 244 rooms (18 suites)*
■ You may "feel like a corporate Scarlett O'Hara" inside this
"Midtown pearl" with an "elegant" marble staircase, where the
staff treats guests to "Southern hospitality times 10"; voters like
"cityscape views", beds "so comfortable even business travel is
a pleasure", health club, lounge and "some of the best hotel
dining around" at Park 75 in this "dependable" star.

Grand Hyatt   22 | 22 | 21 | 22 |$191
(fka Nikko)
*3300 Peachtree Rd.; 404-365-8100; fax 404-364-3952; 800-233-1234;
www.hyatt.com; 438 rooms (21 suites)*
☑ "A cut above your standard chain hotel" observe guests of this
flagship with a "must-see Japanese garden and waterfall" near
the lobby; "spacious" but "simple" rooms on high floors offer views
of Downtown, and all appreciate the location – a "good central
point to work and eat"; still, a few sniff "not very grand."

JW Marriott Hotel Lenox   24 | 23 | 20 | 22 |$188
*3300 Lenox Rd.; 404-262-3344; fax 404-262-8689; 800-228-9290;
www.marriott.com; 371 rooms (4 suites)*
☑ "Good for conventions" and business, this "dependable" "heart-
of-Buckhead" link in the chain provides "transportation to the
airport" via Atlanta's nearby transit system; surveyors who leave
work behind ring up some "serious shopping" at Lenox Mall, and all
admire "stylish" rooms, "eager-to-please employees" and "well-
laid-out" public spaces – the only downside: "yawn"-worthy dining.

RITZ-CARLTON, THE   26 | 26 | 26 | 25 |$237
*181 Peachtree St.; 404-659-0400; fax 404-688-0400; 800-241-3333;
www.ritzcarlton.com; 441 rooms (22 suites)*
☑ With service that's "more than we ever dreamed of" (when "my
shoes were stolen" management "bought new ones"), travelers
regard this business hotel as "the best Downtown", convenient for
conventioneers, with a "top conference-service staff", "freeway
access" and Lobby Lounge; guests eat up the "awesome" Southern
food at the new Atlanta Grill, though a few casual reviewers are
irked when it's inferred to "refrain from wearing jeans."

RITZ-CARLTON BUCKHEAD   27 | 28 | 27 | 27 | $256
3434 Peachtree Rd., NE; 404-237-2700; fax 404-239-0078;
800-241-3333; www.ritzcarlton.com; 553 rooms (29 suites)
■ Impressed by "a responsive" but "unobtrusive" staff, voters
agree that this "almost-perfect hotel" "pays attention to details"
(and wins the top rating in the city); "traditional" rooms with the
"best toiletries anywhere" complement "rich appointments" in
the public areas and "excellent food" at the Dining Room, which
is frequented by investment bankers and well-heeled ladies who
like "easy access to fine shopping" at the Lenox Square Mall.

Swissôtel   24 | 24 | 23 | 22 | $223
3391 Peachtree Rd., NE; 404-365-0065; fax 404-365-8787;
800-253-1397; www.swissotel.com; 365 rooms (11 suites)
☑ For travelers who think hotels should be "contemporary" and
"convenient", this "favorite" offers "sleek" "rooms with a European
feel" – "just right for the business traveler" thanks to fax and
modem hookups, "excellent service" and "fair prices"; diners dig
into hearty steak and lobster at The Palm restaurant; still, some
find the overall experience "too sparse."

W   ▽ 25 | 21 | 22 | 24 | $172
111 Perimeter Ctr. W.; 770-396-6800; fax 770-399-5514;
800-683-6100; www.whotels.com; 274 rooms (154 suites)
☑ "City chic in the suburbs" impresses most in this "funky" hotel's
"large rooms" with signature pillow-top mattresses, Aveda
amenities and simple but "trendy" blonde-wood furnishings; a
"great club" for martinis, Asian-inspired Savu restaurant and an
informal cafe just off the "hip lobby" are manned by a "nice
staff", but the "disappointed" few say this "remodel" is really "a
supermodel with no brains."

Braselton

Château Elan   24 | 24 | 21 | 25 | $203
100 Rue Charlemagne; 678-425-0900; fax 678-425-6000;
800-233-9463; www.chateauelan.com; 306 rooms (20 suites)
☑ This large resort about an hour north of Atlanta is "like being in
a fantasy" stocked with "great golf", winery tours, an equestrian
show center and spa; "large" conference facilities and rooms are
boons to business travelers, and the lobby, "pretty grounds" and
seven restaurants create a spot that "far exceeds expectations",
though naysayers give "mixed reactions" to "faux grandeur."

Jekyll Island

Jekyll Island Club Hotel   24 | 24 | 25 | 25 | $174
371 Riverview Dr.; 912-635-2600; fax 912-635-2818; 800-535-9547;
www.jekyllclub.com; 157 rooms (26 suites, 2 cottages)
☑ Visitors "live with the ghosts of millionaires" at this "well-run"
landmark where Vanderbilts and Rockefellers once played; most
who stay in the refurbished building enjoy "huge, quiet rooms"
with "shabby-chic" Victorian reproductions and the "stunning
sunsets" that punctuate "excellent" seafood dining; still, some
complain that "time has passed this lady by."

Little St. Simons Island

Lodge on Little St. Simons ▽ | 24 | 27 | 24 | 28 | $333 |
912-638-7472; fax 912-634-1811; 888-733-5774;
www.littlestsimonsisland.com; 15 rooms (2 suites)
☑ "Like summer camp for adults" (fishing, boating, horseback
riding, hiking and canoeing) but "with much better food", this lodge
on a 10,000-acre "serene barrier island" is "the perfect place for an
outdoors person"; "sanity is restored" in the "wild" environment
where most appreciate "rustic" accommodations, though some
grouse about "mosquitoes" and wonder if the "wilderness
elegance" isn't "too understated."

Pine Mountain

Callaway Gardens | 20 | 22 | 20 | 23 | $165 |
US Hwy. 27; 706-663-2281; fax 706-663-5068; 800-225-5292;
www.callawaygardens.com; 787 rooms (10 suites)
■ "Rent a log cabin" and "smell the pine" at this family resort
that offers a wide range of all-inclusive activities such as
swimming, tennis and golf; the staff "works hard to make this an
awesome vacation" spot with "beautiful flowers and butterflies"
filling "spectacular gardens."

Savannah

Ballastone Inn | 25 | 26 | 22 | 25 | $229 |
14 E. Oglethorpe Ave.; 912-236-1484; fax 912-236-4626;
800-822-4553; www.ballastone.com; 16 rooms (3 suites)
☑ Soak up "mellow Southern hospitality" at this "romantic inn"
occupying an 1838 mansion, where "nice folks" lend a "personal
touch" to public spaces and "comfortable" rooms decorated with
period antiques (towering four-poster and canopy beds); the
hotel sits in an "excellent location" in the heart of the historic
district, but a few find the whole experience "a little Martha
Stewart-y"; N.B. no children under 16, please.

Mulberry Inn ▽ | 23 | 23 | 21 | 22 | $139 |
601 E. Bay St.; 912-238-1200; fax 912-236-2600; 800-465-4329;
www.savannahhotel.com; 145 rooms (25 suites)
■ Built in 1860 as a livery stable, this "small hotel", "well located"
on Washington Square and one block from River Street, exudes
"charm, charm, charm"; guests "delight" in the "above-standard"
rooms and ample lobby where "afternoon tea and cookies" are
served to live piano music; add in "good service" and "reasonable
prices" and the sum is a "really nice getaway."

River Street Inn | 23 | 22 | 20 | 21 | $145 |
115 E. River St.; 912-234-6400; fax 912-234-3618; 800-678-8946;
www.riverstreetinn.com; 86 rooms (1 suite)
☑ At this "find" on the waterway, guests "enjoy the feel of the
city" while watching paddleboats and freighters from river-view
rooms with balconies; antiques in public spaces and the staff
bolster an "inviting" ambiance, but light sleepers be forewarned:
"don't expect quiet" from adjacent River Street, which can be
"mad" at times, "especially on St. Patrick's Day."

Westin Savannah Harbor Resort 23 | 20 | 22 | 21 | $183
1 Resort Dr.; 912-201-2000; fax 912-201-2001; 800-937-8461;
www.westin.com; 403 rooms (19 suites)
☑ Vacationers like the "views of the city" from the Hutchinson
Island locale of this new (some say "still raw") resort; guests putter
on the golf course, dine in the two restaurants, hang out in "large
rooms" furnished with "unbelievable beds", indulge in the spa or
take a water taxi across the river for shopping and sight-seeing.

Sea Island

CLOISTER, THE 27 | 28 | 26 | 28 | $315
100 Hudson Pl.; 912-638-3611; fax 912-638-5159; 800-732-4752;
www.seaisland.com; 286 rooms (32 suites)
■ "A lifetime must", this "old-fashioned" resort on 10,000 acres has
"something for everyone", from three golf courses to a "gorgeous
beach", nature-study classes and children's programs; rooms "vary
from nice to luxurious", and staff "goes the extra mile" to deliver
hospitality and "great quantities" of food in the dining room; N.B.
gentlemen should bring a jacket and tie; for more, see Spa section.

Hawaii

★ **Best in State**
29 Four Seasons, *Big Is.*/R
    Lodge at Koele, *Lanai*/R
    Four Seasons, *Maui*/R
28 Halekulani, *Oahu*/R
    Manele Bay, *Lanai*/R
27 Mauna Lani Bay, *Big Is.*/R
    Ritz-Carlton, *Maui*/R
    Kahala Mandarin, *Oahu*/R

    Princeville, *Kauai*/R
    Kea Lani, *Maui*/R
    Grand Wailea, *Maui*/R
    Hyatt, *Kauai*/R
    Orchid Mauna Lani, *Big Is.*/R
26 Kona Village, *Big Is.*/R
    Ihilani, *Oahu*/R
    Westin Mauna Kea, *Big Is.*/R

Big Island

FOUR SEASONS HUALALAI 29 | 29 | 28 | 29 | $380
100 Ka'upulehu Dr., Kona; 808-325-8000; fax 808-325-8100;
888-336-5662; www.fourseasons.com; 243 rooms (31 suites)
■ "Ahhh … perfection" coo sybarites, naming this low-rise resort
"paradise found" (No. 1 resort in the U.S.); an "especially attentive
staff" greets guests by name – every time – and "superb" Island-
style Continental fare at Pahu i'a, oversized rooms, small beach,
golf that's reserved for guests only and open-air spa all make this
"one of the greatest places on earth"; for more, see Spa section.

Hilton Waikoloa Village 25 | 25 | 24 | 27 | $244
425 Waikoloa Beach Dr., Waikoloa; 808-886-1234; fax 808-886-2900;
800-445-8667; www.hilton.com; 1,240 rooms (57 suites)
☑ Guests get giddy about this "tropical fantasyland" where you
navigate 62 acres by boat, monorail or foot; water lovers encounter
dolphins, speed down a water slide, snorkel a lagoon or comb the
man-made beach, while culture vultures view a multimillion-
dollar Pacific art collection and foodies head to nine restaurants;
"kids love this place", but some grown-ups grumble the resort is
so huge "you'll need a compass"; for more, see Spa section.

KONA VILLAGE RESORT   27 | 27 | 25 | 27 | $414

Kaupulehu Dr., Kailua-Kona; 808-325-5555; fax 808-325-5124;
800-367-5290; www.konavillage.com; 125 bungalows

For "funky luxury", "God would stay here" say fans of the "peace and quiet" at this "100-percent Polynesian" low-rise hideaway; accommodations come "loaded with romance" – oceanside grass shacks with coconuts for 'do not disturb' signs and no phone, TV or radio; there's acclaim for "outstanding" food ("don't miss the Friday night luau") and a "friendly" staff, but a few heat-sensitive folk note "air conditioners would be an improvement."

MAUNA LANI BAY HOTEL   28 | 28 | 27 | 28 | $345

68-1400 Mauna Lani Dr., Kohala Coast; 808-885-6622; fax 808-881-7000;
800-367-2323; www.maunalani.com; 350 rooms (10 suites, 5 bungalows)

This "enchanting" six-story oceanfront resort sits on a "beach that dreams are made of", and no one seems disappointed with the facilities either, which include "well-appointed" rooms, golf course and spa ("must get a massage on the beach"), or the "attentive service" (you "feel like a guest, not a customer") and "world-class" Pacific Rim cuisine at Canoe House; "find a hammock on the beach" and "watch for whales" advise reviewers, or let the "sounds of surf lull you to sleep."

ORCHID AT MAUNA LANI, THE   27 | 27 | 26 | 28 | $299

1 N. Kaniku Dr., Kohala Coast; 808-885-2000; fax 808-885-5778;
800-845-9905; www.orchid-maunalani.com; 538 rooms (54 suites)

This Kohala Coast beachfront "oasis" has reviewers sputtering superlatives; "five-star service" tops a roster of raves about the pool area with cabanas, tennis facilities, Hawaii Regional (fusion) cuisine at Brown's Beach House and "sophisticated" spa without walls; most extol the little niceties, like "fresh orchids on your pillow at bedtime", but a few whiners find this former Ritz-Carlton "too formal"; for more, see Spa section.

Westin Hapuna Beach Prince Hotel   26 | 26 | 24 | 27 | $289

62-100 Kauna'oa Dr., Kohala Coast; 808-880-1111; fax 808-880-3142;
800-882-6060; www.westin.com; 351 rooms (37 suites)

There's "not a bad room in the house" at this "serene" resort on "one of the most gorgeous beaches in the world" ("snorkel early to see giant sea turtles"); private balconies or patios and open-air lobby and hallways capture panoramic views, especially at sunset, the staff "makes you feel like the most important guest", and dining at six restaurants "surprises with each dish" – all of which can compensate for "long walks to everything."

WESTIN MAUNA KEA   26 | 26 | 25 | 27 | $322
BEACH HOTEL

62-100 Mauna Kea Beach Dr., Kohala Coast; 808-882-7222;
fax 808-882-5700; 800-882-6060; www.westin.com; 310 rooms
(10 suites, 1 private house)

"The epitome of class" declare enthusiasts of this "old-money" oceanfront resort that has an "almost spiritual aesthetic", as evidenced by "dramatic" architecture, an open-air lobby with fish stream and "impressive artwork"; guests relax in rooms with "tile floors and teakwood shutters" when not playing the golf course, sunning on the "secluded crescent beach" or sampling "creative food" at five restaurants.

Kauai

Hanalei Bay Resort

25 | 24 | 23 | 25 | $201

5380 Honoiki Rd., Princeville; 808-826-6522; fax 808-922-8785;
800-922-7866; www.hanaleibaykauai.com; 280 rooms

☑ A "dream location", this North Shore resort facing the "ethereal Bali-Hai" peaks of Hanalei shares "ocean views" and beach with "pricier" neighbors, making this a "great bargain"; "lush grounds", "soft breezes and sweet smells" (from nine types of ginger plants) surround two pools and an open-air restaurant that serves an "extensive" menu; the only cloud on the horizon: "small" rooms.

HYATT REGENCY

27 | 27 | 26 | 28 | $290

1571 Poipu Rd., Koloa; 808-742-1234; fax 808-742-1557;
800-554-9288; www.hyatt.com; 602 rooms (37 suites)

■ This resort on the Poipu coast gives some guests a "completely satisfying hotel orgasm"; still others find the old-Hawaiian low-rise architecture, saltwater lagoon and Anara Spa "intoxicating and addictive"; "friendly to kids" and honeymooners ("utterly romantic private oceanside dinners") alike, it earns accolades for "comfy rooms", golf and tennis facilities, "entertaining shows" and "exceptional service", leaving only a "less-than-swimmable beach" to dampen the 'surf's up!' cry; for more, see Spa section.

PRINCEVILLE

28 | 27 | 26 | 28 | $309

5520 Ka Haku Rd., Princeville; 808-826-9644; fax 808-826-1166;
800-826-4400; www.princeville.com; 252 rooms (51 suites)

■ The view alone of the Napali Coast could sustain guests at this clifftop resort filled with "more flowers than a state dinner"; marble, tapestries and "ornate furniture" (some say "un-Hawaiian") "take your breath away", as do "amazing bathrooms" with opaque-glass windows that turn on or off for privacy or water views; "impeccable service" and "buffet bonanzas" lessen "worry about rain" (this is the wetter side of the island); for more, see Spa section.

Lanai

LODGE AT KOELE

29 | 28 | 28 | 29 | $352

1 Keomoku Hwy., Lanai City; 808-565-7300; fax 808-565-4561;
800-321-4666; www.lanai-resorts.com; 102 rooms (14 suites)

■ There's "no place like" this "unusual combination" of a "classic English lodge" and island resort with croquet, lawn bowling, chess and skeet at an "estate" in the "misty" hills – "so beautiful, you don't need a beach"; "huge rooms" with fireplaces are "truly special", "service is superb" and the "golf astonishing" with pines and bonsai-like greens; formal dining ("pineapple cider to die for") rounds out accolades for "one of the best spots in the world."

MANELE BAY HOTEL

28 | 27 | 27 | 29 | $345

1 Manele Bay Rd., Lanai; 808-565-7700; fax 808-565-2483;
800-321-4666; www.lanai-resorts.com; 250 rooms (27 suites)

■ Spinner dolphins in the bay "make you never want to leave your lounge chair" at this "paradise in paradise" ("there's a reason Bill Gates got married here"); a staff "at your beck and call" makes guests imagine they're visiting "a potentate's palace" filled with large rooms and even larger bathrooms; outside, golf along lava rocks and the ocean helps build an appetite for the restaurants' "fresh food"; for more, see Spa section.

Maui

Embassy Vacation Resorts   25 | 22 | 21 | 23 | $237
104 Kaanapali Beach, Kaanapali Beach; 808-661-2000; fax 808-667-5821;
800-362-2779; www.embassyvacationresorts.com; 413 suites
■ This "airy", "self-contained" oceanfront resort is "chock-full"
of "Hawaiian ambiance" with a "great big pool" that's "terrific"
for families; "attractive" suites (with kitchenettes, large tubs and
two TVs), a "friendly" staff, "accommodating" room service and
"on-site" restaurants make it a "great deal for the money"
(breakfast buffets are included in the rate).

FOUR SEASONS WAILEA   29 | 29 | 28 | 29 | $363
3900 Wailea Alanui, Wailea; 808-874-8000; fax 808-874-2222;
800-334-6284; www.fourseasons.com; 380 rooms (75 suites)
■ "Is this heaven, or just a dream?" ask the smitten as they're
"spritzed with Evian and handed cold face towels" under cabanas
at the pool (a sure spot for celebrity sightings); rooms furnish "the
most comfortable beds" and "gigantic" bathrooms, while staff
orchestrates "a level of service beyond expectations", from "utterly
perfect" dining at three restaurants to entertaining children
"amazingly well"; for more, see Spa section.

GRAND WAILEA   28 | 26 | 26 | 28 | $360
3850 Wailea Alanui, Wailea; 808-875-1234; fax 808-879-4077;
800-888-6100; www.grandwailea.com; 780 rooms (60 suites)
■ "Grand, grand, grand!", this resort, "perfectly positioned on
the beach", "lives up to its name" with design like "a tropical
Vegas" ("I expected to see Liberace playing by the pool"); "large
rooms and bathrooms" can barely compete with the water park
slides, "fabulous dining" in a "multitude of restaurants" and a spa
(the largest in Hawaii); there's only one drawback at this "flashy"
"slice of heaven" – "I cry every time we leave."

HANA-MAUI, HOTEL   27 | 26 | 23 | 26 | $366
Hana Hwy., Hana-Maui; 808-248-8211; fax 808-248-7202; 800-321-4262;
www.hotelhanamaui.com; 66 rooms (18 suites, 7 sea ranch cottages)
☑ "Hey! this is nice" say surprised guests at this "most Hawaiian"
hotel in the "wonderful little town of Hana" ("far removed from
tourists and high-rise commercialism"); a "sybaritic" experience
includes "quiet rooms" ("stay in the sea-ranch cottages" and
"get a whirlpool on your porch"), "charming staff" and "relaxing"
atmosphere with the "sound of crashing waves on one side,
mooing livestock on the other"; critics perceive a "downhill"
slump and suggest that "updating" would make it "what it could
be", particularly the dining ("a low point").

Hyatt Regency   25 | 25 | 25 | 27 | $269
200 Nohea Kai Dr., Lahaina; 808-661-1234; fax 808-667-4498;
800-233-1234; www.hyatt.com; 806 rooms (33 suites)
☑ "Forget your troubles" as you enter an open-air lobby filled with
roaming exotic birds (do penguins count?), orchids and priceless
Oriental art at this "fantasy"-style resort; a "family-friendly" place
with "a pool that never ends" (plus swim-up bar and water slide),
dining at the Swan Court and new oceanfront spa, this isn't the
spot for "quiet seclusion" – indeed, guests report it's a "bit of a
zoo", so avoid rooms directly over the nightly luau.

Kapalua Bay Hotel | 25 | 25 | 24 | 26 | $296 |

*1 Bay Dr., Kapalua; 808-669-5656; fax 808-669-4694; 800-367-8000;
www.kapaluabayhotel.com; 194 rooms (5 suites, 12 villas)*

☑ From its "relatively secluded" roost on a point of land jutting out to sea, this "alternative to big resorts" flaunts a vista "that'll knock your socks off" and "some of the best snorkeling" on the island; there's applause for a "welcoming" staff, the neighboring golf course and contemporary cuisine at the Bay Club, but some protest "dated decor", "oddly angular, '70s-style" architecture and nearby condo construction that threatens to "spoil the view from half the rooms."

Kapalua Villas | 26 | 22 | 22 | 25 | $251 |

*500 Office Rd., Kapalua; 808-669-8088; fax 808-669-5234; 800-545-0018;
www.kapaluavillas.com; 282 rooms (11 suites, 8 private homes)*

☑ "Another day in paradise – golf in the morning, snorkeling in the afternoon, perfect weather" sigh surveyors about this large resort with "blissfully comfortable" condos that share the nearby Ritz-Carlton pool and beach; "views" from "roomy" quarters make a shutterbug's dream come true ("I took a half roll of pictures out my window"), though critics warn that "getting a lot for the money" "depends which unit you stay in" – some "need serious updating."

KEA LANI RESORT | 28 | 27 | 26 | 28 | $334 |

*4100 Wailea Alanui Dr., Wailea; 808-875-4100; fax 808-875-1200;
800-659-4100; www.kealani.com; 450 rooms (413 suites, 37 villas)*

■ Some call the architecture "Moorish", others "Moroccan" or "Mediterranean", but there's no disputing the "beauty" of this white-stucco resort where it's "easy to be spoiled" by a "pool boy who brings around pineapple slices and cool towels", suites with "marble bathrooms big enough to live in" (plus private villas with plunge pools), a restaurant that serves "fabulously presented nouvelle Pacific-Rim cuisine" and a beach where "stars hang out" – in a word, "decadence!"

Plantation Inn ▽ | 26 | 25 | 27 | 23 | $188 |

*174 Lahainaluna Rd., Lahaina; 808-667-9225; fax 808-667-9293;
800-433-6815; www.theplantationinn.com; 19 rooms (4 suites)*

■ Vacationers who don't like big resorts "love" this "little-known" "gem" ("best value in Maui") where even natives go for "superior" French cuisine at Gerard's restaurant; "small, sweet and romantic", the hotel's turn-of-the-century architecture houses "wonderfully appointed rooms", most with a private lanai or balcony; Hawaiian "hospitality" and the courtyard pool and Jacuzzi lure guests to stay on the premises, but it's just a short walk to the waterfront, shops and restaurants.

Renaissance Wailea | 25 | 25 | 24 | 26 | $232 |

*3550 Wailea Alanui Dr., Wailea; 808-879-4900; fax 808-874-5370;
800-992-4532; www.renaissancehotels.com; 345 rooms (12 suites)*

■ For those "who don't want hubbub", this "affordable" resort tempts vacationers with 16 acres of tropical grounds and "quiet" Ulua and Mokapu beaches; "terrific service", "lack of tackiness" and "comfortable rooms" refresh guests for snorkeling and laps in the two freshwater pools; snack lovers take note: the Maui Onion prepares "not-to-be-missed onion rings" and some of "the best burgers on the island."

RITZ-CARLTON KAPALUA   28 | 27 | 27 | 28 | $329

1 Ritz-Carlton Dr., Kapalua in Lahaina; 808-669-6200;
fax 808-665-0026; 800-262-8440; www.ritzcarlton.com; 548 rooms
(58 suites)

■ "Elegant, yes – Hawaiian, no", this secluded island retreat on
the northwest shore keeps guests in "sheer amazement" with its
"pampering" (mint-scented washcloths at the pool, anyone?); staff
tends to the "spacious" rooms, "superb" local cuisine in the
Anuenue Room and "world-class" golf course; the "only bummers":
iffy weather and rough surf; for more, see Spa section.

Sheraton   23 | 22 | 22 | 23 | $222

2605 Kaanapali Pkwy., Lahaina; 808-661-0031; fax 808-661-0458;
800-782-9488; www.sheraton.com; 510 rooms (44 suites)

☑ "Terrific snorkeling and diving on Black Rock earn giant brownie
points" for this "standard Sheraton"; the beach couldn't be more
"awesome" nor the view more "breathtaking", but despite "well
laid out" grounds, "friendly" service and a snaking swimming pool,
a few are miffed by "small", "boring" rooms and "long walks" at
this "affordable" resort.

Westin   23 | 23 | 22 | 25 | $243

(fka Westin Kaanapali Beach)
2365 Kaanapali Pkwy., Lahaina; 808-667-2525; fax 808-661-5764;
888-625-4949; www.westin.com; 759 rooms (28 suites)

☑ "I dream of this resort's" open-air lobby teeming with "live birds,
fish and waterfalls" confess veteran guests, who also favor the
artwork in public spaces, beach, "pleasant staff" and one of the
"best pools" in Kaanapali; some, however, resent extra "resort
fees", "small" rooms and "crowded conditions."

Westin Maui Prince   24 | 24 | 23 | 23 | $231

5400 Makena Alanui, Kihei; 808-874-1111; fax 808-879-8763;
800-321-6248; www.westin.com; 310 rooms (19 suites)

■ Away from crowded tourist areas, this "unpretentious resort" on
the island's more isolated southern tip "delights" snorkelers with a
"prime spot right off perfect Makena Beach" – and close to "nude
Little Beach"; "tastefully appointed" rooms possess an "airy feel"
and "ocean views", while "polite" service and "a smorgasbord of
meals" add to this "tropical haven."

Molokai

Molokai Ranch & Lodge   ▽ 23 | 23 | 19 | 22 | $162

100 Maunaloa Hwy., Maunaloa; 808-531-0158; fax 808-534-1606;
877-726-4656; www.molokai-ranch.com; 120 rooms
(81 tentalows)

☑ "Luxury plus camping" at this "rustic" resort in the upcountry
hills attracts "families in the right frame of mind" and "the cowboy
in us all" (no cars allowed, so take the shuttle to the beach); guests
stay in a two-story lodge or eco-friendly "tentalows" (half tent,
half bungalow), outfitted with flannel sheets and minimal amenities,
and chow down on "adequate food" served at set times ("if you
miss lunch, no food until dinner"); get-up-and-go types warn
"bring a book" to ward off "boredom."

Oahu

HALEKULANI　　　　　28 ⎮ 29 ⎮ 28 ⎮ 27 ⎮ $336

2199 Kalia Rd., Honolulu; 808-923-2311; fax 808-926-8004;
800-367-2343; www.halekulani.com; 456 rooms (44 suites)
■ Delivering "near-perfection" in the "midst of madness", this
oceanfront resort has guests likening it to "an orchid floating in
champagne"; with "white-glove service" (were they "trained at
Buckingham Palace"?), "exquisite public spaces", "contemporary"
Asian-inspired rooms and "magical" dining at La Mer, staying
this "close to paradise" is "worth" every penny.

Hilton Hawaiian Village　　　23 ⎮ 22 ⎮ 22 ⎮ 24 ⎮ $218

2005 Kalia Rd., Honolulu; 808-949-4321; fax 808-951-5458;
800-445-8667; www.hilton.com; 2,545 rooms (363 suites)
☑ More "like a city" than a hotel, this "commercial" mega-resort is
a "great escape for families with children", since "everything is at
your fingertips" (pools, shops, "lots of restaurants" and activities);
surveyors favor rooms with "fantastic views" in the Alii and
Rainbow Towers but caution: this place is "run like a factory";
N.B. a new tower is being added in 2001.

JW MARRIOTT IHILANI　　　28 ⎮ 26 ⎮ 24 ⎮ 27 ⎮ $268

(fka Ihilani Resort & Spa)
92-1001 Olani St., Kapolei; 808-679-0079; fax 808-679-0080;
800-626-4446; www.marriott.com; 387 rooms (36 suites)
☑ "Be ready to relax" at this complete resort that's "worth the
30-minute drive" from the airport; the staff is "friendly", particularly
in the "world-class spa", and big rooms overlook an extensive
oceanfront walk; critics, however, eschew the "fake beach" and
"absence of waves" at the lagoon swimming cove and food that
may have improved with the addition of three new restaurants;
for more, see Spa section.

KAHALA MANDARIN ORIENTAL　28 ⎮ 28 ⎮ 27 ⎮ 27 ⎮ $311

5000 Kahala Ave., Honolulu; 808-739-8888; fax 808-739-8800;
800-367-2525; www.mandarin-oriental.com; 371 rooms
(33 suites)
■ "What could be better than a room overlooking a lagoon where
they let guests play with dolphins?" wonder fans of this resort
that's only "10 minutes from touristville" but feels "a million miles
away"; a "wall of orchids in the lobby", "lovely" "refurbished"
rooms, "divine beach", "superb" service and "hip dining" at Hoku's
Restaurant are why many guests declare: "I never want to leave!"

Royal Hawaiian Hotel, The　　24 ⎮ 25 ⎮ 24 ⎮ 26 ⎮ $273

2259 Kalakaua Ave., Honolulu; 808-923-7311; fax 808-924-7098;
800-325-3589; www.royal-hawaiian.com; 527 rooms (34 suites)
☑ Torches in the courtyard and a "royal coconut grove" "whisper
old Hawaii" at this resort built in 1927; fans of the oceanfront
landmark are split on the best rooms – "the old section" for original
"ambiance" vs. "tower rooms for ocean views"; all agree that
"everyone should stay here at least once" to experience the island
"the way it was and should always be", though a few recommend
the "Pink Palace" get a "makeover."

Sheraton Moana Surfrider
23 | 24 | 23 | 25 | $232

2365 Kalakaua Ave., Honolulu; 808-922-3111; fax 808-923-0308;
800-782-9488; www.sheraton.com; 793 rooms (46 suites)

☑ Waikiki's first resort centers on a restored 1901 plantation house wrapped around a 75-foot banyan tree (accommodations now also include a modern tower); habitués like to sit on rocking chairs on the front porch for afternoon high tea and Sunday brunch or watch surfers, outrigger races and "eclectic crowds" troll the "crowded" beach; but not all is perfect at this "vintage" "paradise" due to "mediocre" rooms and a pool that's "shaded" half the day.

W Diamond Head
▽ 23 | 23 | 22 | 19 | $239

2885 Kalakaua Ave., Honolulu; 808-922-1700; fax 808-924-2249;
877-946-8357; www.whotels.com; 48 rooms (4 suites)

■ "Please don't tell readers" about this place implore surveyors who've found an "intimate" hotel nestled between "a beach park" (Kapiolani) and the Pacific, a half-mile from the Waikiki crowds; purchased by W Hotels in 1999, its recently renovated rooms are "hip" and "cozy" with handcrafted teak furniture; views of Diamond Head are "stunning" from the terrace, restaurant and all guest quarters.

Westin Hawaii Prince
23 | 23 | 22 | 22 | $201

100 Holomoana St., Honolulu; 808-956-1111; fax 808-946-0811;
800-321-6248; www.westin.com; 521 rooms (57 suites)

☑ "Fit for a princess", this high-rise resort – with a "view" of the yachts in Ala Wai Marina – is "just far enough from the crowds" of Waikiki but close enough to walk to attractions; guests praise the "colorful seafood buffet" at Prince Court restaurant and rooms facing the ocean; but wish the other on-site dining weren't so "average" and that the property had a beach.

Idaho

Coeur d'Alene

Coeur d'Alene, The
25 | 24 | 23 | 24 | $197

115 S. Second St.; 208-765-4000; fax 208-664-7276; 800-688-5253;
www.cdaresort.com; 336 rooms (15 suites)

■ "What a view" exclaim admirers of this lakeside resort that's "haunting and misty in winter"; you can appreciate vistas from beds in split-level suites that are "so nice" you could stay in and miss the boating and golfing; a "cordial" staff and treats like "huckleberry soufflé" at Beverly's restaurant further this "pleasant surprise."

Ketchum

Knob Hill Inn
▽ 25 | 23 | 25 | 23 | $230

960 N. Main St.; 208-726-8010; fax 208-726-2712; 800-526-8010;
www.knobhillinn.com; 26 rooms (4 suites)

■ "Delightful" at any time of year, this "European-style" chalet hotel close to Sun Valley grants balcony views of Bald Mountain and the Boulder range from rooms with "great" loos; when not skiing, hiking or relaxing in the sauna or hot tub, guests savor one of the "best breakfasts anywhere"; multilingual service – including "a Saint Bernard" to greet you – puts the finishing touches on a "charming" experience.

Sun Valley

Sun Valley Resort   22 | 24 | 22 | 25 | $234
1 Sun Valley Rd.; 208-622-4111; fax 208-622-2030; 800-786-8259;
www.sunvalley.com; 520 rooms (12 suites, 252 condos, 7 houses)
☑ "Good enough for Hemingway, good enough for me" declare
loyalists of this "classic resort" where Papa still seems "to roam
the halls"; guests like the lodge "at any time of the year" ("loved the
summer ice-skating", "I think I saw Sonja Henie") and keep busy
with outdoor sports for the whole family, including skiing, "miles of
bike trails", golf and tennis; the less-impressed cite "declining"
dining standards and rooms that need "further renovation" to
"maintain the old charm."

Illinois

Chicago

★ **Best in City**
28 Four Seasons/H
     Ritz-Carlton/H
24 Fairmont/H
     Drake/H

23 Monaco/H
     Renaissance/H
     Swissôtel/H
     Whitehall/H

Burnham, The Hotel   ▽ 26 | 25 | 23 | 22 | $179
1 W. Washington St.; 312-782-1111; fax 312-782-0899;
877-294-9712; www.burnhamhotel.com; 122 rooms (19 suites)
■ Spend "a night in architectural history" (the 1895 Reliance
Building, America's first steel-and-glass skyscraper) at this "comfy"
new hotel – an "oh-so-trendy" "find" in a "great Loop location";
"fun" room decor makes an "interesting" contrast with this
"preserved" landmark, and "food and service" at the Atwood
Café prompt reviewers to dub this "my kind of place!"

Drake Hotel, The   23 | 25 | 24 | 24 | $242
140 E. Walton Pl.; 312-787-2200; fax 312-787-1431; 800-553-7253;
www.thedrakehotel.com; 535 rooms (63 suites)
☑ "Wonderful doormen" greet guests at this "well-preserved"
hotel with a "great Lake location" (at the north end of the
Magnificent Mile); this "institution" is "entitled to respect" say
admirers of the views, newly redecorated rooms, "classic
cocktails" in Coq d'Or bar and "fine" seafood in the Cape Cod
Room, but a few might disagree, citing "smallish" accommodations
and a wee bit of "elegant disrepair."

Fairmont   25 | 24 | 23 | 24 | $227
200 N. Columbus Dr.; 312-565-8000; fax 312-946-5311;
800-526-2008; www.fairmont.com; 692 rooms (66 suites)
☑ "Spacious rooms" ("suites the size of apartments") with "views"
and "immaculate marble baths" captivate guests at this large hotel,
located off Michigan Avenue (a tad "inconvenient for walkers");
however, opinions split when it comes to service, which ranges
from "very nice" to "not helpful", and the Regional American fare
at Entre Nous that strikes some as "top-notch" and others
as "strictly standard."

FOUR SEASONS
| 29 | 29 | 28 | 27 | $322 |

120 E. Delaware Pl.; 312-280-8800; fax 312-280-1748; 800-332-3442; www.fourseasons.com; 343 rooms (197 suites)
■ It's "a quality experience all around" at this Magnificent Mile hotel ("great shopping in the building when the weather is foul") with multiple "views" of Lake Michigan; rooms have "great beds" ("we bought one"), service is "consistently superb" and "there's no need to leave for dining" at this "good-as-it-gets" "classic" that ranks best overall in the city; N.B. sometimes the building "moans" "when the wind blows", so the staff "offers earplugs" at night.

House of Blues Hotel, A Loews Hotel
| 24 | 21 | 20 | 22 | $189 |

333 N. Dearborn St.; 312-245-0333; fax 312-923-2444; 877-569-3742; www.loewshotels.com; 367 rooms (22 suites)
☑ "The most fun place to stay" in the Windy City, this "funky" boutique Downtowner carries a "bordello-blue" theme throughout its "interesting but smallish rooms", attached bowling alley and adjacent nightclub of the same name; some commend the "free CD at check-in", famous Sunday gospel brunch at the Club and chance to mingle with "rock stars", but others protest that this "three-ring horror circus of design" is too much of "a young person's hotel."

Monaco
| 25 | 23 | 23 | 22 | $199 |

225 N. Wabash Ave.; 312-960-8500; fax 312-960-1883; 800-397-7661; www.monaco-chicago.com; 192 rooms (22 suites)
☑ Tucked among Downtown buildings, this "cool" boutique hotel may have "a few too many carnival colors" in its guestrooms (think "pink and pistachio green"), but "sample CDs", whirlpools in some of the "great bathrooms", an "adopt-a-goldfish" program and "top service" (not to mention neck massages) move this "adorable find" up several notches on the praise gauge.

Renaissance
| 24 | 23 | 21 | 22 | $212 |

1 W. Wacker Dr.; 312-372-7200; fax 312-372-0834; 800-228-9290; www.renaissancehotels.com; 550 rooms (40 suites)
■ "A big hotel with a small hotel feel", this place between the Loop and Magnificent Mile is the "best location in town for theater-going" (and not bad for shopping, either, just one block from Marshall Field's); highest praise goes to "elegantly appointed guestrooms", an indoor pool, jazz in the lobby, river views and an "attentive staff."

RITZ-CARLTON (A FOUR SEASONS HOTEL)
| 28 | 28 | 28 | 27 | $312 |

160 E. Pearson St.; 312-266-1000; fax 312-266-1194; 800-621-6906; www.fourseasons.com; 435 rooms (90 suites)
■ "A great hotel in every respect", this link in the Four Seasons chain has "suites larger than most homes", individual TVs and VCRs at each StairMaster and treadmill in the gym, a "fabulous Dining Room" and "doting staff" ("I asked the concierge where to buy cufflinks; she whipped out two sets and asked if I preferred black or gray") – no wonder it's a "favorite" among expense-accounters and travelers who like being "pampered."

Sutton Place
25 | 23 | 20 | 19 | $213

21 E. Bellevue Pl.; 312-266-2100; fax 312-246-4250; 800-606-8188;
www.suttonplace.com; 246 rooms (40 suites)

☑ "High-tech" and "sleek", this hotel in a "hip" Downtown location
doesn't scrimp on room details, which include "big tubs" and "lots
of gadgets" (such as "great stereo CD systems"); the city's "best-
looking people" hang out at Whiskey Bar & Grill ("so cool!"), but
surveyors take a dim view of the boutique lodging's "spotty and
somewhat snotty" service.

Swissôtel
24 | 23 | 22 | 21 | $209

323 E. Wacker Dr.; 312-565-0565; fax 312-565-0540; 800-654-7263;
www.swissotel.com; 632 rooms (35 suites)

☑ "Commanding views of Lake Michigan", "reasonable weekend
rates" and a "courteous staff" keep fans of this "business hotel"
checking in at the chain's "*très charmant*" yet out-of-the-way
location north of Grant Park; "marble bathrooms" stocked with
Neutrogena, a nearby golf course and "yummy" Swiss chocolates
in the lobby help most overlook the "generic" room decor.

Whitehall Hotel, The
23 | 25 | 22 | 21 | $224

105 E. Delaware Pl.; 312-944-6300; fax 312-944-8552; 800-948-4255;
www.whitehallchicago.com; 221 rooms (8 suites)

☑ "Clubby and quaint", this 1928 hideaway just a block and a half
off Michigan Avenue is more "small pensione" than business
hotel; regulars like the "hospitality" ("Vernon is the best doorman
in Chicago") and "happening" bar "fit for celeb-watching"; most
hail this as a "civilized" "home away from home", but a few blanch
at "disappointing" bathrooms.

Galena

Eagle Ridge Inn & Resort
23 | 23 | 20 | 23 | $167

444 Eagle Ridge Dr.; 815-777-2444; fax 815-777-4502; 800-892-2269;
www.eagleridge.com; 80 rooms (2 suites)

☑ A "good base for visiting" the countryside of northwest
Illinois, this resort offers four championship links ("the General
golf course is a gem"), a fitness center, children's programs,
boating and fishing; most agree this "relaxing" vacation spot earns
the quintessentially Midwestern accolade of "super-friendly",
but some turn up their noses at the "tatty" rooms ("I had hoped
for more amenities").

Indiana

Indianapolis

Canterbury Hotel
23 | 25 | 23 | 22 | $193

123 S. Illinois St.; 317-634-3000; fax 317-685-2519; 800-538-8186;
www.preferredhotels.com; 99 rooms (25 suites)

☑ "A little bit of Europe", this 1928 Downtowner supplies "a rare
taste of civilization in a murky sea of bad convention hotels";
"well-appointed" rooms come with "great bathrobes", plus
there's a "fine" "dark bar downstairs" and dining in the "parlor";
a few, however, fret that the "charmer" is "old and getting older":
"someone give this tired place an IV" to assist 1999 renovations.

Kentucky

Harrodsburg

Inn at Shaker Village   ▽   24 | 23 | 25 | 24 | $122
3501 Lexington Rd.; 859-734-5411; fax 859-734-5411; 800-734-5611;
www.shakervillageky.org; 81 rooms (8 suites, 2 houses)
■ "Run to Shakertown, but take it easy when you get there" advise
surveyors; this historic resort southwest of Lexington is called
"a don't-miss experience" of "early-American" ambiance and
signature Shaker decor; rooms come with unexpected modern
amenities despite a "pioneer theme and reproduction furnishings"
that set the scene for "good, solid" home cooking served "family-
style" (the town is dry, but some "BYOB and sneak it in").

Louisville

Camberley Brown Hotel   21 | 22 | 21 | 21 | $159
335 W. Broadway; 502-583-1234; fax 502-587-7006; 800-555-8000;
www.camberleyhotels.com; 292 rooms (6 suites)
☑ "It won't blow you away, but it doesn't let you down either" say
veterans of this "beautiful old hotel" in "pleasant surrounds near
the Theater District"; wood and marbled-plaster detailing add
"elegance" to the lobby and rooms are rated best on the club floor,
though some point out that "'worn out' does not mean 'charming.'"

Seelbach Hilton   22 | 22 | 23 | 23 | $157
500 Fourth Ave.; 502-585-3200; fax 502-585-9240; 800-445-8667;
www.hilton.com; 321 rooms (30 suites)
☑ "Bring your Derby hat" to this 1905 "time warp" of a Downtown
hotel brimming with history (perhaps "after a day at Churchill
Downs" racetrack?); fans find the "beautifully redone" rooms –
all with four-poster beds – best on the concierge floor, while
others grumble about the "small", "sad" standard accommodations.

Louisiana

New Orleans

★ **Best in City**
28 Windsor Court/H
26 Soniat House/H
24 Maison de Ville/H
23 Omni Royal Orleans/H
   Royal Sonesta/H

Columns Hotel   ▽   21 | 22 | 20 | 23 | $143
3811 St. Charles Ave.; 504-899-9308; fax 504-899-8170;
800-445-9308; www.thecolumns.com; 20 rooms (3 suites)
☑ The front porch of this Garden District mansion is the "best
place to sip a mint julep" overlooking St. Charles Avenue; "Southern
charm" melds with "earthy decor" (that's a "little" "run-down"),
creating an experience "just like New Orleans": full of "old-bordello
passion" but "so real" that some caution it's "not for tourists."

Fairmont
21 │ 22 │ 21 │ 22 │$193

123 Baronne St.; 504-529-7111; fax 504-522-2303; 800-866-5577;
www.fairmont.com; 700 rooms (87 suites)

☑ "A little worn, but with fabulous bones", this "classic" is a bit
off the usual path (but still close to the French Quarter), making
for "quiet nights"; guests like the "attentive staff" ("they bought an
item I needed to give a client because I was stuck in a meeting"),
"must-see" lobby and Ramos Gin Fizzes in the Sazerac Bar, but
some say that the "graciously old" rooms "need refurbishment."

International House
▽ 24 │ 23 │ 23 │ 24 │$192

221 Camp St.; 504-553-9550; fax 504-553-9560; 800-633-5770;
www.ihhotel.com; 119 rooms (3 suites)

☑ "The hippest lodging to hit the city" declare travelers about this
"funky" hotel where "nouveau-meets-N'Awlins" in "chic" quarters
(one top-floor room with landscaped balcony is "superb"); the bar
and lounge are "great spots to hang out" and watch locals and
"fabulous party-goers" flock to this "stylish" spot minutes from the
Quarter, even if "service needs to follow through" more quickly.

Le Meridien
24 │ 23 │ 22 │ 21 │$199

614 Canal St.; 504-525-6500; fax 504-525-8068; 800-225-5843;
www.meridiennewworleans.com; 494 rooms (7 suites)

■ "Convenient" to all that's "crazy" in the French Quarter but
without "the noise", this hotel has a staff that's "seen it all" and
does a "great job with crowd control during Mardi Gras" – a knack
welcomed by business folk who stay for "proximity to convention
centers", "rooms with lots of work space" and "speedy meals."

Le Pavillon Hotel
22 │ 23 │ 21 │ 22 │$169

833 Poydras St.; 504-581-3111; fax 504-620-4130; 800-535-9095;
www.lepavillon.com; 226 rooms (15 suites)

☑ Late-night snacks of PB&J sandwiches and cocoa in a lobby full
of "authentic antiques" prompt loyalists to remark that this "quiet
hotel" just outside the French Quarter "doesn't get the attention it
should"; "European-style" "rococo-a-rama" rooms come off as
both "quirky" and "tasteful" (suites can be "excessively gaudy"),
and the staff seems to "actually enjoy its profession."

Maison de Ville &
The Audobon Cottages
24 │ 25 │ 26 │ 23 │$234

727 Rue Toulouse; 504-561-5858; fax 504-528-9939; 800-634-1600;
www.maisondeville.com; 23 rooms (2 suites, 7 cottages)

☑ "The charm drapes over you like the moss on the trees" at this
French Quarter townhouse where "each room is unique"; the
"atmospheric old place" ("I saw Tennessee Williams' ghost") has a
courtyard that's "perfect for a drink or breakfast", and its "Bistro
restaurant is among the top" in the city; all this and pampering by
staff can make up for complaints of "cramped" quarters.

Maison Dupuy
22 │ 21 │ 23 │ 20 │$185

1001 Rue Toulouse; 504-586-8000; fax 504-525-5334; 800-535-9177;
www.maisondupuy.com; 200 rooms (10 suites)

☑ Guests keep "close to the action" at this property deep in the
Quarter, where chef Dominique Macquet creates French-Thai
cuisine; regulars request a courtyard view of fountains or a balcony
with their rooms, which can be "small"; a piano bar facing a lively
street and "helpful staff" further foster a "feeling of coziness."

| R | S | D | P | $ |

Omni Royal Orleans

| 23 | 23 | 23 | 23 | $209 |

621 St. Louis St.; 504-529-5333; fax 504-529-7089; 800-843-6664;
www.omnihotels.com; 346 rooms (25 suites)

■ For "reliable digs in the Big Easy" (within walking distance of everything), travelers like this large hotel for "small but nicely appointed" rooms, "charming" ambiance and "great staff"; "solid" fare in the Rib Room, "people-watching" in the lobby bar and views of the mighty Mississippi from a rooftop pool supply "pleasant distractions" at this French Quarter "bargain."

Ritz-Carlton, The

| – | – | – | – | E |

931 Canal St.; 504-524-1331; fax 504-524-7675; 800-241-3333;
www.ritzcarlton.com; 452 rooms (71 suites)

Revelers who want to party down in the French Quarter can now also live it up at this super-deluxe chain's new outpost (opened October 2000) in the landmark Maison Blanche and Kress buildings; the $200 million restoration preserves the glazed terra cotta exterior and punctuates the interior decor with antebellum touches throughout the property, which includes a day spa, two ballrooms, boardroom, 13 meeting rooms, fitness center and outdoor pool, plus Creole and Continental dining at Victor's; guest quarters come with all the amenities one expects, and the Club floor provides even more (for a price), such as private lounge, concierge and complimentary food and drink.

Royal Sonesta

| 23 | 24 | 23 | 23 | $203 |

300 Bourbon St.; 504-586-0300; fax 504-586-0335; 800-766-3782;
www.sonesta.com; 500 rooms (32 suites)

■ This "favorite" "in the middle of the party zone" means "every night is Mardi Gras", so book "an inner courtyard room if you want to sleep" advise veteran guests; dubbed "king" of the Quarter, the large hotel provides "Southern charm at every turn", from acres of rose-colored marble in the lobby to a "great oyster bar" and "quiet lounge" with "good music", all of which help combat the local "iniquity."

SONIAT HOUSE

| 27 | 27 | 24 | 25 | $234 |

1133 Chartres St.; 504-522-0570; fax 504-522-7208; 800-544-8808;
www.soniathouse.com; 33 rooms (8 suites)

■ Expect "ambiance aplenty" (but no children under 12) at this "delight" tucked away "from the noise and fury" in the Quarter; antiques fill rooms inside the "romantic", "historically significant" inn, while out in the courtyard, breakfast ("best biscuits and coffee of our lives") is served with silver service by "gracious hosts."

W

| – | – | – | – | E |

333 Poydras St.; 504-525-9444; fax 504-586-9928; 877-946-8357;
www.whotels.com; 423 rooms (23 suites)

In a town that loves to party, it comes as no surprise that the boutique chain's location near the French Quarter (the larger of two that opened mid-2000 in the Big Easy) puts an emphasis on socializing; scenesters are already lounging in the Living Room lobby, pouring into Rande Gerber's hot bar Whiskey Blue and eating it up at Zoe Bistrot; when it's time to 'fais dodo', rooms' soothing and standard extras include feather beds, preloaded CD players and – a little less comforting – their very own voodoo dolls.

W French Quarter
20 | 21 | 21 | 18 | $168

(fka De La Poste)
*316 Chartres St.; 504-581-1200; fax 504-522-3208; 800-448-4927;
www.whotels.com; 98 rooms (2 suites)*

☑ The French Quarter location and Italian restaurant Bacco
make visitors "smile" at this small hotel with "friendly service";
"eclectically appointed" rooms supply "minimalist luxury" (many
have balconies overlooking the courtyard); purists say there's
"not as much local" character since this facility became a W.

WINDSOR COURT HOTEL
28 | 28 | 28 | 27 | $288

*300 Gravier St.; 504-523-6000; fax 504-596-4513; 800-262-2662;
www.windsorcourthotel.com; 324 rooms (264 suites)*

■ "Forget the robe, bring home the furniture" from the "high-
English-style" rooms at this hotel that rates best overall in the city;
a "quiet spot in a hot town", the "antiques-filled" lobby blends
"urban sophistication" with the staff's "Cajun hospitality"; cuisine
at The Grill Room ("make reservations early") "can hold its own
with the best in the food-crazed" Big Easy, though some think it
may be "too perfect for such a down-and-dirty" town.

Wyndham at Canal Place
23 | 22 | 21 | 23 | $205

(fka Westin Canal Place)
*100 Rue Iberville; 504-566-7006; fax 504-553-5120; 800-996-3426;
www.wyndham.com; 438 rooms (40 suites)*

■ This towering complex, within earshot of (but still "a hike" to) the
French Quarter, commands "sweeping views of the Mississippi"
from its 11th-floor lobby; a rooftop pool, "comfortable" rooms and
"attentive service" appeal mainly to convention-goers and high-
rollers (there's an on-site casino), who like the proximity to "serious
shopping" at Canal Place.

White Castle

Nottoway Plantation
▽ 23 | 23 | 21 | 24 | $174

*30970 Hwy. 405 (The Great River Rd.); 225-545-2730;
fax 225-545-8632; www.nottoway.com; 13 rooms (3 suites)*

■ It's "a grand step back in time" at this 1859 antebellum mansion
in a "romantic setting along the Mississippi"; the "theme-oriented"
experience includes a sherry greeting and tour from the staff;
surveyors insist "stay in the main building to watch boats ply the
river" by this inn, where it's a "quiet stay despite tour buses."

Maine

Bar Harbor

Bar Harbor Inn
22 | 22 | 22 | 21 | $184

*Newport Dr.; 207-288-3351; fax 207-288-8454; 800-248-3351;
www.barharborinn.com; 153 rooms (10 suites)*

☑ "Not for young swingers", this "comforting place to stay" close
to Acadia National Park draws nature-lovers to its eight-acre
waterfront location for "must-see" views of Frenchman Bay and
"lobster-bake lunches on the lawn" (dining room fare rates "just
ok"); "clean" but "kind of shabby" rooms come at "affordable"
prices, and the "friendly" staff gives the kind of "good, old-
fashioned service" that you'd expect in Vacationland.

Cape Elizabeth

Inn by the Sea   23 | 23 | 22 | 23 | $220
40 Bowery Beach Rd.; 207-799-3134; fax 207-799-4779;
800-888-4287; www.innbythesea.com; 43 rooms
■ The "wonderful" ocean views from this "sweet" gray-clapboard inn close to Portland set the tone for other Downeast pleasures, like the nearby "classic lighthouse", lobster bisque, wildlife sightings ("a moose appeared on the lawn") and "friendly" service; all the "well-cared-for" rooms come with patio or balcony but lack a/c, which is usually an issue only one month out of the year.

Deer Isle

Pilgrims Inn   ▽ 24 | 23 | 25 | 22 | $193
Main St.; 207-348-6615; fax 207-348-7769; www.pilgrimsinn.com;
15 rooms (2 cottages)
■ A "true getaway", this "secluded" island "treasure" offers "beautiful rooms" and "total peace and quiet" (only a few private TVs and phones) for "those who like the outdoors"; "friendly" innkeepers serve "freshly prepared and very creative" dinners each evening (except off-season) to guests who stay in either the 1793 wooden-frame house or in two freestanding cottages.

Freeport

Harraseeket Inn   23 | 23 | 24 | 22 | $193
162 Main St.; 207-865-9377; fax 207-865-1684; 800-342-6423;
84 rooms (2 suites)
■ Shop and then drop at this "quaint", family-owned clapboard inn surrounded by myriad outlets and L.L. Bean; guests can shake off bargain mania by sipping a "wonderful afternoon tea" (while a huge stuffed polar bear "plays" the piano), imbibing at the tavern or floating beneath a painted-cloud ceiling at the indoor pool; "great lobster rolls" and "cozy" rooms with modern facilities further epitomize this "New England cliché" (in a good way).

Kennebunkport

Colony Hotel   21 | 22 | 21 | 23 | $191
140 Ocean Ave.; 207-967-3331; fax 207-967-8738; 800-552-2363;
www.thecolonyhotel.com; 123 rooms
◪ A summer tradition since 1914, this "grand" resort perched above the Atlantic offers "fewer amenities than a top-of-the-line hotel" (no TV or a/c), but "Georgian charm", views and a saltwater pool keep vacationers coming back, despite the "staid" ambiance, "creaky" rooms and "undistinguished" New England food.

WHITE BARN INN, THE   25 | 27 | 28 | 25 | $274
37 Beach Ave.; 207-967-2321; fax 207-967-1100;
www.whitebarninn.com; 25 rooms (9 suites)
■ "Surprisingly sophisticated", this 1860s inn located seven miles from the center of town attracts the likes of former President Bush with its "superb" cuisine and "enchanting" "country barn decor"; "romantic" rooms "approach perfection" ("the food is already there"), while the staff at this "formal but homey" hideaway provides some of "the best service under the sun."

Northeast Harbor

Asticou Inn   19   22   21   22 $219
15 Peabody Dr.; 207-276-3344; fax 207-276-3373; 800-258-3373;
www.asticou.com; 47 rooms (15 suites)
☑ "Yankee tradition" rules at this "Mount Desert Island institution"
where "yachters and Rockefeller preteens do the polka on the
porch"; to some, this escape with a bay view "lives on its rep"
(have they seen the recent rehab?), but fans "keep going back."

Ogunquit

Cliff House, The   22   22   21   22 $192
Shore Rd.; 207-361-1000; fax 207-361-2122; www.cliffhousemaine.com;
162 rooms (2 suites)
☑ "Dramatic" ocean views from every room of this cliffside resort
lure fans to drive 45 minutes from the Portland jetport to the "large"
(some say "ordinary") quarters at this historic inn; guests can soak
in a "great hot tub" or listen to music in the lobby, where the "barny
ambiance" and "fresh seafood" evoke a "New England feeling."

Prouts Neck

Black Point Inn Resort   22   23   22   23 $248
510 Black Point Rd.; 207-883-2500; fax 207-883-9976; 800-258-0003;
www.blackpointinn.com; 85 rooms (12 suites)
☑ "Preppy families" and "New Yorkers" find that "antique is fun"
at this "throwback to traditional New England" where you can eat
"lobster three times a day"; most savor the "change of pace" in
"simply furnished rooms", a library and porches with ocean views,
but a few say this "romantic getaway" is "overpriced."

Rockport

Samoset Resort   21   22   20   23 $199
220 Warrenton St.; 207-594-2511; fax 207-594-0048; 800-341-1650;
www.samoset.com; 178 rooms (22 suites, 72 condos,
41 townhouses, 1 cottage)
■ "Golf nuts" say this "coastal charmer's" course on Penobscot
Bay affords "spectacular views" and ranks "better than Pebble
Beach" during good weather; an "organized staff" keeps activities
moving apace while families nosh on "fairly good food" and bunk in
the hotel's "fine, modern rooms", private condos and townhouses;
still, a few think recent major renovations were long "overdue."

Maryland

Baltimore

Admiral Fell Inn   22   22   22   20 $165
888 S. Broadway, Historic Fell's Point; 410-522-7377; fax 410-522-0707;
800-292-4667; www.admiralfell.com; 80 rooms (4 suites)
☑ "Excellent for those who like historic inns", this hotel in the
heart of Fell's Point garners reactions that range from "adorable"
to a "little run-down"; as "part of the Baltimore experience", let
the "pleasant" staff direct you to nearby attractions or the sights
Downtown that are only a water-taxi ride away.

Harbor Court Hotel   26 | 25 | 25 | 24 |$232
550 Light St.; 410-234-0550; fax 410-659-5925; 800-824-0076;
www.harborcourt.com; 202 rooms (25 suites)
■ For "classy digs" (imagine "if Dixie Carter were a hotel . . ."), this
spot overlooking the harbor adds a touch of "elegance in the midst
of honky-tonk" establishments; guests applaud the "attentive
service" and "fabulous food" in the "underrated" Brightons and
Hamptons restaurants and revel in "lot of extras to spoil you",
like late check-out times (good "for a weekend away or wedding
night"); the meeting facilities and "convenience to Downtown"
also make it "the place to stay for business."

Inn at Henderson's Wharf, The ▽ 26 | 23 | 22 | 23 |$162
1000 Fell St.; 410-522-7777; fax 410-522-7087; 800-522-2088;
www.hendersonswharf.com; 38 rooms
■ "Another secret hits prime time" lament those who know about
this 1800s tobacco warehouse turned inn that combines "built-in
peace and quiet" with proximity to Fell's Point hubbub; veterans
value the "friendly service", room views of the water or garden,
"step-on, step-off access to water taxis" and "50 pubs and
restaurants within walking distance", which counter minor
complaints about "no dining options" (other than free breakfast).

Renaissance Harborplace   22 | 21 | 21 | 22 |$184
202 E. Pratt St.; 410-547-1200; fax 410-539-5786; 800-468-3571;
www.renaissancehotels.com; 622 rooms (40 suites)
☑ Standing "right smack on the harbor", this big hotel is "a
great base for touring the Inner Harbor's" dining, shopping and
sightseeing; "comfy rooms" (many with water views) and "good
service" clinch it as a "business traveler's delight" – as long as
you don't mind "noisy traffic" and "tourists"; nitpickers insist that
the "service could improve" and warn of "weekend overbooking."

Oxford

Robert Morris Inn   21 | 22 | 23 | 20 |$168
314 N. Morris St.; 410-226-5111; fax 410-226-5744; 888-823-4012;
www.robertmorrisinn.com; 35 rooms (6 suites)
☑ "The best crab cakes in the world" highlight this Eastern shore
inn that capitalizes on history and "river proximity"; rooms succeed
in creating "timeless charm" that surveyors find "extremely
romantic" (the policy against children under 10 doesn't hurt the
ambiance either), but "creaking stairs and floor" in the original
structure prompt many to ask for rooms at the inn's other building,
"the Sandaway", half a block away.

St. Michaels

INN AT PERRY CABIN   27 | 27 | 27 | 26 |$309
308 Watkins Ln.; 410-745-2200; fax 410-745-3348; 800-722-2949;
www.perrycabin.com; 41 rooms (6 suites)
■ "Laura Ashley comes to life" with "chintz in spades" throughout
"generous rooms" that make "even a lurid affair seem chaste" at
this "gentrified" manor; gourmets laud the "excellent food" and
"tea with cookies" in the public areas, where "top-notch" service
"and Scrabble abound", while a shoreline setting makes for "great
sailing" if you "arrive by private yacht."

Massachusetts

Boston

★ **Best in City**
28 Four Seasons/H
26 Ritz-Carlton/H
     Boston Harbor/H
24 Eliot/H

     Regal Bostonian/H
     Le Meridien/H
     Fairmont Copley Plaza/H
23 Charles Harvard Square/H

BOSTON HARBOR HOTEL, THE   26 | 25 | 25 | 26 | $275
70 Rowes Wharf; 617-439-7000; fax 617-330-9450; 800-752-7077;
www.bhh.com; 230 rooms (26 suites)
■ "Hop a water taxi from the airport" to this "impeccable"
Financial District "knockout" with "old-Boston charm", a "can't-
miss location" and rooms with "stunning harbor views" (a "must"
unless you prefer monitoring "the big dig" construction project);
the "elegant" Rowes Wharf restaurant wins raves for "excellence
in design and dining" and "kudos for brunch" (although a few
casual sorts snipe at the "no jeans" policy) in a hotel that's "a
little stiff (like most Yankees), but stunning."

Charles Hotel Harvard Square   23 | 23 | 24 | 21 | $256
1 Bennett St., Cambridge; 617-864-1200; fax 617-661-5053;
800-882-1818; www.charleshotel.com; 293 rooms (45 suites)
◪ "Tasteful simplicity" distinguishes this boutique hotel in the
heart of "Haaa-vaaad", replete with "memorable perks" like T1
Internet in all rooms, a lending library, spa and "super gym", along
with "excellent live" jazz in the Regatta Bar and brunches from
Henrietta's Table; surveyors are mixed on whether "smallish",
"spare" rooms embody "understated elegance" or a "tragic
combination" of "modern architecture" and "New England charm",
but most enjoy "snuggling under down comforters" and quilts.

Eliot Suite   26 | 25 | 25 | 21 | $245
370 Commonwealth Ave.; 617-267-1607; fax 617-536-9114;
800-443-5468; www.eliothotel.com; 95 rooms (83 suites)
■ "Don't tell too many people about this" "intimate", "clubby"
Back Bay hotel plead fans who say it's "like home – with room
service" and praise its "British feel", "quiet", "trendy and comfy"
locale just steps from Newbury Street, "welcoming staff" and
"great value" to boot, with "beautiful" pastel-toned rooms sporting
French doors and Italian marble baths; "too bad there's no public
space" to speak of, but "super" dinners at the adjacent "upscale
winner" Clio outshine even the bold leopard-print rug.

Fairmont Copley Plaza   23 | 24 | 23 | 24 | $242
138 St. James Ave.; 617-267-5300; fax 617-267-7668; 800-441-1414;
www.fairmont.com; 379 rooms (54 suites)
◪ This "traditional" 1912 landmark with an "ideal location" may
be a sibling to The Plaza in New York, but it personifies "Boston
Brahmin" to the core that "oozes old money"; its public spaces
include a "breathtaking lobby" with gilded coffered ceilings and a
"spectacular" Oak Bar, but the "quaint" guestrooms "vary widely"
with "too many" that are "dated" and "tiny"; still, most find this
"well-to-do-gentleman-down-at-the-heels" icon endearing.

XV Beacon   ▽ 28 | 26 | 27 | 24 |$330

15 Beacon St.; 617-670-1500; fax 617-670-2525; 877-982-3226; www.xvbeacon.com; 61 rooms (2 suites)

■ "This is not your parents' hotel": "high-tech high-class" is the hallmark of this "cool" Beacon Hill newcomer that's "over the top in every way", from the "posh" rooms with "21st-century" amenities like speedy Internet access and remote-controlled fireplaces to the "excellent" Federalist restaurant that tweaks classic American dishes; a future-shocked few claim it's "too much", but for its "sleek" clientele it's an "antidote to hotel blahs."

FOUR SEASONS   28 | 28 | 28 | 27 |$322

200 Boylston St.; 617-338-4400; fax 617-423-0154; 800-819-5053; www.fourseasons.com; 288 rooms (72 suites)

■ The top-ranking hotel in the city, this "posh" "Cadillac" in the Back Bay lures the "jet set" with "style and elegance", from the "spacious" rooms and "very thick robes" to other "wonderful amenities" like "the best fitness center around", an indoor rooftop pool and "amazing" American dining at Aujourd'hui; the staff "will do backflips for you", plus hand out "free duck food and cookies for kids"; N.B. "ask for a room overlooking the Public Garden."

Le Meridien   24 | 24 | 24 | 23 |$253

250 Franklin St.; 617-451-1900; fax 617-423-2844; 800-543-4300; www.lemeridien-hotels.com; 326 rooms (17 suites)

◪ For a "*très* special" Downtown experience, business travelers find it "easy to get to the Financial District" from this "ooh-la-la" hotel with "French flair", from the "elegant furnishings" and "staff that pampers" to the "great chocolate bar" at the "delightful" restaurant Julien; although some grouse about "small rooms at big prices" and warn that the area is "dead for weekend visitors", most are *très contents* at this bit of "France without the jet lag."

Regal Bostonian, The   25 | 25 | 23 | 22 |$244

Faneuil Hall Mktpl.; 617-523-3600; fax 617-523-2454; 800-343-0922; 201 rooms (14 suites)

◪ With its "great location beside Faneuil Hall", this brick hotel is "a good choice for tourists" or for a "romantic weekend" because it's so close to everything; for many, the "nicely furnished", "quirky" quarters and "personal", "extremely pleasant" service provide a "much-preferred" "change from monster hotels", although some warn "beware rear rooms over the fruit market" on weekends ("noise" and "smells"); fans praise dinner at Seasons, a restaurant that's "launched many of Boston's culinary luminaries."

RITZ-CARLTON, THE   26 | 27 | 26 | 25 |$306

15 Arlington St.; 617-536-5700; fax 617-536-1335; 800-241-3333; www.ritzcarlton.com; 275 rooms (46 suites)

■ "Reserved propriety" reigns at this "grande dame" that "still has class and mystique", from the "white-glove service" ("smart doormen with lots of travelers' tips", a "concierge who works miracles") to the "classic English decor" ("perfumed elevators"); despite a few comments about "tight" quarters that are "in need of a makeover", the elegant guestrooms earn high ratings from traditionalists who also swoon over afternoon tea with "blue-haired ladies and silver-haired men" and French "gourmet delights" in the Dining Room overlooking the Public Garden.

Seaport Hotel
22 | 22 | 20 | 22 | $214

1 Seaport Ln.; 617-385-4000; fax 617-385-4001; 877-732-7678; www.seaporthotel.com; 426 rooms (26 suites)

■ "A refreshing new choice" for conventioneers at the nearby World Trade Center, with "modern" rooms that combine "high-design elements" with "spartan elegance" plus techie touches like T1 lines; guests like the all-services-included policy ("no tipping") and "considerate" staff, but note that the waterfront location "in the middle of nowhere" is a drag for those not headed for the WTC.

University Park Hotel @ MIT
– | – | – | – | M

20 Sidney St., Cambridge; 617-577-0200; fax 617-494-8366; 800-222-8733; www.hotelmit.com; 210 rooms (17 suites)

Three blocks from the high-tech campus, this hotel/conference center that opened in late 1998 is shaping up as the Intown place for the *Wired* crowd; circuit-board-accented rooms come equipped with dataports and PlayStations, and meeting spaces sport the latest presentation hardware, of course, but guests can also go offline with a workout in the fitness center or by cocooning with room service from Sidney's Grille, the New American downstairs.

Westin Copley Place
23 | 22 | 21 | 22 | $216

10 Huntington Ave.; 617-262-9600; fax 617-351-7775; 800-937-8461; www.westin.com; 805 rooms (49 suites)

☑ There's "great shopping attached" to this "all-purpose" hotel near Newbury Street and the convention center, as well as "comfy" rooms, some with "killer views" of the Back Bay and Charles River; critics say the "vast" property has "all the charm of a mall" and long for "better cuisine", but others hail the new Bar 10 restaurant and lounge and note a nearby "culinary virtue": Legal Sea Foods.

Brewster

Ocean Edge Resort
23 | 22 | 21 | 23 | $226

2907 Main St.; 508-896-9000; fax 508-896-2721; 800-343-6074; www.oceanedge.com; 320 rooms (62 suites, 193 villas)

■ "Weather-beaten charm" and an ocean setting ("breathtaking dunes") distinguish this 19th-century mansion and carriage house, a "good family resort" that also attracts conference attendees and "septuagenarians" with "clean-as-a-whistle" rooms, "impeccable grounds" and a "very accommodating staff" (it's especially popular for a "pleasant golf getaway" or access to the 26-mile Cape Cod Rail Trail); clinching a villa with a kitchen means you'll have a "semiprivate" "escape from Cape crowds."

Chatham

Chatham Bars Inn
23 | 24 | 23 | 25 | $256

297 Shore Rd.; 508-945-0096; fax 508-945-6785; 800-527-4884; www.chathambarsinn.com; 205 rooms (35 suites)

■ This "fine old stunner" evokes Currier & Ives with colonnaded brick, striped awnings and a wraparound porch; inside the main building (which sits on 22 acres right in the center of town) guests find "homey, country-style rooms" that are "incredibly romantic" (despite "weak a/c"), but many opt for "cozy cottages by the seaside – a must"; loyalists "travel hours just for a lobster roll" and "cocktails on the great veranda" – "the perfect ending to a day."

Wequassett Inn
| 24 | 22 | 23 | 24 | $264 |

Rte. 28, Pleasant Bay; 508-432-5400; fax 508-432-5032;
800-225-7125; www.wequassett.com; 104 rooms (6 suites)
☑ Tucked away "in a peaceful cove with sailboats", this "upscale hideaway" lures vacationers with "great access to the Cape Cod National Golf course" and plenty of water sports; country-pine furniture and handmade quilts accentuate the "local ambiance" in 20 "cozy" cottages and villas scattered around the "self-contained resort", but despite high ratings, "not all rooms are equal" warn surveyors, so some complain that it's "a bit overpriced."

Deerfield

Deerfield Inn, The
| 22 | 22 | 23 | 22 | $179 |

81 Old Main St.; 413-774-5587; fax 413-775-7221; 800-926-3865;
www.deerfieldinn.com; 23 rooms
■ For a "step back in time", devotees of "classic Colonial" style opt for this historic setting smack on the main drag of a reconstructed pre-Revolution village; a "pretty old place" with individually decorated rooms, an "enjoyable patio", "good, old-fashioned American food" and an "unpretentious air", it feels like "New England through and through."

Lenox

BLANTYRE
| 27 | 27 | 27 | 27 | $338 |

16 Blantyre Rd.; 413-637-3556; fax 413-637-4282;
www.blantyre.com; 23 rooms (8 suites, 3 cottages)
■ "Like an Errol Flynn movie set" say those enchanted by the "fairy-tale" Tudor castle, carriage house and cottages of this "opulent" resort with conservatory-style public spaces (a harpist plays nightly), "formal" dining and "luxury" accommodations with spindled beds ("the main building is the place to be"); 100 acres of "beautiful grounds" (three miles from Tanglewood) offer croquet, tennis, trails and an outdoor pool; N.B. no guests under 12.

Cranwell Resort
| 22 | 22 | 21 | 22 | $231 |

55 Lee Rd.; 413-637-1364; fax 413-637-4364; 800-272-6935;
www.cranwell.com; 107 rooms (27 suites)
☑ "Beautiful grounds and vistas" come "fully loaded" with a Berkshire "mountain landscape" suited for both cross-country skiing and golf at this 1894 Tudor mansion where the links and training school are "never too crowded"; fans prefer the "casually elegant" main building with its "large" Arts-and-Crafts-style rooms, and though a minority cites "inattentive service", its amenities and location near Tanglewood more than compensate for most.

Wheatleigh
| 24 | 24 | 26 | 24 | $373 |

Hawthorne Rd.; 413-637-0610; fax 413-637-4507;
www.wheatleigh.com; 19 rooms (9 suites)
■ "So Italian!" swoon reviewers taken with this Berkshire estate modeled after a 16th-century palazzo, a "splendid romantic getaway" ("pretend it's your own villa" or you're "a CEO having an affair") with an "attentive staff" and what enthusiasts call the "best food this side of Mars"; a few with more modest tastes find it all "overdone", but even they "couldn't ask to be closer to Tanglewood"; N.B. no children under the age of nine.

Martha's Vineyard

CHARLOTTE INN, THE
27 | 26 | 26 | 26 | $304

27 S. Summer St.; 508-627-4751; fax 508-627-4652; 25 rooms (2 suites)

■ "Martha Stewart would love" this "total charmer" with "utterly tasteful" guest rooms (each with "its own flair" and "stuffed with upmarket antiques") set on a "manicured property" within walking distance of everything; the five-building complex centers around a "lovely, formal" white-clapboard whaling merchant's home attended to by a "cultured" staff that creates an ambiance both "casual and caring"; it's "perfection at a price", with "excellent" French haute cuisine at L'Etoile and a no-children-under-14 policy.

Harbor View Hotel
21 | 22 | 21 | 22 | $265

131 N. Water St.; 508-627-7000; fax 508-627-8417; 800-225-6005; www.harbor-view.com; 124 rooms (9 suites, 2 townhouses)

■ "If you like lighthouses and coastal scenery", then take in the "stunning views from rocking chairs" on the big wraparound porch facing the water at this hotel that's a short stroll from Edgartown and the beach; honeymooners and families appreciate "crisp, clean", "reasonable rooms", "hospitable service" and meals that send you to "lobster heaven" – in short, "charming" overall, but "not fancy" (and maybe "a little too quaint" for a few).

Nantucket

Jared Coffin House
22 | 23 | 23 | 22 | $235

29 Broad St.; 508-228-2400; fax 508-228-8549; 800-248-2405; www.jaredcoffinhouse.com; 60 rooms

☑ Guests "step back in time" at this 1845 "architectural marvel" (some fear "it'll blow over in the next storm") "convenient" to the heart of town; insiders say rooms in the hotel "can be supersmall", so "request a canopy bed" ("code for 'something larger'") or "stay in the newer of the buildings"; "wonderful chowder" in The Tap Room tops off this "all-around" Federal-period experience that "doesn't come cheap."

WAUWINET INN
27 | 26 | 27 | 25 | $380

Wauwinet Rd.; 508-228-0145; fax 508-325-0657; 800-426-8718; www.wauwinet.com; 30 rooms (5 cottages)

■ "Cherish the solitude" (without children) at this "exclusive and expensive" resort aside a "pristine" beach that's "isolated" from town but near Great Point Wildlife Refuge; the "beautiful and bright" "Ralph Lauren" decor warms the hearts of "the martini set", who enjoy being "spoiled by the service" and "wonderful food" at Topper's; loyalists make the "Gray Lady's best spot" a "once-a-year must" for "picture-postcard-perfect" sunset views.

White Elephant Hotel
22 | 23 | 22 | 21 | $278

50 Easton St.; 508-228-2500; fax 508-325-1195; 800-475-2637; www.whiteelephanthotel.com; 66 rooms (30 suites, 12 cottages)

■ Built in the '20s, this island resort with a "spectacular" Intown location (close to the ferry) recently underwent a transformation by the Wauwinet owners, so "it's too soon to tell" if rooms and cottages (many with fireplaces) grouped around courtyards "keep their charm"; but recent reports confirm modern amenities like Molton Brown toiletries and high-speed Internet access, plus "fresh food", a "good bar" and "better service."

Sandwich

Dan'l Webster Inn 23 23 22 23 $177

149 Main St.; 508-888-3622; fax 508-888-5156; 800-444-3566;
www.danlwebsterinn.com; 54 rooms (16 suites)

■ "If you want to touch base with history", then this old inn that did
time as a Patriot's tavern is "pure delight"; service "that couldn't be
nicer", "low-key" decor in rooms (many with canopied beds and
fireplaces) and "good" American fare in four "beautiful dining
rooms" or a conservatory keep a Cape trip "traditional."

Williamstown

Orchards Hotel, The 25 24 23 22 $204

222 Adams Rd.; 413-458-9611; fax 413-458-3273; 800-225-1517;
www.orchardshotel.com; 47 rooms

■ Near the Williamstown Playhouse, this small "country-style"
hotel "with a welcoming" staff is "perfect for a getaway" in any
season; rooms have a "New England elegance" – some with four-
poster beds, fireplaces – that carries through to public areas where
high tea is served; some find the "delicious" Continental fare a tad
"heavy", but heartier sorts love the "great cookies" left at turndown.

Michigan

Birmingham

Townsend Hotel, The 26 25 24 23 $255

100 Townsend St.; 248-642-7900; fax 248-645-9061; 800-548-4172;
www.townsendhotel.com; 150 rooms (58 suites)

☑ "Superior rooms" make this "diamond in the rough" a "top"
choice for "rock stars", business-trippers and "anyone who's big"
(some think even "Barbra Streisand stays here"); in a "trendy"
suburb, the "polished mahogany" details, "wonderful concierge"
and floral arrangements bring "a little sophistication to the
Midwest", though quibblers note that "fussy" dining "falls short."

Dearborn

Dearborn Inn, The 21 22 22 22 $171

20301 Oakwood Blvd.; 313-271-2700; fax 313-271-7464;
800-228-9290; www.marriott.com; 222 rooms (31 suites)

☑ Close to the Henry Ford Museum, this Georgian-style Marriott
"with a true inn ambiance" "takes you back to the horse-and-buggy
era" on 23 private acres; fans praise the "great service" and public
rooms (the "lobby's a treat"), while others criticize a "cloying"
atmosphere and "business-style" digs that "need improvement."

RITZ-CARLTON, THE 26 26 25 24 $222

300 Town Ctr. Dr.; 313-441-2000; fax 313-441-2051; 800-241-3333;
www.ritzcarlton.com; 308 rooms (15 suites)

■ "Quiet, posh" and "reliable", this best bet in Dearborn – plunked
adjacent to a massive shopping mall – "does what it can" to bring
"style" to its "drab" surroundings; "A+" rooms, "attentive service"
and "fancy dining room" are good for business travelers and local
auto execs who prefer staying at what they consider "probably
the best hotel in the area."

Mackinac Island

Grand Hotel　　　　　　　23 | 25 | 24 | 26 | $265
Mackinac Is.; 906-847-3331; fax 906-847-3259; 800-334-7263;
www.grandhotel.com; 343 rooms (36 suites)

☑ It's "so beautiful they charge nonguests $5 to see" this 1887
resort between Lakes Huron and Michigan, famous for the "world's
longest porch" ("one yearns for ladies in long dresses and straw
hats"); "service exceeds" and there's "a great kids' program", but
those less lost somewhere in time feel "like part of a production
line" and dislike the food and "dated rooms" (without a/c).

Saugatuck

Wickwood Inn　　　　　　▽ 27 | 26 | 26 | 24 | $207
510 Butler St.; 616-857-1465; fax 616-857-1552; 800-385-1174;
www.wickwoodinn.com; 11 rooms (4 suites)

■ "Don't miss the homemade breakfast" advise fans of this "treat"
run by Julee Rosso (of *Silver Palate Cookbook* fame) and husband
Bill Miller; the "decor is perfect" in four common areas and
individually themed rooms that mix "style and class" ("around
every corner is something more breathtaking than the last") with
modern amenities (CD players, feather beds).

Minnesota

Minneapolis/St. Paul

Hyatt Whitney　　　　　　25 | 23 | 21 | 20 | $182
150 Portland Ave.; 612-375-1234; fax 612-376-7512; 800-633-7313;
www.hyatt.com; 97 rooms (40 suites)

■ "Where the celebs stay", this "cleverly converted old flour mill"
with a "river location" offers large, strikingly decorated suites,
"superb service" and "outstanding food" in the Grille; while it's
"not in an attractive part of the city", most find its "European style"
and "quaint, intimate" character to be the Twin Cities' best.

Nicollet Island Inn　　　　▽ 23 | 23 | 23 | 20 | $156
95 Merriam St.; 612-331-1800; fax 612-331-6528; 800-331-6528;
www.nicolletislandinn.com; 24 rooms

■ An historic building turned small hotel in a "fun location" – an
island in the middle of the Mississippi River (yet surprisingly near
Downtown) – this inn has "cozy rooms" with "extremely comfy
beds", "sweet" service and American Heartland food that add
more than a dash of "romance" to this "charming" hideaway.

Saint Paul Hotel, The　　　24 | 25 | 25 | 24 | $184
350 Market St., St. Paul; 651-292-9292; fax 651-228-9506;
800-292-9292; www.stpaulhotel.com; 254 rooms (32 suites)

■ "An extensive scotch whisky bar" and the "best steaks, hash
browns and Sunday brunches" at the St. Paul Grill are two reasons
this "classic" is a Twin Cities favorite; built in 1910, the "grand old
lady is holding up well", pleasing regulars with "lovely restored
rooms", "attentive" service and heaping helpings of "charm" –
all within walking distance of the "verrry quiet" Downtown.

Red Wing

St. James Hotel   ▽ 24 | 23 | 23 | 23 | $136
406 Main St.; 651-388-2846; fax 651-388-5226; 800-774-8372;
www.st-james-hotel.com; 61 rooms
■ In an "undiscovered" river town (one hour southeast of
Minneapolis), this "restored" hotel (built in 1875) is a "charming"
"period piece"; rooms with handmade quilts are "romantic" (if a
tad "faded"), and some have views; there's "good food" in the
Port of Red Wing restaurant, but the real attractions here are
"wonderful antiques shops and hikes" nearby.

Mississippi

Biloxi

Beau Rivage Resort   26 | 23 | 22 | 24 | $145
875 Beach Blvd.; 228-386-7111; fax 228-386-7414; 800-567-6667;
www.beaurivage.com; 1,780 rooms (66 suites)
☑ "All fixed up pretty", this "better-than-Vegas" coastal casino
has "spotless" rooms (some with Gulf views) that are "calming
after a long night of gambling"; fans overlook "too much smoke" in
public areas – many hope the "huge ficus trees in the lobby" don't
go into "shock" – and the staff who doesn't seem to "smile."

Natchez

Monmouth Plantation   ▽ 26 | 24 | 25 | 27 | $179
36 Melrose Ave.; 601-442-5852; fax 601-446-7762; 800-828-4531;
www.monmouthplantation.com; 31 rooms (16 suites)
■ "Miss Marguerite greets her guests with Southern charm" at this
"upscale" "antebellum" mansion full of "romance" and "fabulous"
rooms in the main house and pond cottage; service is "attentive",
menus "innovative" and the grounds conducive to strolling.

Missouri

Kansas City

Fairmont   25 | 24 | 24 | 24 | $196
(fka Ritz-Carlton)
401 Ward Pkwy.; 816-756-1500; fax 816-756-1635; 800-866-5577;
www.fairmont.com; 366 rooms (20 suites)
☑ You might "forget you're in Kansas" at this "comfortable" hotel,
though "views" of the Country Club Plaza serve as a good reminder;
transformed from a Ritz-Carlton in February 2000, this staying spot
is considered "the nicest in town", with "impeccable" service
and "great" decor that a few critics point out is "worn."

Raphael Hotel, The   23 | 24 | 22 | 21 | $159
325 Ward Pkwy.; 816-756-3800; fax 816-802-2131; 800-821-5343;
www.raphaelkc.com; 123 rooms (88 suites)
☑ "Local rich people put up guests" in this former 1927 apartment
building across from historic Country Club Plaza because it's "small
enough so the staff remembers you, big enough to accommodate
everyone grandly"; the boutique hotel's "quaint rooms" may be
"growing long in the tooth", but most find its age "charming."

St. Louis

Hyatt Regency
| 21 | 21 | 20 | 24 | $158 |

1 St. Louis Union Station; 314-231-1234; fax 314-923-3971;
800-233-1234; www.hyatt.com; 539 rooms (21 suites)

☑ "Tourists love the location" of this hotel inside a restored train station ("the most beautiful lobby I've ever seen") and also take to shopping in the adjacent "upscale" mall; surveyors, however, were less impressed by the rooms – deemed both "pedestrian" and "overpriced for Missouri" – and the lack of an outdoor pool.

RITZ-CARLTON, THE
| 27 | 27 | 26 | 26 | $222 |

100 Carondelet Plaza; 314-863-6300; fax 314-863-3525;
800-241-3333; www.ritzcarlton.com; 301 rooms (34 suites)

■ "Great as usual", the "relaxed Midwestern luxury" at this crystal-and-marble hotel about 15 minutes from Downtown may be "a little out of the way" but "it's the only choice for high-end travelers", who focus on "expansive suites", "two excellent restaurants" (with "superb" wine lists) and the "attentive staff."

Montana

Gallatin

Gallatin Gateway Inn
▽ | 20 | 22 | 23 | 24 | $143 |

76405 Gallatin Rd.; 406-763-4672; fax 406-763-4672; 800-676-3522;
www.gallatingatewayinn.com; 34 rooms (4 suites)

■ Once the last stop before Yellowstone, this former railroad depot, now a renovated small inn, is "fun for train buffs", "fantastic for weddings" and "a surprising treat" for those in search of "good" service and dining and a wine list in such "a remote area."

Whitefish

Grouse Mountain Lodge
| 23 | 23 | 21 | 23 | $164 |

2 Fairway Dr.; 406-862-3000; fax 406-862-0326; 877-862-1505;
www.grmtlodge.com; 145 rooms (12 suites)

■ "If you want to roll out of bed and be on a golf course" – the only 36-hole course in the state – put this "serene" four-season inn 30 minutes from Glacier National Park on your list; active types can ski, mountain bike, play tennis or swim laps, while an "attentive staff" caters to the laid-back, who relax in "rustic elegance", be it dining on "fresh game" or lolling beside "roaring stone fireplaces."

Nevada

Lake Tahoe

Hyatt Regency Resort & Casino
| 22 | 22 | 21 | 21 | $186 |

(fka King's Castle)

111 Country Club Dr., Incline Village; 775-832-1234; fax 775-831-7508;
800-233-1234; www.hyatt.com; 450 rooms (28 suites, 24 cottages)

■ High and low rollers who need a break from "honky-tonk" gambling at this "high-quality" casino can retire to "laid-back" lakeside cottage suites on the "woodsy" north shore for a gander at "great scenery"; "good service", outdoor barbecue and "pleasant Western motif" throughout "never overwhelm the natural beauty."

Las Vegas

★ **Best in City**

28 Four Seasons/H	**24** Paris, Las Vegas/R
Bellagio/R	**23** Mirage/R
26 Venetian/R	Caesars Palace/R
25 Mandalay Bay/R	Rio Suite/R

BELLAGIO ⎹ 28 ⎹ 26 ⎹ 28 ⎹ 28 ⎹ $236 ⎹

3600 Las Vegas Blvd. S.; 702-693-7444; fax 702-693-8546; 888-987-6667; www.bellagioresort.com; 3,005 rooms (388 suites, 9 villas)

■ "Losing your shirt never felt so great" as in this "class act for the senses" (like "Lake Como in the desert"); book a so-called water-view room to gaze at dancing fountains, marvel at the lobby ceiling of glass sculptures by Dale Chihuly, "mortgage your house" for tickets to Cirque de Soleil's 'O' show and by all means indulge in a "decadent" dinner at Aqua or Le Cirque; for more, see Spa section.

Caesars Palace ⎹ 24 ⎹ 22 ⎹ 23 ⎹ 24 ⎹ $182 ⎹

3570 Las Vegas Blvd. S.; 702-731-7110; fax 702-697-5890; 800-634-6661; www.caesars.com; 2,454 rooms (448 suites)

■ You "feel like part of the *Sopranos* on vacation" by indulging with "lots of European playboys" at this landmark of "supreme" Greco-Roman "kitsch"; at the center of the Strip, "classic Vegas" comes alive with togas and "unique Forum shops" in a mall under a faux sky; those in the know go for new rooms in the Palace Tower and Wolfgang Puck's Chinois restaurant.

FOUR SEASONS ⎹ 29 ⎹ 28 ⎹ 27 ⎹ 28 ⎹ $271 ⎹

3960 Las Vegas Blvd. S.; 702-632-5000; fax 702-632-5222; 877-632-5000; www.fourseasons.com; 424 rooms (86 suites)

■ Seasoned travelers expect "elegance and exceptional service" from this chain, but surveyors truly relish the combo on the Sin City strip, where it's "a luxury to find a hotel with no casino" (it ranks as the town's No. 1 overall); guests swoon over "carefree check-in", a "hushed" lobby and "elevators that smell good", then recover with a pool, spa treatments and "sophisticated" rooms (with Bulgari toiletries in suites) before venturing out to "all the action nearby."

Hard Rock Hotel & Casino ⎹ 22 ⎹ 20 ⎹ 21 ⎹ 23 ⎹ $163 ⎹

4455 Paradise Rd.; 702-693-5000; fax 702-693-5010; 800-693-7625; www.hardrockhotel.com; 657 rooms (63 suites)

■ "Twenty-four hours in a place like this is still not enough!" shout "rocking 'n' rolling" reviewers of this "change from huge resorts on the Strip", but be warned, these digs are "as sexy as it gets without being illegal", filled with the "good-looking" who flock to the bar scene, on-site concerts and dining at Nobu before chilling out in "slick rooms" tended by the "coolest employees."

Hyatt Regency Lake Resort ▽ ⎹ 25 ⎹ 24 ⎹ 22 ⎹ 25 ⎹ $200 ⎹

67 Montelago Blvd., Henderson; 702-457-1234; fax 702-567-6067; 800-233-1234; www.hyatt.com; 496 rooms (42 suites, 10 villas)

◪ The hybrid of "Moroccan decor" and "Vegas glitz" at this out-of-the-way resort on a lake 17 miles south of the Strip is at once "a haven of calm" and "a happening"; rooms maintain the "tasteful" theme while a casino with windows feels "Mediterranean"; fans praise the "always-friendly service" and myriad water sports, but detractors lament the "restaurants are less than spectacular."

Luxor

21 | 19 | 18 | 21 | $126

3900 Las Vegas Blvd. S.; 702-262-4000; fax 702-262-4405;
800-288-1000; www.luxor.com; 4,455 rooms (444 suites)

☑ "King Tut-meets-Liberace" at this south Strip resort where rooms look "like a Pharaoh's tomb"; guests reach favored "corner suites with whirlpool tubs" and "sloping walls" via "dizzying" "inclinator" elevators that shoot "diagonally" from the lobby, but many laud newer Tower rooms as less "kitschy"; some report "getting lost" on the "confusing casino floor" and bemoan "zombied staff" and dining that's "about quantity not quality" at this "bizarre" "bargain."

Mandalay Bay

26 | 24 | 25 | 26 | $183

3950 Las Vegas Blvd. S.; 702-632-7777; fax 702-632-7190;
877-632-7000; www.mandalaybay.com; 3,220 rooms (673 suites)

■ "Bold and beautiful" sums up this "gargantuan" resort with a beach, wave pool and "lazy river" ("perfect for kids" who "won't want to leave"); the "cheese factor is minimal" in "gigantic rooms", bathrooms that are "plain gorgeous" and "exciting restaurants" like Aureole, Border Grill and Red Square; more than a few suggest "bringing walking shoes" to this "self-contained city" well off the main drag near the airport.

MGM Grand

21 | 19 | 21 | 21 | $151

3799 Las Vegas Blvd. S.; 702-891-1111; fax 702-891-1030;
800-929-1111; www.mgmgrand.com; 5,034 rooms (794 suites)

☑ "Your room could be in a different area code than the lobby" at this "family-friendly" "amusement park" resort with Oz-inspired "green, glitter and gold as far as the eye can see"; brace for "a complete sensory overload" and "constantly getting lost" down "mile-long corridors" on the way to "reliably good facilities" like a Studio 54 Club, pool and "endless food choices" such as Emeril Lagasse's New Orleans Fish House and Wolfgang Puck Cafe; happily, the staff "comes through when there's a room mix-up" (a frequent occurrence with surveyors).

Mirage

24 | 23 | 23 | 24 | $166

3400 Las Vegas Blvd. S.; 702-791-7111; fax 702-791-7414;
800-374-9000; www.mirage.com; 3,044 rooms (218 suites)

☑ The faithful claim that this "is where it all started, and is still going strong" with a famed shark aquarium at check-in, rain-forest lobby, Siegfried & Roy white-tiger show and volcano that erupts every 15 minutes ("what a blast!"); "perfectly located mid-Strip", the hotel provides a spa, "lots for families to do" 24 hours a day, a buffet that's "better than most" and, of course, "there's a casino too"; "monochromatic" rooms are showing signs of "wear and tear" and "chairs at the mile-long pool go fast, so arrive early."

Paris, Las Vegas

24 | 23 | 23 | 24 | $157

3655 Las Vegas Blvd. S.; 702-946-7000; fax 702-946-4405;
888-266-5687; www.parislasvegas.com; 2,916 rooms (295 suites)

■ "*C'est magnifique!*" to "swim under the Eiffel Tower" at a casino "where the theme actually works": cobblestone streets in the mall, boys on bicycles delivering baguettes, "pseudo-French accents" from the staff and "all those pastry shops" tempt guests to pant "*oui oui*"; with "wet face towels and fruit" at poolside and an all-around *je ne sais quoi,* it's "easy to forget" you're in Vegas; for a reality check, request a room facing the Strip.

Regent
∇ 29 25 24 27 $219

221 N. Rampart Blvd.; 702-869-7777; fax 702-869-7058;
877-869-8777; www.regenthotels.com; 541 rooms (75 suites)

■ "The perfect escape from tackiness", this new golf resort 20 minutes from the Strip is already earning praise (and a near-perfect rating) for its "elegant" rooms; private poolside cabanas, "no crowds", "no gambling in the lobby" and "endless luxury" make it a refuge for adults who seek pampering at the Aquae Sulis spa.

Rio Suite
25 21 23 22 $138

3700 W. Flamingo Rd.; 702-252-7777; fax 702-579-6565;
888-746-7482; www.playrio.com; 2,563 suites

☑ The *carnivale* never stops at this "boisterous" resort where hoots of approval go to a "fun" Mardi Gras parade and 51st-floor Voodoo Lounge; "big" rooms offer "a lot for your buck", including a voyeuristic "window between shower and bedroom" in most; nitpickers note these "technically aren't suites" and some carp that the hotel is "way too far from the action", even by shuttle or taxi.

Venetian, The
28 23 25 27 $201

3355 Las Vegas Blvd. S.; 702-414-1000; fax 702-414-1100;
877-883-6423; www.venetian.com; 3,036 suites

☑ Take a gondola ride at this "tasteful reproduction of Venice" that's "totally Vegas"; suites "the size of airplane hangars" may make you "forget to gamble", and the Canyon Ranch Spa takes care of non-casino-goers, as do shopping and "top of the line" eateries, including Wolfgang Puck's Postrio, Emeril Lagasse's Delmonico Steakhouse and Lutèce; critics slam "gaudy" decor, "hideous service" and "long lines" at check-in and check-out; for more, see Spa section.

Stateline

Harrah's Hotel & Casino
23 22 21 21 $146

Hwy. 50; 775-588-6611; fax 775-586-6607; 800-427-7247;
www.harrahs.com; 540 rooms (62 suites)

■ "Two bathrooms are heaven for a husband and wife", not to mention the three TVs and Nintendo that come standard in rooms at this "enormous casino" that has "lake and mountain views"; most like the "luxury at a bargain price", "good service" and "average food", but some wonder "is there such a thing as a nice casino?"

New Hampshire

Bretton Woods

Mount Washington Hotel & Resort, The
22 23 22 25 $198

Rte. 302; 603-278-1000; fax 603-278-8838; 800-258-0330;
www.mtwashington.com; 334 rooms (48 condos)

☑ "You can't beat the views" of the Presidential Range, and there's not a hint of "glitz" at this "old and simple" resort best suited to golfers and cross-country skiers who like to "step back" in time to fully appreciate the Victorian "charm", "superior staff" and 900-foot wrap-around veranda; but skeptics contend that no a/c, "low-brow food" and a "dilapidated elegance" fit for a "Hercule Poirot mystery" mean "the old gray mare ain't what she used to be."

Dixville Notch

Balsams Grand Resort Hotel, The　22 | 25 | 24 | 26 | $241

Rte. 26, Lake Gloriette; 603-255-3400; fax 603-255-4221;
800-255-0600; www.thebalsams.com; 185 rooms (18 suites)

■ "Yankee hospitality" and "phenomenal vistas" keep sports fans and seekers of "low-key" solace coming back to this "idyllic setting" in the Great North Woods, a "world apart" from other large resorts; stalwarts tout "spending a holiday with family or friends" at the 1866 hotel on 15,000 acres for the best in "New England charm."

Franconia

Franconia Inn　▽ 22 | 23 | 23 | 21 | $359

1300 E. Valley Rd.; 603-823-5542; fax 603-823-8078; 800-473-5299;
www.franconiainn.com; 34 rooms (4 suites)

■ A "peaceful retreat", this "quaint" 1863 country inn "with lots of character" set on 100 acres amid scenic mountains soothes stressed-out sojourners with "comfortable" furnishings and "good country food"; rooms may be "rather simple", but "wonderful staff", all-season sports and stunning views "revive the soul."

North Conway

White Mountain Hotel & Resort　▽ 22 | 22 | 21 | 22 | $151

W. Side Rd.; 603-356-7100; fax 603-356-7100; 800-533-6301;
www.whitemountainhotel.com; 80 rooms (13 suites)

☑ This hotel at the foot of a cliff "in the most beautiful region of the state" affords "spectacular scenery" and maintains a "consistent" staff ("the same faces every year"); while rooms are "comfortable" (a few snipe "tacky", "thin walls"), most guests spend their time at the five nearby ski areas or the North Conway factory outlets.

New Jersey

Absecon

Seaview Marriott Resort　22 | 23 | 21 | 23 | $192

401 S. New York Rd.; 609-652-1800; fax 609-652-2307; 800-228-9290;
www.marriott.com; 297 rooms (57 suites)

■ Away from the "noise and glitz" of AC, this "golfers' paradise" proffers a "great way" to log casino and tee time; "service-oriented", with "comfortable furnishings for work and relaxation", "it's surprisingly charming for a Marriott", and most think this "well-run" resort is "what 'Down at the Shore' should be like."

Atlantic City

Caesars Atlantic City　22 | 21 | 21 | 21 | $155

2100 Pacific Ave.; 609-348-4411; fax 609-343-2486; 800-223-7277;
www.caesars.com; 1,144 rooms (186 suites)

☑ "Interestingly over the top", this stalwart makes guests who stay in the Centurian oceanfront towers feel "like emperors" and those stuck in "noisy" rooms overlooking the casino like they're being "fed to the lions"; avoid holiday weekends if you want to savor the "hokum" of the "Roman lobby" and Temple Bar, though some wish "the salt air would blow all the glitz out to sea."

Harrah's Atlantic City   22 | 21 | 20 | 20 | $131
777 Harrah's Blvd.; 609-441-5000; fax 609-348-6057; 800-427-7247; www.harrahs.com; 1,174 rooms (254 suites)
■ Providing "calm in a crazy world of frenzied blue-haired gamblers", this "off-the-beaten-Boardwalk" bayfront resort has "some good bargains"; "the casino is the allure, not the rooms", but water views from the Marina Tower are "a big plus"; what's more, "good house shows", six restaurants and an "eager-to-please" staff make "losing your shirt" at the gaming tables "less painful."

Trump Taj Mahal   22 | 20 | 19 | 21 | $159
1000 Boardwalk; 609-449-1000; fax 609-449-6794; 800-825-8888; www.trumptaj.com; 1,250 rooms (237 suites)
☑ Guess who "dreamed up the color scheme" at this "mega-hotel" and casino with "the best people-watching in Atlantic City"?; easy "access to the Boardwalk", a terrific spa and "gaudy" yet "good-sized rooms" are all pluses for this "classic Donald", who "would have it no other way."

Bernardsville

Bernards Inn   24 | 26 | 27 | 22 | $185
27 Mine Brook Rd.; 908-766-0002; fax 908-766-4604; 888-766-0002; www.bernardsinn.com; 20 rooms (2 suites)
■ This "wonderful respite in horse country" serves "four-star" Progressive American cuisine amid a "club atmosphere" ("not showy, just like old money"); "first-class service" and "cozy" rooms in the 1907 country inn "exude luxury", making for a "romantic" "getaway" where guests can watch trains go by at the piano bar.

Cape May

Inn of Cape May   22 | 21 | 21 | 23 | $157
7 Ocean St.; 609-884-5555; fax 609-884-3871; 800-582-5933; www.innofcapemay.com; 52 rooms (15 suites)
■ "Lovers unite" amid "Victorian splendor" and lounge on a wrap-around porch to "converse and watch the ocean" at this historic inn across from the beach; "hospitable" owners also encourage folks to "bring the kids" (if well-behaved, of course) and "take advantage of special packages" for a "Jersey shore summer vacation" in a "quiet" (no phones in rooms), "pleasant" atmosphere.

Short Hills

HILTON AT SHORT HILLS   26 | 26 | 26 | 25 | $216
41 JFK Pkwy.; 973-379-0100; fax 973-379-6870; 800-445-8667; www.hilton.com; 304 rooms (37 suites)
■ "This place should be in Beverly Hills", rave patrons who appreciate "luxury" 30 minutes from New York City (and across from the "best mall in the Northeast"); "caring service for weary travelers" ("someone at your beck and call 24/7"), "gorgeous spa", gym (they "lend you shoes, shorts and a T-shirt") and "superior brunch" at the The Terrace prompt some to ponder, "I thought it was the Ritz" (hence "steep prices"); for more, see Spa section.

New Mexico

Santa Fe

Bishop's Lodge Resort   23 | 24 | 22 | 23 | $220
Bishop's Lodge Rd.; 505-983-6377; fax 505-989-8739; 800-732-2240; www.bishopslodge.com; 111 rooms (19 suites)
■ A family vacation here is the stuff of "fond lifelong memories": horseback ride, fish, play tennis or "hike in the forested canyons" surrounding this "old adobe resort" – "almost a dude ranch" – in foothills only two miles from the Plaza; rooms are "comfortable", grounds "beautiful" and staff "goes that extra mile"; one caveat: "don't stay by the horse corral in the summer heat."

Eldorado Hotel   23 | 23 | 22 | 23 | $209
309 W. San Francisco St.; 505-988-4455; fax 505-995-4555; 800-955-4455; www.eldoradohotel.com; 219 rooms (19 suites)
■ "The largest hotel in town" (but only five stories tall), this property "handles big groups well" for receptions and conferences, and most tourists insist it's "much more charming than you'd expect"; for a "real Southwestern feel", request a "homey" suite (some have kiva fireplaces), walk to shopping and sites during the day and take in the evening entertainment at the lounge.

INN OF THE ANASAZI   26 | 26 | 26 | 25 | $255
113 Washington Ave.; 505-988-3030; fax 505-988-3277; 800-688-8100; www.innoftheanasazi.com; 59 rooms (8 suites)
■ Right by the Plaza, this top-rated "intimate inn" offers "the full Santa Fe experience"; rooms are appointed with "authentic SW decor", fireplaces and "robes you'd love to take home"; Native American and cowboy flavors mingle in "exquisite food" served in the dining room, and service is "as good as it gets"; in short, "everything you love about the Southwest is realized to pricey perfection", except perhaps for a paucity of views.

Inn on the Alameda   24 | 23 | 21 | 22 | $208
303 E. Alameda; 505-984-2121; fax 505-986-8325; 800-289-2122; www.inn-alameda.com; 69 rooms (10 suites)
■ "Opt for a room with a romantic fireplace", handmade furniture and local artwork at this small Pueblo Revival–style inn that's "convenient to Canyon Road" art galleries and "near the Plaza, but removed from tourist chaos"; behind its adobe walls, staff dishes out "warm hospitality" and "sumptuous breakfasts" on a garden patio – making this a "good value" for haute Southwestern style.

Taos

Taos Inn, The Historic   21 | 21 | 22 | 21 | $173
125 Paseo del Pueblo Norte; 505-758-2233; fax 505-758-5776; 800-826-7466; www.taosinn.com; 36 rooms (3 suites)
■ "Even the soap is fabulous" at this modestly priced historic inn in the center of a town with "lots of character and characters" (especially at the "cozy Adobe Bar" with live jazz music); "tasteful" "Southwest" decor in the guestrooms (most with fireplaces, which make for "a romantic winter evening") extends to the "lovely courtyard" and Doc Martin's restaurant.

New York

★ **Best in State**
29 Point, *Saranac Lake*/SR
28 Four Seasons, *New York City*/H
27 St. Regis, *New York City*/H
    Lake Placid Lodge, *Lake Placid*/SR
26 Pierre, *New York City*/H

Amenia

Troutbeck Country Inn   22 | 24 | 23 | 23 | $235
20 Leedsville Rd.; 845-373-9681; fax 845-373-7080; 800-978-7688;
www.troutbeck.com; 42 rooms (9 suites)
☑ Just two hours from NYC, this Dutchess County country retreat
is ideal for special occasions and off-site business meetings; its
English-style manor house on 600 acres of "breathtaking grounds"
insures that "every room's a winner", though some find the
"eclectic" decor "not up to par" with the "seasonal food" and
"low-key service" that's "among the finest."

Bolton Landing

Sagamore, The   23 | 24 | 23 | 26 | $247
110 Sagamore Rd.; 518-644-9400; fax 518-644-2626; 800-358-3585;
www.thesagamore.com; 350 rooms (175 suites)
■ "What can be more beautiful than a view of Lake George when
you get up in the morning?" ask aficionados of the "unspoiled"
wilderness outside this "upscale" Adirondacks "idyll"; though
meeting facilities help boost the adult ratio, "it's a fun place to go
with family without surrendering to a kids' resort", and if "some
rooms are exquisite and some are broom closets", most guests
consider this sprawling resort hotel to be an overall "outstanding
place to visit" and play, even if "everything costs extra."

Cooperstown

Otesaga Resort Hotel, The   20 | 23 | 20 | 24 | $221
60 Lake St.; 607-547-9931; fax 607-547-9675; 800-348-6222;
www.otesaga.com; 136 rooms (12 suites)
■ This "piece of 'Leatherstocking' history" may be "the only game
in town", but it scores a homerun with baseball fans making the
pilgrimage to Cooperstown; "cool off in Lake Otsego, play golf or
go to the Hall of Fame – it's all a short walk" from the 1909 hotel
"with lovely public rooms and the best back porch", which makes
the Middle-American food seem fitting.

Garden City

Garden City Hotel   24 | 24 | 25 | 23 | $245
45 Seventh St.; 516-747-3000; fax 516-747-1414; 800-547-0400;
www.gchotel.com; 272 rooms (16 suites)
■ Fans relish the "luxury of a city hotel" set in one of NYC's
richest suburbs in Long Island; "comfy" rooms and "two gourmet
restaurants" raise the "romantic" stakes, while still others groove
on the weekend "singles scene" in the "disco" downstairs.

Lake Placid

LAKE PLACID LODGE 27 | 26 | 26 | 27 | $339

Whiteface Inn Rd.; 518-523-2700; fax 518-523-1124;
www.lakeplacidlodge.com; 34 rooms (4 suites, 17 cabins)

■ "Gore-Tex meets Dom Perignon" inside this Relais & Châteaux "rustic deluxe" Adirondack inn where a staff "caters with finesse and skill"; "fabulous lake views", "individually decorated" rooms and "big cabins" with "great fireplaces" combine with "fantastic" food, to cause guests to conclude that, though "pricey," it's "still cheaper than having your own camp."

Mirror Lake Inn 24 | 24 | 23 | 24 | $204

5 Mirror Lake Dr.; 518-523-2544; fax 518-523-2871;
www.mirrorlakeinn.com; 128 rooms (18 suites)

■ There's hiking, biking and fishing on the doorstep of this recently renovated, 19th-century family-run mini-resort for "the active traveler" that's a "less expensive and hoity-toity" Lake Placid–area alternative; for a "great lodge feel", skiers end their day with cocktails by the "cozy" common room's "huge fireplace" before retiring to "attractively furnished" rooms.

Mt. Tremper

Emerson Inn, The – | – | – | – | E

146 Mt. Pleasant Rd.; 845-688-7900; fax 845-688-2789;
877-688-2828; www.the-emerson.com; 24 rooms (4 suites)

Two hours from Manhattan (close to Woodstock), this Catskills hideaway offers chic suites surprisingly themed along Persian, African, Caribbean, and Asian lines with quirky flourishes; the all-inclusive price covers champagne upon arrival, five-course dinners, breakfast and sports facilities topped off with a full-service health spa; however, many guests get their exercise in their rooms.

New Paltz

Mohonk Mountain House 20 | 22 | 19 | 25 | $255

1000 Mountain Rest Rd.; 914-255-1000; fax 914-256-2161;
800-772-6646; www.mohonk.com; 261 rooms (27 suites)

◪ "Favored by the lockjaw crowd" and " blondes in Lilly Pulitzer" attire, this grand 19th-century "throwback" resort may be "past its peak", but its "breathtaking" mountain setting by a glacier lake lures loyalists for "annual retreats" that come with fireplaces and balconies instead of TV; organized activities "keep the whole family busy", but "obligatory" food and lack of modern amenities ("hello! this is 2000 – get some air conditioning") in the "large", "simple accommodations" may dampen the experience.

New York City

★ **Best in City**

28 Four Seasons/H	Plaza Athénée/H
27 St. Regis/H	**25** New York Palace/H
26 Pierre/H	Inn at Irving Place/SI
Peninsula/H	Mercer/H
Mark/H	Trump International/H
Carlyle/H	**24** Regency/H
Lowell/H	Plaza/H

Algonquin, The
18 | 21 | 20 | 21 | $227

59 W. 44th St.; 212-840-6800; fax 212-944-1419; 165 rooms (23 suites)

☑ "Old New York charm" and "literary ghosts" imbue this "well-located" Theater District hotel, once home to the famed Round Table literary clique; devotees relish the "clubby atmosphere", "classic bar" and "outstanding cabaret" in the Oak Room, which some say make up for the "claustrophobic" guest rooms and "dreary decor" (despite a 1998 renovation); "personal service" and the resident "lobby cat" add to the "intimate" ambiance.

Benjamin, The
26 | 25 | 23 | 22 | $283

122 E. 50th St.; 212-715-2500; fax 212-715-2525; 888-423-6526; www.thebenjamin.com; 209 rooms (97 suites)

■ "A wonderful escape from the busy streets" rave fans of this "classy" East Sider (ex Beverly Hotel) that was gutted in 1999 to suit vacationers and business travelers alike; "first-rate rooms" (all equipped with high-speed Internet access and kitchenettes), "exceptional" room service, an on-site spa and extras like a choice of eight pillows have guests gushing "this is living!"

Box Tree, The
24 | 24 | 26 | 22 | $303

250 E. 49th St.; 212-758-8320; fax 212-308-3899; 13 rooms (4 suites)

☑ You might walk right past this "romantic hideaway" tucked away on an East Midtown block, but if so you'll be sorry you missed the "creatively decorated" and "themed" rooms with gas fireplaces that make this "true NY brownstone" "feel like a small country inn"; add "attentive service" and pricey but "superb" food in the first-floor French restaurant and you'll understand why few object to "lots of stairs"; most guests consider the "spirited establishment" "a jewel", even if a minority faults it as "pretentious."

CARLYLE, THE
26 | 27 | 26 | 25 | $375

35 E. 76th St.; 212-744-1600; fax 212-717-4682; 800-227-5737; 190 rooms (64 suites)

■ "It doesn't get much better than this" declare guests of this elite East Side hotel steps from New York's museum mile; here "dowager widows and rich orphans" mix with "celebrities galore", spending top dollar for an "island of civility" with "elegant" lobby, "well-appointed rooms", "gracious" service and "superb food"; the "old-world" attitude may be "intimidating" and amenities lacking for the business traveler ("no voice mail"), but all agree on the musical charms of "legendary" Bobby Short in the Cafe Carlyle, and it's intriguing that your room may well have once housed a Kennedy.

Crowne Plaza Manhattan Hotel, The
– | – | – | – | M

1605 Broadway; 212-977-4000; fax 212-333-7393; 800-243-6969; www.crowneplaza.com; 770 rooms (19 suites)

Putting guests in the middle of Midtown's buzz, this Times Square mega-hotel is within walking distance of Broadway shows, Radio City Music Hall and the shops of Fifth Avenue; during downtime from the maddening crowd, there's dipping in the indoor pool, connecting with the in-room dataport or taking in the cityscape or river views afforded on the high-rise's upper floors.

DoubleTree Guest Suites   22 | 20 | 18 | 18 | $228
1568 Broadway; 212-719-1600; fax 212-921-5212; 800-222-8733;
www.nyc.doubletreehotels.com; 460 rooms (460 suites)

☑ You "actually have space to relax" in "clean rooms" "high above
the noise and grime" of Times Square at this "Broadway lover's"
pick, well located for scoring "reduced-price" show tickets at the
nearby TKTS pavilion; families, business travelers, even squads of
bachelor parties appreciate the "good security" and "chocolate
chip cookies at check-in", but most are loathe to dine here, and out-
of-towners chalk up "temperamental service" to "NYC attitude."

Elysée, Hotel   23 | 25 | 23 | 21 | $285
60 E. 54th St.; 212-753-1066; fax 212-980-9278; 800-535-9733;
99 rooms (14 suites)

■ This prewar boutique hotel in Midtown is a "lovely cross
between Euro-chic and a bed and breakfast"; each "charming"
room is decorated with refurbished and reproduction antiques,
and guests are "amazed at the quiet" (even "facing the street");
for a bit of noise, join a hip crowd at the Monkey Bar downstairs
or try the excellent restaurant; "first-class public rooms" and
complimentary breakfast and hors d'oeuvres add allure.

Embassy Suites Hotel   – | – | – | – | VE
102 North End Ave.; 212-945-0100; fax 212-945-3012; 800-362-2779;
www.embassysuites.com; 463 suites

The June 2000 opening of this 15-story Downtown hotel presents
a roomier-than-usual New York option, with suites ranging from
450 to 800 square feet (all equipped with high-speed Internet
access) atop a 16-screen cinema and tens of thousands more
feet of retail space; in contrast to all the commercialism is an
A-list of specially commissioned art works from Sol LeWitt and
Pat Steier, among others, and dining appears promising, thanks
to chef Larry Forgione, who's running both a steakhouse and
casual restaurant here.

FOUR SEASONS   29 | 28 | 28 | 28 | $418
57 E. 57th St.; 212-758-5700; fax 212-758-5711; 800-332-3442;
www.fourseasons.com; 370 rooms (60 suites)

■ Not just NYC's but the U.S.'s No. 1–rated hotel is this I.M. Pei–
designed "masterpiece of modern elegance"; it immerses its
necessarily well-heeled clientele in minimalist chic from the
grand lobby to closets, including huge rooms with "sheets like
butter", bathtubs that fill in 60 seconds and automated drape
pulls; everything is "top-notch" – rooms, staff, dining and public
spaces – which means it's unusually hard to get a reservation; for
more, see Spa section.

Helmsley Park Lane, The   22 | 21 | 20 | 20 | $263
36 Central Park S.; 212-371-4000; fax 212-521-6259; 800-221-4982;
www.helmsleyhotels.com; 622 rooms (41 suites)

☑ Some say "look out for Leona" (who lives on the top floors), but
you're better off looking at the "park views" from this "well-run"
Midtowner that's within easy walking distance to Lincoln Center;
many fans praise the "luxurious feel" and "welcoming" staff, while
equal numbers "don't understand what all the fuss is about", given
the "mediocre public areas" and "bordello-esque rooms" that
are currently being renovated.

Hilton New York
| 19 | 18 | 17 | 18 | $228 |

1335 Sixth Ave.; 212-586-7000; fax 212-315-1374; 800-445-8667;
www.hilton.com; 2,086 rooms (51 suites)

■ You can expect to see "stampedes of conventioneers" swarming this newly renovated and centrally located Midtown mega-hotel, where the huge amount of meeting space is an event planner's dream; insiders know that "the lower the floor, the louder it is", so they "head to the executive floors" for "better" service and "modern", "nice-sized rooms."

Hilton Times Square
| 20 | 20 | 19 | 19 | $232 |

234 W. 42nd St.; 212-840-8222; fax 212-840-5516; 800-445-8667;
www.hilton.com; 440 rooms (15 suites)

■ Modernism meets high-cultured whimsy 20 stories above Times Square at the city's newest Hilton, opened in May 2000; geometric shapes on the outside encase a specially commissioned sculpture by Tom Otterness of Lilliputian-like figures toppling a giant clock; for the pragmatist in you, each room comes with high-speed Internet access, wireless keyboard and safe to store your laptop while you're out exploring the wax museum, cinema and stores in the complex below or wining and dining at chef Larry Forgione's Above restaurant or Pinnacle bar in the Sky Lobby.

Hudson
| – | – | – | – | I |

356 W. 58th St.; 212-554-6000; fax 212-554-6139; 800-444-4786;
www.hudsonhotel.com; 1,000 rooms (58 studios)

More than 20 years after his reign at the height of hip via his Studio 54, Ian Schrager has returned chic to the Columbus Circle area with designer Philippe Starck; look-at-me touches start at the glass-encased entry escalator, spread to the baroque lobby bar, meander past a courtyard garden and end up at Hudson Cafeteria, where the "in" crowd downs haute comfort food (like mac 'n' cheese topped with foie gras) at communal tables; the tiny, but cheap, rooms (some with river views) are reminiscent of ship's cabins, with crisp white linens offsetting dark wood paneling; in sum, ya gotta see it to believe it, and you may not believe it anyway.

INN AT IRVING PLACE
| 27 | 26 | 24 | 24 | $303 |

56 Irving Pl.; 212-533-4600; fax 212-533-4611; 800-685-1447;
www.innatirving.com; 12 rooms (6 suites)

■ "A charming retreat in Gramercy Park" where "perfect service" is the norm, this small "gem" is located in an 1834 brownstone with antiques, four-poster beds and ornamental fireplaces; you start the day with complimentary breakfast followed by "exquisite high tea" at Lady Mendl's or room service from nearby Verbena restaurant and cocktails at Cibar; N.B. business travelers are in, but children under 12 are out.

Inter-Continental Central Park South
| 22 | 22 | 19 | 18 | $295 |

112 Central Park S.; 212-757-1900; fax 212-757-9620; 800-327-0200;
www.interconti.com; 208 rooms (16 suites)

☑ If you get an "upper floor with a view of Central Park, it's like a fairy tale and you're the prince(ss)" at this former Ritz-Carlton; despite solid ratings, and having the city's best park to play in, there's not much indoor "public space to speak of" and some rooms are "postage-stamp size" and pretty pricey by non-NYC standards.

Inter-Continental New York | 21 | 22 | 21 | 21 | $266 |
111 E. 48th St.; 212-755-5900; fax 212-644-0079; 800-327-0200;
www.interconti.com; 686 rooms (86 suites)
☑ Reviews are mixed for this large Midtown hotel that caters to a constant barrage of business folk; some rave about an "impressive lobby" and "lovely rooms" while naysayers call it a "monument to mediocrity", ranting about "inedible food", "disappointing" service and rooms so "teeny" that "if you bring a big suitcase there'll be no room for you"; all agree, however, that the location is hard to beat.

Kitano, The | 23 | 25 | 23 | 21 | $277 |
66 Park Ave.; 212-885-7000; fax 212-885-7100; 800-548-2666;
www.kitano.com; 131 rooms (18 suites)
☑ "A bit of Japan in NYC", this "lovely boutique hotel" in Murray Hill wins accolades for its "minimalist Asian decor", sushi room service and "quiet" atmosphere; admirers also applaud its "refreshing" staff and "plush rooms" ("down comforters are a great touch") with marble baths, but dissenters complain that "the small" size "doesn't work" and would rather not pay all those yen.

Le Parker Meridien | 23 | 22 | 22 | 21 | $271 |
118 W. 57th St.; 212-245-5000; fax 212-708-7471; 800-543-4300;
www.lemeridien-hotels.com; 698 rooms (224 suites)
☑ Despite being near Central Park, Carnegie Hall and Fifth Avenue shopping, it's the views from the rooftop pool, outstanding brunch at Norma's, "public spaces that feel almost sacred" and "world-class" gym that keep guests at this "sleek" high-rise; but surveyors split on service, with fans cooing over an "exceptionally helpful" staff and foes saying it's like a "true taste of France."

Library Hotel, The | – | – | – | – | E |
299 Madison Ave.; 212-983-4500; fax 212-499-9099; 877-793-7323;
www.libraryhotel.com; 60 rooms (9 suites)
Traveling bibliophiles will want to book this boutique hotel opened in August 2000 a block away from the New York Public Library; floors are arranged by the Dewey decimal system and the sleek tan-and-black rooms assigned appropriate themes and reading collections; but scholars do not live by words alone, so a volume-lined common area hosts breakfast and evening wine and cheese.

LOWELL, THE | 27 | 27 | 25 | 23 | $365 |
28 E. 63rd St.; 212-838-1400; fax 212-319-4230; 800-221-4444;
www.preferredhotels.com; 68 rooms (47 suites)
■ Loyalists flock to this "discreet" East Side landmark that "feels like a 19th-century hotel in London" for "excellent" service and "European charm" that they say is worth the high price; go for tea in the Pembroke Room or for startlingly good steak in the Post House; but if you're looking for romance, book one of the "heavenly rooms" upstairs with a fireplace.

Mansfield, The | 18 | 22 | 19 | 21 | $222 |
12 W. 44th St.; 212-944-6050; fax 212-764-4477; 877-847-4444;
www.mansfieldhotel.com; 124 rooms (27 suites)
■ "Diet before you check in" to the "Lilliputian" rooms at this "groovy Euro-chic" boutique in Midtown; "friendly" staff, "hip decor", "great amenities" (in-room CD player, 24-hour cappuccino bar) and the hot M Bar keep 'em coming back – or maybe it's the "bargain" price that includes breakfast and a dessert buffet.

MARK, THE
26 | 27 | 26 | 25 | $352

25 E. 77th St.; 212-744-4300; fax 212-744-2749; 800-843-6275; www.mandarinoriental.com; 177 rooms (60 suites)

■ A "flawless, unpretentious staff" led by Ray Bickson, possibly the "world's best" general manager, make this Upper East Side hotel a destination for "privacy" and "paradise in the big, bad city"; "perfect elegance" in the marble lobby, the "cozy Mark's Bar" and "super" food ("the dining room is a real sleeper") are just the downstairs introduction to lovely, comfortable rooms, which together with "sumptuous baths" produce an elegant "English home" ambiance for business and pleasure travelers.

Mercer, The
26 | 24 | 26 | 24 | $350

147 Mercer St.; 212-966-6060; fax 212-965-3838; 888-918-6060; 75 rooms (6 suites)

☑ The "calm, cool and sexy" new boutique SoHo hotel from André Balazs renders some fans speechless ("too hip for words") with its "stylish" postmodern decor, "celeb-watching in the lobby" and "small" but loftlike rooms ("very New York"); guests seem to revel in "wanna-be cool" service that's "attentive" but "snooty" and advise "don't miss [Jean-Georges Vongerichten's] Mercer Kitchen" for "wonderful" New American food (and room service); "bothersome street noise" irks light sleepers at this "prime locale."

Michelangelo, The
25 | 24 | 22 | 22 | $286

152 W. 51st. St.; 212-765-1900; fax 212-581-7618; 800-237-0990; www.michelangelohotel.com; 178 rooms (55 suites)

■ "A piece of Florence in Midtown", this "absolutely charming" hotel maintains a "small town feel in the big city", treating guests to a "pretty lobby", "spacious" "soundproofed rooms" and bathrooms "with nice tubs for a long soak"; first-timers call it "a happy surprise" and disciples consider it "a home away from home" with "all the amenities for business travelers" or sybarites alike.

Millenium Hilton
23 | 22 | 20 | 21 | $243

55 Church St.; 212-693-2001; fax 212-571-2316; 800-445-8667; www.hilton.com; 561 rooms (102 suites)

■ "Good for working folks", this "sleek" high-rise in the heart of Wall Street provides all the necessary business amenities (e.g. dataports, two-line speaker phones) as well as after-hours recreation with a "decent gym" and "chic" bar scene (otherwise this area becomes "no man's land after 6 PM"); lest the "efficient" service, "modern" room decor and "fabulous" river views go unnoticed on non-work days, this "above-average" chain outpost tempts families and couples with weekend "bargain" deals.

Millennium Broadway
22 | 21 | 20 | 20 | $232

145 W. 44th St.; 212-768-4400; fax 212-768-0847; 800-622-5569; www.millennium-broadway.com; 752 rooms (14 suites)

☑ Just off Times Square ("outstanding for the theatergoer"), this "non-crowd-seeker's paradise in the center of all the action" is "great for meetings" with the onsite Hudson Theater serving as "conference center"; "modern rooms" come with "snappy decor" and the restaurant may serve the "best carrot-ginger soup under the sun", but critics warn that the "food needs a little work" and "you'll have to climb over the bed to get to the bathroom" if you bring too much luggage.

Morgans
22 | 23 | 23 | 21 | $268

237 Madison Ave.; 212-686-0300; fax 212-779-8352; 800-334-3408;
113 rooms (18 suites)

⚊ You have to know where Ian Schrager's "eclectic" Murray Hill
"hangout" is or you'll never find this "cool" boutique hotel with
"no name on the door"; "subdued, fashionable travelers" dig the
"modern" decor, "fun CD and video library", "totally chic bar" and
hot Asia De Cuba restaurant, while dissenters fault this "silly place"
as "all form over function" with "spartan", "sardine-can rooms"
"so dark you can't see" and a "suffocatingly chic" attitude from a
"mod squad" staff.

New York Helmsley Hotel, The
22 | 21 | 21 | 20 | $253

212 E. 42nd St.; 212-490-8900; fax 212-490-8909; 800-221-4982;
www.helmsleyhotels.com; 788 rooms (11 suites)

⚊ "Gold, gold, gold everywhere" at this hotel in Midtown East has
reviewers lamenting the "1970s decorator kitch", but "it wouldn't be
a Helmsley if it weren't a bit in your face" (though a '99 renovation
may have changed things); "impersonal" ambiance prompts many
to say it's "lost the luster of the days when Leona ruled", but
"believe it or not, it's not a bad value for NYC", especially the
"attention to service", which makes it "ok for business meetings."

New York Marriott Brooklyn
23 | 22 | 20 | 21 | $185

333 Adams St., Brooklyn; 718-246-7000; fax 718-246-0563;
800-228-9290; www.marriott.com; 376 rooms (20 suites)

⚊ "A hotel in Brooklyn worth staying at? yes!" – this may come
as a shock to some; "well-priced" meeting rooms, "beautiful
bedrooms" and "excellent service" make this newcomer a "great
place to unwind after business"; even if a few Manhattanophiles
find the hotel "overpriced", "somewhat bland" and too far "from
Midtown", they're outvoted by those who enjoy dining in Brooklyn
Heights and checking out the "stunning promenade views."

New York Marriott Marquis
23 | 22 | 19 | 23 | $221

1535 Broadway; 212-398-1900; fax 212-704-8930; 800-228-9290;
www.marriott.com; 1946 rooms (60 suites)

⚊ "Yes, it's in Times Square and it's a zoo, but that's ok" exclaim
adrenalin-junkies ready to check into this "Broadway behemoth"
with a "terrific location for theaters" and the "ultimate feeling of
being in New York"; this "virtual city under one roof" provides "big,
clean rooms" (many with "excellent views") and a "professional"
staff that "manages the crowds", but beware "a weird entrance",
"waits for elevators" and only-"acceptable" in-house dining.

NEW YORK PALACE, THE
26 | 25 | 25 | 25 | $312

455 Madison Ave.; 212-888-7000; fax 212-303-6000; 800-697-2522;
www.newyorkpalace.com; 896 rooms (85 suites)

⚊ Check into this "luxury" Midtown hotel and you'll still be "treated
like royalty", even though "Queen Leona" has abdicated to the
"Royal Family of Brunei"; accommodations inside the landmark
Villard House base and the new modern tower are "plush to the
extreme", from "spectacular lobby" and "spacious", "enchanting
Cinderella rooms" to views of Saint Patrick's Cathedral and the
city beyond; though the "wonderful service", "wow" dinners at
Le Cirque 2000, "fluffy beds"and "amazing health club" "can't be
beat", a few find too much "glitz" and prices to match.

Omni Berkshire Place
– – – – VE

21 E. 52nd St.; 212-753-5800; fax 212-754-5020; 800-843-6664;
www.omnihotels.com; 396 rooms (47 suites)

"Possibly the nicest of the Midtown hotels" say surveyors who voted on this "great central location"; with "the feel of a small hotel", it offers "good value for the money", such as an "excellent health club", a "willing staff" and "lovely rooms" (with marble baths and dataports) like those of the fanciest chains but "at an Omni price"; most "would stay there again anytime", though some complain of "brain-dead service at front desk."

Paramount
21 22 19 21 $195

235 W. 46th St.; 212-764-5500; fax 212-354-5237; 800-225-7474;
610 rooms (15 suites)

■ Bargain prices, a great Theater District location and Schrager/Starck design draw the young, "funky" and "trendy" of the world to this totally renovated old-timer where the lobby "looks like a bat cave" suitable for "fashionable spies or rock stars"; most appreciate the "friendly" service from an "ultra-cute" staff and forgive the tight rooms built with "great design" elements "for hipsters who don't need to spread out" (bring "a shoehorn"); "low-lighting" throughout the hotel "hides hangovers" well – a testament to the continuing "chic" of the "fab" "Whiskey Bar" downstairs.

PENINSULA
27 26 26 26 $372

700 Fifth Ave.; 212-956-2888; fax 212-903-3949; 800-262-9467;
www.peninsula.com; 239 rooms (56 suites)

☑ "First class in every way" and "expense-account heaven" are how guests sum up this landmark hotel; "magnificent views from the rooftop bar" or glass-enclosed rooftop pool, an "elegant restaurant", "top-notch service", spa treatments and in-room "gadgets" add up to an "almost unsettling level of luxury" and cause guests to forgive "itty-bitty rooms" and occasional glitches.

PIERRE, THE
26 27 26 26 $372

2 E. 61st St.; 212-838-8000; fax 212-940-8109; 800-743-7734;
www.fourseasons.com; 202 rooms (53 suites)

☑ "Doesn't everyone already know how wonderful this is?" ask visitors to this "consistently superb" Four Seasons–run "favorite" that extends "elegance and style without fanfare" to "old money" types; "first-class" public areas and ballrooms, an "exotic tearoom" (The Rotunda), "caring" staff and the "prime location" on Central Park all win accolades, but there are minor grumbles: unless you're in the "suite crowd", regular rooms are "small" and "a bit dated"; plus, there's a constant parade of weddings and "prissy socialites."

Plaza, The
23 24 24 25 $325

768 Fifth Ave.; 212-759-3000; fax 212-759-3167; 800-759-3000;
www.fairmont.com; 805 rooms (96 suites)

☑ Bowing to "an American classic", fans say this "granddaddy of them all" "should be given a lifetime-achievement award" for "elegance"; most guests love having the "city at your fingertips", the "plush" Palm Court for afternoon tea and drinks in the Oak Bar, but critics warn that rooms can be "inconsistent" (ergo, "approve before unpacking") and could do without the tourist "hordes" who "trip over themselves" to view this "fairy tale" of "legend and lore."

PLAZA ATHÉNÉE, HÔTEL   26 | 27 | 25 | 24 | $400

37 E. 64th St.; 212-734-9100; fax 212-772-0958; 800-447-8800;
www.plaza-athenee.com; 152 rooms (35 suites)

■ "So good, so French" and so "costly", recite reviewers made to "feel like family" at this "superb", "small and lovely" "European-style" hotel on the quiet East Side; "suites with balconies" are considered "fabulous", but traditional rooms take a drubbing for being "postage-stamp size"; even so, most guests trust the "gracious" staff and say the "exquisite" modern global cuisine served in the "ornate" Le Régence is a "special occasion" treat.

Regency Hotel, The   25 | 26 | 23 | 23 | $321

540 Park Ave.; 212-759-4100; fax 212-826-5674; 800-233-2356;
www.loewshotels.com; 351 rooms (87 suites)

■ It's the Midtown "place to be" for the "original power breakfast" and a "quiet walk on the Avenue"; "understated but outstanding service" makes this a "refuge for celebs", business execs and the just plain rich; "remembered" regulars stay in "spare but beautifully done" rooms, partake of "amazing hot chocolate in winter", quaff cocktails in the "beautiful Library Lounge" and applaud "great value" even at high prices.

Regent Wall Street   – | – | – | – | VE

55 Wall St.; 212-845-8600; fax 212-845-8601; 800-545-4000;
www.regenthotels.com; 144 rooms (47 suites)

Behind the Greek Revival columns that testify to the original purpose (Mercantile Exchange) of this Wall Street landmark emerges a new boutique property (the first luxury hotel in the Financial District), which looks to the future while embracing the past; rooms are equipped with the digital amenities 21st-century business types have come to expect (DVDs, CDs, fax/printer/copy machines), and the marble-and-gilt ballroom is grand enough to fete any IPO.

Renaissance   23 | 23 | 21 | 21 | $226

714 Seventh Ave.; 212-765-7676; fax 212-765-1962; 800-468-3571;
www.renaissancehotels.com; 310 rooms (5 suites)

☑ At this "solid hotel" right on Times Square, most are pleased by "unexpectedly" "clean, elegant rooms", "a helpful concierge", good lobby security and convenience to the theaters that they say add up to "an overall great NY experience"; still a few others groan "all sizzle and no steak" and are vexed by the "awkward" second-floor lobby and "hassle" of "changing elevators to get to your room"; Foley's Fish House pleases with its panoramic view of Times Square.

RIHGA Royal   26 | 24 | 23 | 22 | $307

151 W. 54th St.; 212-307-5000; fax 212-765-6530; 800-937-5454;
www.rihga.com; 496 suites

☑ "Comfort and space abound" at this Midtown hotel where "beautiful furnishings", "to-die-for marble bathrooms" (complete with "heated toilet seats – oh my god!"), "service so friendly you forget you're in Manhattan" and "reasonable prices" are a big hit with business travelers, families and "rock, movie and sports stars"; a few whimper that the "lobby is nondescript" and Halcyon Restaurant "needs work", but most pray the "show-biz" clientele won't start overbooking their "secret hideaway."

Royalton Hotel   23 │ 22 │ 23 │ 25 │ $291
44 W. 44th St.; 212-869-4400; fax 212-869-8965; 800-635-9013;
169 rooms (24 suites)
■ "Can a lobby get any cooler than this?" ponder patrons of this
ultra-chic hotel with "ultramodern decor" and "dimly lit" rooms for
the "best night's sleep in Midtown" (scour the "mini-bar stocked
with condoms"); a few call the hotel "a classic case of design over
function" with "pricey", "oh-so-tiny" rooms but are easily outvoted
by "power brunchers" at Restaurant 44 to cure "morning-after"
blues and the "meat-market" bar that causes the need for the cure.

Sheraton New York Hotel & Towers   18 │ 19 │ 18 │ 18 │ $227
811 Seventh Ave.; 212-581-1000; fax 212-262-4410; 800-325-3535;
www.sheraton.com; 1,750 rooms (29 suites)
■ "Not exciting, but consistent" this "reliable business hotel" in
Midtown West "serves its purpose well as long as the purpose
isn't romance"; "typically undersized New York rooms" are "ok
for working" and the "staff is quite good", but the "dearth of
restaurants" (the chain's three casual spots don't seem to satisfy)
sends travelers hunting and gathering in nearby Times Square.

Sheraton Russell Hotel   22 │ 23 │ 20 │ 22 │ $229
45 Park Ave.; 212-685-7676; fax 212-889-3193; 800-325-3535;
www.sheraton.com; 146 rooms (26 suites)
■ "An escape from Midtown madness", this Murray Hill "surprise"
has a "cozy", "clubby" personality – and "no feeling of a chain";
cyber-surfers and business travelers appreciate its "large rooms"
with oversized "dream desks", dataports, fax/printer/copier
machines and voicemail, plus coffeemakers and Starbucks beans;
consult the "cordial" concierge for dinner reservations, since the
Club Lounge serves only continental breakfast.

Sherry-Netherland, The   25 │ 25 │ 24 │ 21 │ $346
781 Fifth Ave.; 212-355-2800; fax 212-319-4306; 800-247-4377;
www.sherrynetherland.com; 90 rooms (33 suites)
✔ "Like fine wine", gush patrons of this "shimmering" landmark
with a "great location" anchoring the southwest corner of Central
Park (it "feels like you live in New York"); staff "greets you like a
member of the family" and stock refrigerators in "spacious" rooms
with complimentary mineral water, soda and Godiva chocolates;
surveyors appreciate the "good value", complimentary breakfast
and views, and even though a few complain that the hotel "caters
to apartment residents", there's no argument about dinner: "try to
get a table at Cipriani's" downstairs.

SoHo Grand Hotel   22 │ 23 │ 23 │ 24 │ $297
310 W. Broadway; 212-965-3000; fax 212-965-3200; 800-965-3000;
www.sohogrand.com; 369 rooms (4 suites)
✔ "Hip, hip, hooray!" applaud "people-watchers" at this "swank"
"eyeful" in "Manhattan's chicest neighborhood"; accolades
abound for the stainless steel "high design", "trendy-with-
manners" staff and "surprising quality of its restaurant", but many
also bemoan "rooms that are smaller than small" ("should be
called SoHo Closet"), even if they do come with Kiehl's toiletries;
"more for the movie star than the CEO", this "in place" lures the
"young hipsters and European travelers" to its "outstanding" bar.

Stanhope (A Park Hyatt Hotel)   25 | 25 | 23 | 23 | $309
995 Fifth Ave.; 212-774-1234; fax 212-650-4705; 800-223-1234;
www.hyatt.com; 185 rooms (57 suites)

☑ "An island of calm civility" in a prime Upper East Side location across from the Metropolitan Museum of Art reminds guests "what success is all about" with "excellent service" and "cozy" yet "luxurious" rooms that afford "beautiful views of Central Park" and "the best turn-down mints"; while some scoff "past its prime" since Hyatt took over in 1999, most "feel at home" and agree that "drinks at the sidewalk cafe is a highlight of life on this planet."

ST. REGIS   28 | 28 | 27 | 26 | $409
2 E. 55th St.; 212-753-4500; fax 212-787-3447; 800-759-7550;
www.stregis.com; 314 rooms (92 suites)

■ "Splurge" at this 1904 beaux-arts landmark that tenders "luxury everywhere you turn" – from "drop-dead white-glove service" to "gilded" rooms with "personal butlers" and public areas that are "what Louis XIV had in mind when he built Versailles"; the King Cole Bar (with the "gorgeous mural painted by Maxfield Parrish") and the Lespinasse restaurant for "sublime" French fare make most agree this "perfect place" is "worth" its astronomic prices.

Swissôtel, The Drake   – | – | – | – | E
440 Park Ave.; 212-421-0900; fax 212-371-4190; 800-372-5369;
www.swissotel.com; 495 rooms (108 suites)

Parked at a tonier address than many Midtown hotels, this haven for the corporate traveler accommodates in contemporary-styled rooms equipped with two-line phones, voice mail and dataport – plus sound-proofing for those confidential conversations; food used to be a major draw when Jean-Georges Vongerichten cooked here, and it's a contender once again since the opening of Quantum 56 restaurant in late 1999, and Fauchon, the first U.S. outpost for the Parisian food retailer, in summer 2000; what's more, the entire property just got a multimillion-dollar renovation.

TriBeCa Grand Hotel   – | – | – | – | VE
2 Sixth Ave.; 212-519-6600; fax 212-519-6700; 877-519-6600;
www.tribecagrand.com; 203 rooms (7 suites)

The gritty-yet-glam nabe of artist studios and dot-com-millionaire lofts got its own luxury staying spot with the May 2000 opening of this high-design hotel; while Internet drones tap away on wireless keyboards, glued to Herman Miller chairs inside minimalist rooms, indie-film types rent the on-site Screening Room and the rest of the crowd heads for Church Lounge, the theatrically lit living room, where meeting, lounging and dining mix in one boozy cocktail.

Trump International Hotel & Tower   26 | 25 | 25 | 22 | $365
1 Central Park W.; 212-299-1000; fax 212-299-1150; 888-448-7867;
www.trumpintl.com; 167 rooms (130 suites)

☑ "You feel like you're staying in a friend's private posh apartment" at this "sybaritic" high-rise off Columbus Circle where room service meals are prepared at the New French restaurant Jean Georges ("one of NYC's best") and you might even catch a glimpse of The Donald downstairs; guest quarters may be a bit small, but they come with Jacuzzis, kitchenettes and "drop-dead park views" (brought into focus by in-room telescopes) and lots of "'80s-style glitz"; most guests conclude that this is "first-class all the way."

UN Plaza Hotel
| 24 | 22 | 21 | 21 | $253 |

1 United Nations Plaza; 212-758-1234; fax 212-702-5048;
800-222-8888; www.unplaza.com; 427 rooms (40 suites)

☑ "The view" and East Side location opposite the United Nations are the main draws at this "quiet respite", where weekenders score "good rates"; a "reliable" favorite among business travelers and diplomats as well, this large hotel also lures guests with a "dynamite pool", "understated staff" and "clean, livable" rooms that start on the 28th floor, but critics harp on the "dated decor" that "needs some refurbishing."

Waldorf-Astoria & Towers
| 24 | 24 | 24 | 25 | $296 |

301 Park Ave.; 212-355-3000; fax 212-872-7272; 800-925-3673;
www.waldorf.com; 1425 rooms (278 suites)

☑ "Still a charmer," this "grand" art deco hotel in Midtown ("convenient" to shopping and sightseeing) sets a "refined atmosphere" in a "fabulous lobby" filled with "romance" and "history in every shadow"; admirers tout comfortable rooms and "great food in Peacock Alley" restaurant, but a few fault this "queen dowager" for being so busy with black-tie charity events that it sometimes feels like "a factory", albeit a fancy one; as for the adjacent but separate Waldorf Towers, only world leaders and billionaires can get in – oh, isn't that Bill and Hillary?

Westin Essex House
| 23 | 24 | 23 | 23 | $283 |

160 Central Park S.; 212-247-0300; fax 212-315-1839; 800-937-8461;
www.westin.com; 605 rooms (170 suites)

☑ "Still the best choice on Central Park South" concur most guests (including "lots of who's who" types) at this art deco "heaven" that's "classy without pretensions"; the generally "lovely" rooms vary from "spacious" to "phone booth" (it's "worth paying more for a park view"), and on occasion the "impeccable staff" "needs a little work", but families like the "short walk to playgrounds", and all agree on the "well-done" Café Botanica and the advisability of reservations for the famed French chef Alain Ducasse's *très cher* new restaurant; N.B. the hotel has recently been divided, with the best accommodations registered under the St. Regis Club brand.

W New York
| 21 | 22 | 23 | 23 | $257 |

541 Lexington Ave.; 212-755-1200; fax 212-832-9673; 877-946-8357;
www.whotels.com; 722 rooms (61 suites)

☑ "Dress in black – everyone else does" at this "fun", "hip" Midtowner; "shoebox-size" rooms "exude style and taste" (and come with feather beds), but most agree the "staff takes itself a little too seriously", which doesn't seem to matter to the "army of twentysomethings" crawling the "cool lobby" and Rande Gerber's "too fabulous" Whiskey Blue bar; soberer sorts work out in the "wonderful gym and spa" or fill up at the "Cool Juice" bar.

W New York – The Tuscany
| 24 | 22 | 21 | 19 | $266 |

120 E. 39th St.; 212-686-1600; fax 212-779-0148; 877-946-8357;
www.whotels.com; 122 rooms (12 suites)

☑ "If Calvin Klein had a hotel, this is what it would look like" quip surveyors about this "friendly" Murray Hill boutique hotel that's "close to everything yet secluded and private"; "large", "modern" rooms with "cool", inconsistent decor make up for no public spaces to speak of – except for "stylish dining" at Icon restaurant.

North Hudson

Elk Lake Lodge
— — — — M

Blue Ridge Rd.; 518-532-7616; fax 518-532-9262; 6 rooms (7 cottages)
Set amid 40,000-plus largely private acres of "spectacular
wilderness", this "authentic, no frills"1904 lakeside lodge "for true
outdoor lovers" may offer only "basic" rooms and food, but there
are also "spacious" cottages with "postcard views" of what
National Geographic magazine has called "the jewel of the
Adirondacks"; with mountain lake swimming, canoeing, fishing,
climbing and 45 miles of hiking trails, as well as an aura of
woodland peace without phones and TVs, all within a five-hour
drive from Boston or New York, it's one of the Northeast's best
bargain sleepers; open May–October, but don't try to get in during
August – it's reserved by families 10 years in advance.

Rhinebeck

Beekman Arms & Delamater House
21 21 23 20 $162

*6387 Mill St.; 845-876-7077; fax 845-876-7077; 800-361-6517;
www.beekmanarms.com; 63 rooms (4 suites)*
☑ "Revolutionary charms abound" at this 1776 vintage inn located
in a "great area for antiquing" and touring Dutchess County; "a
dark, warm" tavern and "incredible lobby fireplace" may cause
main house guestrooms to appear "disappointing" in comparison,
so some say "stay in the [newer] Delamater House across the
street"; high expectations about dining under the long-distance
direction of star chef Larry Forgione have not always been met.

Saranac Lake

POINT, THE
29 29 28 29 $811

*Saranac Lake; 518-891-5674; fax 518-891-1152; 800-255-3530;
www.thepointresort.com; 11 rooms (1 suite)*
■ Vacationing "tycoons" find "expensive perfection" at this former
Rockefeller camp where they're treated "like private guests in
a billionaire's country lodge"; located in "God's country" amid
the Adirondack Mountains, the "rustic, romantic" waterfront
"hideaway" for adults constantly "exceeds" "highest expectations"
for "heavenly food", "gracious" service and "divine" rooms all
with down comforters and fireplaces (but no TVs or phones); if
you have to ask, the all-inclusive price is simply beyond the point.

Tarrytown

Castle at Tarrytown, The
25 25 25 26 $256

*400 Benedict Ave.; 914-631-1980; fax 914-631-4612; 800-616-4487;
www.castleattarrytown.com; 31 rooms (11 suites)*
■ "A fairy tale comes true" at this "special occasion" spot just
outside the "hubbub of New York City", where you can play "king
or queen for a day" in a Relais & Châteaux castle overlooking the
Hudson River; four-poster canopied beds in "huge" suites (some
with fireplaces) charm guests, as does "wonderful service that
includes many extras", while the view of Manhattan "does it" for
diners in Equus restaurant, which serves Contemporary American/
French "gourmet delights."

North Carolina

Asheville

Grove Park Inn, The   23 | 24 | 23 | 26 | $195
290 Macon Ave.; 828-252-2711; fax 828-253-7053; 800-438-5800; www.groveparkinn.com; 510 rooms (12 suites)
☑ Guests come in droves for "views" of the Blue Ridge Mountains and "old Southern charm and service" at this 1913 Arts and Crafts huge stone inn with "fireplaces you can stand in"; a few complain about "cramped" rooms and conventioneers, but most agree it's "one of the area's finest in all respects" – especially "if you love to golf" or relax in a rocker on the porch; N.B. a spa opens in 2001.

RICHMOND HILL INN   28 | 28 | 27 | 26 | $242
87 Richmond Hill Dr.; 828-252-7313; fax 828-252-8726; 800-545-9238; www.richmondhillinn.com; 33 rooms (3 suites, 9 cottages)
■ "Unforgettable", sigh devotees of this inn minutes from Downtown with "impeccable accommodations" in an 1889 Queen Anne–style mansion and cottages around a croquet lawn; all "love" the "exceptional" food, "views of the mountains" and "unbelievable service" ("it even snowed on cue!"); romantics can request "a room with a fireplace" and flower lovers should stroll the Victorian-style Parterre Garden with period plantings.

Chapel Hill

Carolina Inn, The   21 | 22 | 20 | 23 | $162
211 Pittsboro St.; 919-933-2001; fax 919-918-2795; 800-962-8519; www.carolinainn.com; 177 rooms (7 suites)
☑ "Tar Heel parents" and others are in for "a treat" at this Southern "belle", a 1924 Colonial inn located "in the heart of the UNC campus"; though rooms are "a bit small" and "old", the atmosphere is appropriately "tradition-filled", and guests appreciate sincere "hospitality"; sports fans note: "book early for football weekends."

Siena Hotel   25 | 25 | 23 | 23 | $178
1505 E. Franklin St.; 919-929-4000; fax 919-968-8527; 800-223-7379; www.sienahotel.com; 80 rooms (12 suites)
■ If you want "a pleasant change from chains" consider this "little slice of Europe" on Chapel Hill's main drag; the small Italian-style hotel maintains "lovely grounds" and "gorgeous rooms" with "earnest college kids" providing "intelligent service"; diners applaud the free breakfast buffet, and what's more, you don't have to leave Fido at home because the hotel allows pets.

Charlotte

Park Hotel, The   24 | 24 | 21 | 22 | $181
2200 Rexford Rd.; 704-364-8220; fax 704-365-4712; 800-334-0331; www.theparkhotel.com; 193 rooms (6 suites)
☑ Surveyors appreciate the details – "softest sheets I've ever slept on" and "great oatmeal soap" – at this "small hotel with personal service" that serves tourists and business travelers alike, causing some to declare it the "best in town"; set on a former estate, the South Park location is "wonderful for shopping", however, a few "disappointed" detractors say it doesn't live up to its reputation.

Duck

Sanderling Inn, The | 26 | 25 | 22 | 25 | $211 |
1461 Duck Rd.; 252-261-4111; fax 252-261-1638; 800-701-4111;
www.sanderlinginn.com; 88 rooms (8 suites)
☑ It's "not easy to get to" this Outer Banks resort, but vacationers
still flock here for the bordering Pine Island bird sanctuary, "sandy
beach" and large rooms with "great bathrobes"; "outstanding
service" and "low-key style" help guests "unwind", and even
though the "exquisite" spot is "great for kids" it's "probably too
romantic to bring them"; the dining room, a restored 1899 Coast
Guard Station, earns novelty points, but a few gripe about the
restaurant's "uninteresting menu."

Lake Toxaway

Greystone Inn, The ▽ | 26 | 26 | 24 | 24 | $267 |
Greystone Ln.; 828-966-4700; fax 828-862-5689; 800-824-5766;
www.greystoneinn.com; 33 rooms (3 suites)
■ Expect "tons of character" at this hideaway along Lake Toxaway;
"outstanding in every way," the 1915 Swiss-style mansion feels as
comfortable as a "second home" for those seeking "seclusion" in a
"beautiful setting"; nearby hiking, water sports (do champagne
cruises count?) and "large rooms" with "balconies overlooking
the lake" make this a vacationer's "dream."

Pinehurst

Pinehurst Resort | 25 | 26 | 25 | 27 | $249 |
Carolina Vista; 910-295-6811; fax 910-295-8503; 800-487-4653;
www.pinehurst.com; 529 rooms (232 suites)
☑ A hole-in-one for sports lovers, this vast hotel and condo
complex maintains eight golf courses – the "best east of Pebble
Beach" – and two dozen tennis courts amid a remote setting south
of Raleigh; staff turns on the "Southern charm" for a "swank"
clientele who eats up the "unbelievable Sunday brunch", but the
less enthusiastic lament "mediocre rooms" and warn "if you don't
golf, you don't get it."

Pittsboro

FEARRINGTON HOUSE | 28 | 27 | 27 | 25 | $225 |
COUNTRY INN, THE
2000 Fearrington Village Ctr.; 919-542-2121; fax 919-542-4202;
www.fearrington.com; 31 rooms (3 suites)
■ Nature lovers discover "heaven among Belted Galloway cows"
at this inn with "plush rooms" and "comfortable beds" that
"exudes charm and serenity" in a village setting "close enough
to Chapel Hill" not to feel "out of the way"; there's "a real sense
of being nurtured without pretense" by the staff, and "elegantly
inexpensive" dining proves an "incredible experience" (though
"food can be overly rich" for some).

Ohio

Cincinnati

Cincinnatian Hotel, The   24 | 24 | 25 | 23 | $197
601 Vine St.; 513-381-3000; fax 513-651-0256; 800-942-9000;
www.cincinnatianhotel.com; 146 rooms (7 suites)
☑ There's "no better in the Queen City" than this Downtown "art
deco–style classic" near convention and performing arts centers;
while surveyors say "dining in the Palace restaurant is cool and
sophisticated" and "service is fabulous" ("I called with a cable
TV question and someone was there in five minutes"), others are
vexed by "dark rooms", "peeling wallpaper" and a health club
that's "too small."

Cleveland

Renaissance   22 | 22 | 22 | 23 | $169
24 Public Sq.; 216-696-5600; fax 216-696-0432; 800-696-6898;
www.renaissancehotels.com; 491 rooms (43 suites)
☑ A "surprising treasure" that's "perfect for Indians or Browns
games, the Rock 'n' Roll Hall of Fame" and The Avenue shopping
mall, this "grand old hotel" earns respect for a "beautiful lobby"
and marble fountain; the landmark may employ "the nicest staff,"
but "really small rooms" irk some guests, while the more practical
regard them as "functional" and "affordable."

RITZ-CARLTON, THE   27 | 27 | 25 | 25 | $213
1515 W. Third St.; 216-623-1300; fax 216-623-0515; 800-241-3333;
www.ritzcarlton.com; 207 rooms (27 suites)
☑ "Who knew Cleveland has this gem?" ask guests who discover
some "great views" of Lake Erie and proximity to the up-and-
coming Warehouse District; dubbed "the place to stay" for
"unparalleled service" and "terrific" rooms, most welcome
"classic" touches like "wonderful afternoon tea" after shopping
at the adjacent Avenue at Tower City Center but a few find the
ambiance slightly "staid and formal" (especially those visiting the
nearby Rock 'n' Roll Hall of Fame).

Oklahoma

Oklahoma City

Waterford Marriott, The   22 | 23 | 21 | 22 | $158
6300 Waterford Blvd.; 405-848-4782; fax 405-848-7810;
800-992-2009; www.marriott.com; 197 rooms (30 suites)
☑ A touch of "class in the Plains" say fans of this midsize hotel
"on the edge of the city, in a nice suburban area" (the location
puts guests within easy reach of the National Cowboy Hall of
Fame); the "down-home feeling" in "modern", "large rooms" and
"helpful staff" add up to a "great value", even if "it tries to be old
world but isn't."

Oregon

Black Butte

Black Butte Ranch ▽ 26 | 24 | 23 | 26 | $263
Hwy. 20; 541-595-6211; fax 541-595-2077; 800-452-7455;
www.blackbutteranch.com; 120 rooms (150 condos & homes)
■ "All outdoor, all the time" chant fans of this vast resort where
high desert meadows and Three Sisters mountains serve as a
backdrop for "unlimited summer and winter activities" at the 4
pools, 2 golf courses, 22 tennis courts and skiing on Mt. Bachelor
and Mt. Hood; "wonderful" accommodations range from rooms
to condos to resort homes (quality "varies with owner") at this
"family vacation spot" where "ranch life was never so good."

Gleneden Beach

Westin Salishan Lodge, The ▽ 25 | 24 | 25 | 23 | $199
7760 Hwy. 101 N.; 541-764-2371; fax 541-764-3681; 800-452-2300;
www.salishan.com; 205 rooms (3 suites)
◪ Fans travel to this "fine coastal resort" on acres of wooded
hillside for its "excellent facilities", especially the Scottish-style
golf course, "warm swimming pool" and rooms with exposed
wood beams and balconies (some sport views of Siletz Bay below
and all have fireplaces); the Dining Room "is worth the visit alone",
but some dislike "unfortunate new decor" that "misses the mark"
of "authentic Northwest styling."

Gold Beach

Tu Tu'Tun Lodge ▽ 27 | 28 | 26 | 27 | $222
96550 N. Bank Rogue; 541-247-6664; fax 541-247-0672;
800-864-6357; www.tututun.com; 20 rooms (2 suites, 2 houses)
■ "What a great place" for "fun" (boating, fishing, hiking)
declare enthusiasts of this resort along the majestic Rogue River
whose "owners make guests feel they are all friends"; the "cozy
atmosphere" lures some to "stay forever" in "huge" rooms that
include balconies or patios "with views" (but no TVs in some) at
"moderate prices" considering extra "details" like freshly baked
cookies, binoculars and private soaking tubs (if requested); the
food is "super", too, and all agree that the name is the only
drawback – "it's so hard to pronounce."

Hood River

Columbia Gorge Hotel ▽ 22 | 24 | 26 | 23 | $189
4000 Westcliff Dr.; 541-386-5566; fax 541-386-9141; 800-345-1921;
www.columbiagorgehotel.com; 40 rooms (4 suites)
■ This "delightful resort" overlooking a gorge (with a waterfall
on the property) proves "romantic, especially during Christmas",
when the grounds are "covered in thousands of white lights";
while river-view dining tastes "great" any season or time of day,
guests rave about the "three-hour", five-course breakfast; a few
say antique-laden rooms were a bit "dated" until renovations in
2000, but note a "pet-friendly staff" greets pooches "with a dog
bowl" at check-in.

Mount Bachelor

Sunriver Resort | 23 | 22 | 21 | 24 | **$149** |

1 Center Dr.; 541-593-1000; fax 541-593-5458; 800-547-3922; www.sunriver-resort.com; 503 rooms (75 suites, 270 homes & cottages)

☑ It's "never too crowded" at this expansive all-seasons resort that sports "rustic-chic" decor in the Cascade Mountains; "lots of great activities" – hiking, riding, rafting, to name a few – make it "ideal for the whole family", and loyalists insist "it's still the best" place to stay for Mt. Bachelor skiing; rooms in the new River Lodges or Wildflower condos are "beautiful", and views from the The Meadows restaurant on the river are "super", but more than a few find the food "mediocre and expensive."

Portland

Benson Hotel, The | 23 | 24 | 23 | 23 | **$176** |

309 SW Broadway; 503-228-2000; fax 503-471-3920; 888-523-6766; www.bensonhotel.com; 287 rooms (56 suites)

☑ "Great design gives this hotel both history and contemporary comfort" with "beautiful wood throughout" (walnut from Russia) and "traditional but not tatty" furnishings; "attentive service", a "convivial lobby bar" ("good jazz", "the best martinis in town") and "cozy" rooms are "venerable" pluses for this downtown brick-and-mortar landmark that some think a "bit long in the tooth."

Fifth Avenue Suites Hotel | 26 | 25 | 22 | 22 | **$173** |

506 SW Washington; 503-222-0001; fax 503-222-0004; 800-711-2971; www.5thavenuesuites.com; 221 rooms (135 suites)

☑ "Look no further" for "gigantic" accommodations "decorated like a Parisian townhouse" at this centrally located hotel housed in a "restored" 1912 department store building; guests rave about the "homey feel" ("teddy bears on every bed", "umbrellas in every room") and "welcoming" staff that serves coffee and tea in the morning, wine in the afternoon by the lobby fireplace; the restaurant rates "ok", with "better nearby."

Governor Hotel, The | 24 | 24 | 23 | 23 | **$179** |

611 SW 10th Ave.; 503-224-3400; fax 503-241-2122; 800-554-3456; www.govhotel.com; 100 rooms (24 suites)

■ "Appropriately old-fashioned", this refurbished Arts & Crafts–style historic "sleeper" maintains "classic" rooms bursting with "regional flavor", such as paintings inspired by the journals of Lewis & Clark; the "well-kept" hotel, likened to "a private club", employs a "knowledgeable staff", serves steak and seafood at Jake's Grill and charges "moderate" rates – all in all, a "bargain" in a "great Downtown location."

Heathman Hotel, The | 23 | 26 | 26 | 23 | **$195** |

1001 SW Broadway; 503-241-4100; fax 503-790-7116; 800-551-0011; www.heathmanhotel.com; 150 rooms (33 suites)

■ The staff's "great people skills" mask their "militant dedication to quality" at this historic hotel near the Performing Arts Center and Pioneer Square where guests savor "understated luxury" and French/Northwest cuisine; note to culture-vultures: browse the "art collection, including Warhols", before rolling into bed to watch a video from the hotel's "outstanding library."

RiverPlace | 24 | 24 | 22 | 22 | $193 |
1510 SW Harbor Way; 503-228-3233; fax 503-295-6161;
800-227-1333; www.riverplacehotel.com; 84 rooms (45 suites)
■ In a "perfect setting" on the Willamette River, this "intimate" hotel is a "great alternative" to high-rises; "beautiful, contemporary decor", waterside jogging paths, and a "charming staff" leave only a few grumbles of feeling "a bit off the beaten track."

Vintage Plaza, The Hotel | 24 | 24 | 22 | 21 | $198 |
422 SW Broadway; 503-228-1212; fax 503-228-3398; 800-243-0555;
www.vintageplaza.com; 107 rooms (20 suites)
■ Oenophiles call this "creatively" restored city center hotel "a find" with a wine theme including "sophisticated decor" and daily tastings; rooms are tended by "thoughtful" staff, and "fun" Pazzo serves "refreshing" (if at times "uneven") Northern Italian fare.

Pennsylvania

Bradford

Glendorn | – | – | – | – | VE |
1032 W. Corydon St.; 814-362-6511; fax 814-368-9923;
800-843-8568; www.glendorn.com; 10 rooms (2 suites, 6 cabins)
Ninety minutes south of Buffalo, this NW PA 'great camp' presents a chance to rough it without forgoing the finer things; guests spend days canoeing, fly-fishing or getting in-room rubdowns and then put the weight back on in the Great Hall dining room at night.

Erwinna

Evermay on-the-Delaware | 23 | 25 | 26 | 23 | $203 |
889 River Rd.; 610-294-9100; fax 610-294-8249; 877-864-2365;
www.evermay.com; 18 rooms (1 suite)
☑ Charmed guests "plan to go back" to this 18th-century inn north of New Hope; "warm hosts" welcome travelers (no kids under 12) to Victorian rooms with river views and grounds "out of a travel magazine"; most like the "faraway" feel, but some say "overrated."

Farmington

Nemacolin Woodlands Resort ▽ | 27 | 24 | 24 | 27 | $244 |
1001 LaFayette Dr.; 724-329-8555; fax 724-329-6947; 800-422-2736;
www.nemacolin.com; 275 rooms (25 suites, 54 townhouses, 2 homes)
■ Sportswise "there's nothing you can't do" at this Laurel Highlands resort and spa; toss in "gorgeous rooms", "reasonable prices" and a top-rate staff and it's clear why this is "ideal for a weekend or business retreat"; for more, see Spa section.

Hershey

Hotel Hershey, The | 22 | 23 | 23 | 24 | $185 |
1 Hotel Dr.; 717-533-2171; fax 717-534-3125; 800-533-3131;
www.hersheypa.com; 235 rooms (27 suites, 1 house)
☑ "With the smell of chocolate everywhere, how can it be bad?" say fans of this updated "golden oldie" near Hershey's factory in PA Dutch country; most throw "kisses" to the "kid-friendly", "well-appointed" setting, but to some it isn't worth the "sugar high."

Philadelphia

FOUR SEASONS   28 | 28 | 28 | 27 | $273
1 Logan Sq.; 215-963-1500; fax 215-963-9506; 800-332-3442;
www.fourseasons.com; 364 rooms (102 suites)

■ "Sleep like a baby" on the "world's most comfy mattresses"
("where can I buy one?" – they'll only "sell their pillows") at "the
hotel equivalent of Prozac"; guests adore public spaces and a staff
that "rolls out the red carpet" at this "class act" near museums;
all agree brunch, which comes "with verbal weather reports", is
"worth waking up for" and dinner is "a celestial experience" at
the Fountain Restaurant.

Omni Hotel at Independence Park   23 | 22 | 21 | 21 | $180
401 Chestnut St.; 215-925-0000; fax 215-925-1263; 800-843-6664;
www.omnihotels.com; 150 rooms (3 suites)

☑ "History buffs" delight over the Downtown setting of this "cozy"
chain outpost that's steps from Independence Hall; "modern
amenities" mix with "friendly" service, lending a "classic Philly
feel" to lobby and "large, comfy rooms"; "good meeting spaces"
also make this perfect for the business crowd, who appreciate the
hotel's "fair prices", and only a few gripe about "paper-thin walls."

Park Hyatt at The Bellevue   24 | 23 | 24 | 24 | $217
1415 Chancellor Ct.; 215-893-1234; fax 215-732-8518; 800-233-1234;
www.hyatt.com; 172 rooms (28 suites)

■ Hyatt's "face-lift" of the Bellevue maintains the "grandeur" at
this century-old hotel that's both "ornate and comfortable", plus
close to everything Downtown; "Bram Stoker once hung out" here,
perhaps to puff a cigar or sip cocktails in the Library Lounge or
steep in the high tea service ("a must"); surveyors appreciate "nice
touches" in rooms, "bold" food, "attentive" staff and gym affiliation
(the Sporting Club draws the city's movers and shakers).

Rittenhouse Hotel, The   26 | 26 | 24 | 24 | $252
210 W. Rittenhouse Sq.; 215-546-9000; fax 215-732-3364;
800-635-1042; www.rittenhousehotel.com; 98 rooms (11 suites)

■ "Now this is city living" exclaim fans of this "chichi" boutique
tucked in the heart of Downtown; "movie stars abound", but even
non-famous folk and business travelers are "pampered" ("the
concierge drove me to get a Philly Steak sandwich!"); and who
wouldn't "treasure" the "biggest standard rooms you'll ever find",
filled with "cherry-wood furniture" and "huge" marble bathrooms?;
N.B. long-term suites are available on the top-floor.

Ritz-Carlton, The   – | – | – | – | E
10 Ave. of the Arts; 215-735-7700; fax 215-735-7710; 800-241-3333;
www.ritzcarlton.com; 330 rooms (46 suites)

Occupying two historic Downtown buildings – one a replica of the
Pantheon in Rome, the other a 1930s, 30-story tower – this new
hotel from the venerable chain opened in late June 2000; under
neo-classical detailing of the Rotunda (with Guastavino tiles
and lead-glass occula) guests mingle over afternoon tea and
dine brasserie-style aside Ionic columns; richly decorated
rooms (with Internet access and portable phones at "Smart
Desks") complement signature-style service, a health club, spa,
meeting facilities – even a tobacco lounge.

Westin   24 | 24 | 22 | 24 | $227
(fka St. Regis & Ritz-Carlton)
Liberty Pl.; 215-563-1600; fax 215-567-2822; 800-937-8461;
www.westin.com; 290 rooms (17 suites)

☑ The jury's out on this hotel "with an identity crisis" (ex St. Regis and Ritz-Carlton) that may have "maintained the look and feel" of "elegance" but still has "a lot of kinks to work out" before it attains "consistency" at this "prime Downtown Center City location"; fans hope rooms remain "comfortable" ("fabulous beds and pillows"), the staff stays "friendly" and that downhill dining will be reversed.

Pittsburgh

Priory, The   ▽ 22 | 23 | 19 | 21 | $159
614 Pressley St.; 412-231-3338; fax 412-231-4838; www.thepriory.com;
24 rooms (3 suites)

☑ A "combination of monastic charm and modern elegance" fills this "cozy" inn within walking distance to the Warhol Museum; a "congenial" staff, happy hour in the library (with complimentary wine) and "wonderful courtyard garden" make up for "spartan" rooms – "but what did you expect" from former clergy quarters?

Westin William Penn   21 | 21 | 20 | 22 | $165
530 William Penn Pl.; 412-281-7100; fax 412-553-5252;
800-937-8461; www.westin.com; 596 rooms (34 suites)

☑ A completed $20 million renovation has resulted in a "beauty makeover" for "the grande dame" of Downtown that's "suited to business travelers" (and "safe for women"); you "feel like a captain of industry" in the lobby while "listening to the piano player", and the staff makes sure "every 'i' is dotted and 't' crossed" – reviewers just hope those "dark and dusty" rooms become a thing of the past.

Skytop

Skytop Lodge   21 | 22 | 21 | 24 | $243
1 Skytop; 570-595-7401; fax 570-595-9618; 800-345-7759;
www.skytop.com; 185 rooms (25 suites)

☑ "Old world, not trailer world", quip guests at this "English manor" resort in the "usually blah" Poconos that's "like stepping back in time"; loyalists like the "clubby feeling", "professional" service and "degree of formality" that surround the golf and other activities, while a minority remark that it's "becoming a little too kid-friendly", the rooms are "small" and the "food needs a spark."

Puerto Rico

Dorado

Hyatt Dorado Beach Resort   24 | 22 | 22 | 24 | $270
Hwy. 693; 787-796-1234; fax 787-796-4647; 800-233-1234;
www.hyatt.com; 262 rooms (18 suites, 17 casitas)

☑ "Others come and go, but this one's hard to beat" say fans of this resort 45 minutes from San Juan (sharing facilities with Hyatt Regency Cerromar Beach); insiders advise "spending more" for ground floor rooms or private casitas that let you "walk to the sea" (other quarters are "ordinary"); the "golf course near the ocean is not to be missed", but the same can't be said for food and service.

Hyatt Regency   22 │ 22 │ 21 │ 24 │ $253
Cerromar Beach Resort
Hwy. 693; 787-796-1234; fax 787-796-4647; 800-233-1234; www.hyatt.com;
506 rooms (20 suites)

▲ The river pool (with rapids slides and waterfalls) is "worth the
trip" to this "complete resort" with a "theme-park atmosphere"
that's "great for families"; a beach and "chirping frogs" on "well-
cared for grounds" are "faves", but it's hard to overlook "crowds",
"all-night music", "surly staff" and "shabby rooms."

Fajardo

Las Casitas Village   ▽ 28 │ 27 │ 24 │ 27 │ $440
1000 El Conquistador Ave., Las Crobas; 787-863-1000;
fax 787-863-6758; 800-996-3426; www.wyndham.com; 90 villas

■ "Sherbet-colored villas enhanced by tropical flowers" are
"picture-perfect" at this "secluded" sib of El Conquistador (right
next door), where "suites overlook the sea", a "butler staff" "takes
pampering to the extreme" and "intimate pools" are "relaxing for
adults, fun for kids" ("like home on the road"); the Golden Door
Spa is a plus as is the "buffet breakfast" served alfresco.

Wyndham El Conquistador   25 │ 23 │ 24 │ 26 │ $292
1000 El Conquistador Ave.; 787-863-1000; fax 787-863-6500;
800-996-3426; www.wyndham.com; 910 rooms (106 suites)

▲ The beach has "little nooks and crannies for alone time" at this
cliff-side spot that gets glowing feedback for its "eager-to-please
staff" ("cold towels and fruit kebabs served around the pool"), 12
restaurants ("people dress for dinner – how refreshing"), "views
from wherever you turn", "roomy rooms", Golden Door Spa and
"great golf"; however, some aren't so keen on the island location
that requires "waiting in line" for a 15-minute boat ride to the beach.

Rincon

HORNED DORSET   28 │ 26 │ 27 │ 26 │ $304
PRIMAVERA, THE
Apartado 1132; 787-823-4030; fax 787-823-5580; 800-633-1857;
www.horneddorset.com; 31 rooms (29 suites)

■ If you "like to be left alone" with "nothing to do" except "sleep
in a four-poster bed", "bathe in a claw-foot tub", pass through
"French doors that open to unobstructed views" of crashing waves,
dine at a "gourmet restaurant" and "watch the sunset", this top-
ranking spot "tucked away" on the island's west coast ("light years
from San Juan") is your own "piece of paradise"; the seaside
setting is "a special place to unwind" ("no kids under 12 allowed").

Rio Grande

Westin Rio Mar   23 │ 22 │ 21 │ 25 │ $250
6000 Rio Mar Blvd.; 787-888-6000; fax 787-888-6600; 888-627-8556;
www.westin.com; 694 rooms (72 suites, 58 villas)

▲ Some vacationers have "no idea life can be this lavish" until
eyeing this "pretty" resort near the rain forest on the eastern end
of the island; "rooms are somewhat small" (with Neutrogena
toiletries) but it's really the "relaxing spa" and "great activities"
(casino, water sports, golf, tennis) that attract families and meetings.

San Juan

Caribe Hilton
21 | 21 | 20 | 22 | $215
*Los Rosales St.; 787-721-0303; fax 787-725-8849; 800-468-8585;
www.hilton.com; 644 rooms (40 suites)*
■ Ongoing renovations should only enhance the "casual, fun
and airy" ambiance at this "standard" resort that still fosters a
"fascinating local social life" with a central location near Old San
Juan; though the casino won't open till July 2001, you should "go for
the piña coladas", advise returnees and definitely "order them on
the secluded beach."

El Convento, Hotel
23 | 22 | 21 | 21 | $210
*100 Cristo St.; 787-723-9020; fax 787-721-2877; 800-468-2779;
www.elconvento.com; 58 rooms (3 suites)*
☑ "The history" "permeates everything" in this "beautifully
restored" 350-year-old Carmelite convent in the heart of Old San
Juan; "friendly service", nightly wine and cheese tasting, a "lively
bar" and courtyard dining make a stay here "quite special", but
reviewers note that rooms vary in size, from "grand to cell-like" –
as "you might expect" in a place with such "character" – and the
pool may be "the world's smallest."

Ritz-Carlton, The
26 | 26 | 25 | 26 | $295
*6961 Ave. of the Governors; 787-253-1700; fax 787-253-1111;
800-241-3333; www.ritzcarlton.com; 419 rooms (12 suites)*
■ "Posh and decadent", this new outpost strikes some as "more
like a city hotel than a resort" where the staff "tries hard to do
everything right" (one disoriented guest discovered they have a
"policy against pointing when giving directions"); "simple, elegant
rooms", an oceanfront pool, spa, casino, kids' camp and dining all
get the thumbs up, but too bad there's "heavy air traffic overhead";
for more, see Spa section.

Wyndham El San Juan
23 | 23 | 23 | 25 | $238
*6063 Isla Verde Ave.; 787-791-1000; fax 787-791-0390;
800-468-2818; www.wyndham.com; 385 rooms (33 suites)*
☑ "Every night feels like a fiesta in the lobby" of this beachfront
resort with "elegant guestrooms", seven restaurants, casino,
"friendly staff", "wild bar scene" and "prime beach"; three
"crowded pool areas" and enough overhead jets to make it
"sound like you're at the airport" are minor drawbacks for
those looking for "one of the more happening places on the
Isla Verde strip."

Wyndham Old San Juan
23 | 22 | 21 | 22 | $222
*100 Brumbaugh St.; 787-721-5100; fax 787-721-1111; 800-996-3426;
www.wyndham.com; 240 rooms (40 suites)*
■ This "old-style" hotel along the renovated waterfront (across the
street from the cruise ship pier) "stands up well to its competition"
with a rooftop pool and views of the port and Old San Juan; a
"small" lobby casino, "clean" rooms and "adequate service" come
as a "pleasant surprise" to many.

Vieques

Martineau Bay Resort   – | – | – | – | VE
Rte. 200, Vieques; 787-741-4100; fax 787-741-4105; 888-767-3966;
www.martineaubay.com; 156 rooms (20 suites)
Like Rosewood siblings Caneel Bay and Little Dix Bay, upon opening
in winter 2000/2001, this island resort on the northern shore is
bound to attract power vacationers (brave enough to hop puddle-
jumper props from San Juan) with in-room TVs, phones and fax
machines (unlike other properties); and while meeting spaces for
more than 200 should become a favorite with the conference
crowd, a fitness center, marina and full roster of activities – plus
the chain's popular kids' programs – could keep things from
getting too businesslike.

Rhode Island

Block Island

1661 Inn & Manisses Hotel, The   21 | 22 | 22 | 21 | $197
1 Spring St.; 401-466-2421; fax 401-466-3162; 800-626-4773; 53 rooms
■ "Block out some time" on this "lovely island" urge cognoscenti
of this New England resort composed of an inn, Victorian
landmark hotel and cottages that overlook a farm with exotic
animals; "cozy" rooms with "beautiful furnishings" (but no a/c)
and a "warm" staff win vacationer loyalty, or maybe it's the
"great socializing" at sunset with cocktails and hors d'oeuvres
before "traditional" dinners of "freshly caught bluefish and herbs
from the garden."

Newport

Castle Hill Inn & Resort   24 | 23 | 25 | 25 | $233
590 Ocean Ave.; 401-849-3800; fax 401-849-3838; 888-466-1355;
www.castlehillinn.com; 25 rooms (2 suites, 10 cottages)
■ "One night is not enough" chirp champions of this Victorian
resort with "knockout" ocean and bay views on a private 40-acre
peninsula; rooms are decorated with "antiques galore" and
"romantic waterfront cottages" equipped with "mini-kitchens";
but don't cook Sunday morning or you'll miss the alfresco brunch
with live jazz.

Cliffside Inn   25 | 24 | 22 | 22 | $233
2 Seaview Ave.; 401-847-1811; fax 401-848-5850; 800-845-1811;
www.cliffsideinn.com; 16 rooms (8 suites)
■ "A great place for romance", this "incredibly charming" inn near
First Beach and Cliff Walk satisfies even the most demanding
sybarites with "beautifully appointed" Victorian rooms featuring
at least one fireplace (some have two or three), bathrooms with
tubs to soak in "for an eternity", outstanding breakfasts and
"homemade cookies" and sandwiches at high tea served by an
"attentive staff" – all a world removed from "noisy crowds and
T-shirt shops."

Francis Malbone House ▽ | 25 | 25 | 27 | 25 | $216 |
392 Thames St.; 401-846-0392; fax 401-848-5956; 800-846-0392;
www.malbone.com; 20 rooms (4 suites)
■ "Second honeymooners" and other "romantics" "can't say
enough" about this circa 1760 small hotel centrally located near the
"bustling harbor"; sleeping quarters come with the "most comfy"
beds (antique and period-reproduction), plus modern amenities
and fireplaces (in most rooms), while "superlative" service and
"five-star breakfasts" (the "French toast will bring you back")
"more than compensate" for street "noise" in peak season.

Hyatt Regency | 19 | 19 | 18 | 20 | $183 |
(fka Doubletree Islander)
1 Goat Island; 401-851-1234; fax 401-851-3201; 800-233-1234;
www.hyatt.com; 264 rooms (17 suites)
☑ It "can only get better" observe guests of this hotel, now under
new management, that has "wonderful vistas" of the harbor from
its Goat Island home ("away from the hustle and bustle" of town
but a quick walk to the action); in the meantime, surveyors turn in
respectable, if not stellar, ratings for the "simple and clean" rooms
and "attentive" service and consider the sports facilities "a
bonus" – but the "nondescript" food needs to "improve."

Vanderbilt Hall ▽ | 23 | 23 | 23 | 23 | $257 |
41 Mary St.; 401-846-6200; fax 401-846-0701; 888-826-4255;
www.vanderbilthall.com; 52 rooms (14 suites)
☑ The "all-around pampering" makes surveyors "feel like guests at
a very wealthy person's home" instead of at this historic small hotel,
where the "understated" rooms are all unique and a "pleasant
surprise" (though some are also "microscopic"); opinions on dining
in front of the "roaring fireplace" range from "decent" to "great",
but overall it's an "excellent" choice – just brace for high prices.

Providence

Westin | 23 | 21 | 20 | 22 | $176 |
1 W. Exchange St.; 401-598-8000; fax 401-598-8200; 800-937-8461;
www.westin.com; 364 rooms (23 suites)
■ "A big fish in a small pond", this "modern" business hotel in a
"newly hip city" boasts a "great location" close to the new mall,
convention center and Brown University, and seems to have more
"charm" than a "typical Westin"; "extremely nice rooms", a multi-
level lobby and "great employee attitude" (though they "need a
good concierge") make this "a pleasant surprise."

South Carolina

Charleston

Charleston Place Hotel | 26 | 25 | 25 | 25 | $225 |
205 Meeting St.; 843-722-4900; fax 843-722-0728; 800-831-3490;
www.charlestonplacehotel.com; 477 rooms (42 suites)
■ "Lots of personality" emanates from this hotel in the center of the
historic district, offering "gracious hospitality" and "immense",
"luxurious rooms" as well as "adventurous chefs" at the Charleston
Grill and "nonstop food" on the concierge floor; boosters swear this
"big hotel in a small city" "has it all", including "Southern charm."

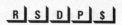
Hilton Charleston Harbor Resort `23` `23` `21` `23` `$153`

20 Patriots Point Rd., Mount Pleasant; 843-856-0028;
fax 843-856-8333; 888-856-0028; www.hilton.com; 131 rooms
(7 suites)

■ Just a boardwalk away from Patriots Point Naval and Maritime Museum, this midsize hotel affords "outstanding panoramic views" and even a chance to see dolphins in the harbor; a water taxi zips guests over to the Historic District, and the concierge can arrange fishing trips; enthusiasts most appreciate the "quiet and pleasant atmosphere" and "accommodating staff" at this "excellent value."

John Rutledge House `27` `26` `23` `23` `$215`

116 Broad St.; 843-723-7999; fax 843-720-2615; 800-476-9741;
19 rooms (4 suites)

■ "Step back in time" at this "beautifully restored" townhouse (built in 1763 by a signer of the United States Constitution); "very welcoming" and "full of charm", the inn maintains a "great courtyard" for breakfast, as well as a choice of "elegant rooms," "large suites" and guest quarters in two carriage houses "for more privacy"; it may be "expensive", but those who call it a "once-in-a-lifetime experience" don't seem to mind; "on-site parking" means you can leave the car and explore Charleston on foot.

Lodge Alley Inn `23` `21` `20` `22` `$178`

195 E. Bay St.; 843-722-1611; fax 843-577-7497; 800-845-1004;
www.lodgealleyinn.com; 93 rooms (93 suites)

☑ Opinions are decidedly divided when it comes to this "Old South" inn with diverse accommodations in a series of renovated 18th-century warehouses (some with sleeping lofts and fireplaces); fans praise the rooms – each "a voyage of discovery" – and come here for "romance" and the "wonderful courtyard with jazz music", while less fanciful sorts declare it just "ok", and even "down at heel"; but no one quibbles about the "location, location, location."

Mills House Hotel, The `22` `23` `21` `22` `$165`

115 Meeting St.; 843-577-2400; fax 843-722-0623; 800-874-9600;
www.millshouse.com; 214 rooms (19 suites)

☑ You're "within strolling distance of everything" at this "classy" midsize "old-time charmer" that serves Low-Country cuisine in the Barbadoes Room; loyalists love the "warm staff" and "comfortable rooms" and "can't imagine staying anywhere else", but a few detractors declare the spot "slightly tarnished" and too expensive for such "thin walls."

Planters Inn `25` `25` `25` `22` `$196`

112 N. Market St.; 843-722-2345; fax 843-577-2125; 800-845-7082;
www.plantersinn.com; 62 rooms (6 suites)

■ "Don't miss the restaurant" advise the many admirers of this "chic" inn that serves "superb creative local cuisine" at the "top-drawer" Peninsula Grill; but that's not the only reason to try this Relais & Châteaux hotel in the heart of Charleston: it's "bursting with hospitality" and surveyors like the rooms with canopied beds, breakfast delivered "with silver service" and "bargain" prices "in a city of few bargains."

Hilton Head

Daufuskie Island
▽ | 26 | 25 | 23 | 26 | $214

1 Seabrook Dr.; 843-842-2000; fax 843-686-3755; 800-648-6778; www.daufuskieresort.com; 89 rooms (37 cottages)

■ "Hope no one discovers this getaway" say respondents who would like to keep this "serene setting" a secret; just a ferry ride away from Hilton Head, the midsize resort makes a "wonderful escape" with two championship golf courses, a camp for kids, horseback riding and fishing; of course, there are also "pristine beaches" for those who prefer "a very quiet, very special" bask in the Carolina sun; a few quibblers cite "mucho bugs in summer" but appreciate the "nesting turtles."

Disney's Hilton Head Island Resort
25 | 23 | 21 | 24 | $194

22 Harbourside Ln.; 843-341-4100; fax 843-341-4130; 800-981-6304; www.disney.com; 102 villas

☑ "Fun for all", this village-style resort by the Shelter Cove Harbor Marina makes for an "exceptional-value" family vacation: parents find "true relaxation" (and nearby golf) while kids delight in "typical Disney" activities plus nature walks, bike tours and campfires; kitchen-equipped, "spacious" villas (one to three bedrooms) are "beautiful", but some bemoan "limited dining choices" and can't get over a "lousy location" "too far from the beach" (even with shuttle service).

Hilton Oceanfront Resort
23 | 22 | 21 | 23 | $191

23 Ocean Ln.; 843-842-8000; fax 843-341-8033; 800-845-8001; www.hilton.com; 323 rooms (22 suites)

☑ "Conveniently located" on a "gorgeous" wide beach, this "dependable" resort has "lots going on, yet is quiet and pleasant"; accommodations cater to families with "large rooms", kitchenettes and balconies, as well as two pools (separated for adults and kids) and "fabulous deals" on room rates; "nice landscaping" for "long walks" within the nearby gated community and "above-average service" are more reasons guests overlook the "boring" dining.

Hyatt Regency
22 | 22 | 21 | 23 | $189

Oceanfront at Palmetto Dunes; 843-785-1234; fax 843-842-4695; 800-554-9288; www.hyatt.com; 505 rooms (31 suites)

☑ "Beautiful beachfront", "great golf", tons of tennis and a "healthy dose of relaxation" attract folks to this "not flashy, but solid" resort that keeps families busy with bike paths, kids' camp and an Olympic-size pool; "they try hard to please here", but that's not enough for some who insist it's "time for a face-lift" at this "typical" property where the "scenery is the thing."

Palmetto Dunes Resort
24 | 22 | 22 | 23 | $195

4 Queens Folly; 843-785-1161; fax 843-686-2877; 800-845-6130; www.palmettodunesresort.com (450 villas, 30 homes)

■ Guests have the run of 2,000 acres at this oceanfront "mind-clearing getaway", a "golfing paradise" and "beach heaven" that some call the "best plantation on the island"; accommodations range from "spacious and well-equipped" villas to six-bedroom houses, surrounded by five swimming pools, 25 tennis courts and three golf courses, providing plenty of recreation and "relaxation" at this "lovely place" that's "maintained its quality."

Sea Pines Resort   25 | 23 | 22 | 25 | $202
32 Greenwood Dr.; 843-785-3333; fax 843-842-1475; 800-732-7463;
www.seapines.com (500 villas & homes)
■ "So much to do" rave fans of this "low-key" "nature lover's
paradise", a huge family resort with golf and tennis, "wonderful
bicycle trails", horseback riding, a five-mile beach and "great
kids' program"; the vast variety of villas and homes in a "beautiful
setting" prompt the question "what's not to like?" – except maybe
"the occasional alligator in the driveway."

Westin   23 | 22 | 21 | 24 | $208
2 Grasslawn Ave.; 843-681-4000; fax 843-681-1087; 800-937-8461;
www.westin.com; 412 rooms (30 suites, 96 villas)
☑ Golfers and beachcombers wallow in the "casual elegance" at
this "nicely laid out" resort with a "secluded beach location" eight
miles from Harbour Town; "spacious" rooms, all with balcony
views, can be a touch "sea beaten" and a few complain about
"uncaring service" and "only fair" food, but the "great sports
facilities" and "pools so large you'll forget about the beach" make
this a family destination "you never have to leave."

Isle Of Palms

Wild Dunes Resort   25 | 22 | 22 | 25 | $204
5757 Palm Blvd.; 843-886-6000; fax 843-886-2916; 800-845-8880;
www.wilddunes.com; 393 rooms (10 suites, 300 villas & homes)
☑ "We liked it so much we stayed for three months" say a few
lucky ones about this "great family getaway" where lodgings
range from rooms and suites at the Boardwalk Inn to homes and
villas with up to six bedrooms ("some nicely decorated, some
not"); the real attractions are a "perfect beach" and "have-it-all"
activities; but some warn "it can feel isolating" and "they could
improve the food."

Kiawah Island

Kiawah Island Resorts   23 | 23 | 21 | 24 | $216
12 Kiawah Beach Dr.; 843-768-2121; 800-654-2924;
www.kiawahresort.com; 730 rooms (580 condos & villas)
☑ "Worries melt away" as guests "kick back" on this barrier island
with "breathtaking scenery"; "if you golf, don't miss this place",
though many also appreciate miles of beach, biking, water sports
and wetland tours; detractors, however, gripe about the "suburban-
like development" and "upscale fast food."

Tennessee

Memphis

Peabody, The   23 | 24 | 23 | 25 | $189
149 Union Ave.; 901-529-4000; fax 901-529-3600; 800-732-2639;
www.peabodymemphis.com; 468 rooms (15 suites)
■ "A cornucopia of Delta charms", this "well-updated" hotel close
to Beale Street is like "The Plaza of the South" with a lobby "that
invites you to relax" with "cowboys, belles, divorcées, tourists" and
"parading ducks"; "big and proper" rooms, service "with style" and
a "don't-miss Sunday brunch" help fortify this "solid institution."

Nashville

Loews Vanderbilt Plaza   23 | 22 | 20 | 21 | $179
*2100 W. End Ave.; 615-320-1700; fax 615-320-5019; 800-235-6397;
www.loewshotels.com; 340 rooms (13 suites)*
☑ This is "the place to stay when you need to find out why your
child is changing majors" (convenient to Vanderbilt University)
that's also a "mecca for alums" close "to local dives and live
music bars" on Music Row; rooms are "clean and comfortable",
and there's a "great staff" but "very average" dining.

Opryland Hotel   21 | 20 | 19 | 23 | $182
*2800 Opryland Dr.; 615-889-1000; fax 615-871-5728; 888-976-2000;
www.oprylandhotels.com; 2884 rooms (200 suites)*
☑ "Magellan could get lost" in this "massive" vacation and
conference resort; nine acres of tropical gardens, waterfalls, rivers
and fountains within a "climate-controlled" atrium "bubble" make
you "wonder if you are inside or outside"; many are "embarrassed
to have had to stay" at the "glitzy spectacle", bemoaning "fast
food" dining and a "smoky" "country music lovers' nirvana."

Union Station,   20 | 19 | 22 | 22 | $147
A Historic Wyndham Hotel
*1001 Broadway; 615-726-1001; fax 615-248-3554; 800-996-3426;
www.wyndham.com; 124 rooms (13 suites)*
☑ The "elegant" 1998 restoration of a Romanesque-style train
station blocks from Downtown provides "a different look" with
a barrel-vaulted lobby, stained-glass windows and slate track
schedule behind the registration counter; "warm" rooms are
adorned in railroad decor ("historical but creepy" say some).

Walland

BLACKBERRY FARM   29 | 29 | 29 | 27 | $406
*1471 W. Millers Cove Rd.; 865-984-8166; fax 865-681-7753;
800-273-6004; www.blackberryfarm.com; 44 rooms (16 cottages)*
■ "The loveliest, most luxurious place ever" swoon surveyors, who
liken this lodge in the Smokies to "staying at a wealthy uncle's
country home"; the rooms provide a "romantic" "getaway for mind,
body and soul", enhanced by the service (the "world should be run
so smoothly"); guests can partake of myriad country activities (fly-
fishing lessons, wildflower hikes), and "you can't beat chef Fleer's"
"outstanding menu with creative selections and presentations"
of "homegrown food" (plus an "open pantry policy" to boot).

Texas

★ **Best in State**

28	Mansion, *Dallas*/H	Adolphus, *Dallas*/H
27	Four Seas. Colinas, *Irving*/R	**24** Barton Cr., *Austin*/R
	Four Seasons, *Austin*/H	St. Regis, *Houston*/H
	Four Seasons, *Houston*/H	Tremont, *Galveston*/H
26	Crescent Court, *Dallas*/H	La Mansion, *San A.*/H
25	Westin La Cantera, *San A.*/R	**23** Omni, *Houston*/H
	Lancaster, *Houston*/H	Plaza, *San A.*/H
	Houstonian, *Houston*/H	**22** Westin Riverwalk, *San A.*/H
	Hyatt Hill Co., *San A.*/R	Omni Mandalay, *Irving*/H

Austin

Barton Creek Resort
24 | 25 | 23 | 25 | $218

8212 Barton Club Dr.; 512-329-4000; fax 512-329-4597; 800-336-6158; www.bartoncreek.com; 295 rooms (16 suites)
■ "I want to go here when I die" – assert duffers and "spa bunnies" over this "secluded" resort on the edge of Hill Country (20 minutes from Downtown); "immaculate grounds" surrounding four championship courses (plus putting greens and three driving ranges) complement "modern" guest rooms and "lively" meeting space, making this "great for business" and "fun for groups."

Driskill, The
22 | 22 | 20 | 24 | $174

604 Brazos St.; 512-474-5911; fax 512-474-2214; 800-252-9367; www.driskillhotel.com; 188 rooms (15 suites)
☑ "She's all gussied up and has a real Texas twang": this 1886 hotel in the heart of town was "restored to glory" in 1999, complete with "cowhide couches and chairs" in the lobby; many savor the "Southern hospitality" (complimentary hot chocolate and milk and PB&J at night) in the "classic" "politico stomping ground" that provides "fresh flowers" in all the rooms, but surveyors advise: "choose carefully – some are Texas size, some Rhode Island size."

FOUR SEASONS
27 | 27 | 26 | 26 | $230

98 San Jacinto Blvd.; 512-478-4500; fax 512-478-3117; 800-332-3442; www.fourseasons.com; 291 rooms (28 suites)
■ "Rub shoulders with Hollywood and music insiders" at the hotel's "river-view bar" and "watch the bats fly" from under Congress Avenue bridge; guests indulge in "a true Austin experience" with "hearty Texas food (lots of steak)" and "hip Western decor that fits the locale perfectly"; rooms come with some of the "best beds in the known universe", and patrons are "always treated like very special guests."

Lake Austin Spa Resort
▽ 24 | 23 | 23 | 23 | $237

1705 S. Quinlan Park Rd.; 512-372-7300; fax 512-266-1572; 800-847-5637; www.lakeaustin.com; 40 rooms
■ The ambiance is "not so chichi that you have to wear earrings while working out" at this "great place to escape the insanity of daily life and shed a few pounds to boot"; the resort offers "activities from canoes to hammocks, hikes to dance classes, and a pool", making it, "financially speaking, the best for your money"; guest savor the respite of "quiet grounds" and dining in a casual restaurant that serves "healthy, tasty, well-prepared" food with global twists.

Renaissance
23 | 22 | 20 | 23 | $147

9721 Arboretum Blvd.; 512-343-2626; fax 512-346-7945; 800-468-3571; www.renaissancehotels.com; 478 rooms (101 suites)
☑ "Big, like Texas" sums up this "solid bet" that's a "convenient" business hotel with "city views"; a "spacious atrium" and grounds in the corner of a 95-acre arboretum set the stage for suites and executive-level rooms, while the "great shopping and eating nearby" bodes well for for foodies who say that the hotel fare is "not memorable."

Dallas/Ft. Worth

Adolphus, Hotel
25 | 24 | 25 | 24 | $208

1321 Commerce St., Dallas; 214-742-8200; fax 214-651-3588; 800-221-9083; www.hoteladolphus.com; 428 rooms (116 suites)
■ Guests revel in this "renovated" hotel (built by beer baron Adolphus Busch in 1912) that's done up in "jaw-dropping elegance" (think "cowboy rococo" decor meets English Country "floral arrangements" in "Texas-size" accommodations); "a lovely place for weddings" and "relaxing" enough to make a "business trip feel like a vacation", this Financial District "classic" boasts "a wonderful dining experience" in the French Room, but "be careful in the neighborhood at night."

CRESCENT COURT, HOTEL
27 | 26 | 26 | 26 | $254

400 Crescent Ct., Dallas; 214-871-3200; fax 214-871-3272; 800-654-6541; www.crescentcourt.com; 218 rooms (27 suites)
■ Dubbed the "Texas Taj Mahal", this hotel was modeled after an English estate by architect Philip Johnson; to-the-manor-born touches start with a lobby of Italian marble and continue in "big, luxurious" rooms ("excellent pillows", "great French balconies" and "rose lotion that's worth the stay"); "inventive fare" and a location on the edge of the Central Business and Uptown Arts districts (near "amazing stores") prompts surveyors to wax "I wish I had a business trip coming up."

Fairmont
22 | 22 | 21 | 21 | $190

1717 N. Akard St., Dallas; 214-720-2020; fax 214-720-5269; 800-441-1414; www.fairmont.com; 550 rooms (50 suites)
◪ "Solid and dependable, the Buick of chains" remark guests of this hotel in a "convenient" location near the Financial District; "a good value" and "a good place for a meetings" it "gets the job done" with "large rooms" and "cool views" of the "concrete city" and "great steakhouse", though some sniff "past its prime."

FOUR SEASONS AT LAS COLINAS
27 | 27 | 26 | 27 | $265

4150 N. MacArthur Blvd., Irving; 972-717-0700; fax 972-717-2550; 800-332-3442; www.fourseasons.com; 357 rooms (12 suites)
■ "Bring the clubs" (and Spandex) to this "golfer and gym-goers' paradise" located off the beaten path yet 15 minutes from Dallas/ Fort Worth airport; two courses (plus a school that "maintains standards even with back-to-back classes"), an "endless pool" and spa renew health and soul; during downtime, guests appreciate the "good food and great bar", large rooms with views and "first-class service"; for more, see Spa section.

MANSION ON TURTLE CREEK, THE
28 | 28 | 29 | 27 | $312

2821 Turtle Creek Blvd., Dallas; 214-559-2100; fax 214-528-4187; 800-527-5432; www.mansiononturtlecreek.com; 141 rooms (15 suites)
■ "I'd live here in a heartbeat if I won the Lotto" sigh surveyors – and the superlatives just keep flowing for the state's and city's top-ranking boutique hotel where the "staff remembers your name from day one"; "lavish" rooms and the "biggest bathtubs ever" are "always a treat", and "even the jaded" agree that "restaurant schools should send students" to study chef Dean Fearing's SW cuisine; some guests consider this "in-town" "favorite" "the best hotel in America" and make "a detour to Dallas just to stay here."

Melrose, The   22 | 23 | 21 | 21 | $180

3015 Oak Lawn Ave., Dallas; 214-521-5151; fax 214-521-2470; 800-635-7673; www.melrosehotel.com; 184 rooms (22 suites)

■ Travelers welcome "relief from big chain hotels" at this 1924 hotel with "odd-shaped", "quaintly decorated" rooms resembling a "rich dowager's apartment"; four-poster beds, "luxury linens" and "large bathrooms that feel almost like home" lend a "cozy atmosphere", as does "personable service" and "wonderful Library Bar" all close to Turtle Creek, the Arts District and "plenty of nightlife."

Omni Mandalay Hotel   24 | 23 | 21 | 22 | $191

221 E. Las Colinas Blvd., Irving; 972-556-0800; fax 972-556-0729; 800-843-6664; www.omnihotels.com; 410 rooms (92 suites)

■ "Overlooked but excellent", this "cavernous" hotel on Mandalay Canal "isn't close to anything but DFW airport" – music to the ears of travelers seeking "quiet luxury"; "large" rooms face either downtown Dallas or Lake Carolyn and the "knowledgeable staff" proves "eager to please"; a "good workout room and pool" make this "value" a "weekender's delight."

Renaissance Worthington, The   21 | 21 | 19 | 21 | $158

200 Main St., Ft. Worth; 817-870-1000; fax 817-882-1756; 800-228-9290; www.renaissancehotels.com; 504 rooms (30 suites)

■ This "super" hotel (under chain management since mid-1999) comes up as surveyors' "first choice" in town for a "good business hotel"; there's close proximity to Sundance Square (20 movie screens within two blocks) and "early-morning walks around the nearby old-stockyard area"; "Texan hospitality", "spacious" suites and rooms and the "best buffet Sunday brunch" further make this corporate option "the pride" of the city.

Wyndham Anatole   23 | 21 | 21 | 23 | $189

2201 Stemmons Frwy., Dallas; 214-748-1200; fax 214-761-7520; 800-996-3426; www.wyndham.com; 1620 rooms (129 suites)

☑ "A city in itself", this "gargantuan" high-rise has "everything needed for business meetings"; it may "look like a prison from the outside", but the art collection ("including a piece of the Berlin Wall") and "oversized" rooms are deemed "worth the visit"; travelers keep fit and fed with the "extraordinary fitness center" and "choice of 11 restaurants" – you might "never need to leave for things to do" ("where else can you find a croquet court?").

El Paso

Camino Real Hotel   21 | 19 | 19 | 20 | $146

101 S. El Paso St.; 915-534-3000; fax 915-534-3023; 800-722-6466; www.caminoreal.com; 359 rooms (33 suites)

☑ The "jewel of a border town" (a "bright spot in a very dull" place), this historic hotel near the Convention and Performing Arts Center comes as "a surprise" that it's "so Mexican" but "full of real Texans"; guests are awed by "an amazing Tiffany ceiling" in the Dome Bar, but the "huge" rooms with Queen Anne-style furniture can be either "great" or "awful", and service "has slipped."

Galveston

Tremont House, The　　　25 | 24 | 23 | 23 | $219
2300 Ship's Mechanic Row; 409-763-0300; fax 409-763-1539;
800-996-3426; www.wyndham.com; 117 rooms (15 suites)
■ Representing "the very best kind of preservation", this "elegantly restored" old warehouse in the "gentrified" Strand Historic District supplies "civilized charm" in black-and-white "high-ceiling" rooms connected by ironwork bridges that surround a "neat" four-story atrium; guests declare the hotel "delightful", boosted by a "friendly staff" and "good" restaurant.

Houston

FOUR SEASONS　　　27 | 28 | 26 | 26 | $241
1300 Lamar St.; 713-650-1300; fax 713-652-6220; 800-332-3442;
www.fourseasons.com; 404 rooms (17 suites)
■ "Flawless service" from an "almost too helpful" staff makes this "superb" Downtown hotel agreeably "predictable" in its "ultra-luxurious" "grace"; guests applaud extra touches in "spacious" rooms ("classical music left on after turn-down") and "super beds" that are "more comfy than home"; dining at Deville restaurant treats business travelers to food with a "French twist", which they can work off at the "marvelous private health club."

Houstonian Hotel, The　　　25 | 25 | 24 | 26 | $199
111 N. Post Oak Ln.; 713-680-2626; fax 713-680-2992; 800-231-2759;
www.houstonian.com; 286 rooms (7 suites)
■ "Where else can you see ex-President Bush walking into a spa for a massage?" ask patrons of this "secluded getaway" on 18 acres smack in the middle of the city; the fitness center ("like having your own country club") and "amazingly accommodating service" draw "weary business travelers"; even though "rooms are not cute or charming", views and "healthy food" help make this "standout" "an excellent welcome to all that's Texas."

Lancaster, The　　　26 | 26 | 25 | 23 | $196
701 Texas Ave.; 713-228-9500; fax 713-223-4528; 800-231-0336;
www.lancaster.com; 93 rooms (9 suites)
■ "So romantic, we call it the Love Shack" confess surveyors who stay at the "jewel box" next door to the Alley Theater; close to the cultural heart of town, this "small hotel" feels "like being in England", with "intimate" rooms decorated with chintz and gilded picture frames; fans of Bistro Lancaster's contemporary American cuisine consider it "the best restaurant post-opera."

Omni Houston Hotel　　　24 | 23 | 22 | 23 | $178
4 Riverway; 713-871-8181; fax 713-871-0719; 800-843-6664;
www.omnihotels.com; 373 rooms (33 suites)
■ A Galleria setting ensures a "serene" ambiance amid "secluded grounds" adjacent to Memorial Park at this "business-type hotel"; "rooms are done in calming sage", staff offers "eager service" and most delight in the "pool", but feel "kind of isolated" from city shops or restaurants (to remedy, the hotel runs a "convenient and reliable" shuttle in an eight-mile radius).

St. Regis | 26 | 24 | 24 | 23 | $227 |

1919 Briar Oaks Ln.; 713-840-7600; fax 713-840-7617; 888-627-8194;
www.stregis.com; 232 rooms (52 suites)

■ "Everything about the hotel is wonderful, especially the people"
rave reviewers about "personalized service"; the hotel "lives up to
its reputation" with a "calm" atmosphere and guestrooms equipped
with CD players and feather duvets and pillows; prime cuts in The
Remington Grill, "great Sunday brunches" in The Astor Court and
the "best bar in town" keep the place filled with "a well-heeled
crowd" on the weekend.

San Antonio

Fairmount Hotel, The | 23 | 23 | 22 | 20 | $195 |

401 S. Alamo St.; 210-224-8800; fax 210-475-0082; 800-996-3426;
www.wyndham.com; 37 rooms (17 suites)

■ "No two rooms are alike (our group had a blast looking at each
other's)" in this "charming, small" Italianate-Victorian hotel built
in 1906 and moved six blocks in 1985 to its current spot next to the
historic La Villita district ("away from the hustle and bustle of the
Riverwalk"); Polo's serves "the best breakfast in town with made-
to-order croissants and homemade butter" tout surveyors.

Hyatt Regency Hill Country Resort | 25 | 24 | 23 | 27 | $221 |

9800 Hyatt Resort Dr.; 210-647-1234; fax 210-681-9681;
800-554-9288; www.hyatt.com; 500 rooms (58 suites)

☑ "Imagine crossing the sets of 'Dallas' and 'Bonanza'" and you'll
picture this resort that's "great to visit with kids"; "everyone will
love the water park" pool with a "rambling lazy river" ("float down it
in an inner tube"), "rounds of golf" and tennis (tuckered adults can
take in the spa or curl up in front of lobby fireplaces); rooms sport
"Texan decor" (rocking chair on the patio, anyone?), but service
can be "spotty" and dining needs "substantial upgrading."

La Mansion del Rio Hotel | 24 | 24 | 23 | 24 | $201 |

112 College St.; 210-518-1000; fax 210-226-0389; 800-292-7300;
www.lamansion.com; 337 rooms (11 suites)

■ This "pretty Spanish Colonial" hotel overlooking a "lovely spot at
the end of the River Walk" treats guests to a "taste of Old Mexico"
with "beautiful interiors"; "rooms with a river view are best" report
surveyors who enjoy "watching the barges and great-tailed
grackles" from balconies ("noisy but worth it"); "helpful" service
at this 1852 converted boys' school extends to "quality" dining on
the terrace at the "romantic" restaurant.

Menger Hotel | 20 | 22 | 20 | 22 | $145 |

204 Alamo Plaza; 210-223-4361; fax 210-228-0022; 800-345-9285;
www.mengerhotel.com; 319 rooms (24 suites)

☑ "Teddy Roosevelt signed up Rough Riders at the bar" of this
landmark that "snuggles up next to the Alamo"; opened in 1859, the
"eccentric" hotel decorates public spaces with antiques, photos
and paintings ("love those great-looking cowboys"), but despite
"reasonable rates and good service", some spirits dampen with
room decor – ranging from "Old West elegance" to "Holiday Inn"
humdrum – and only "merely good" dining.

Plaza San Antonio   24 | 23 | 21 | 23 |$168
555 S. Alamo St.; 210-229-1000; fax 210-229-1418; 800-727-3239;
www.plazasa.com; 252 rooms (6 suites)
■ "Away from tourist traffic" but still close to the River Walk, this
Marriott hotel with a "Spanish-Mexican feel" has a "beautiful
courtyard and pool area" and gardens on six and a half acres
("check out the roaming peacocks", or peddle yourself to the
nearby La Villita Historic District and markets on free bikes);
"quiet, comfortable" rooms prove "better than expected" at this
"reasonable" low-rise that employs a "friendly" staff.

Westin La Cantera   26 | 24 | 24 | 25 |$204
16641 La Cantera Pkwy.; 210-558-6500; fax 210-558-2400;
800-937-8461; www.westin.com; 508 rooms (25 suites, 38 bungalows)
■ "An exciting new destination" (opened in May 1999), this resort
(well "suited for families, meetings and conventions") requires "a
bit of a hike to the River Walk" action, but most guests like the
outdoor setting near Six Flags theme park and "Mexican firepots"
that illuminate "alfresco cocktails" in the evening; rooms are
"spacious" and service "hospitable."

Westin Riverwalk   23 | 23 | 21 | 23 |$174
420 W. Market St.; 210-224-6500; fax 210-444-6000; 800-937-8461;
www.westin.com; 474 rooms (40 suites)
☑ You "can't beat" the "great location" along a "quiet stretch of the
River Walk"; both "elegant and personable (a rare combination)",
this recently opened hotel "tries hard to please" with "modern"
rooms (most with balconies and views), however, reviewers warn
that the place can be "overwhelmed" with conferences, tourists
and "too many weddings" while it "works out some fledgling kinks."

U.S. Virgin Islands

St. Croix

Buccaneer, The   24 | 23 | 20 | 23 |$251
Gallows Bay; 340-773-2100; fax 340-778-8215; 800-255-3881;
www.thebuccaneer.com; 138 rooms (5 suites)
☑ Both a "honeymoon" retreat and "welcoming" family destination
("great place to bring a baby"), this large resort has "amazing
ocean views", a "beautiful beach" ("I learned to snorkel here"),
golf course, tennis courts and "wonderful service"; a handful of
critics crab about "ordinary food" and grounds that sometimes
"seem to have been trashed by pirates."

Carambola Beach   25 | 24 | 22 | 24 |$270
(fka Westin)
Estate Davis Bay; 340-778-3800; fax 340-778-1682; 800-424-1943;
www.sunterra.com; 144 rooms
☑ "A tropical gem" surrounded by white sand and green hills, this
resort has "large" villa-pods (with six rooms each), "exquisite
grounds", a "great golf course" and "marvelous breakfasts";
reviewers love it when the "extremely friendly staff" serves up
the "best piña coladas at the bar", but snorkelers complain that
the "ocean is rough", making waters potentially "unswimmable."

St. John

CANEEL BAY
27 | 27 | 26 | 27 | $378

*N. Shore Rd.; 340-776-6111; fax 340-693-8280; 888-767-3966;
www.caneelbay.com; 166 cottages*

■ Seven "pristine", "never-crowded" beaches let guests "escape everyday life" while "snorkeling, swimming and beachcombing"; loyalists say this "paradise" is "incomparable if you want to do nothing but relax" (no phones or TVs in private cottages), and the staff "caters to your every need"; a rule about "appropriate attire in the evening" turns off T-shirt-and-shorts types, but the "classy crowd" of annual returnees rave about the food.

Westin
26 | 23 | 23 | 25 | $267

(fka Hyatt Regency)
*Great Cruz Bay; 340-693-8000; fax 340-779-4500; 800-937-8461;
www.westin.com; 285 rooms (7 suites, 15 townhouses)*

☑ Guests take in some of the "best sunsets in the world" from the "modern" accommodations at this resort overlooking Great Cruz Bay; high marks go to the "quiet and romantic" gardens, pool, on-site scuba diving and other water activities, though a few wish the harbor water was more of a "crystal-clear turquoise"; dining earns mixed reviews, as does service, which some find "friendly" and others report as "close to dreadful."

St. Thomas

Marriott Frenchman's Reef & Morningstar Beach Resort
23 | 22 | 21 | 23 | $237

*5 Estate Bakkeroe; 340-776-8500; fax 340-715-6191; 800-524-2000;
www.marriott.com; 504 rooms (88 suites)*

☑ Sisters and next-door neighbors, these chain resorts share many facilities (and "lots of action" on the same strand of beach) but retain their own flavors; cliff-top Frenchman's Reef boasts "beautiful grounds", "pretty pool area" and "views of the harbor", while at the more exclusive beachfront Morningstar, some "large rooms" spill into gardens; few sing about the supper here, so diners looking elsewhere take a "convenient" boat ride to town.

RITZ-CARLTON, THE
27 | 26 | 25 | 27 | $329

*6900 Great Bay; 340-775-3333; fax 340-775-4444; 888-856-4407;
www.ritzcarlton.com; 148 rooms (4 suites)*

☑ "Plush" rooms fill this Italian palazzo high atop a hill overlooking Great Bay; "everything's top-notch" say those who favor "beautiful grounds", an infinity pool and beach (though a few deem the stretch of sand "a little small"); reviewers really like unwinding with the "magnificent view" while their "kids are entertained elsewhere" at one of the resort's many children's programs.

Wyndham Sugar Bay
23 | 22 | 22 | 23 | $241

*6500 Estate Smith Bay; 340-777-7100; fax 340-779-1740;
800-927-7100; www.wyndham.com; 300 rooms (9 suites)*

☑ This resort's price tag covers "all you can eat and drink" plus views of Smith Bay, access to three interconnecting pools and all water sports, including diving, snorkeling, windsurfing, sailing, kayaking and parasailing from the "small beach"; service is part of the package, though some say you wouldn't know it, and the "decent rooms" seem intentionally "sparse – to get you outside."

Utah

Deer Valley

Deer Valley Lodging 28 | 24 | 25 | 25 | $318
1375 Deer Valley Dr. S.; 435-649-4040; fax 435-645-8419; 800-782-4813; www.deervalleylodging.com; 520 rooms (450 condos, 20 houses)
■ This "first-class" "skiers' paradise" has a "diverse selection" of accommodations in multiple locations so you "can choose your own style" from rooms to condos (some look like "log cabins"), all in an "excellent location" right on the mountain for ski-in and ski-out access; add "delicious food" at Mariposa and McHenry's restaurants (a part of Deer Valley Resort) and admirers declare "all you need is snow."

Goldener Hirsch Inn ▽ 27 | 27 | 26 | 25 | $299
7570 Royal St. E.; 435-649-7770; fax 435-649-7901; 800-252-3373; www.goldenerhirschinn.com; 20 rooms (17 suites)
■ "It's like being in Salzburg" (home of the namesake sister lodge) at this chalet right on the ski slopes; public spaces full of "traditional Austrian" antiques lead to rooms that can be even "more interesting than the mountain" with hand-carved and hand-painted furniture, fabrics and "wonderful" amenities (balconies and fireplaces in some); indeed, so "fabulous" is the entire "experience", including service and dining, that guests find it "hard to leave to ski."

Park City

STEIN ERIKSEN LODGE 27 | 27 | 27 | 26 | $318
7700 Stein Way; 435-649-3700; fax 435-649-5825; 800-453-1302; www.steinlodge.com; 129 rooms (47 suites)
■ "When you care enough to have the very best" ski buffs head to this lodge in the mountains with "homelike" rooms (knotty pine furniture and Scandinavian colors) equipped with whirlpool tubs that "could fit a party"; "impeccable service" ("they put my ski boots on for me") and a "food and wine list worth the trip alone" might keep you "by the fire" (a "good place to spot the rich and famous") instead of on the "ski runs right outside the door"; N.B. as of June 2001, the lodge will expand to 170 rooms.

Salt Lake City

Hotel Monaco, The ▽ 27 | 24 | 23 | 20 | $151
15 W. 200 S.; 801-595-0000; fax 801-532-8500; 877-294-9710; www.monaco-saltlakecity.com; 225 rooms (32 suites)
■ Surveyors weren't "expecting anything this bright" in town, but rave about French Deco-inspired rooms with bold striped walls and mahogany furniture at this "boutique hotel par excellence" that's "well located" Downtown in a former bank building; "get a guppy for your room" or partake of "jolly service" and "Western-friendly" amenities (complimentary wine and back-rubs at cocktail hour) suggest the converted.

Snowbird

Cliff Lodge 22 | 21 | 21 | 23 | $220

*Little Cottonwood Canyon; 801-742-2222; fax 801-933-2119;
800-453-3000; www.snowbird.com; 511 rooms (21 suites)*

☑ The "avalanche-resistant" "concrete monstrosity" looks "somewhat Soviet", but this resort is very convenient for "serious skiers" by being directly on the slopes; guests wax poetic about a rooftop pool and spa, and remain practical about "enormous" rooms ("sterile" but "good value") so it's no surprise that when the "pretentious dining room" serves "amateurish food" most remember that "beautiful scenery" and a "five-star" mountain are the real draws at this "bunker in paradise."

Sundance

Sundance 27 | 24 | 25 | 26 | $248

*N. Fork Provo Canyon; 801-225-4107; fax 801-226-1937; 800-892-1600;
www.sundanceresort.com; 107 rooms (95 suites, 12 cabins)*

■ "Gorgeous views at any time of year" boost this "perfect blend of nature and resort" on the north fork of the roaring Provo River; "unparalleled ambience" imbues "rustic rooms" and "romantic" "cabins hidden in the pines", or you can rent large homes or suites decorated "Western style"; for all reviewers, "watching the hummingbirds while dining" in the Tree Room on food made with "herbs and vegetables from Robert Redford's own garden" is hardly "roughing it."

Vermont

Barnard

TWIN FARMS 29 | 29 | 29 | 29 | $851

*Stage Rd.; 802-234-9999; fax 802-234-9990; 800-894-6327;
www.twinfarms.com; 14 rooms (6 suites, 8 cottages)*

■ Rated the top small hotel in the nation, and with the No. 1 ranking for rooms as well, this "glorious" inn is where those with deep pockets "go to be coddled" in "the height of luxury"; guests swoon over "beautiful cottages in private woods" and rooms at the Main House (which has one of "the best contemporary art collections of any hotel in America"), as well as "fabulous" dinners made from estate-grown produce and served by an "exceptional staff"; those "who can afford" this "enchanting" spot near Woodstock insist it "should be experienced at least once in a lifetime"; N.B. adults only.

Essex

Inn at Essex, The 23 | 24 | 24 | 22 | $155

*70 Essex Way; 802-878-1100; fax 802-878-0063; 800-727-4295;
www.innatessex.com; 120 rooms (38 suites)*

■ "The only thing missing is Bob Newhart" at this country inn staffed by New England Culinary School students (their "pastries are a specialty"), where the "lovely grounds and pool" and "wonderful service" lend themselves to a "romantic getaway", wedding or "gourmet weekend" that amounts to a "genuine bargain"; N.B. spend the savings on "nearby antiquing that's not to be missed."

Grafton

Old Tavern at Grafton, The   22 | 23 | 23 | 24 | $186

92 Main St.; 802-843-2231; fax 802-843-2245; 800-843-1801;
www.old-tavern.com; 59 rooms (8 suites, 6 houses)

■ Luddites who yearn for "the way it used to be" embrace this "wonderfully restored" country inn that revives the "golden days of civility" with two "great front porches", no phones or TVs and "marvelous food"; "beautiful in summer or winter", the resort has "cozy rooms" in the main building and six "lovely houses."

Lower Waterford

Rabbit Hill Inn   ▽ 28 | 28 | 29 | 28 | $233

Pucker St. & Rte. 18; 802-748-5168; fax 802-748-8342;
800-762-8669; www.rabbithill.com; 20 rooms (9 suites)

■ "Bunnies on the table, bunnies on the bed" at this "sleeper" inn that folks "hate to tell us" about (it's "that great"); earning sky-high ratings, the "wonderful" Regional American dining (included in the room rate) is backed up by "gracious" service and "lovely" rooms (some with "fireplaces" and whirlpools, all with baskets of snacks and drinks) at this "romantic" spot "in the middle of nowhere."

Manchester

Equinox, The   23 | 24 | 23 | 24 | $231

Rte. 7A; 802-362-4700; fax 802-362-4861; 800-362-4747;
www.equinoxresort.com; 183 rooms (29 suites)

☑ After long days on the slopes or shopping at nearby outlets, this "superior" all-year resort feels like "a full-service gentlemen's club" with fly fishing, falconry and golf; an "elegant" atmosphere (some say "as stuffy as the animals above the fireplace") and "well-appointed" country rooms are maintained by "quiet service", however, many point out that the facility is "too big to be quaint."

Quechee

Quechee Inn at Marshland Farm   21 | 21 | 21 | 21 | $170

Quechee Main St.; 802-295-3133; fax 802-295-6587; 800-235-3133;
www.quecheeinn.com; 24 rooms (2 suites)

☑ Outdoor types find this sprawling country inn overlooking the Ottauquechee River "great in the fall", "nice for skiing" and "beautiful" for summer trekking that "transports you from meadows to forests"; most praise "warm welcomes" and "wholesome breakfasts", but some warn of "slightly worn-out" rooms.

Shelburne

INN AT SHELBURNE FARMS   25 | 26 | 27 | 27 | $215

1611 Harbor Rd.; 802-985-8498; fax 802-985-8123;
www.shelburnefarms.org; 26 rooms (2 cottages)

■ "The 19th century rules" at this "elegant" mansion resort aside Lake Champlain; a staff that "makes you feel like a Vanderbilt" compensates for rooms so "old-fashioned" they're devoid of heat (this working dairy farm is open only from May–October), and everything else achieves "absolute perfection" – including "excellent" dining and "quiet time" to nourish "body and spirit."

Stowe

Green Mountain Inn
| 22 | 22 | 21 | 22 | $171 |

18 Main St.; 802-253-7301; fax 802-253-5096; 800-253-7302; www.greenmountaininn.com; 100 rooms (19 suites)
■ This "homey inn" in "a great little town" hides a "delightful" year-round heated swimming pool out back that "feels perfect after a day of skiing"; surveyors recommend booking "a suite with a gas fireplace" for "romantic memories", though all rooms (even if "small") are "attractively" furnished with antiques.

Topnotch at Stowe
| 23 | 24 | 23 | 24 | $228 |

4000 Mountain Rd.; 802-253-8585; fax 802-253-9263; 800-451-8686; www.topnotch-resort.com; 118 rooms (10 suites, 18 townhouses)
■ "The epitome of what a New England ski lodge should be" sigh proponents of this "classy and woodsy" resort, but you don't have to slide the slopes to enjoy "the best health vacation ever" with tennis, golf, swimming, hiking and a spa; "public areas full of nooks and crannies" create a "nice atmosphere" while a "wonderful" staff watches over "top-notch townhouses and junior suites that can handle a whole family."

Trapp Family Lodge
| 23 | 24 | 22 | 24 | $190 |

700 Trapp Hill Rd.; 802-253-8511; fax 802-253-5740; 800-826-7000; www.trappfamily.com; 116 rooms (18 suites)
☑ Even if the "Tyrolean atmosphere" and twice-weekly sing-alongs are a touch "hokey", this mountain resort with "grounds that would make Julie Andrews" warble retains "a certain charm" from the days when it was home to the von Trapp family; "exquisite" views, "light, airy rooms", "wonderful hospitality" and dining to the tunes of a "harpist" create a "very restful and complete escape" – with a "good variety of activities" "no matter what time of the year."

Vergennes

Basin Harbor Club
| 20 | 23 | 21 | 24 | $239 |

Basin Harbor Rd.; 802-475-2311; fax 802-475-6545; 800-622-4000; www.basinharbor.com; 136 rooms (77 cottages)
■ The "granddaddy of family resorts", this "lively" colony with loads of activities (but no TVs) feels like a "summer camp for grown-ups" on Lake Champlain; "public areas are tastefully done", but the "cute cottages" "near the water's edge" may be best for indulging in this "all-American" "classic" that lures "many back year after year", even with a "rigid dress code" in the Main Dining Room.

Warren

Pitcher Inn, The
| ▽ 26 | 24 | 26 | 23 | $380 |

275 Main St.; 802-496-6350; fax 802-496-6354; 888-867-4824; www.pitcherinn.com; 11 rooms (2 suites)
■ Relais & Châteaux finds a winner with this "romantic hideaway"; a "wonderful old place, recently redone with tons of charm" leaving surveyors feeling this is "as much a museum and work of art, as an inn"; "a great experience any time of the year" for "superb" food, wine and setting; you can even sleep in the "hayloft with luxury."

West Dover

INN AT SAWMILL FARM, THE   26 │ 26 │ 28 │ 25 │ $307
Crosstown Rd. & Rte. 100; 802-464-8131; fax 802-464-1130;
800-493-1133; www.relaischateaux.com; 20 rooms (3 suites)
■ A "*House & Garden* look" (flowered wallpaper, beams, trout
pond and "authentic antiques") saturates this converted dairy
farm (and member of the Relais & Châteaux group) where gourmets
head for "refined", "romantic getaways" with "impeccable food"
and a "stellar" wine list; "hands-on owners oversee every detail",
from "superb", "cozy" rooms – half with fireplaces – to the "super"
and "unobtrusive" staff; N.B. no TV, no phones and they suggest
no children under eight.

Woodstock

Woodstock Inn & Resort   23 │ 24 │ 23 │ 24 │ $215
14 The Green; 802-457-1100; fax 802-457-6699; 800-448-7900;
www.woodstockinn.com; 144 rooms (7 suites)
■ "Posh, plush" and "picture-perfect" in a "quintessential town",
this "classy" resort "seems to get better" each season; guests
revel in touches like "quiet nooks", coffee in front of a "roaring
fire in the lobby" and "cozy" rooms with "lovely quilts"; for the
more energized, the inn offers a "convenient" shuttle to ski
slopes, a "tough golf course", a newly renovated health center
and proximity to local shops.

Virginia

Alexandria

MORRISON HOUSE   26 │ 26 │ 26 │ 25 │ $206
116 S. Alfred St.; 703-838-8000; fax 703-684-6283; 800-367-0800;
www.morrisonhouse.com; 45 rooms (3 suites)
■ Considered to be Old Town's "hidden delight", this "romantic"
small hotel displays "country estate style" in "petite but lovely"
rooms; the Elysium restaurant serves acclaimed eclectic American
fare, and an "informal" piano bar and sing-along in The Grille
"makes you feel like you're in a Broadway show"; plus, the service
is "unbeatable" – "I've never been treated better."

Arlington

RITZ-CARLTON PENTAGON CITY   27 │ 27 │ 26 │ 26 │ $223
1250 S. Hayes St.; 703-415-5000; fax 703-415-5061; 800-241-3333;
www.ritzcarlton.com; 366 rooms (12 suites)
☑ "Lovely, comfortable" rooms come with "all the trappings" at
this "mature" hotel; commendations go to the "pampering" service,
"good meeting set-ups", "excellent" dining room and "clubby"
lounge (where Linda tripped up Monica); the Metro at the door
gives "easy access" to DC, yet some are chafed by the "strange"
"suburban" location "linked to an upscale shopping mall"; in
addition, returnees worry that all the "good staffers" are being
drafted by the chain's new Downtown property.

Boyce

L'Auberge Provencal ▽ 25 26 27 24 $213
*13630 Lord Fairfax Hwy.; 540-837-1375; fax 540-837-2004;
800-638-1702; www.laubergeprovencale.com; 14 rooms
(4 suites)*
■ "French innkeepers" Alain and Celeste have concocted a
"fantastic" "formula for romance" by blending "cheerful" antique-
filled rooms in an old farmhouse with "divine" food ("boy, can they
cook!"); if the breakfast leaves you lazy, settle in by a "crackling
fire", peruse authentic Picasso and Matisse artwork, lounge by a
"secluded pool" or nap in "comfortable beds" before gearing up
for the "incredible" dinner.

Charlottesville

KESWICK HALL AT MONTICELLO 27 26 26 26 $305
*701 Club Dr.; 804-979-3440; fax 804-977-4171; 800-274-5391;
www.keswick.com; 48 rooms (2 suites)*
☑ It's easy to play "lord of the manor" at this "English country-
style" resort, with tea on the terrace (or garden) or sherry on "plump
sofas by the fireplace"; a "great golf course", "scrumptious"
dinners in the "dressy dining room" and slumbering nights in
"beautiful rooms" filled with antiques quell minor murmurs
of "snotty service."

Hot Springs

HOMESTEAD, THE 25 27 26 27 $286
*Rte. 220; 540-839-1766; fax 540-839-7670; 800-838-1766;
www.thehomestead.com; 510 rooms (87 suites)*
☑ A "tried and true" "favorite", this "stately" resort sports more
recreation choices than you could ever sample (golf, tennis, riding,
fishing, shooting, carriage rides, hiking, biking and swimming in a
"Roman-revival pool"); while hot-spring-fed baths were the original
draw, nowadays a convention crowd mixes with families and
seniors to enjoy waterfall cascade walks, a spa and "outstanding
breakfasts" served by a "cheerful" staff, which make up for
"redecorated but small" rooms and a hard-to-reach location; for
more, see Spa section.

Irvington

Tides Resorts, The 22 25 24 24 $209
*480 King Carter Dr.; 804-438-5000; fax 804-438-5222; 800-843-3746;
www.the-tides.com; 181 rooms (5 suites)*
■ A "laid-back" "ambiance of yesteryear" imbues this waterside
resort "managed by multiple generations of the same family"; a
"golfing paradise" (3 courses) that's "great for boaters" too and the
"lovely setting in the middle of nowhere" provide "lots to do with
kids" but it's mostly about "relaxing", "watching the Washington
power set at play" and savoring "good food" (just a little "too
Southern" for some).

Leesburg

Lansdowne Resort | 24 | 24 | 23 | 25 | $205 |
44050 Woodridge Pkwy.; 703-729-8400; fax 703-729-4096;
800-541-4801; www.lansdowneresort.com; 305 rooms (14 suites)
◩ A "convention spot" with "lots of small areas for conversation",
this resort (in a rapidly developing high-tech corridor) also offers
"special golf or spa packages" – a "great value" for the leisurely
minded; most recommend "basic, comfy" rooms and dining at the
three restaurants, and while the "uniformed staff" "can be counted
on to be polite", a few observe that the hotel's "large" size and
"impersonal" ambiance comes off a "bit cold."

McLean

RITZ-CARLTON TYSON'S CORNER | 27 | 27 | 26 | 26 | $242 |
1700 Tysons Blvd.; 703-506-4300; fax 703-506-2694; 800-241-3333;
www.ritzcarlton.com; 398 rooms (48 suites)
■ "A civilized place to rest and do business", this "top-drawer
hotel" in the suburbs (you "must have a car") accommodates with
"comfortable" rooms ("opt for the club-level" executive suites) that
may be "cookie-cutter" but are "from the greatest cookie cutters
on earth"; staff provides "everything you'd expect", and a "perfect
(indoor) pool" and high tea add to this "pure luxury" that's
connected to the "upscale" Tysons Corner shopping complex.

Richmond

Jefferson Hotel, The | 25 | 25 | 24 | 26 | $196 |
Adams & Franklin Sts.; 804-788-8000; fax 804-225-0334;
800-424-8014; www.jefferson-hotel.com; 274 rooms (26 suites)
◩ "Beautifully restored" and "maintained", this beaux arts
classic's "grand staircase" (think *Gone With the Wind*) descends
from the "stunning Palm Court"; credited with "true Southern
hospitality", the hotel "works well for corporate meetings" (in-room
modem access and a pool were recently added) and is touted as
the "only place" the "society page" considers "worth holding an
event"; dining ranges from "sumptuous" to "overrated", so some
find the "shuttle to nearby restaurants" handy.

Washington

INN AT LITTLE WASHINGTON, THE | 29 | 29 | 29 | 27 | $398 |
Main & Middle Sts.; 540-675-3800; fax 540-675-3100; 14 rooms
(5 suites)
■ If you're "not sure you'll make it to heaven" get a taste of it all at
this "magnificent gourmet retreat for lovers" where "Washington's
elite" eat chef Patrick O'Connell's top-rated "stratospheric" cuisine
before retiring to an "interior decorator's dream" of a room;
"nothing is overlooked" by the "superb" staff who serve tea in
the "Victorian" inn's garden; even if mere mortals dare to ask: are
the "astronomical prices" for "nirvana" "in the boonies" "really
necessary?" the answer is "but of course!"

Williamsburg

Kingsmill Resort   24 | 23 | 22 | 25 | $211
1010 Kingsmill Rd.; 757-253-1703; fax 757-253-8237; 800-832-5665;
www.kingsmill.com; 400 rooms (185 suites)
■ "Pretty marsh views" and a "setting on the James River" (near
Busch Gardens and Colonial Williamsburg) enhance the cachet
of this resort known for one of the "best golf courses in the East"
(63 holes); reviewers report that "simple but spacious" rooms and
suites ("great for large families"), an "accommodating" staff and
"food reflecting local Colonial flavors (peanut soup!)" make this a
"most enjoyable" albeit "ordinary property."

Williamsburg Colonial Houses   24 | 23 | 23 | 23 | $200
136 E. Francis St.; 757-229-1000; fax 757-565-8444; 800-447-8679;
www.colonialwilliamsburg.org; 76 rooms
☑ Add a "unique dimension to visiting" Colonial Williamsburg by
reserving a room ("well ahead of time") in one of it's dwellings in
a tavern, cottage or shop quarters; though living spaces are
"small" and "sparse in spirit", they're "decorated with period
pieces" and furnished with "thoughtful details" such as air-
conditioning and televisions (which can help drown out "noise
at street-level"); adjoining resort facilities (golf, tennis, fitness,
dining) supplement this "delightful" experience of "history,
not creature comforts."

Williamsburg Inn   25 | 25 | 24 | 25 | $229
136 E. Francis St.; 757-220-7978; fax 757-565-8444; 800-447-8679;
www.colonialwilliamsburg.org; 111 rooms (7 suites)
☑ "George Washington never had it so good" claim history
buffs about this "gracious" resort that's like "living in Colonial
America"; "period rooms" with no lack of "modern amenities"
rate best in the "old" main inn (currently being renovated and
enlarged), and guests appreciate the "consistent and graceful
quality" of the "huge pool and fitness center", gardens and
Regency restaurant, even if the "coat-and-tie" rule for dining
comes off as "stuffy."

Washington

Blaine

Resort Semiahmoo   24 | 23 | 22 | 25 | $179
9565 Semiahmoo Pkwy.; 360-371-2000; fax 360-371-5490;
800-770-7992; www.semiahmoo.com; 198 rooms (12 suites)
■ The "sheer beauty" of the surrounding Canadian Rockies and
Puget Sound, especially at "sunset", awes guests at this "pastoral
resort" on the water that's "close enough to Vancouver for day-
trippers"; rooms are "spacious but not luxe" and the staff "handles
big groups well", keeping them busy with kayaking, sailing, beach
bonfires, golf, "excellent beachcombing" and nature tours.

Kirkland

Woodmark Hotel   ▽ │ 26 │ 26 │ 25 │ 25 │ $228
on Lake Washington
1200 Carillon Point; 425-822-3700; fax 425-822-3699; 800-822-3700;
www.thewoodmark.com; 100 rooms (21 suites)
■ This "quiet lakeside retreat" makes a "great place for a weekend
getaway", "romantic" interlude or corporate meeting ("Microsoft
uses it often") seven miles from Downtown Seattle; guests gawk
at "sweeping views" of the marina, shoreline, Olympic mountains
and city skyline from their rooms, "relax" with spa treatments and
nibble (between feasts at Waters bistro) on "nighttime snacks"
provided by an "always excellent" staff.

Seattle

Alexis Hotel, The   25 │ 25 │ 24 │ 22 │ $215
1007 First Ave.; 206-624-4844; fax 206-621-9009; 800-426-7033;
www.alexishotel.com; 109 rooms (44 suites)
■ It's the "staff that makes this hotel special" with "prompt,
friendly" service at the "European-style" boutique near Pioneer
Square that accommodates business travelers and vacationers
in rooms that have "more space than you need"; decor honors
greats like John Lennon and Miles Davis, and seasonal art
exhibits adorn public rooms, while Northwest cuisine at the
Painted Table "holds its own among Seattle restaurants."

BELLEVUE CLUB HOTEL   27 │ 26 │ 23 │ 26 │ $217
11200 SE Sixth St., Bellevue; 425-454-4424; fax 425-688-3101;
800-579-1110; www.bellevueclub.com; 67 rooms (3 suites)
■ "No detail is overlooked", making this "luxury" spot 15 minutes
east of the city "popular with a business crowd", who stays in
large, art-filled rooms ("wish it were my bedroom at home"); a
"friendly staff" and "creative" cuisine draw guests to Polaris
restaurant, and should you want to toughen up after indulgences,
the facilities at a "second-to-none" athletic club include an
Olympic-size pool, track, tennis, racquetball and squash courts.

FOUR SEASONS OLYMPIC   27 │ 27 │ 26 │ 26 │ $258
411 University St.; 206-621-1700; fax 206-623-2271; 800-223-8772;
www.fourseasons.com; 450 rooms (208 suites)
■ "The Four Seasons does it again" rejoice guests at this Italian
Renaissance landmark in the heart of the city; service provides
"flawlessly executed" "friendly touches" like welcome cookies
for kids, making it "a real joy to be a guest here"; the recently
renovated rooms furnish "the most comfortable beds ever", while
public areas and "ultimate dining" are "sublime."

Inn at the Market   26 │ 26 │ 25 │ 22 │ $219
86 Pine St.; 206-443-3600; fax 206-448-0631; 800-446-4484;
www.innatthemarket.com; 70 rooms (7 suites)
■ "Shush, don't tell" beg fans of this boutique hotel on a hill
overlooking Pike Place Market and Puget Sound (the "perfect
location from which to explore the city"); "first-rate modern rooms"
may be "small", but have "big bathrooms", and the "exceptional
staff" pays attention to "details"; reviewers rate this "most
romantic" for its ivy-covered courtyard, lobby with wood-burning
fireplace and rooftop deck with "breathtaking views."

Mayflower Park Hotel, The   22   23   22   21 $167

405 Olive Way; 206-623-8700; fax 206-382-6996; 800-426-5100;
www.mayflowerpark.com; 171 rooms (20 suites)

☑ An "excellent value" "in these post-software fortune days" quip
loyalists of this "European-type hotel" near Pike's Place Market
"attractions" ("eat, shop and catch the monorail without ever
walking outside"); "friendly service" and "world-class" "martinis
in the lounge" keep most "happy", even if rooms in the "well-
renovated" hotel may be "dimly lit" or on occasion "disappointing."

Monaco, Hotel   27   26   24   24 $198

1101 Fourth Ave.; 206-621-1770; fax 206-621-7779; 800-945-2240;
www.monaco-seattle.com; 189 rooms (45 suites)

■ "Jazzy", "colorful rooms", some with "deep-soaking tubs for
two" (please spare the complimentary "goldfish"), keep this "funky"
Downtown hotel "boutiquey without going overboard"; a "quirky
yet professional" staff caters "wine tastings in the lobby" and "the
food at Sazerac restaurant is excellent"; all laud this "whimsical"
spot "filled with advertising execs" as "ultra-hip and lots of fun."

Sorrento Hotel, The   23   26   25   23 $214

900 Madison St.; 206-622-6400; fax 206-343-6155; 800-426-1265;
www.hotelsorrento.com; 76 rooms (42 suites)

☑ "Personalized service" with "attention to detail" stands out at
this Italianate villa overlooking Downtown; an "extraordinary
ambiance" harmonizes with the "super food in the Hunt Club" and
drinks by the "fireplace in the lounge", but a few grumble about
"standard-rate rooms" so "small" you can "change TV channels
with your toes" and the "hilly" hike to "the center of town."

Vintage Park, Hotel   24   24   23   21 $188

1100 Fifth Ave.; 206-624-8000; fax 206-623-0568; 800-624-4433;
www.vintagepark.com; 126 rooms (36 suites)

■ "Let it rain" as much as it likes because "gorgeous rooms"
(including a luxury suite with four-poster bed, whirlpool and
fireplace) and a "friendly" staff can't be dampened by gray skies
at this "upmarket" hotel in Downtown; "good" Italian food, "great
evening wine reception" and "port nightcaps" almost "guarantee
romance" – and encourage business travelers to "definitely return."

W   28   25   23   26 $227

1112 Fourth Ave.; 206-264-6000; fax 206-264-6100; 877-946-8357;
www.whotels.com; 426 rooms (9 suites)

■ Out-of-towners love the "nontraditional approach to everything"
at this "hip" Downtown hotel filled with "beautiful people" and a
"whatever-you-want, whenever-you-want-it" philosophy (there's a
special button on portable phones to assist); rooms that "combine
high-tech with eastern spirituality" possess "amazing beds" and
"decadent amenities", all managed by a "too-cool-for-school" staff.

Westin   23   23   22   21 $188

1900 Fifth Avenue; 206-728-1000; 800-937-8461; www.westin.com;
891 rooms (33 suites)

☑ Besides its "distinctive 'Jetsons' architecture" and "views of
the city, Puget Sound and the Olympic Mountains", this "busy
Downtown hotel" is all business, with "good conference facilities"
and "heavenly beds"; dissenters call it "an average convention
hotel" that "will not blow you away with individual gestures."

Snoqualmie

SALISH LODGE　　　27　25　26　25　$228
6501 Railroad Ave. SE; 425-888-2556; fax 425-831-6589;
800-826-6124; www.salishlodge.com; 87 rooms (4 suites)
■ A waterfall lures travelers to this "romantic" resort at the
foothills of the Cascade Mountains to unwind in "large rooms
with fireplaces and whirlpool tubs" or in the spa with "Asian
flair"; like "elegant living in the trees", the experience at this
"special place" delivers "civilized service" and "superior dining"
("don't miss Sunday brunch"), but "make sure your room" comes
with a view.

Whidbey Island

Inn at Langley, The　　　27　25　26　22　$229
400 First St.; 360-221-3033; fax 360-221-3033;
www.innatlangley.com; 26 rooms (2 suites, 2 cottages)
■ Soak in "great karma" at this "Arts & Crafts paradise" with
views of the Saratoga Passage; "quiet" guestrooms (no children
under 12, please) are designed for "comfort" with whirlpools,
fireplaces and porches that surveyors find "so romantic"; service
is "friendly" and there's "no lack of confidence" in the Country
Kitchen, where innkeeper/chef Steven Nogal prepares "exquisite
food" using "fresh local ingredients."

West Virginia

White Sulphur Springs

GREENBRIER, THE　　　27　28　27　29　$332
300 W. Main St.; 304-536-1110; fax 304-536-7854; 800-624-6070;
www.greenbrier.com; 637 rooms (32 suites, 67 cottages, 4 houses)
■ Dubbed "America's country home", this "tried-and-true" resort
commands thousands of acres of the Allegheny Mountains, "where
every view is postcard-quality"; "individual attention (despite
convention attendees)" proves service is "white-glove all the
way", and "romantic rooms with luxurious baths" use bold colors
and designs; recreational facilities, including golf, tennis and
culinary programs, and "very formal" dining combine to create
"elegance par excellence"; for more, see Spa section.

Wisconsin

Chetek

Canoe Bay　　　▽　27　23　27　25　$291
Rte. 1; 715-924-4594; fax 715-924-2078; www.canoebay.com;
19 rooms (10 cottages)
■ A two-hour drive from Minneapolis or six from Chicago, this
280-acre Relais & Châteaux "secluded" hideaway is ideal for
"romance"; enjoy Frank Lloyd Wright–inspired cottages with
"tubs for two", "great food", an awarding-winning wine list,
"friendly service" and "total privacy"; some think the "perfect
Midwest setting" on a crystal clear lake and no-children policy
make it so "quiet you can hardly think."

Kohler

AMERICAN CLUB, THE   27   27   26   26 $246
Highland Dr.; 920-457-8000; fax 920-457-0299; 800-344-2838;
www.americanclub.com; 236 rooms (21 suites)
■ "Rural sophistication" that's "ritzy but practical" keeps this
complete resort "always special" for regulars, who return
for rooms that almost "pale in comparison" to their "deluxe
bathrooms" (this is, after all, the "toilet-manufacturing capital of
the world"); "golf by day and hot tub at night", a staff that "does it
all well" and "fantastic food" add to the "all-out fun"; for more,
see Spa section.

Lake Geneva

Grand Geneva Resort & Spa   24   23   22   23 $190
7036 Grand Geneva Way; 262-248-8811; fax 262-249-4763;
800-558-3417; www.grandgeneva.com; 355 rooms (32 suites)
☑ Despite its racy past as a Playboy club, this resort between
Chicago and Milwaukee has "impressive facilities for business
meetings" and is "fun for families" who come for the "excellent
golf", "spacious grounds" (with tennis courts and swimming
pools) and spa; after renovations, most agree its "fair rooms"
(some with winter "views of the frozen lake"), "nice" service and
"average food" at three restaurants are "greatly improved", but
"not yet top-flight."

Milwaukee

Pfister Hotel, The   23   24   23   24 $178
424 E. Wisconsin Ave.; 414-273-8222; fax 414-273-5025;
800-558-8222; www.thepfisterhotel.com; 307 rooms (82 suites)
■ This "majestic" hotel has hosted travelers since 1893 with "New
York quality and gentle Wisconsin service"; from the "high tea in
the lobby" that resembles "a ballroom on the Titanic" and the
"fabulous Sunday brunch" in the Café Rouge to the "traditional"
yet "comfortable" "rooms in the old section" with their "great
bathrooms" and "cozy blankets" on a "cold winter night", most
agree this is one "old-timer" that has "maintained its charm."

Wyoming

Grand Teton National Park

Jenny Lake Lodge   24   24   25   25 $265
Hwy. 89, Moran; 307-733-4647; fax 307-543-3358; www.gtlc.com;
37 rooms (6 suites)
☑ "Don't expect to stay connected to the world" at this "luxurious"
but "rustic" "Wild West lodge", "magically placed at the foot of the
Tetons"; some say it's "the perfect getaway" for "couples", once
the initial surprise – "no TVs or phones" in suites and cabins – gives
way to fascination with creatures that roam this "stunningly
beautiful locale"; most marvel at the "high-quality food", lobby
warmed by a huge stone fireplace and "wooded isolation", but a
few growl about "arrogant service."

Jackson

AMANGANI   29 26 25 29 $455

*1535 NE Butte Rd.; 307-734-7333; fax 307-734-7332; 877-734-7333;
www.amanresorts.com; 40 suites*
■ Built on a butte overlooking Jackson Hole and Grand Teton
National Park, this "chic" small resort (the only American outpost
of the prestigious Amanresort chain) is "at one with its natural
surroundings", offering "ever-changing views" from "dramatic
windows" in the lobby and off guestroom patios; with "hip",
"noncowboy" furnishings and "understated luxury" this "paradise
on the hill" has many "hoping for more" in the U.S.; N.B. reviewers
advise "not a place for families."

RUSTY PARROT LODGE   26 27 24 24 $244

*175 N. Jackson St.; 307-733-2000; fax 307-733-5566; 800-458-2004;
www.rustyparrot.com; 31 rooms (1 suite)*
☑ "Deluxe in de snow" joke fans of this small, river-rock-and-pine
lodge three blocks from town, where a "friendly and professional
staff" "makes you feel at home"; most chirp about "cozy",
"immaculately clean" rooms (some with whirlpools or fireplaces),
"gourmet breakfasts" in the morning, "fresh cookies" at night,
and treatments at the spa, but a handful squawk "too cutesy!"

Teton Pines Resort & Country Club   24 21 21 24 $217

*3450 North Clubhouse Drive; 307-733-1005; fax 307-733-2860;
800-238-2223; www.tetonpines.com; 16 rooms (2 townhouses)*
☑ At this "gorgeous resort" that's "a little out of the way" in the
Jackson Hole valley, guests "live like a success" surrounded by "all
the amenities: double baths, excellent service" and "the mountains
that take top billing"; while most praise the guestrooms (all of
which can be turned into suites), some naysayers call the property
"very country clubby" and insist "there are much better choices"
in the area.

Spas

Arizona

Catalina

MIRAVAL, LIFE IN BALANCE
28 | 29 | 28 | 29 | VE

5000 E. Via Estancia; 520-825-4000; fax 520-818-5870; 800-825-4000; www.miravalresort.com; 106 rooms (6 suites)

■ Even hardcore Type As can't help but find a "sense of calm the minute they arrive" at this desert retreat meant to heighten the senses, increase spiritual awareness and manage stress; praise goes to an "equine experience" (participants communicate with horses), rock climbing and "biking and hiking on mountain trails" ("very rewarding"); "delicious" "fresh food" makes the newly soothed "forget this is a spa."

Phoenix/Scottsdale

ARIZONA BILTMORE
27 | 27 | 27 | 26 | E

Missouri & 24th Sts., Phoenix; 602-955-6600; fax 602-954-2548; 800-950-0086; www.arizonabiltmore.com; 730 rooms (80 suites)

◪ Derived from Native American healing rituals, "therapeutic and relaxing" treatments like "Raindrop Therapy", "Bindi Body Massage" and Ayurvedic elemental balancing are dubbed "cutting-edge" by fans and "weird" by foes, but all agree this recently renovated "architectural gem", inspired by Frank Lloyd Wright and "beautifully set" in the Phoenix Mountain foothills, has "great food", "classic accommodations" and an "outstanding staff."

BOULDERS, THE
29 | 29 | 28 | 27 | VE

34631 N. Tom Darlington Dr., Carefree; 480-488-9009; fax 480-488-4118; 800-553-1717; www.wyndham.com; 210 rooms (160 casitas, 50 villas)

■ "Try the hot-rock massage" urge guests who decompress at this consistently top-rated resort's "all-around wonderful" Sonoran Spa; adding to the wow-factor are "terrific classes", two championship golf courses, "comfy rooms", "exquisite" food, a staff that "caters to all needs" and "beautiful" desert scenery.

FOUR SEASONS AT TROON NORTH
28 | 28 | 28 | 27 | E

10600 E. Crescent Moon Dr., Scottsdale; 480-515-5700; fax 480-515-5599; 888-207-9696; www.fourseasons.com; 210 rooms (22 suites, 4 villas, 3 haciendas)

■ In keeping with the chain's stellar reputation, this top resort's new outpost for pampering has "beautiful decor and great service"; the spa area may seem "small", but it's actually 12,000 sq. ft. with 14 treatment rooms, offset by two "great" golf courses, tennis and a free year-round kids' program at this "fabulous" facility.

PHOENICIAN, THE
28 | 28 | 28 | 28 | E

6000 E. Camelback Rd., Scottsdale; 480-941-8200; fax 480-423-2452; 800-888-8234; www.thephoenician.com; 654 rooms (66 suites, 7 villas)

■ "At the base of beautiful Camelback Mountain", this acclaimed resort provides the "decadent" Centre for Well-Being to guests who aren't involved in golf, tennis, swimming or sightseeing; "you can't do better than this" say reviewers of the "relaxing meditation room", treatments, products, restaurants and technicians that "outdo any staff elsewhere."

Sedona

ENCHANTMENT RESORT | 28 | 27 | 27 | 26 | M |
525 Boynton Canyon Rd.; 520-282-2900; fax 520-282-9249;
800-826-4180; www.enchantmentresort.com; 222 rooms (115 suites)
■ Eliciting ahhs for its setting, casitas and "peaceful aura", this
"place to pamper body and soul" sits amid the red boulders of
Boynton Canyon; exercise and beauty play second fiddle to mind-
expanding pursuits like dream analysis and energy healing; hikers
head to 1,000-year-old Sinagua ruins, fitness fiends practice tai
chi and everyone has epiphanies: "have a massage in the gazebo-
like areas – you'll feel like the whole planet is yours."

Tucson

CANYON RANCH HEALTH RESORT | 26 | 29 | 27 | 29 | VE |
8600 E. Rockcliff Rd.; 520-749-9655; fax 520-749-1646;
800-742-9000; www.canyonranch.com; 175 rooms (43 suites)
☑ "I'm addicted" say fans of this "crème de la crème" property in
the "rustic" Southwest; bravos go to "supervised fitness activities"
(e.g. sunrise hiking, mountain biking, kick-boxing), "awesome food",
a staff that "does everything for you" and spirituality guidance;
cynics sniff "ridiculously expensive", but enthusiasts who return
"two or three times a year" to "lose weight", beat burnout and
stifle stress insist it's "cheaper and better than a therapist."

Loews Ventana Canyon | 26 | 26 | 25 | 25 | E |
7000 N. Resort Dr.; 520-299-2020; fax 520-299-6832; 800-234-5117;
www.loewshotels.com; 398 rooms (27 suites)
■ Golfing among the cacti is the primary pursuit at this desert
resort in the foothills of the Santa Catalinas, but sybarites also
seek out the spa treatments (facials, aromatherapy, shiatsu,
reflexology); the consensus: "I'd go back in a heartbeat."

California

Big Sur

POST RANCH INN | 29 | 28 | 28 | 27 | VE |
Hwy. 1; 831-667-2200; fax 831-667-2512; 800-527-2200;
www.postranchinn.com; 30 cottages
■ "The best massage I've ever had – it spoiled me for life" rave
recipients of the revered rubdowns that, like all treatments at this
little spa, are performed as "you overlook heaven" in your own eco-
friendly guestroom (built between redwoods on a craggy Pacific
coast cliff); dining also rates well – "the food is superb, the wine
list incomparable" – and classes in "the yoga yurt are great."

VENTANA INN | 27 | 27 | 27 | 27 | E |
Hwy. 1; 831-667-2331; fax 831-667-2419; 800-628-6500;
www.ventanainn.com; 62 rooms (30 suites, 2 private houses)
■ "Holy-moly – it's so relaxing" exclaim acolytes of Allegria, the
"supreme spa" at this "rustic yet luxurious" refuge "for deep-
pocketed sybarites"; raves go to "massages that turn you into
putty", "soaking baths", astrology and color readings and "privacy
galore" at this setting where "at night, you walk to the restaurant on
a magically lit path, through woods, along the side of a mountain."

Carmel Area

Lodge at Pebble Beach, The   27 | 27 | 26 | 26 | E
17 Mile Dr., Pebble Beach; 831-624-3811; fax 831-644-7960;
800-654-9300; www.pebblebeach.com; 185 rooms (11 suites)
■ "Tranquil and innovative", the spa at this Monterey Coast golf
resort offers "pampering" and "relaxation at its best": energy-
balancing massages, facials and revitalizing body wraps using
fragrant herbs from the surrounding forest, plus hairstyling in a full-
service salon; naturally, hoorays also go to "spectacular scenery."

Desert Hot Springs

Two Bunch Palms   21 | 25 | 22 | 27 | E
67-425 Two Bunch Palms Trail; 760-329-8791; fax 760-329-1317;
800-472-4334; www.twobunchpalms.com; 45 rooms (6 suites, 16 villas)
◪ It's "adult camp" ("no children allowed") at this "sanctuary"
outside Palm Springs for those who "love the secluded hot tub",
"great mud baths" and "water massages to die for"; while some
complain "rooms are peculiar", realists maintain "you don't go
for the rooms, you go for the treatments, which are superior."

Escondido

GOLDEN DOOR   28 | 29 | 28 | 29 | VE
777 Deer Springs Rd.; 760-744-5777; fax 760-471-2393;
800-424-0777; www.goldendoor.com; 39 rooms
■ "Splurge – you won't regret it" at this "standard-bearer" of spas,
set on 377 acres of Japanese gardens; with a "devoted" staff
member to "pampered" guest ratio of four to one, clients (including
"many celebs") undergo "vigorous" schedules of exercise,
massage, skincare and spiritual nourishment (in between they dine
on "delicious" cuisine that's low everything); rooms are spartan
but "serene", and loyalists leave with a "sense of purity."

Los Angeles

PENINSULA BEVERLY HILLS, THE   28 | 28 | 27 | 26 | E
9882 S. Santa Monica Blvd., Beverly Hills; 310-551-2888;
fax 310-975-2854; 800-462-7899; www.peninsula.com; 196 rooms
(32 suites, 16 villas)
■ "Forget reality, pamper yourself" at this "expensive" hotel spa
(also available to day guests) that offers fruit scrubs, mud masks
and post-operative skincare lymphatic massages (this is, after all,
Beverly Hills), plus a full fitness facility; it's definitely "first-class" –
and just a tweezer's toss from Rodeo Drive.

Napa

Meadowood Napa Valley   27 | 26 | 26 | 25 | E
900 Meadowood Ln., St. Helena; 707-963-3646; fax 707-963-3532;
800-458-8080; www.meadowood.com; 85 rooms (45 suites)
■ "Sip wine while they restore your body" at this "small" spa
attached to a top-rated hideaway in the hills; the health-minded
savor "rooms big enough for ballroom dancing", "excellent" food,
winery tours and skincare treatments that use the local specialty –
Chardonnay cream body wraps and grapeseed facials.

Villagio Inn & Spa
28 | 25 | 22 | 26 | M |

6481 Washington St.; 707-944-8877; fax 707-944-8855;
800-351-1133; www.villagio.com; 112 rooms (26 suites)

■ With its lap pool, fitness room and "friendly and informative staff", this "outstanding" new 3,500 sq. ft. spa is becoming almost as big a draw as the wineries and vineyards that surround it; like the bottled elixir the area is known for, a few of the "good massages" here take advantage of the native produce, in the form of grapeseed products that soothe and polish.

Palm Springs Area

La Quinta Resort & Club
25 | 26 | 25 | 26 | E |

49-499 Eisenhower Dr., La Quinta; 760-564-4111; fax 760-564-5758;
800-598-3828; www.laquintaresort.com; 851 rooms (26 suites,
193 casitas)

■ The crowning glory of this glamorous, golf-obsessed desert resort is its new spa, a "beautiful" sanctuary where the Santa Rosa Mountains provide the backdrop for an array of "open-air" face and body treatments, including the signature Celestial Shower; guests soak in private tubs and "have massages on their own patios", where they can "smell the lavender, hear the birds and just bliss out."

Marriott's Desert Springs
25 | 25 | 24 | 27 | M |

74855 Country Club Dr., Palm Desert; 760-341-2211;
fax 760-862-1631; 800-255-0848; www.desertspringsresort.com;
884 rooms (51 suites)

■ "Awesome" rave fans of this "serene" facility set apart from the large and "crowded" main hotel, where business travelers chill out between meetings and golf; "world-class" treatments include "the most relaxing facials and massages" ("I fell asleep!"), Ayurvedic rituals (to rebalance body and mind) and makeovers at the trendy Jose Eber salon.

RITZ-CARLTON RANCHO MIRAGE
27 | 28 | 27 | 26 | E |

68-900 Frank Sinatra Dr., Rancho Mirage; 760-321-8282;
fax 760-770-8178; www.ritzcarlton.com; 240 rooms (21 suites)

■ With "typical Ritz attention to detail and service", this cliffside hotel's "top-of-the-line" spa pacifies patrons with 30 treatments, from craniosacral therapy to reflexology; toss in tennis, croquet, golf and "superb" dining, and you've got "an unforgettable experience – must return soon."

San Diego Area

FOUR SEASONS AVIARA
29 | 28 | 27 | 27 | E |

7100 Four Seasons Point, Carlsbad; 760-603-6800; fax 760-603-6801;
800-332-3442; www.fourseasons.com; 331 rooms (44 suites)

■ "They've done everything right" at this "well-run" hotel spa (opened in 1997 and renovating in 2001) where "TVs at every treadmill", massages, loofah scrubs, body wraps, "soothing colors" and "lots of open space" promote "overall relaxation"; "first-rate service" and a challenging golf course also win praise, while "exquisite artwork throughout" leads guests to observe "it could pass as a gallery."

Santa Barbara

Four Seasons Biltmore   26 | 27 | 26 | 25 | E
1260 Channel Dr.; 805-969-2261; fax 805-565-8323; 800-332-3442;
www.fourseasons.com; 215 rooms (17 suites)

☑ "Luxurious" typifies reactions to the spa at this Spanish Colonial
oceanside resort offering assorted treatments using the upscale
Guinot skincare line (for facials and body treatments); champions
cheer the "homey garden cottages" and "early-California feel",
but critics say the site is "overrun with kids and senior citizens."

Sonoma

Sonoma Mission Inn   24 | 25 | 24 | 25 | E
18140 Hwy. 12, Boyes Hot Springs; 707-938-9000; fax 707-996-5358;
800-862-4945; www.sonomamissioninn.com; 230 rooms (60 suites)

■ Devotees recommend the "decadent and addictive Bathing
Ritual" – hydrotherapy treatments that offer the "splendor" of an
ancient Roman bathhouse – at this newly renovated spa above
a centuries-old mineral spring "in the midst of wine country";
boosters also praise service ("everything is a finger snap away")
for "the most hedonistic experience I could ever imagine."

Vista

Cal-a-Vie   26 | 27 | 27 | 28 | E
2249 Somerset Rd.; 760-945-2055; fax 760-630-0074; 866-772-4283;
www.cal-a-vie.com; 24 cottages

☑ "A great experience and worth it" say fans who "would live
permanently" at this retreat 40 miles north of San Diego; "great
meals and tons of treatments" are on the bill of fare, and
customers report "I lost weight" and "looked like I had a face-lift after a
week"; the less impressed deem it "worn and in need of updating."

Colorado

Beaver Creek

Hyatt Regency   26 | 26 | 25 | 25 | E
50 W. Thomas Pl.; 970-949-1234; fax 970-949-4164; 800-554-9288;
www.hyatt.com; 275 rooms (26 suites)

■ "After skiing, there's nothing better than a shiatsu massage" say
sore-muscled sportsfolk who like the Allegria Spa's "exceptional
treatments and qualified staff"; an "outdoor fireplace, great for
toasting marshmallows in winter or summer", is also on the ahh-list.

Colorado Springs

Broadmoor, The   26 | 27 | 25 | 27 | E
1 Lake Ave.; 719-634-7711; fax 719-577-5779; 800-634-7711;
www.broadmoor.com; 700 rooms (107 suites)

■ "Try the Broadmoor Falls [hydrotherapy extravaganza] for a real
treat" suggest surveyors smitten by this "super" spa located at the
foot of the Rockies, with a "picture-postcard view of Cheyenne
Mountain"; a "friendly, informative staff" performs facials and body
treatments with products derived from native Colorado plants and
herbs; the initiated marvel "everything I need in life is right here."

Edwards

Lodge & Spa at Cordillera, The   27 | 25 | 27 | 25 | E

2205 Cordillera Way; 970-926-2200; fax 970-926-2486; 800-877-3529; www.cordillera-vail.com; 56 rooms (11 suites, 10 houses)

■ "Fantastic setting – definitely go" implore admirers of this mountaintop chateau's "small" but "efficient" spa overlooking Vail Valley; upscale travelers unjangle their nerves with state-of-the-art facials, massages, body treatments and fitness equipment, plus skiing, hiking, biking, swimming, golfing and "fabulous" eating at Restaurant Picasso (one of three dining options).

Telluride

Peaks   27 | 27 | 25 | 27 | E

136 Country Club Dr.; 970-728-6800; fax 970-728-6175; 800-789-2220; www.wyndham.com; 174 rooms (34 suites)

■ "Good for families with skiers and spa-ers", this alpine resort is home to a Rocky Mountain branch of the famed California refuge, the Golden Door, where "top-notch" pampering includes beauty treatments and spiritual guidance, "the best hot-rock massages and detox baths" and soaks in the hot tub with a view of the slopes.

Vail

Sonnenalp   25 | 26 | 25 | 26 | VE

20 Vail Rd.; 970-476-5656; fax 970-476-1639; 800-654-8312; www.sonnenalp.com; 90 rooms (88 suites)

■ In the heart of Vail village, this spa is "tops" with fans who go to the European chalet–style hotel not only to ski but also to beautify, detoxify, shape up and calm down with "great massages", facials, body treatments, aromatherapy and hydrotherapy; refreshed reviewers then recommend "sinking into the world's fluffiest robes."

Florida

Amelia Island

Ritz-Carlton, The   27 | 27 | 27 | 26 | E

4750 Amelia Island Pkwy.; 904-277-1100; fax 904-277-9064; 800-241-3333; www.ritzcarlton.com; 449 rooms (45 suites)

■ "A perfect balance of sea, sand and relaxed formality" sums up the experience at this top-rated resort's Fitness Center and Day Spa on the windswept Atlantic shore; kudos go to Thalassotherapy body wraps, facials and sunset massages on the beach.

Miami

Turnberry Isle Resort & Club   27 | 26 | 26 | 25 | E

19999 W. Country Club Dr.; 305-932-6200; fax 305-933-6560; 800-327-7028; www.turnberryisle.com; 395 rooms (41 suites)

■ At this well-established golf, tennis and marina resort 10 minutes from the Atlantic, country-clubbers who used to balk at "the need to take a shuttle bus to the old gym" and spa should be delighted by a new 25,000 sq. ft. on-site facility – set to open at press time – that will have a full menu of treatments, state-of-the-art equipment and a juice bar serving fruit, veggie and nutraceutical elixirs.

Naples

RITZ-CARLTON, THE   28 | 28 | 28 | 27 | E
280 Vanderbilt Beach Rd.; 941-598-3300; fax 941-598-6690;
800-241-3333; www.ritzcarlton.com; 463 rooms (36 suites)
■ "A spa at such a glorious hotel – on such an exquisite beach – is
almost sinful" swoon souls soothed by services like deep-tissue
massage and full-body paraffin wraps; a new and improved 51,000
sq. ft. tri-level fitness and spa facility above the Gulf of Mexico –
set to open spring 2001 – should be an instant passport to Blissville.

Orlando

Disney's Grand Floridian   27 | 27 | 26 | 27 | M
4401 Floridian Way, Lake Buena Vista; 407-934-7639;
fax 407-824-3186; www.waltdisneyworld.com; 867 rooms (61 suites)
◪ "Who needs all that Mickey Mouse stuff" wonder fans of
"the best facials", "manicures and pedicures like nothing you've
experienced before" and "indulgent massages"; a "shortage of
treatment rooms" makes it "difficult to get reservations", but
"relaxation at its finest" is worth any wait.

Palm Beach

Breakers, The   25 | 25 | 25 | 24 | E
1 S. County Rd.; 561-655-6611; fax 561-653-6656; 888-273-2537;
www.thebreakers.com; 569 rooms (45 suites)
◪ Beside the "grand" landmark hotel sits its "beautiful new spa"
complex – with pools, workout facilities and lots of treatment
rooms (17) – specializing in "decadent, knee-weakening" massages
and facials using upscale Guerlain products; faultfinders say it's
"elegant" but "stuffy" (the tony clientele speaks in "hushed"
tones) and "too expensive."

FOUR SEASONS   28 | 28 | 28 | 27 | VE
2800 S. Ocean Blvd.; 561-582-2800; fax 561-355-3715; 800-432-2335;
www.fourseasons.com; 210 rooms (12 suites)
■ In a city known for opulence, this "fabulous" spa caters to
well-heeled (and already pampered) guests with a full menu of
"luxurious" body treatments, facials, massage and personal
trainers; "I felt overwhelmingly relaxed after they took care of
me" trill contented and cosseted clients.

Georgia

Sea Island

CLOISTER, THE   27 | 28 | 26 | 27 | E
100 Hudson Pl.; 912-638-3611; fax 912-638-5159; 800-732-4752;
www.seaisland.com; 286 rooms (32 suites)
■ "Fun and manners do mix" at this beachfront "real Southern
family resort" that still enforces a dress code for dinner; an
exhaustive array of recreational options (including golf, horseback
riding, tennis, sailing and boating) is supplemented by "lovely"
beauty treatments and consultations with personal trainers,
nutritionists and stress-management experts.

Hawaii

Big Island

FOUR SEASONS HUALALAI | 30 | 30 | 29 | 29 | VE |
100 Ka'upulehu Dr., Kona; 808-325-8000; fax 808-325-8100;
888-340-5662; www.fourseasons.com; 243 rooms (31 suites)
■ Guests flip over the "imaginative treatments" offered in an
"open-air spa" amid the "mind-boggling scenery" of the Kona
Coast; glowing reviews also go to "outdoor exercise and massage",
"a helpful staff" and "superb golf"; in short, the spa at this top-
rated "paradise" is "the best around."

Hilton Waikoloa Village | 26 | 27 | 26 | 27 | M |
425 Waikoloa Beach Dr., Waikoloa; 808-886-1234;
fax 808-886-2902; 800-445-8667; www.hilton.com; 1,240 rooms
(57 suites)
■ In the name of *ho'oponopono* (translation: healing), the "well-
managed" Kohala Spa at this sprawling "Disneyland-esque"
resort offers body wraps with the oil from native orchids as well
as *limu* (seaweed) and coco-mango extract, "women-only" baths
in an infused whirlpool and a variety of massages, including Lomi
Lomi (an ancient therapeutic technique to boost blood flow) and
hot *pohaku* (healing stones).

Orchid at Mauna Lani, The | 27 | 27 | 25 | 26 | E |
1 N. Kaniku Dr., Kohala Coast; 808-885-2000; fax 808-885-5778;
800-845-9905; www.orchid-maunalani.com; 538 rooms (54 suites)
■ "Superb ecstasy" awaits patrons of the spa at this "fairy-tale
resort", "magically nestled" beside volcano and beach; to promote
physical and spiritual fitness, offerings include tai chi and yoga
under palm trees, speed-walks through lava flows and open-air
massages at the high-tide mark in the sand.

Kauai

HYATT REGENCY | 28 | 28 | 27 | 29 | E |
1571 Poipu Rd., Koloa; 808-742-1234; fax 808-742-1557;
800-554-9288; www.hyatt.com; 602 rooms (37 suites)
■ "So amazing it's off the charts" gasp those who sample the lava
rock shower, Ti Leaf Cool Wrap (for sunburn) and red colloidal
clay body mask (revs up circulation) at this plantation-style resort's
ANARA Spa; dubbed "tops in paradise", it offers an impressive
menu of cleansing, relaxing and revitalizing treatments beneath
"clear blue skies", as "singing birds" provide background music.

Princeville | 27 | 27 | 26 | 26 | E |
5520 Ka Haku Rd., Princeville; 808-826-9644; fax 808-826-1166;
800-826-4400; www.princeville.com; 252 rooms (51 suites)
■ "The absolute best spa in the world – no kidding" insist
reviewers who've undergone the "beachside massages", facials,
body wraps and personal fitness training at this "resort with
wonderful perks" like "daily 10-minute rain showers" followed by
"enchanting rainbows at no extra charge", plus robes, slippers,
flowers and "Aveda bath products."

Lanai

MANELE BAY HOTEL   28 | 27 | 27 | 26 | E

1 Manele Bay Rd., Lanai; 808-565-7700; fax 808-565-2483;
800-321-4666; www.lanai-resorts.com; 250 rooms (27 suites)
■ Surrounded by multi-level Asian-style gardens, this "dream getaway" overlooking the ocean is "great if you want to rub elbows with celebrities" while indulging in a wide range of body treatments and massages offered alfresco – "watch the dolphins" while being kneaded; N.B. guests at sister resort Lodge at Koele are invited to share the spa facilities, which are currently being expanded.

Maui

FOUR SEASONS WAILEA   29 | 29 | 29 | 28 | E

3900 Wailea Alanui, Wailea; 808-874-8000; fax 808-874-6449;
800-334-6284; www.fourseasons.com; 380 rooms (75 suites)
■ For "pampering to the max", "try the massage by the beach" say those who find serenity at the "elegant" resort's "small" but "superb" Health Centre spa; "every detail" is designed to "make you feel comfortable and beautiful" – from "free water bottles in the gym" to "first-class" mud treatments and "doting" personal trainers.

Ritz-Carlton Kapalua   28 | 27 | 27 | 25 | E

1 Ritz-Carlton Dr., Kapalua; 808-669-6200; fax 808-669-1566;
800-241-3333; www.ritzcarlton.com; 548 rooms (58 suites)
■ "Morning rain" on the northern part of the island is "great for surfers" and early-risers who like to work out or have facials, beauty treatments and massages – Swedish, Lomi Lomi, shiatsu – without missing a moment of precious sunshine time; surveyors find the Fitness Center and Spa, like the resort itself, "world-class."

Oahu

JW MARRIOTT IHILANI   28 | 27 | 26 | 27 | E

92-100 Olani St., Kapolei; 808-679-0079; fax 808-679-0080;
800-626-4446; www.ihilani.com; 387 rooms (36 suites)
■ On a "secluded part of Oahu", "far from touristy Waikiki", the "wonderful" staff at Ihilani Spa leads visitors on a daily fitness walk around four lagoons and promotes an all-over glow with assorted facials and body treatments using herbs, salt, seaweed and island gardenia and hibiscus; all in all, "a great escape" marvel guests.

Massachusetts

Lenox

CANYON RANCH
IN THE BERKSHIRES   25 | 28 | 26 | 28 | VE

165 Kemble St.; 413-637-4400; fax 413-637-0057; 800-742-9000;
www.canyonranch.com; 126 rooms
■ Four-season "pampering" and "purification" are on the agenda at this estate-like mecca in a Berkshire setting; "the most amazing experience I've ever had – athletic, spiritual, relaxing – with surprisingly good food" chant supporters (though "you're dying for butter by the time you leave"); the "caring staff" pushes a primarily "yuppie" crowd to work out, so this is not for "couch potatoes."

Nevada

Las Vegas

BELLAGIO   29 | 26 | 28 | 26 | M
3600 Las Vegas Blvd. S.; 702-693-7444; fax 702-693-8546;
888-987-7111; www.bellagioresort.com; 3,005 rooms (388 suites,
9 villas)
■ "Taste in Vegas – miracles never cease" remark reviewers of
the "beautiful spa area" at this upscale, amenity-driven hotel;
raves go to herbal wraps, "rejuvenating treatments", "invigorating
sauna", "great products" and "friendly attendants"; the gym may
be "small" but "has all the necessities"; P.S. cognoscenti suggest
checking out the "high-rollers room" – a spa within a spa for VIPs.

Venetian, The   28 | 26 | 26 | 27 | M
3355 Las Vegas Blvd. S.; 702-414-1000; fax 702-414-4805;
888-283-6423; www.venetian.com; 3,036 suites
☑ Canyon Ranch and Vegas seem like unlikely bedfellows, but
enthusiasts say this "mega-property" (aka "Venice by the Strip")
pulls it off with a "spacious gym", climbing wall, step aerobics
classes, "large variety of pampering treatments" and "excellent
menu in the spa's Canyon Ranch Cafe"; naysayers groan about
crowds ("you have to wait in line to use the relaxation room; I felt
like I was in a herd of cows – moo").

New Jersey

Short Hills

Hilton at Short Hills   25 | 26 | 26 | 25 | M
41 JFK Pkwy.; 973-379-0100; fax 973-379-6870; 800-774-1500;
www.hilton.com; 304 rooms (37 suites)
■ "This mini-oasis close to NYC" offers hotel guests and outsiders
a potpourri of massages (including shiatsu and reflexology) as well
as body treatments, lap pool, exercise equipment, "poolside spa
cuisine" and "the very best motivator of all – the Short Hills Mall
across the street" (shuttle buses available).

New Mexico

Santa Fe

Ten Thousand Waves   24 | 26 | 21 | 27 | M
3451 Hyde Park Rd.; 505-982-9304; fax 505-989-5077;
www.tenthousandwaves.com; 8 suites
☑ "Like entering another world", these Japanese hot springs
make for a "Zen retreat" "right there in ole New Mexico"; while a
few complain the collection of "sparse" buildings and outdoor
hot tubs is "slipping and too crowded", those who say the
day-spa treatments (the operation's mainstay) are "a must if
in the area" recommend "the watsu [aquatic massage] and
hot-stone treatment."

New York

New York City

FOUR SEASONS | 29 | 28 | 28 | 27 | E |
57 E. 57th St.; 212-350-6420; fax 212-893-6818; 800-819-5053;
www.fourseasons.com; 370 rooms (60 suites)
■ Manhattan's "best-kept secret" may be this 5,000 sq. ft. spa
and fitness center located three floors beneath this "gorgeous"
I.M. Pei–designed hotel's lobby; open to guests only, it's the
place for "creative" and "consistently amazing massages", a
"clean and comfortable gym" and "incredibly relaxing treatments."

Pennsylvania

Farmington

Nemacolin Woodlands Resort | 28 | 26 | 25 | 27 | E |
1001 La Fayette Dr.; 724-329-8555; fax 724-329-6947; 800-422-2736;
www.nemacolin.com; 275 rooms (25 suites, 54 townhouses, 2 homes)
■ At this "too-good-to-be-true" chateau-style resort in the "rural"
Laurel Highlands Mountains, the newly renovated spa features a
"great variety" of cutting-edge services, including hydrotherapy,
reflexology, meditation and counseling for weight loss, nutrition
and stress; "play Mystic Rock" implore golfers, referring to the
hotel's challenging Pete Dye–designed golf course.

Puerto Rico

San Juan

Ritz-Carlton, The | 26 | 25 | 26 | 26 | M |
6961 Ave. of the Governors; 787-253-1700; fax 787-253-1777;
800-241-3333; www.ritzcarlton.com; 419 rooms (12 suites)
■ The "best place for pampering in the area", this "subdued" spa
with a "great staff" gets pulses racing with aerobics, hiking,
waterskiing and windsurfing (not to mention Latin dance classes),
then calms things down a notch or two with aromatherapy, herbal
wraps and mud masks.

Texas

Arlington

Greenhouse, The | 28 | 28 | 27 | 28 | VE |
817-640-4000; fax 817-649-0422; 800-473-3646;
www.thegreenhousespa.com; 36 suites
■ "Like a sorority for well-pampered women of a certain age",
this "small, relaxing" Dallas/Ft. Worth–area spa hosts "a very
motivating fitness staff and large number of exercise classes";
though a few veterans sniff "1999 was not good, as they were
remodeling", recent visitors deem the "redo a success."

Dallas/Ft. Worth

Four Seasons at Las Colinas   28 | 27 | 26 | 25 | E

4150 N. MacArthur Blvd., Irving; 972-717-0700; fax 972-717-2550; 800-332-3442; www.fourseasons.com; 357 rooms (12 suites)

■ Like "some of Dallas' star athletes", you "can get a very good sports massage" at this "tremendous" sports club, spa and salon only 15 minutes from Downtown; also noteworthy are indoor and outdoor jogging tracks, four pools, eight outdoor and four indoor (air-conditioned) tennis courts, facials, body treatments and two PGA golf courses.

Utah

St. George

Green Valley   24 | 24 | 22 | 25 | VE

1871 W. Canyon View Dr.; 435-628-8060; fax 435-673-4084; 800-237-1068; www.greenvalleyspa.com; 35 rooms

■ "You don't know what relaxation is until you go" to this retreat amid "St. George's spectacular scenery" that furnishes "great canyon hikes"; after the "best spa treatments in my experience" (there are more than 60 to choose from), "beautiful people" gather at mealtime around "community tables" to down the "healthy yet tasty" food; N.B. suite accommodations will be available early next year.

Vermont

Ludlow

Green Mountain at Fox Run   23 | 26 | 24 | 22 | E

Fox Ln.; 802-228-8886; fax 802-228-8887; 800-448-8106; www.fitwoman.com; 26 rooms

☑ "I do not recommend this place unless you are in real trouble" say veterans of this decades-old, women-only weight-loss retreat; in its namesake Vermont mountain range (which provides "great hiking" nearby), the program, designed to adjust guests' attitudes toward food and exercise, "is excellent" ("it changed my life"), but some "don't like the style."

Virginia

Hot Springs

Homestead, The   26 | 27 | 26 | 26 | E

US Rte. 220 N.; 540-839-1766; fax 540-839-7656; 800-838-1766; www.thehomestead.com; 510 rooms (87 suites)

■ The clientele ("old money everywhere") comes for "innovative" treatments at this historic, recently renovated mountaintop resort known for its hot springs; traditional hydrotherapy treatments – soaking in a marble tub of mineral-rich thermal water, getting hosed off with a Scotch spray – are joined by newer-fangled body wraps and facials, while "Georgian elegance" reigns supreme.

West Virginia

White Sulphur Springs

GREENBRIER, THE   27 | 27 | 27 | 27 | E

300 W. Main St.; 304-536-1110; fax 304-536-7854; 800-624-6070;
www.greenbrier.com; 637 rooms (32 suites, 67 cottages, 4 houses)
■ Surveyors fondly remember the therapeutic sprays of powerful
jets of hot, then cold water (known as a Swiss Shower) at this
legendary "Shangri-la for Southern belles" in the Allegheny
Mountains; aside from the "old-world" comforts of the sulfur
water baths, spa-goers partake of seaweed body wraps, facials
and aromatherapy, among other services; as for the atmosphere,
this "century-old place" is "stiff, but good – no, make that great."

Wisconsin

Kohler

American Club, The   27 | 27 | 26 | 26 | M

Highland Dr.; 920-457-8000; fax 920-451-2118; 800-344-2838;
www.americanclub.com; 236 rooms (21 suites)
■ It's no coincidence – this "great Midwest getaway", with
"fabulous bathrooms" and "remarkably good" hydrotherapy
treatments, shares its hometown, Kohler, with the headquarters
for the plumbing manufacturer of the same name; country-inn
charm is paired with "terrific food" and pampering at the Kohler
Waters Spa, while River Wildlife, a 500-acre preserve, is where
outdoorsy types go to commune with nature.

Hotel & Resort Indexes*

All-Inclusive Price

ARIZONA
Tucson
Tanque Verde Guest Ranch
Wickenburg
Merv Griffin's Wickenburg
CALIFORNIA
Albion
Albion River Inn
Carmel Area
John Gardiner's Ranch
Solvang
Alisal Guest Ranch
GEORGIA
Little St. Simons Island
Lodge on Little St. Simons
HAWAII
Big Island
Kona Village
NEW YORK
North Hudson
Elk Lake Lodge
Saranac Lake
Point
NORTH CAROLINA
Pinehurst
Pinehurst Resort
PENNSYLVANIA
Skytop
Skytop Lodge
SOUTH CAROLINA
Hilton Head
Daufuskie Island Club
TEXAS
Austin
Lake Austin Spa Resort
VERMONT
Barnard
Twin Farms
Essex
Inn at Essex

Beach Settings
(ocean or lake)

ALABAMA
Point Clear
Marriott's Grand
CALIFORNIA
Carmel Area
Highlands Inn
Lodge at Pebble Beach
Dana Point
Ritz-Carlton Laguna Niguel

Gualala
St. Orres
Laguna Beach
Surf & Sand
Los Angeles
Casa Del Mar
Le Merigot Santa Monica
Loews Santa Monica
Malibu Beach Inn
Shutters on the Beach
Monterey
Monterey Plaza Hotel
Spindrift Inn
San Diego Area
del Coronado
Santa Barbara
Four Seasons Biltmore
FLORIDA
Amelia Island
Amelia Island Plantation
Ritz-Carlton
Boca Raton
Boca Raton Resort
Captiva Island
South Seas Resort
Fort Lauderdale
Lago Mar
Marriott's Harbor Beach
Keys
Cheeca Lodge
Hawk's Cay Resort
Hyatt Key West
Ocean Reef Club
Pier House
Sheraton Suites Key West
Wyndham Casa Marina
Marco Island
Hilton Beach Resort
Marriott
Miami
Beach Hse. Bal Harbour
Delano
Fisher Island Club
Hotel
Loews Miami Beach
Nash
Raleigh
Sonesta Key Biscayne
Tides
Turnberry Isle Resort
Naples
Registry
Ritz-Carlton

Hotel & Resort Indexes

Palm Beach
Breakers
Ritz-Carlton
Ponte Vedra
Lodge & Club
Ponte Vedra Inn & Club
Sanibel Island
Casa Ybel
Sanibel Harbor Resort
Sarasota
Resort/Longboat Key Club
Tampa/St. Petersburg
Colony Beach
Don CeSar
Vero Beach
Disney's Vero Beach
GEORGIA
Jekyll Island
Jekyll Island Club
Sea Island
Cloister
HAWAII
Big Island
Hilton Waikoloa Village
Orchid at Mauna Lani
Westin Hapuna Beach
Westin Mauna Kea Beach
Kauai
Hanalei Bay Resort
Princeville
Lanai
Manele Bay
Maui
Embassy Suites Kaanapali
Four Seasons Wailea
Grand Wailea
Hyatt Regency
Kapalua Bay Hotel
Kapalua Villas
Kea Lani Resort
Renaissance Wailea
Ritz-Carlton Kapalua
Sheraton
Westin
Westin Maui Prince
Oahu
Halekulani
Hilton Hawaiian Village
JW Marriott Ihilani
Kahala Mandarin Oriental
Royal Hawaiian
Sheraton Moana Surfrider

IDAHO
Coeur d'Alene
Coeur d'Alene
MAINE
Cape Elizabeth
Inn by the Sea
Kennebunkport
Colony
White Barn Inn
Prouts Neck
Black Point Inn
MARYLAND
Oxford
Robert Morris Inn
MASSACHUSETTS
Brewster
Ocean Edge Resort
Chatham
Chatham Bars Inn
Wequassett Inn
Nantucket
Wauwinet
MICHIGAN
Mackinac Island
Grand
MISSISSIPPI
Biloxi
Beau Rivage Resort
NEVADA
Las Vegas
Hyatt Reg. Lake Resort
NEW JERSEY
Absecon
Marriott's Seaview
Atlantic City
Caesars
Trump Taj Mahal
NEW YORK
Cooperstown
Otesaga
Lake Placid
Mirror Lake Inn
Saranac Lake
Point
NORTH CAROLINA
Duck
Sanderling Inn
OREGON
Gleneden Beach
Westin Salishan Lodge
Gold Beach
Tu Tu'Tun Lodge

PUERTO RICO
Dorado
Hyatt Dorado Beach
Hyatt Regency Cerromar
Fajardo
Las Casitas
Wyndham El Conquistador
Rincon
Horned Dorset Primavera
Rio Grande
Westin Rio Mar
San Juan
Caribe Hilton
Wyndham El San Juan
Wyndham Old San Juan
Vieques
Martineau Bay
SOUTH CAROLINA
Hilton Head
Disney's Hilton Head
Hilton Oceanfront Resort
Hyatt Regency
Palmetto Dunes
Westin
Isle of Palms
Wild Dunes
U.S. VIRGIN ISLANDS
St. Croix
Carambola
St. Thomas
Marriott's French/Morn.
Ritz-Carlton
Wyndham Sugar Bay
VERMONT
Vergennes
Basin Harbor Club
WASHINGTON
Blaine
Resort Semiahmoo
Whidbey Island
Inn at Langley

Beautiful Grounds

ALABAMA
Point Clear
Marriott's Grand
ALASKA
Girdwood
Westin Alyeska
ARIZONA
Phoenix/Scottsdale
Arizona Biltmore
Hyatt Reg. Gainey Rch.
Phoenician

Renaissance
Royal Palms
Tucson
Arizona Inn
Westward Look
CALIFORNIA
Big Sur
Post Ranch Inn
Carmel Area
Carmel Valley Ranch
Inn at Spanish Bay
Lodge at Pebble Beach
Los Angeles
Bel-Air
Ritz-Carlton Huntington
Mendocino
Stanford Inn by the Sea
Monterey
Pacific
Napa
Auberge du Soleil
Meadowood
Silverado
Villagio Inn
Ojai
Ojai Valley Inn
Palm Springs Area
Marriott's Rch. Las Palmas
Merv Griffin's Resort
Renaissance Esmeralda
Westin Mission Hills
San Diego Area
Inn at Rancho Santa Fe
Marriott's Coronado Island
Rancho Bernardo Inn
Rancho Valencia
Santa Barbara
Bacara
Four Seasons Biltmore
Santa Rosa
Vintners Inn
Sonoma
Kenwood Inn
Madrona Manor
COLORADO
Colorado Springs
Broadmoor
CONNECTICUT
Norwich
Norwich Inn
Washington
Mayflower Inn

Hotel & Resort Indexes

Business Oriented

ARIZONA

Phoenix/Scottsdale
Hyatt Reg. Gainey Rch.
Ritz-Carlton

Tucson
Omni Tucson Nat'l Golf

CALIFORNIA

Carmel Area
Quail Lodge

Los Angeles
Biltmore
Century Plaza
Hyatt Regency
L'Ermitage
Loews Santa Monica
New Otani
Omni Hotel
Park Hyatt
Peninsula Bev. Hills
Regent Bev. Wilshire
Sofitel
St. Regis
Wyndham Checkers

Menlo Park
Stanford Park Hotel

Napa
Meadowood

Newport Beach
Four Seasons
Sutton Place

Palo Alto
Garden Court

San Diego Area
Hilton La Jolla Torrey Pines
Hyatt Regency
San Diego Marriott
Westgate

San Francisco
Argent
Fairmont
Hyatt Regency
Nikko
Pan Pacific
Park Hyatt

San Jose
Fairmont Hotel

COLORADO

Denver
Inverness Hotel
Westin Tabor Center

CONNECTICUT

Greenwich
Hyatt Regency

DELAWARE

Wilmington
Du Pont

DISTRICT OF COLUMBIA

Washington
Hay-Adams
Jefferson
JW Marriott Penn. Ave
Madison
Monarch
Ritz-Carlton
St. Regis
Swissôtel

FLORIDA

Miami
Hyatt Regency Coral Gables
Loews Miami Beach

Orlando
Marriott's Orlando World
Peabody
Walt Disney World Dolphin
Walt Disney World Swan

Tampa/St. Petersburg
Hyatt Regency Westshore
Saddlebrook

GEORGIA

Atlanta
Grand Hyatt
JW Marriott Lenox
Ritz-Carlton
Swissôtel

HAWAII

Oahu
Westin Hawaii Prince

ILLINOIS

Chicago
Renaissance
Ritz-Carlton
Swissôtel

LOUISIANA

New Orleans
Le Meridien
Omni Royal Orleans
Ritz-Carlton
Royal Sonesta
Wyndham at Canal Place

MARYLAND

Baltimore
Renaissance Harborpl.

Casinos

CONNECTICUT
Ledyard
Foxwoods
LOUISIANA
New Orleans
Wyndham at Canal Place
MISSISSIPPI
Biloxi
Beau Rivage Resort
NEVADA
Lake Tahoe
Hyatt Regency
Las Vegas
Bellagio
Caesars Palace
Hard Rock
Hyatt Reg. Lake Resort
Luxor
Mandalay Bay
MGM Grand
Mirage
Paris, Las Vegas
Regent
Rio Suite
NEW JERSEY
Atlantic City
Caesars
Harrah's
Trump Taj Mahal
PUERTO RICO
Dorado
Hyatt Regency Cerromar
Fajardo
Wyndham El Conquistador
Rio Grande
Westin Rio Mar
San Juan
Ritz-Carlton
Wyndham El San Juan
Wyndham Old San Juan

Child/Family Friendly

ARIZONA
Phoenix/Scottsdale
Fairmont Scottsdale Prin.
Hyatt Reg. Gainey Rch.
Pointe Hilton Tapatio Cliffs
Renaissance
Tucson
Loews Ventana Canyon
Sheraton El Conquistador

Tanque Verde Guest Ranch
Westin La Paloma
Wickenburg
Merv Griffin's Wickenburg
CALIFORNIA
Los Angeles
Hollywood Roosevelt
Ojai
Ojai Valley Inn
Palm Springs Area
Marriott's Desert Springs
Marriott's Rch. Las Palmas
Renaissance Esmeralda
San Diego Area
Four Seasons Aviara
San Luis Obispo
Apple Farm
Santa Barbara
Four Seasons Biltmore
Solvang
Alisal Guest Ranch
COLORADO
Beaver Creek
Beaver Creek Lodge
Charter at Beaver Creek
Durango
Sheraton Tamarron
Keystone
Keystone Lodge
Vail
Vail Cascade
DISTRICT OF COLUMBIA
Washington
JW Marriott Penn. Ave
FLORIDA
Amelia Island
Amelia Island Plantation
Boca Raton
Boca Raton Resort
Captiva Island
South Seas Resort
Fort Lauderdale
Lago Mar
Marriott's Harbor Beach
Keys
Cheeca Lodge
Hawk's Cay Resort
Sheraton Suites Key West
Wyndham Casa Marina
Marco Island
Marriott

Miami
Doral
Sonesta Key Biscayne
Naples
Registry
Orlando
Disney Institute
Disney's Beach Club
Disney's Boardwalk
Disney's Polynesian
Disney's Wilderness Lodge
Disney's Yacht Club
Loews Portofino Bay
Marriott's Orlando World
Walt Disney World Dolphin
Walt Disney World Swan
Palm Beach
Four Seasons
Sanibel Island
Casa Ybel
Sarasota
Resort/Longboat Key Club
Vero Beach
Disney's Vero Beach
GEORGIA
Pine Mountain
Callaway Gardens
Sea Island
Cloister
HAWAII
Big Island
Hilton Waikoloa Village
Kauai
Hyatt Regency
Maui
Embassy Suites Kaanapali
Four Seasons Wailea
Grand Wailea
Hyatt Regency
Renaissance Wailea
Oahu
Hilton Hawaiian Village
IDAHO
Coeur d'Alene
Coeur d'Alene
Sun Valley
Sun Valley
MAINE
Prouts Neck
Black Point Inn
MASSACHUSETTS
Brewster
Ocean Edge Resort

Martha's Vineyard
Harbor View Hotel
MINNESOTA
Minneapolis/St. Paul
Hyatt Whitney
NEVADA
Las Vegas
Mandalay Bay
MGM Grand
Paris, Las Vegas
NEW HAMPSHIRE
Dixville Notch
Balsams Grand
NEW JERSEY
Cape May
Inn of Cape May
NEW MEXICO
Santa Fe
Bishop's Lodge
NEW YORK
Bolton Landing
Sagamore
Lake Placid
Mirror Lake Inn
New Paltz
Mohonk Mtn. House
NORTH CAROLINA
Duck
Sanderling Inn
OREGON
Mount Bachelor
Sunriver
PENNSYLVANIA
Bradford
Glendorn
Farmington
Nemacolin Woodlands
Hershey
Hershey
PUERTO RICO
Dorado
Hyatt Regency Cerromar
Fajardo
Las Casitas
Rio Grande
Westin Rio Mar
SOUTH CAROLINA
Hilton Head
Daufuskie Island Club
Disney's Hilton Head
Hilton Oceanfront Resort
Hyatt Regency
Palmetto Dunes

Sea Pines
Westin
Isle of Palms
Wild Dunes
TEXAS
San Antonio
Hyatt Reg. Hill Country
Westin La Cantera
U.S. VIRGIN ISLANDS
St. Croix
Buccaneer
VERMONT
Stowe
Topnotch at Stowe
Vergennes
Basin Harbor Club
VIRGINIA
Irvington
Tides Inn
Williamsburg
Kingsmill

Children Not Recommended
(call to confirm policies)
CALIFORNIA
Big Sur
Post Ranch Inn
Ventana Inn
Carmel Area
Bernardus Lodge
Napa
Auberge du Soleil
Sonoma
Kenwood Inn
FLORIDA
Keys
Little Palm Island
GEORGIA
Savannah
Ballastone Inn
HAWAII
Maui
Plantation Inn
LOUISIANA
New Orleans
Maison de Ville
Soniat House
MARYLAND
Oxford
Robert Morris Inn
MASSACHUSETTS
Lenox
Blantyre
Weathleigh

Martha's Vineyard
Charlotte Inn
NEW JERSEY
Short Hills
Hilton at Short Hills
NEW YORK
New York City
Inn at Irving Place
PENNSYLVANIA
Erwinna
Evermay on-the-Delaware
PUERTO RICO
Rincon
Horned Dorset Primavera
WASHINGTON
Whidbey Island
Inn at Langley
WISCONSIN
Chetek
Canoe Bay

Condos, Cottages & Villas
ARIZONA
Phoenix/Scottsdale
Boulders
Four Seasons/Troon North
Hermosa Inn
Hyatt Reg. Gainey Rch.
Phoenician
Sedona
L'Auberge de Sedona
Tucson
Arizona Inn
Hacienda del Sol
Tanque Verde Guest Ranch
CALIFORNIA
Big Sur
Post Ranch Inn
Ventana Inn
Carmel Area
La Playa
Seven Gables Inn
Stonepine
Tickle Pink
Gualala
St. Orres
Los Angeles
Chateau Marmont
Fairmont Hotel
Hollywood Roosevelt
Peninsula Bev. Hills
Sunset Marquis

Napa
Auberge du Soleil
Oakhurst
Chateau du Sureau
Palm Springs Area
Hyatt Grand Champions
La Quinta Resort & Club
Miramonte
San Diego Area
del Coronado
Inn at Rancho Santa Fe
La Casa Del Zorro
Santa Barbara
Upham
Sausalito
Casa Madrona
Yosemite
Ahwahnee
COLORADO
Aspen
L'Auberge
Edwards
Lodge & Spa at Cordillera
CONNECTICUT
Norwich
Norwich Inn
FLORIDA
Captiva Island
South Seas Resort
Keys
Hawk's Cay Resort
Hilton Key West
Little Palm Island
Ocean Reef Club
Miami
Fisher Island Club
Sonesta Key Biscayne
Orlando
Disney Institute
Disney's Boardwalk
Sanibel Island
Sanibel Harbor Resort
Vero Beach
Disney's Vero Beach
GEORGIA
Jekyll Island
Jekyll Island Club
HAWAII
Big Island
Kona Village
Mauna Lani Bay Hotel
Westin Mauna Kea Beach
Maui
Hana-Maui

Kapalua Bay Hotel
Kapalua Villas
Kea Lani Resort
Molokai
Molokai Ranch Lodge
IDAHO
Sun Valley
Sun Valley
KENTUCKY
Harrodsburg
Inn at Shaker Village
LOUISIANA
New Orleans
Maison de Ville
MAINE
Deer Isle
Pilgrims Inn
Rockport
Samoset
MASSACHUSETTS
Brewster
Ocean Edge Resort
Lenox
Blantyre
Martha's Vineyard
Harbor View Hotel
Nantucket
Wauwinet
White Elephant Inn
NEVADA
Lake Tahoe
Hyatt Regency
Las Vegas
Bellagio
Hyatt Reg. Lake Resort
NEW HAMPSHIRE
Bretton Woods
Mount Washington Resort
NEW YORK
Lake Placid
Lake Placid Lodge
North Hudson
Elk Lake Lodge
NORTH CAROLINA
Asheville
Richmond Hill Inn
OREGON
Black Butte
Black Butte Ranch
Gold Beach
Tu Tu'Tun Lodge
Mount Bachelor
Sunriver

PENNSYLVANIA
Bradford
Glendorn
Farmington
Nemacolin Woodlands
Hershey
Hershey
PUERTO RICO
Dorado
Hyatt Dorado Beach
Fajardo
Las Casitas
Rio Grande
Westin Rio Mar
RHODE ISLAND
Newport
Castle Hill Inn
SOUTH CAROLINA
Hilton Head
Daufuskie Island Club
Disney's Hilton Head
Palmetto Dunes
Sea Pines
Westin
Isle of Palms
Wild Dunes
Kiawah Island
Kiawah Island Resort
TENNESSEE
Walland
Blackberry Farm
TEXAS
San Antonio
Westin La Cantera
U.S. VIRGIN ISLANDS
St. John
Caneel Bay
Westin
UTAH
Deer Valley
Deer Valley Lodging
Sundance
Sundance
VERMONT
Barnard
Twin Farms
Grafton
Old Tavern at Grafton
Shelburne
Inn at Shelburne Farms
Stowe
Topnotch at Stowe
Vergennes
Basin Harbor Club

WASHINGTON
Whidbey Island
Inn at Langley
WEST VIRGINIA
White Sulphur Springs
Greenbrier
WISCONSIN
Chetek
Canoe Bay
WYOMING
Jackson
Teton Pines Resort

Dining Excellence

ARIZONA
Phoenix/Scottsdale
Boulders
Fairmont Scottsdale Prin.
Hermosa Inn
Phoenician
Royal Palms
Sedona
L'Auberge de Sedona
Tucson
Loews Ventana Canyon
Westin La Paloma
CALIFORNIA
Albion
Albion River Inn
Big Sur
Post Ranch Inn
Carmel Area
Inn at Spanish Bay
Lodge at Pebble Beach
Dana Point
Ritz-Carlton Laguna Niguel
Los Angeles
Bel-Air
Four Seasons Bev. Hills
L'Ermitage
Peninsula Bev. Hills
Regent Bev. Wilshire
Shutters on the Beach
Wyndham Bel Age
Wyndham Checkers
Napa
Auberge du Soleil
Newport Beach
Four Seasons
Oakhurst
Chateau du Sureau
Palm Springs Area
Ritz-Carlton Rancho Mirage

MGM Grand
Venetian
NEW JERSEY
Bernardsville
Bernards Inn
NEW MEXICO
Santa Fe
Eldorado
Inn of the Anasazi
NEW YORK
New York City
Box Tree
Embassy Suites
Four Seasons
Le Parker Meridien
Mark
Mercer
New York Palace
Plaza Athénée
St. Regis
Trump International
Waldorf-Astoria
Westin Essex House
Rhinebeck
Beekman Arms
Saranac Lake
Point
NORTH CAROLINA
Pittsboro
Fearrington House
OREGON
Hood River
Columbia Gorge
Portland
Heathman
PENNSYLVANIA
Erwinna
Evermay on-the-Delaware
Philadelphia
Four Seasons
PUERTO RICO
Rincon
Horned Dorset Primavera
TENNESSEE
Walland
Blackberry Farm
TEXAS
Dallas/Ft. Worth
Adolphus
Mansion on Turtle Creek
Houston
Four Seasons
Omni

UTAH
Deer Valley
Deer Valley Lodging
Park City
Stein Eriksen Lodge
VERMONT
Barnard
Twin Farms
Lower Waterford
Rabbit Hill Inn
Warren
Pitcher Inn
West Dover
Inn at Sawmill Farm
VIRGINIA
Boyce
L'Auberge Provencal
Washington
Inn at Little Washington
WASHINGTON
Seattle
Four Seasons Olympic
Sorrento
Whidbey Island
Inn at Langley
WISCONSIN
Chetek
Canoe Bay

Dramatic Designs

ARIZONA
Phoenix/Scottsdale
Arizona Biltmore
Phoenician
Wyndham Buttes Resort
CALIFORNIA
Big Sur
Post Ranch Inn
Gualala
St. Orres
Palm Springs Area
Marriott's Desert Springs
San Diego Area
Hyatt Regency La Jolla
San Francisco
Argent
Hyatt Regency
Triton
Squaw Valley
Plumpjack's
Yosemite
Ahwahnee

Hotel & Resort Indexes

FLORIDA
Miami
Biltmore
Delano
Orlando
Disney's Grand Floridian
Loews Portofino Bay
Walt Disney World Dolphin
Walt Disney World Swan
GEORGIA
Atlanta
Grand Hyatt
HAWAII
Big Island
Hilton Waikoloa Village
Westin Mauna Kea Beach
Lanai
Lodge at Koele
Maui
Grand Wailea
Kea Lani Resort
Westin
ILLINOIS
Chicago
Burnham
NEVADA
Las Vegas
Bellagio
Caesars Palace
Luxor
Mandalay Bay
MGM Grand
Paris, Las Vegas
Venetian
NEW MEXICO
Santa Fe
Inn of the Anasazi
NEW YORK
New York City
Four Seasons
Hudson
Mercer
Morgans
Paramount
Royalton
SoHo Grand
TENNESSEE
Nashville
Opryland Hotel
TEXAS
Dallas/Ft. Worth
Crescent Court

VERMONT
Warren
Pitcher Inn
WASHINGTON
Seattle
Westin
WISCONSIN
Chetek
Canoe Bay
WYOMING
Jackson
Amangani

Exotic

CALIFORNIA
Los Angeles
Chateau Marmont
San Luis Obispo
Madonna Inn
FLORIDA
Boca Raton
Boca Raton Resort
Captiva Island
South Seas Resort
Fort Lauderdale
Marriott's Harbor Beach
Keys
Cheeca Lodge
Hawk's Cay Resort
Little Palm Island
Marquesa
Miami
Turnberry Isle Resort
Orlando
Disney's Polynesian
HAWAII
Big Island
Four Seasons Hualalai
Hilton Waikoloa Village
Kona Village
Orchid at Mauna Lani
Westin Hapuna Beach
Westin Mauna Kea Beach
Kauai
Hyatt Regency
Maui
Hyatt Regency
Westin
PUERTO RICO
Vieques
Martineau Bay

Fireplaces
(in-room; *wood-burning)

ARIZONA
Phoenix/Scottsdale
Boulders*
Four Seasons/Troon North
Royal Palms
Wickenburg
Merv Griffin's Wickenburg*
CALIFORNIA
Albion
Albion River Inn*
Big Sur
Post Ranch Inn*
Carmel Area
Bernardus Lodge
Carmel Valley Ranch*
Highlands Inn*
Inn at Spanish Bay
Los Angeles
Malibu Beach Inn
Mendocino
Stanford Inn by the Sea*
Monterey
Pacific
Spindrift Inn
Napa
Auberge du Soleil*
Silverado*
Villagio Inn*
Vintage Inn*
Oakhurst
Chateau du Sureau*
San Francisco
Sherman House*
White Swan Inn
San Luis Obispo
Apple Farm
Santa Barbara
San Ysidro Ranch*
Solvang
Alisal Guest Ranch*
Fess Parker's
Sonoma
Kenwood Inn*
COLORADO
Aspen
L'Auberge
Little Nell
Beaver Creek
Beaver Creek Lodge
Charter at Beaver Creek*

Vail
Sonnenalp
MASSACHUSETTS
Boston
XV Beacon
NEW MEXICO
Santa Fe
Inn of the Anasazi
NEW YORK
Lake Placid
Lake Placid Lodge*
New York City
Box Tree
Inn at Irving Place
Saranac Lake
Point*
OREGON
Gleneden Beach
Westin Salishan Lodge
Mount Bachelor
Sunriver*
RHODE ISLAND
Newport
Cliffside Inn*
UTAH
Deer Valley
Deer Valley Lodging*
VERMONT
Barnard
Twin Farms*
WASHINGTON
Snoqualmie
Salish Lodge*
Whidbey Island
Inn at Langley
WYOMING
Jackson
Amangani

Fishing

CALIFORNIA
Solvang
Alisal Guest Ranch
COLORADO
Durango
Sheraton Tamarron
Telluride
Peaks
FLORIDA
Captiva Island
South Seas Resort
Keys
Cheeca Lodge

Hawk's Cay Resort
Little Palm Island
GEORGIA
Little St. Simons Island
Lodge on Little St. Simons
ILLINOIS
Galena
Eagle Ridge Inn
MONTANA
Whitefish
Grouse Mountain Lodge
NEW HAMPSHIRE
Dixville Notch
Balsams Grand
NEW MEXICO
Santa Fe
Bishop's Lodge
NEW YORK
Lake Placid
Mirror Lake Inn
North Hudson
Elk Lake Lodge
OREGON
Gold Beach
Tu Tu'Tun Lodge
PENNSYLVANIA
Bradford
Glendorn
SOUTH CAROLINA
Charleston
Hilton Charleston Harbor
Hilton Head
Daufuskie Island Club
Isle of Palms
Wild Dunes
TENNESSEE
Walland
Blackberry Farm
VERMONT
Manchester
Equinox
Warren
Pitcher Inn
VIRGINIA
Hot Springs
Homestead

Golf

ALABAMA
Point Clear
Marriott's Grand
ARIZONA
Phoenix/Scottsdale
Arizona Biltmore

Boulders
Fairmont Scottsdale Prin.
Hyatt Reg. Gainey Rch.
Marriott's Camelback Inn
Phoenician
Pointe Hilton Tapatio Cliffs
Wigwam
Tucson
Lodge at Ventana
Loews Ventana Canyon
Omni Tucson Nat'l Golf
Westin La Paloma
CALIFORNIA
Carmel Area
Carmel Valley Ranch
Inn at Spanish Bay
Lodge at Pebble Beach
Quail Lodge
Napa
Meadowood
Silverado
Ojai
Ojai Valley Inn
Palm Springs Area
Hyatt Grand Champions
La Quinta Resort & Club
Marriott's Desert Springs
Marriott's Rch. Las Palmas
Miramonte
Renaissance Esmeralda
Westin Mission Hills
San Diego Area
Four Seasons Aviara
Hilton La Jolla Torrey Pines
La Costa
Rancho Bernardo Inn
Squaw Valley
Resort at Squaw Creek
COLORADO
Beaver Creek
Hyatt Regency
Colorado Springs
Broadmoor
Denver
Inverness Hotel
Durango
Sheraton Tamarron
Edwards
Lodge & Spa at Cordillera
Keystone
Keystone Lodge

Pinehurst
Pinehurst Resort
OREGON
Black Butte
Black Butte Ranch
Gleneden Beach
Westin Salishan Lodge
PENNSYLVANIA
Farmington
Nemacolin Woodlands
Skytop
Skytop Lodge
PUERTO RICO
Dorado
Hyatt Dorado Beach
Hyatt Regency Cerromar
Fajardo
Wyndham El Conquistador
Rio Grande
Westin Rio Mar
SOUTH CAROLINA
Hilton Head
Daufuskie Island Club
Hyatt Regency
Sea Pines
Westin
Isle of Palms
Wild Dunes
Kiawah Island
Kiawah Island Resort
TEXAS
Austin
Barton Creek Resort
Dallas/Ft. Worth
Four Seasons/Las Colinas
San Antonio
Hyatt Reg. Hill Country
Westin La Cantera
U.S. VIRGIN ISLANDS
St. Croix
Buccaneer
Carambola
VERMONT
Manchester
Equinox
Vergennes
Basin Harbor Club
Woodstock
Woodstock Inn
VIRGINIA
Charlottesville
Keswick Hall
Hot Springs
Homestead

Irvington
Tides Inn
Leesburg
Lansdowne
Williamsburg
Kingsmill
Williamsburg Inn
WASHINGTON
Blaine
Resort Semiahmoo
WEST VIRGINIA
White Sulphur Springs
Greenbrier
WISCONSIN
Kohler
American Club
Lake Geneva
Grand Geneva

Gyms/Health Clubs

ARIZONA
Phoenix/Scottsdale
Arizona Biltmore
Boulders
Fairmont Scottsdale Prin.
Four Seasons/Troon North
Marriott's Camelback Inn
Tempe Mission Palms
Tucson
Lodge at Ventana
Loews Ventana Canyon
Omni Tucson Nat'l Golf
Westward Look
CALIFORNIA
Berkeley
Claremont Resort
Big Sur
Ventana Inn
Carmel Area
Carmel Valley Ranch
Stonepine
Dana Point
Ritz-Carlton Laguna Niguel
Los Angeles
Barnabey's
Bel-Air
Biltmore
Hyatt Regency
Le Merigot Santa Monica
Mondrian
New Otani
Omni Hotel
Regent Bev. Wilshire

Ritz-Carlton Huntington
Ritz-Carlton Marina del Rey
Shutters on the Beach
W
Napa
Meadowood
Silverado
Newport Beach
Four Seasons
Palm Springs Area
La Quinta Resort & Club
Marriott's Rch. Las Palmas
Merv Griffin's Resort
Ritz-Carlton Rancho Mirage
San Diego Area
Four Seasons Aviara
Hyatt Regency La Jolla
La Costa
Rancho Bernardo Inn
Rancho Valencia
San Francisco
Fairmont
Huntington
Monaco
Nikko
Palace
Park Hyatt
Ritz-Carlton
San Jose
Fairmont Hotel
Santa Barbara
Bacara
Squaw Valley
Resort at Squaw Creek
COLORADO
Aspen
Little Nell
Beaver Creek
Charter at Beaver Creek
Hyatt Regency
Colorado Springs
Broadmoor
Denver
Inverness Hotel
Telluride
Peaks
Vail
Vail Cascade
CONNECTICUT
Greenwich
Hyatt Regency
DISTRICT OF COLUMBIA
Washington
Four Seasons

Latham Georgetown
Madison
Monarch
Park Hyatt
Ritz-Carlton
FLORIDA
Amelia Island
Amelia Island Plantation
Ritz-Carlton
Boca Raton
Boca Raton Resort
Captiva Island
South Seas Resort
Keys
Ocean Reef Club
Marco Island
Hilton Beach Resort
Miami
Biltmore
Doral
Fisher Island Club
Hyatt Regency Coral Gables
Loews Miami Beach
Turnberry Isle Resort
Orlando
Loews Portofino Bay
Marriott's Orlando World
Palm Beach
Breakers
Ritz-Carlton
Ponte Vedra
Lodge & Club
Ponte Vedra Inn & Club
Sanibel Island
Sanibel Harbor Resort
Sarasota
Resort/Longboat Key Club
Tampa/St. Petersburg
Saddlebrook
GEORGIA
Atlanta
Ritz-Carlton Buckhead
Savannah
Westin Savannah Harbor
HAWAII
Big Island
Four Seasons Hualalai
Orchid at Mauna Lani
Kauai
Hyatt Regency
Maui
Hyatt Regency
Kea Lani Resort

ILLINOIS
Chicago
Fairmont
Four Seasons
House of Blues Hotel
Renaissance
Ritz-Carlton
LOUISIANA
New Orleans
Fairmont
Omni Royal Orleans
MAINE
Rockport
Samoset
MARYLAND
Baltimore
Renaissance Harborpl.
MASSACHUSETTS
Boston
Boston Harbor Hotel
Seaport Hotel
Lenox
Cranwell Resort
MISSISSIPPI
Biloxi
Beau Rivage Resort
NEVADA
Lake Tahoe
Hyatt Regency
Las Vegas
Bellagio
Caesars Palace
Four Seasons
Hard Rock
Hyatt Reg. Lake Resort
MGM Grand
Mirage
Venetian
Stateline
Harrah's
NEW JERSEY
Atlantic City
Trump Taj Mahal
NEW YORK
Bolton Landing
Sagamore
New York City
Crowne Plaza
Embassy Suites
Four Seasons
Helmsley Park Lane
Hilton Times Square
Inter-Continental CPS
Le Parker Meridien

Millennium Broadway
Millennium Hilton
New York Palace
Omni Berkshire Place
Peninsula
Plaza
RIHGA Royal
Sheraton New York
Swissôtel
Trump International
UN Plaza Hotel
Waldorf-Astoria
Westin Essex House
W New York
NORTH CAROLINA
Asheville
Grove Park Inn
Duck
Sanderling Inn
OKLAHOMA
Oklahoma City
Waterford Marriott
OREGON
Portland
Governor
PENNSYLVANIA
Farmington
Nemacolin Woodlands
Hershey
Hershey
Philadelphia
Park Hyatt at the Bellevue
Rittenhouse
PUERTO RICO
Rio Grande
Westin Rio Mar
RHODE ISLAND
Providence
Westin
SOUTH CAROLINA
Charleston
Charleston Place
Isle of Palms
Wild Dunes
TEXAS
Austin
Barton Creek Resort
Four Seasons
Lake Austin Spa Resort
Dallas/Ft. Worth
Crescent Court
Four Seasons/Las Colinas
Omni Mandalay Hotel

Houston
Four Seasons
Houstonian Hotel
Omni
San Antonio
Westin La Cantera
VERMONT
Manchester
Equinox
Stowe
Topnotch at Stowe
Woodstock
Woodstock Inn
VIRGINIA
Hot Springs
Homestead
Williamsburg
Kingsmill
WASHINGTON
Blaine
Resort Semiahmoo
Seattle
Bellevue Club
Westin
WEST VIRGINIA
White Sulphur Springs
Greenbrier
WISCONSIN
Kohler
American Club
Lake Geneva
Grand Geneva

High-Speed Internet Access
(in-room)

ALASKA
Anchorage
Regal Alaskan
ARIZONA
Phoenix/Scottsdale
Fairmont Scottsdale Prin.
Four Seasons/Troon North
Hyatt Reg. Gainey Rch.
Marriott's Camelback Inn
Ritz-Carlton
Wyndham Buttes Resort
ARKANSAS
Little Rock
Capital Hotel
CALIFORNIA
Carmel Area
Bernardus Lodge
Carmel Valley Ranch

Dana Point
Ritz-Carlton Laguna Niguel
Lafayette
Lafayette Park
Laguna Beach
Surf & Sand
Los Angeles
Avalon
Bel-Air
Beverly Hills Hotel
Beverly Hilton
Biltmore
Century Plaza
Four Seasons Bev. Hills
Hollywood Roosevelt
Mondrian
Renaissance Bev. Hills
Sofitel
St. Regis
W
Wyndham Checkers
Monterey
Monterey Plaza Hotel
Newark
W Suites
Newport Beach
Four Seasons
Sutton Place
Palm Springs Area
Hyatt Grand Champions
La Quinta Resort & Club
Marriott's Desert Springs
Marriott's Rch. Las Palmas
Merv Griffin's Resort
Miramonte
Renaissance Esmeralda
Westin Mission Hills
Riverside
Mission Inn
San Diego Area
Hilton La Jolla Torrey Pines
La Valencia
Loews Coronado Bay
San Francisco
Archbishop's Mansion
Donatello
Huntington
Mark Hopkins Inter-Cont.
Monaco
Palomar
Pan Pacific
Park Hyatt
Renaissance Stanford Court
Ritz-Carlton

Library
Millennium Hilton
Morgans
New York Marriott Brooklyn
New York Marriott Marquis
Omni Berkshire Place
Peninsula
Regency
St. Regis
Tribeca Grand
Trump International
UN Plaza Hotel
Waldorf-Astoria
W New York - Tuscany
NORTH CAROLINA
Charlotte
Park
OHIO
Cincinnati
Cincinnatian
Cleveland
Ritz-Carlton
OREGON
Portland
Riverplace
PENNSYLVANIA
Philadelphia
Four Seasons
Rittenhouse
Pittsburgh
Westin William Penn
PUERTO RICO
San Juan
Ritz-Carlton
SOUTH CAROLINA
Hilton Head
Hilton Oceanfront Resort
Isle of Palms
Wild Dunes
TENNESSEE
Nashville
Union Station Hotel
TEXAS
Austin
Driskill
Four Seasons
Dallas/Ft. Worth
Fairmont
Mansion on Turtle Creek
Melrose, The
Houston
Four Seasons
San Antonio
Fairmount

VERMONT
Essex
Inn at Essex
VIRGINIA
Arlington
Ritz-Carlton Pentagon City
McLean
Ritz-Carlton Tyson's Corner
Richmond
Jefferson
WASHINGTON
Seattle
Bellevue Club
Monaco
W
WISCONSIN
Lake Geneva
Grand Geneva

Historic Interest

ARIZONA
Grand Canyon
El Tovar
Phoenix/Scottsdale
Arizona Biltmore
Tucson
Tanque Verde Guest Ranch
ARKANSAS
Little Rock
Capital Hotel
CALIFORNIA
Berkeley
Claremont Resort
Los Angeles
Biltmore
Hollywood Roosevelt
Shangri-La
Riverside
Mission Inn
San Diego Area
del Coronado
San Francisco
Archbishop's Mansion
Clift
Mark Hopkins Inter-Cont.
Palace
Westin St. Francis
Yosemite
Ahwahnee
COLORADO
Aspen
Jerome
Colorado Springs
Broadmoor

Denver
Brown Palace Hotel
Oxford Hotel
DELAWARE
Montchanin
Inn at Montchanin Village
Wilmington
Du Pont
DISTRICT OF COLUMBIA
Washington
Hay-Adams
Jefferson
Madison
Mayflower
Morrison-Clark Inn
Willard Inter-Continental
FLORIDA
Boca Raton
Boca Raton Resort
Keys
Gardens
Marquesa
Miami
Biltmore
Palm Beach
Breakers
Tampa/St. Petersburg
Belleview Biltmore
Don CeSar
Renaissance Vinoy
HAWAII
Oahu
Royal Hawaiian
Sheraton Moana Surfrider
ILLINOIS
Chicago
Burnham
INDIANA
Indianapolis
Canterbury
KENTUCKY
Harrodsburg
Inn at Shaker Village
Louisville
Seelbach Hilton
LOUISIANA
New Orleans
Fairmont
Maison de Ville
White Castle
Nottoway Plantation
MAINE
Kennebunkport
Colony

MASSACHUSETTS
Boston
Fairmont Copley Plaza
Nantucket
Jared Coffin House
Sandwich
Dan'l Webster Inn
MICHIGAN
Mackinac Island
Grand
MINNESOTA
Minneapolis/St. Paul
Hyatt Whitney
Saint Paul Hotel
Red Wing
St. James
MISSISSIPPI
Natchez
Monmouth Plantation
NEW HAMPSHIRE
Bretton Woods
Mount Washington Resort
Dixville Notch
Balsams Grand
NEW MEXICO
Santa Fe
Bishop's Lodge
NEW YORK
Bolton Landing
Sagamore
Cooperstown
Otesaga
New Paltz
Mohonk Mtn. House
New York City
Algonquin
New York Palace
Plaza
St. Regis
Waldorf-Astoria
Rhinebeck
Beekman Arms
NORTH CAROLINA
Asheville
Grove Park Inn
OREGON
Portland
Governor
PENNSYLVANIA
Erwinna
Evermay on-the-Delaware
Pittsburgh
Priory

PUERTO RICO
San Juan
El Convento
SOUTH CAROLINA
Charleston
John Rutledge House
TENNESSEE
Nashville
Union Station Hotel
TEXAS
Austin
Driskill
San Antonio
Fairmount
La Mansion del Rio
Menger
VERMONT
Shelburne
Inn at Shelburne Farms
VIRGINIA
Hot Springs
Homestead
Williamsburg
Williamsburg Colonial Hses.
WEST VIRGINIA
White Sulphur Springs
Greenbrier
WISCONSIN
Milwaukee
Pfister

"In" Places

CALIFORNIA
Los Angeles
Argyle
Avalon
Bel-Air
Beverly Hills Hotel
Casa Del Mar
Chateau Marmont
L'Ermitage
Mondrian
Peninsula Bev. Hills
Shutters on the Beach
Standard
Sunset Marquis
W
Napa
Auberge du Soleil
San Francisco
Campton Place
Donatello
Laurel Inn
Palomar

Prescott
W
San Luis Obispo
Madonna Inn
Squaw Valley
Plumpjack's
COLORADO
Aspen
Little Nell
Denver
Monaco
Oxford Hotel
Teatro
DISTRICT OF COLUMBIA
Washington
George
FLORIDA
Miami
Beach Hse. Bal Harbour
Delano
Hotel
Loews Miami Beach
Nash
Tides
GEORGIA
Atlanta
W
HAWAII
Oahu
W
ILLINOIS
Chicago
House of Blues Hotel
Monaco
Sutton Place
LOUISIANA
New Orleans
International House
W
W French Quarter
MASSACHUSETTS
Boston
XV Beacon
NEVADA
Las Vegas
Bellagio
Hard Rock
NEW YORK
New York City
Mansfield
Mercer
Morgans
Paramount
Royalton

SoHo Grand
W New York
W New York - Tuscany
PUERTO RICO
Fajardo
Las Casitas
TEXAS
Austin
Four Seasons
UTAH
Salt Lake City
Monaco
WASHINGTON
Seattle
Monaco
W
WYOMING
Jackson
Amangani

Island Settings

CALIFORNIA
San Diego Area
del Coronado
Marriott's Coronado Island
FLORIDA
Amelia Island
Amelia Island Plantation
Ritz-Carlton
Captiva Island
South Seas Resort
Keys
Cheeca Lodge
Gardens
Hawk's Cay Resort
Hilton Key West
Hyatt Key West
Little Palm Island
Marquesa
Ocean Reef Club
Pier House
Wyndham Casa Marina
Marco Island
Hilton Beach Resort
Marriott
Miami
Fisher Island Club
Grove Isle Club
Sarasota
Resort/Longboat Key Club
Tampa/St. Petersburg
Colony Beach

GEORGIA
Jekyll Island
Jekyll Island Club
Little St. Simons Island
Lodge on Little St. Simons
Savannah
Westin Savannah Harbor
Sea Island
Cloister
HAWAII
Big Island
Four Seasons Hualalai
Hilton Waikoloa Village
Kona Village
Mauna Lani Bay Hotel
Orchid at Mauna Lani
Westin Hapuna Beach
Westin Mauna Kea Beach
Kauai
Hanalei Bay Resort
Hyatt Regency
Princeville
Lanai
Manele Bay
Maui
Four Seasons Wailea
Grand Wailea
Hana-Maui
Hyatt Regency
Kapalua Bay Hotel
Kapalua Villas
Kea Lani Resort
Plantation Inn
Renaissance Wailea
Ritz-Carlton Kapalua
Sheraton
Westin
Molokai
Molokai Ranch Lodge
Oahu
Halekulani
JW Marriott Ihilani
Kahala Mandarin Oriental
Royal Hawaiian
Sheraton Moana Surfrider
MAINE
Bar Harbor
Bar Harbor Inn
Deer Isle
Pilgrims Inn
Northeast Harbor
Asticou Inn

MASSACHUSETTS
Martha's Vineyard
Charlotte Inn
Harbor View Hotel
Nantucket
Jared Coffin House
Wauwinet
MICHIGAN
Mackinac Island
Grand
NEW YORK
Bolton Landing
Sagamore
NORTH CAROLINA
Duck
Sanderling Inn
PUERTO RICO
Dorado
Hyatt Dorado Beach
Hyatt Regency Cerromar
Fajardo
Las Casitas
Wyndham El Conquistador
Rincon
Horned Dorset Primavera
Rio Grande
Westin Rio Mar
San Juan
Caribe Hilton
El Convento
Ritz-Carlton
Wyndham El San Juan
Wyndham Old San Juan
Vieques
Martineau Bay
RHODE ISLAND
Block Island
1661 Inn & Manisses Hotel
Newport
Francis Malbone House
Hyatt Regency
Vanderbilt Hall
SOUTH CAROLINA
Hilton Head
Daufuskie Island Club
Disney's Hilton Head
Hilton Oceanfront Resort
Hyatt Regency
Palmetto Dunes
Sea Pines
Westin
Isle of Palms
Wild Dunes

Kiawah Island
Kiawah Island Resort
U.S. VIRGIN ISLANDS
St. Croix
Buccaneer
Carambola
St. John
Caneel Bay
Westin
St. Thomas
Marriott's French/Morn.
Ritz-Carlton
Wyndham Sugar Bay

Kitchens
(in-room)
ARIZONA
Tucson
Lodge at Ventana
CALIFORNIA
Los Angeles
Oceana
Wyndham Bel Age
Napa
Silverado
Newark
W Suites
San Francisco
Donatello
COLORADO
Aspen
L'Auberge
Beaver Creek
Beaver Creek Lodge
Charter at Beaver Creek
Durango
Sheraton Tamarron
DELAWARE
Montchanin
Inn at Montchanin Village
FLORIDA
Captiva Island
South Seas Resort
Palm Beach
Brazilian Court
Sanibel Island
Casa Ybel
Tampa/St. Petersburg
Colony Beach
HAWAII
Maui
Embassy Suites Kaanapali
Kapalua Villas

MAINE
Cape Elizabeth
Inn by the Sea
NEW YORK
New York City
Benjamin
Trump International
NORTH CAROLINA
Duck
Sanderling Inn
PUERTO RICO
Fajardo
Las Casitas
SOUTH CAROLINA
Hilton Head
Hilton Oceanfront Resort
Palmetto Dunes
Sea Pines
U.S. VIRGIN ISLANDS
St. Croix
Carambola

Mountain Settings/Views

ALASKA
Denali
Mt. McKinley Princess
Girdwood
Westin Alyeska
ARIZONA
Phoenix/Scottsdale
Four Seasons/Troon North
Phoenician
Pointe Hilton Tapatio Cliffs
Sedona
Enchantment
Tucson
Loews Ventana Canyon
Sheraton El Conquistador
Westin La Paloma
CALIFORNIA
Oakhurst
Chateau du Sureau
Ojai
Ojai Valley Inn
Palm Springs Area
Hyatt Grand Champions
Marriott's Desert Springs
Marriott's Rch. Las Palmas
Miramonte
Ritz-Carlton Rancho Mirage
Santa Barbara
San Ysidro Ranch

Squaw Valley
Plumpjack's
Resort at Squaw Creek
Yosemite
Ahwahnee
COLORADO
Aspen
Jerome
L'Auberge
Little Nell
St. Regis
Beaver Creek
Beaver Creek Lodge
Charter at Beaver Creek
Hyatt Regency
Inn at Beaver Creek
Durango
Sheraton Tamarron
Edwards
Lodge & Spa at Cordillera
Keystone
Keystone Lodge
Telluride
Peaks
Vail
Lodge at Vail
Sonnenalp
Vail Cascade
HAWAII
Lanai
Lodge at Koele
Molokai
Molokai Ranch Lodge
IDAHO
Coeur d'Alene
Coeur d'Alene
Ketchum
Knob Hill Inn
Sun Valley
Sun Valley
MASSACHUSETTS
Lenox
Cranwell Resort
MONTANA
Gallatin
Gallatin Gateway Inn
NEVADA
Lake Tahoe
Hyatt Regency
Stateline
Harrah's
NEW HAMPSHIRE
Bretton Woods
Mount Washington Resort

Dixville Notch
Balsams Grand
Franconia
Franconia Inn
NEW MEXICO
Santa Fe
Bishop's Lodge
NEW YORK
Bolton Landing
Sagamore
Lake Placid
Lake Placid Lodge
Mirror Lake Inn
Mt. Tremper
Emerson Inn
New Paltz
Mohonk Mtn. House
Saranac Lake
Point
NORTH CAROLINA
Asheville
Grove Park Inn
Richmond Hill Inn
Lake Toxaway
Greystone Inn
OREGON
Black Butte
Black Butte Ranch
Mount Bachelor
Sunriver
PENNSYLVANIA
Farmington
Nemacolin Woodlands
Skytop
Skytop Lodge
TENNESSEE
Walland
Blackberry Farm
UTAH
Deer Valley
Deer Valley Lodging
Goldener Hirsch
Park City
Stein Eriksen Lodge
Snowbird
Cliff Lodge
Sundance
Sundance
VERMONT
Barnard
Twin Farms
Lower Waterford
Rabbit Hill Inn

Manchester
Equinox
Stowe
Green Mountain Inn
Topnotch at Stowe
Trapp Family Lodge
West Dover
Inn at Sawmill Farm
VIRGINIA
Hot Springs
Homestead
WASHINGTON
Blaine
Resort Semiahmoo
Snoqualmie
Salish Lodge
WEST VIRGINIA
White Sulphur Springs
Greenbrier
WYOMING
Grand Teton National Park
Jenny Lake Lodge
Jackson
Amangani
Rusty Parrot Lodge

Noteworthy Newcomers

ARIZONA
Phoenix/Scottsdale
Four Seasons/Troon North
CALIFORNIA
Los Angeles
Avalon
Maison 140
Omni Hotel
St. Regis
Newark
W Suites
San Francisco
Laurel Inn
Serrano
Santa Barbara
Bacara
COLORADO
Denver
Teatro
DISTRICT OF COLUMBIA
Washington
Ritz-Carlton
FLORIDA
Miami
Beach Hse. Bal Harbour

Mandarin Oriental
Nash
GEORGIA
Savannah
Westin Savannah Harbor
HAWAII
Oahu
W
LOUISIANA
New Orleans
Ritz-Carlton
W
MASSACHUSETTS
Boston
XV Beacon
NEVADA
Las Vegas
Hyatt Reg. Lake Resort
NEW YORK
Mt. Tremper
Emerson Inn
New York City
Embassy Suites
Hudson
Library
Regent Wall Street
Tribeca Grand
PENNSYLVANIA
Philadelphia
Ritz-Carlton
PUERTO RICO
Vieques
Martineau Bay

No TVs/Phones
(in-room)

ALASKA
Glacier Bay
Glacier Bay Lodge
ARIZONA
Tucson
Tanque Verde Guest Ranch
CALIFORNIA
Albion
Albion River Inn
Big Sur
Post Ranch Inn
Carmel Area
Seven Gables Inn
Gualala
St. Orres
Oakhurst
Chateau du Sureau

Solvang
Alisal Guest Ranch
Sonoma
Kenwood Inn
Madrona Manor
FLORIDA
Keys
Little Palm Island
GEORGIA
Little St. Simons Island
Lodge on Little St. Simons
HAWAII
Big Island
Kona Village
Molokai
Molokai Ranch Lodge
MAINE
Deer Isle
Pilgrims Inn
Kennebunkport
Colony
Northeast Harbor
Asticou Inn
MICHIGAN
Saugatuck
Wickwood
NEW HAMPSHIRE
Dixville Notch
Balsams Grand
NEW JERSEY
Cape May
Inn of Cape May
NEW YORK
Lake Placid
Lake Placid Lodge
New Paltz
Mohonk Mtn. House
North Hudson
Elk Lake Lodge
Saranac Lake
Point
OREGON
Gold Beach
Tu Tu'Tun Lodge
PUERTO RICO
Rincon
Horned Dorset Primavera
U.S. VIRGIN ISLANDS
St. John
Caneel Bay
VERMONT
Grafton
Old Tavern at Grafton

Lower Waterford
Rabbit Hill Inn
Quechee
Quechee Inn
Vergennes
Basin Harbor Club
West Dover
Inn at Sawmill Farm
VIRGINIA
Boyce
L'Auberge Provencal
Washington
Inn at Little Washington
WYOMING
Grand Teton National Park
Jenny Lake Lodge

Offbeat/Funky

CALIFORNIA
Gualala
St. Orres
Los Angeles
Avalon
Chateau Marmont
Hollywood Roosevelt
Mondrian
Standard
Mendocino
Stanford Inn by the Sea
Riverside
Mission Inn
San Francisco
Monaco
Palomar
Serrano
Triton
San Jose
de Anza
San Luis Obispo
Madonna Inn
COLORADO
Aspen
L'Auberge
Denver
Monaco
Teatro
Vail
Sonnenalp
DISTRICT OF COLUMBIA
Washington
George

FLORIDA
Keys
Cheeca Lodge
Pier House
Lake Wales
Chalet Suzanne
Miami
Delano
Hotel
Mayfair House
Raleigh
Orlando
Disney's Polynesian
Disney's Wilderness Lodge
HAWAII
Big Island
Kona Village
Lanai
Lodge at Koele
Molokai
Molokai Ranch Lodge
ILLINOIS
Chicago
House of Blues Hotel
Monaco
KENTUCKY
Harrodsburg
Inn at Shaker Village
LOUISIANA
New Orleans
Columns
International House
Le Pavillon
W
MASSACHUSETTS
Boston
XV Beacon
University Park Hotel @ MIT
MISSISSIPPI
Natchez
Monmouth Plantation
NEVADA
Las Vegas
Hard Rock
Rio Suite
NEW YORK
Mt. Tremper
Emerson Inn
New York City
Hudson
Library
Mercer
Morgans

Paramount
Royalton
PUERTO RICO
San Juan
Caribe Hilton
TENNESSEE
Nashville
Union Station Hotel
TEXAS
Austin
Driskill
San Antonio
Menger
VERMONT
Stowe
Trapp Family Lodge
Warren
Pitcher Inn
WASHINGTON
Seattle
Monaco

Pet Friendly

ARIZONA
Grand Canyon
El Tovar
Phoenix/Scottsdale
Arizona Biltmore
Boulders
Fairmont Scottsdale Prin.
Four Seasons/Troon North
Marriott's Camelback Inn
Renaissance
Tucson
Loews Ventana Canyon
Westward Look
CALIFORNIA
Carmel Area
Lodge at Pebble Beach
Los Angeles
Avalon
Barnabey's
Beverly Hills Hotel
Beverly Hilton
Century Plaza
Chateau Marmont
Four Seasons Bev. Hills
Le Merigot Santa Monica
L'Ermitage
Loews Santa Monica
Regent Bev. Wilshire
Ritz-Carlton Marina del Rey
Sofitel
W

Mendocino
Stanford Inn by the Sea
Napa
Harvest Inn
Villagio Inn
Vintage Inn
Newport Beach
Four Seasons
Sutton Place
Ojai
Ojai Valley Inn
Palm Springs Area
La Quinta Resort & Club
Miramonte
San Diego Area
Inn at Rancho Santa Fe
La Costa
La Valencia
Loews Coronado Bay
Marriott's Coronado Island
San Francisco
Best Western Tuscan Inn
Campton Place
Clift
Mandarin Oriental
Monaco
Palomar
Prescott
Serrano
Triton
Westin St. Francis
San Jose
Fairmont Hotel
COLORADO
Aspen
Little Nell
St. Regis
Denver
Loews Giorgio
Monaco
Durango
Sheraton Tamarron
Telluride
Peaks
Vail
Lodge at Vail
DELAWARE
Wilmington
Du Pont
DISTRICT OF COLUMBIA
Washington
Four Seasons
Hay-Adams
Jefferson

Jefferson
Madison
Willard Inter-Continental
FLORIDA
Naples
Ritz-Carlton
GEORGIA
Atlanta
Four Seasons
Ritz-Carlton
ILLINOIS
Chicago
Four Seasons
LOUISIANA
New Orleans
Windsor Court
MASSACHUSETTS
Boston
Four Seasons
Nantucket
Wauwinet
MINNESOTA
Minneapolis/St. Paul
Hyatt Whitney
NEVADA
Las Vegas
Bellagio
NEW YORK
New York City
Carlyle
Four Seasons
New York Palace
Peninsula
Pierre
Plaza Athénée
Regent Wall Street
RIHGA Royal
Trump International
UN Plaza Hotel
Waldorf-Astoria
Westin Essex House
Saranac Lake
Point
PENNSYLVANIA
Philadelphia
Park Hyatt at the Bellevue
Rittenhouse
Ritz-Carlton
Pittsburgh
Westin William Penn
TEXAS
Austin
Driskill

Dallas/Ft. Worth
Adolphus
Mansion on Turtle Creek
El Paso
Camino Real El Paso
Houston
Four Seasons
Houstonian Hotel
VIRGINIA
Arlington
Ritz-Carlton Pentagon City
Richmond
Jefferson

Remote
ALASKA
Denali
Mt. McKinley Princess
Glacier Bay
Glacier Bay Lodge
CALIFORNIA
Gualala
St. Orres
Oakhurst
Chateau du Sureau
San Diego Area
La Casa Del Zorro
CONNECTICUT
Ledyard
Foxwoods
FLORIDA
Keys
Little Palm Island
GEORGIA
Little St. Simons Island
Lodge on Little St. Simons
HAWAII
Maui
Hana-Maui
Molokai
Molokai Ranch Lodge
MAINE
Deer Isle
Pilgrims Inn
MASSACHUSETTS
Nantucket
Wauwinet
MONTANA
Gallatin
Gallatin Gateway Inn
NEW YORK
Saranac Lake
Point

OREGON
Black Butte
Black Butte Ranch
PENNSYLVANIA
Bradford
Glendorn
PUERTO RICO
Rincon
Horned Dorset Primavera
Vieques
Martineau Bay
RHODE ISLAND
Block Island
1661 Inn & Manisses Hotel
SOUTH CAROLINA
Hilton Head
Daufuskie Island Club
VERMONT
Warren
Pitcher Inn
WISCONSIN
Chetek
Canoe Bay
WYOMING
Grand Teton National Park
Jenny Lake Lodge
Jackson
Amangani
Teton Pines Resort

Romantic

ARIZONA
Phoenix/Scottsdale
Boulders
Sedona
L'Auberge de Sedona
CALIFORNIA
Albion
Albion River Inn
Big Sur
Post Ranch Inn
Ventana Inn
Carmel Area
Bernardus Lodge
Highlands Inn
Quail Lodge
Tickle Pink
Dana Point
Ritz-Carlton Laguna Niguel
Laguna Beach
Surf & Sand

Los Angeles
Bel-Air
Malibu Beach Inn
Shutters on the Beach
Monterey
Spindrift Inn
Napa
Auberge du Soleil
Villagio Inn
Vintage Inn
Oakhurst
Chateau du Sureau
San Diego Area
La Valencia
Rancho Valencia
San Francisco
Archbishop's Mansion
Sherman House
White Swan Inn
San Luis Obispo
Apple Farm
Santa Barbara
El Encanto
Four Seasons Biltmore
San Ysidro Ranch
Sausalito
Casa Madrona
CONNECTICUT
Norwich
Norwich Inn
Washington
Mayflower Inn
Westport
Inn at National Hall
DISTRICT OF COLUMBIA
Washington
Henley Park
Latham Georgetown
FLORIDA
Boca Raton
Boca Raton Resort
Keys
Gardens
Little Palm Island
Marquesa
Miami
Mayfair House
Naples
Ritz-Carlton
Vero Beach
Disney's Vero Beach

VIRGINIA
Alexandria
Morrison House
Boyce
L'Auberge Provencal
Washington
Inn at Little Washington
WASHINGTON
Snoqualmie
Salish Lodge
Whidbey Island
Inn at Langley

Rural Settings

ARIZONA
Grand Canyon
El Tovar
Sedona
Enchantment
Tucson
Lodge at Ventana
Tanque Verde Guest Ranch
Wickenburg
Merv Griffin's Wickenburg
CALIFORNIA
Albion
Albion River Inn
Big Sur
Ventana Inn
Carmel Area
Carmel Valley Ranch
Quail Lodge
Stonepine
Gualala
St. Orres
Mendocino
Stanford Inn by the Sea
Napa
Auberge du Soleil
Harvest Inn
Meadowood
Silverado
Santa Barbara
El Encanto
San Ysidro Ranch
Santa Rosa
Vintners Inn
Solvang
Alisal Guest Ranch
Sonoma
Kenwood Inn
Madrona Manor

CONNECTICUT
New Preston
Boulders
Norwich
Norwich Inn
Washington
Mayflower Inn
FLORIDA
Lake Wales
Chalet Suzanne
GEORGIA
Braselton
Chateau Elan
Pine Mountain
Callaway Gardens
ILLINOIS
Galena
Eagle Ridge Inn
KENTUCKY
Harrodsburg
Inn at Shaker Village
LOUISIANA
White Castle
Nottoway Plantation
MAINE
Kennebunkport
White Barn Inn
Ogunquit
Cliff House
MASSACHUSETTS
Deerfield
Deerfield Inn
Lenox
Weathleigh
Sandwich
Dan'l Webster Inn
NEW HAMPSHIRE
Bretton Woods
Mount Washington Resort
Franconia
Franconia Inn
North Conway
White Mountain Hotel
NEW YORK
Amenia
Troutbeck Country Inn
Cooperstown
Otesaga
Saranac Lake
Point
NORTH CAROLINA
Lake Toxaway
Greystone Inn

Pinehurst
Pinehurst Resort
Pittsboro
Fearrington House
OREGON
Black Butte
Black Butte Ranch
Gold Beach
Tu Tu'Tun Lodge
Hood River
Columbia Gorge
PENNSYLVANIA
Erwinna
Evermay on-the-Delaware
VERMONT
Barnard
Twin Farms
Grafton
Old Tavern at Grafton
Quechee
Quechee Inn
Shelburne
Inn at Shelburne Farms
Vergennes
Basin Harbor Club
VIRGINIA
Boyce
L'Auberge Provencal
Charlottesville
Keswick Hall
Hot Springs
Homestead
Washington
Inn at Little Washington
WISCONSIN
Lake Geneva
Grand Geneva
WYOMING
Jackson
Amangani

Scuba Diving

FLORIDA
Boca Raton
Boca Raton Resort
Fort Lauderdale
Marriott's Harbor Beach
Keys
Cheeca Lodge
Hawk's Cay Resort
Hilton Key West
Hyatt Key West
Ocean Reef Club
Wyndham Casa Marina

Miami
Sonesta Key Biscayne
Palm Beach
Breakers
Ritz-Carlton
HAWAII
Big Island
Four Seasons Hualalai
Hilton Waikoloa Village
Kona Village
Mauna Lani Bay Hotel
Kauai
Hyatt Regency
Princeville
Lanai
Manele Bay
Maui
Embassy Suites Kaanapali
Four Seasons Wailea
Grand Wailea
Hyatt Regency
Kapalua Bay Hotel
Kea Lani Resort
Renaissance Wailea
Sheraton
Westin
Westin Maui Prince
Oahu
Kahala Mandarin Oriental
PUERTO RICO
Rincon
Horned Dorset Primavera
Rio Grande
Westin Rio Mar
SOUTH CAROLINA
Charleston
Charleston Place
U.S. VIRGIN ISLANDS
St. Croix
Buccaneer
Carambola
St. John
Caneel Bay
Westin
St. Thomas
Marriott's French/Morn.
Ritz-Carlton
Wyndham Sugar Bay

Skiing

ALASKA
Girdwood
Westin Alyeska

CALIFORNIA
Squaw Valley
Plumpjack's
Resort at Squaw Creek
COLORADO
Aspen
L'Auberge
Little Nell
St. Regis
Beaver Creek
Beaver Creek Lodge
Charter at Beaver Creek
Hyatt Regency
Durango
Sheraton Tamarron
Edwards
Lodge & Spa at Cordillera
Keystone
Keystone Lodge
Telluride
Peaks
Vail
Lodge at Vail
Sonnenalp
Vail Cascade
IDAHO
Sun Valley
Sun Valley
MASSACHUSETTS
Lenox
Cranwell Resort
MONTANA
Whitefish
Grouse Mountain Lodge
NEVADA
Lake Tahoe
Hyatt Regency
Stateline
Harrah's
NEW HAMPSHIRE
Bretton Woods
Mount Washington Resort
Dixville Notch
Balsams Grand
Franconia
Franconia Inn
North Conway
White Mountain Hotel
NEW YORK
Bolton Landing
Sagamore
Lake Placid
Lake Placid Lodge
Mirror Lake Inn

Saranac Lake
Point
OREGON
Black Butte
Black Butte Ranch
PENNSYLVANIA
Farmington
Nemacolin Woodlands
Skytop
Skytop Lodge
UTAH
Deer Valley
Goldener Hirsch
Park City
Stein Eriksen Lodge
Snowbird
Cliff Lodge
Sundance
Sundance
VERMONT
Barnard
Twin Farms
Grafton
Old Tavern at Grafton
Quechee
Quechee Inn
Stowe
Green Mountain Inn
Topnotch at Stowe
Trapp Family Lodge
Woodstock
Woodstock Inn
VIRGINIA
Hot Springs
Homestead
WISCONSIN
Lake Geneva
Grand Geneva
WYOMING
Jackson
Amangani
Rusty Parrot Lodge

Spa Facilities

ARIZONA
Phoenix/Scottsdale
Arizona Biltmore
Boulders
Four Seasons/Troon North
Marriott's Camelback Inn
Phoenician
Sedona
Enchantment

Regent
Venetian
NEW JERSEY
Short Hills
Hilton at Short Hills
NEW YORK
Lake Placid
Mirror Lake Inn
New York City
Benjamin
Four Seasons
Peninsula
NORTH CAROLINA
Asheville
Grove Park Inn
PENNSYLVANIA
Farmington
Nemacolin Woodlands
PUERTO RICO
Fajardo
Las Casitas
Wyndham El Conquistador
San Juan
Ritz-Carlton
TEXAS
Austin
Lake Austin Spa Resort
Dallas/Ft. Worth
Four Seasons/Las Colinas
Houston
Houstonian Hotel
San Antonio
Hyatt Reg. Hill Country
UTAH
Snowbird
Cliff Lodge
VERMONT
Stowe
Topnotch at Stowe
VIRGINIA
Hot Springs
Homestead
Leesburg
Lansdowne
WASHINGTON
Kirkland
Woodmark
Snoqualmie
Salish Lodge
WEST VIRGINIA
White Sulphur Springs
Greenbrier

WISCONSIN
Kohler
American Club
Lake Geneva
Grand Geneva
WYOMING
Jackson
Rusty Parrot Lodge

Super Deluxe

ARIZONA
Phoenix/Scottsdale
Four Seasons/Troon North
Phoenician
CALIFORNIA
Carmel Area
Inn at Spanish Bay
Lodge at Pebble Beach
Stonepine
Dana Point
Ritz-Carlton Laguna Niguel
Los Angeles
Bel-Air
Four Seasons Bev. Hills
L'Ermitage
Peninsula Bev. Hills
Regent Bev. Wilshire
Ritz-Carlton Huntington
Shutters on the Beach
St. Regis
Napa
Auberge du Soleil
Oakhurst
Chateau du Sureau
San Diego Area
Four Seasons Aviara
San Francisco
Campton Place
Mandarin Oriental
Ritz-Carlton
Sherman House
Santa Barbara
Bacara
Four Seasons Biltmore
COLORADO
Aspen
Little Nell
St. Regis
Edwards
Lodge & Spa at Cordillera
CONNECTICUT
Washington
Mayflower Inn

Westport
Inn at National Hall
DISTRICT OF COLUMBIA
Washington
Four Seasons
Ritz-Carlton
St. Regis
FLORIDA
Amelia Island
Ritz-Carlton
Boca Raton
Boca Raton Resort
Keys
Little Palm Island
Miami
Fisher Island Club
Grove Isle Club
Turnberry Isle Resort
Naples
Ritz-Carlton
Orlando
Disney's Grand Floridian
Palm Beach
Breakers
Four Seasons
Ritz-Carlton
GEORGIA
Atlanta
Four Seasons
Ritz-Carlton Buckhead
HAWAII
Big Island
Four Seasons Hualalai
Mauna Lani Bay Hotel
Orchid at Mauna Lani
Westin Mauna Kea Beach
Kauai
Princeville
Lanai
Lodge at Koele
Manele Bay
Maui
Four Seasons Wailea
Grand Wailea
Kea Lani Resort
Ritz-Carlton Kapalua
Oahu
Halekulani
Kahala Mandarin Oriental
ILLINOIS
Chicago
Four Seasons
Ritz-Carlton

LOUISIANA
New Orleans
Ritz-Carlton
Windsor Court
MAINE
Kennebunkport
White Barn Inn
MARYLAND
St. Michaels
Inn at Perry Cabin
MASSACHUSETTS
Boston
Four Seasons
Ritz-Carlton
Lenox
Blantyre
Nantucket
Wauwinet
MISSOURI
St. Louis
Ritz-Carlton
NEVADA
Las Vegas
Bellagio
Four Seasons
Regent
NEW MEXICO
Santa Fe
Inn of the Anasazi
NEW YORK
New York City
Carlyle
Four Seasons
Mark
Omni Berkshire Place
Pierre
Plaza Athénée
St. Regis
Swissôtel
Trump International
Saranac Lake
Point
PENNSYLVANIA
Bradford
Glendorn
Philadelphia
Four Seasons
Rittenhouse
Ritz-Carlton
PUERTO RICO
Dorado
Hyatt Dorado Beach

Fajardo
Las Casitas
Wyndham El Conquistador
Rincon
Horned Dorset Primavera
San Juan
Ritz-Carlton
Wyndham El San Juan
Vieques
Martineau Bay
SOUTH CAROLINA
Charleston
Planters Inn
TENNESSEE
Memphis
Peabody
Walland
Blackberry Farm
TEXAS
Austin
Four Seasons
Dallas/Ft. Worth
Adolphus
Crescent Court
Four Seasons/Las Colinas
Mansion on Turtle Creek
Houston
Four Seasons
St. Regis
U.S. VIRGIN ISLANDS
St. John
Caneel Bay
St. Thomas
Ritz-Carlton
UTAH
Deer Valley
Goldener Hirsch
VERMONT
Barnard
Twin Farms
Warren
Pitcher Inn
VIRGINIA
Charlottesville
Keswick Hall
Washington
Inn at Little Washington
WASHINGTON
Seattle
Bellevue Club
Four Seasons Olympic
WEST VIRGINIA
White Sulphur Springs
Greenbrier

WISCONSIN
Chetek
Canoe Bay
WYOMING
Jackson
Amangani

Swimming Pools

ARIZONA
Phoenix/Scottsdale
Arizona Biltmore
Four Seasons/Troon North
Phoenician
Renaissance
Tucson
Arizona Inn
Sheraton El Conquistador
Westin La Paloma
CALIFORNIA
Los Angeles
Argyle
Avalon
Beverly Hills Hotel
Mondrian
Park Hyatt
Wyndham Bel Age
Palm Springs Area
La Quinta Resort & Club
Marriott's Desert Springs
Westin Mission Hills
FLORIDA
Fort Lauderdale
Marriott's Harbor Beach
Miami
Biltmore
Delano
Loews Miami Beach
Raleigh
Orlando
Disney's Beach Club
Disney's Yacht Club
Hyatt Regency Gr. Cypress
Loews Portofino Bay
Marriott's Orlando World
HAWAII
Kauai
Hanalei Bay Resort
Maui
Four Seasons Wailea
Grand Wailea
Hyatt Regency
Sheraton
Westin

MASSACHUSETTS
Boston
Four Seasons
NEVADA
Las Vegas
Four Seasons
NEW YORK
New York City
Le Parker Meridien
PENNSYLVANIA
Philadelphia
Park Hyatt at the Bellevue
PUERTO RICO
Dorado
Hyatt Regency Cerromar
TEXAS
Dallas/Ft. Worth
Four Seasons/Las Colinas
Wyndham Anatole
San Antonio
Hyatt Reg. Hill Country
U.S. VIRGIN ISLANDS
St. Thomas
Wyndham Sugar Bay
VERMONT
Stowe
Green Mountain Inn
VIRGINIA
Hot Springs
Homestead

Swimming Pools, Private

ARIZONA
Phoenix/Scottsdale
Marriott's Camelback Inn
Sedona
Enchantment
CALIFORNIA
San Diego Area
Rancho Valencia
HAWAII
Big Island
Mauna Lani Bay Hotel
Westin Mauna Kea Beach
LOUISIANA
White Castle
Nottoway Plantation
PUERTO RICO
Rincon
Horned Dorset Primavera

SOUTH CAROLINA
Hilton Head
Palmetto Dunes

Tennis

ARIZONA
Phoenix/Scottsdale
Arizona Biltmore
Boulders
Fairmont Scottsdale Prin.
Four Seasons/Troon North
Phoenician
Wigwam
Sedona
Enchantment
Tucson
Lodge at Ventana
Loews Ventana Canyon
Sheraton El Conquistador
Westin La Paloma
Westward Look
CALIFORNIA
Berkeley
Claremont Resort
Carmel Area
Bernardus Lodge
Carmel Valley Ranch
John Gardiner's Ranch
Lodge at Pebble Beach
Dana Point
Ritz-Carlton Laguna Niguel
Los Angeles
Beverly Hills Hotel
Napa
Meadowood
Silverado
Ojai
Ojai Valley Inn
Palm Springs Area
Hyatt Grand Champions
La Quinta Resort & Club
Marriott's Desert Springs
Marriott's Rch. Las Palmas
Ritz-Carlton Rancho Mirage
Westin Mission Hills
San Diego Area
Four Seasons Aviara
Hyatt Regency
Hyatt Regency La Jolla
La Costa
Rancho Valencia

RHODE ISLAND
Newport
Hyatt Regency
SOUTH CAROLINA
Hilton Head
Daufuskie Island Club
Palmetto Dunes
Sea Pines
Westin
Isle of Palms
Wild Dunes
Kiawah Island
Kiawah Island Resort
TEXAS
Austin
Barton Creek Resort
Dallas/Ft. Worth
Four Seasons/Las Colinas
VERMONT
Stowe
Topnotch at Stowe
WEST VIRGINIA
White Sulphur Springs
Greenbrier

Views

ALASKA
Denali
Mt. McKinley Princess
Girdwood
Westin Alyeska
Glacier Bay
Glacier Bay Lodge
ARIZONA
Grand Canyon
El Tovar
Phoenix/Scottsdale
Hyatt Reg. Gainey Rch.
Pointe Hilton Tapatio Cliffs
Tucson
Loews Ventana Canyon
CALIFORNIA
Berkeley
Claremont Resort
Carmel Area
Carmel Valley Ranch
Highlands Inn
Inn at Spanish Bay
Seven Gables Inn
Tickle Pink

Dana Point
Ritz-Carlton Laguna Niguel
Laguna Beach
Surf & Sand
Los Angeles
Fairmont Hotel
Le Merigot Santa Monica
Loews Santa Monica
Malibu Beach Inn
Ritz-Carlton Marina del Rey
Shangri-La
Shutters on the Beach
Sofitel
Napa
Auberge du Soleil
Palm Springs Area
Marriott's Desert Springs
Ritz-Carlton Rancho Mirage
San Diego Area
Hyatt Regency
Marriott's Coronado Island
San Francisco
Fairmont
Huntington
Mandarin Oriental
Santa Barbara
Bacara
El Encanto
Sausalito
Casa Madrona
Yosemite
Ahwahnee
COLORADO
Denver
Inverness Hotel
Telluride
Peaks
DISTRICT OF COLUMBIA
Washington
Hay-Adams
FLORIDA
Keys
Hyatt Key West
Miami
Tides
Naples
Registry
Orlando
Walt Disney World Dolphin
Walt Disney World Swan

WYOMING
Jackson
Amangani
Teton Pines Resort

Waterside Settings

ALASKA
Glacier Bay
Glacier Bay Lodge
CALIFORNIA
Albion
Albion River Inn
Big Sur
Post Ranch Inn
Carmel Area
Inn at Spanish Bay
Lodge at Pebble Beach
Seven Gables Inn
Tickle Pink
Gualala
St. Orres
Los Angeles
Ritz-Carlton Marina del Rey
Shangri-La
Monterey
Monterey Plaza Hotel
San Diego Area
Loews Coronado Bay
San Diego Marriott
CONNECTICUT
Westport
Inn at National Hall
FLORIDA
Miami
Mandarin Oriental
Orlando
Walt Disney World Dolphin
Walt Disney World Swan
GEORGIA
Savannah
Westin Savannah Harbor
MAINE
Bar Harbor
Bar Harbor Inn
Ogunquit
Cliff House
Rockport
Samoset

MARYLAND
Baltimore
Renaissance Harborpl.
St. Michaels
Inn at Perry Cabin
MASSACHUSETTS
Boston
Boston Harbor Hotel
Seaport Hotel
Martha's Vineyard
Harbor View Hotel
MICHIGAN
Mackinac Island
Grand
MINNESOTA
Minneapolis/St. Paul
Hyatt Whitney
Nicollet Island Inn
NEVADA
Lake Tahoe
Hyatt Regency
Las Vegas
Hyatt Reg. Lake Resort
NEW JERSEY
Atlantic City
Harrah's
Cape May
Inn of Cape May
NEW YORK
Cooperstown
Otesaga
Lake Placid
Mirror Lake Inn
New Paltz
Mohonk Mtn. House
North Hudson
Elk Lake Lodge
Saranac Lake
Point
NORTH CAROLINA
Lake Toxaway
Greystone Inn
OREGON
Gold Beach
Tu Tu'Tun Lodge
PENNSYLVANIA
Erwinna
Evermay on-the-Delaware
RHODE ISLAND
Newport
Castle Hill Inn

SOUTH CAROLINA
Charleston
Hilton Charleston Harbor
TEXAS
Austin
Lake Austin Spa Resort
VERMONT
Shelburne
Inn at Shelburne Farms
VIRGINIA
Irvington
Tides Inn
WASHINGTON
Blaine
Resort Semiahmoo
Kirkland
Woodmark
WISCONSIN
Chetek
Canoe Bay

Water Sports
(on-site)

CALIFORNIA
San Diego Area
Hyatt Regency
FLORIDA
Boca Raton
Boca Raton Resort
Captiva Island
South Seas Resort
Fort Lauderdale
Marriott's Harbor Beach
Keys
Cheeca Lodge
Hawk's Cay Resort
Hilton Key West
Hyatt Key West
Ocean Reef Club
Wyndham Casa Marina
Miami
Sonesta Key Biscayne
Naples
Ritz-Carlton
Palm Beach
Breakers
Four Seasons
Ritz-Carlton
Tampa/St. Petersburg
Colony Beach

GEORGIA
Sea Island
Cloister
HAWAII
Big Island
Four Seasons Hualalai
Hilton Waikoloa Village
Kona Village
Mauna Lani Bay Hotel
Orchid at Mauna Lani
Westin Hapuna Beach
Westin Mauna Kea Beach
Kauai
Hanalei Bay Resort
Hyatt Regency
Princeville
Lanai
Manele Bay
Maui
Embassy Suites Kaanapali
Four Seasons Wailea
Grand Wailea
Hyatt Regency
Kapalua Bay Hotel
Kea Lani Resort
Renaissance Wailea
Sheraton
Westin
Westin Maui Prince
Molokai
Molokai Ranch Lodge
Oahu
JW Marriott Ihilani
Kahala Mandarin Oriental
W
NEVADA
Lake Tahoe
Hyatt Regency
NEW YORK
Bolton Landing
Sagamore
Lake Placid
Lake Placid Lodge
Saranac Lake
Point
NORTH CAROLINA
Lake Toxaway
Greystone Inn

Aerobics/Exercise

ARIZONA
Catalina
Miraval, Life in Balance
Phoenix/Scottsdale
Arizona Biltmore
Boulders
Four Seasons/Troon North
Phoenician
Sedona
Enchantment
Tucson
Canyon Rch. Health Resort
Loews Ventana Canyon
CALIFORNIA
Escondido
Golden Door
Napa
Meadowood
Palm Springs Area
La Quinta Resort
Marriott's Desert Springs
Ritz-Carlton Rcho Mirage
Sonoma
Sonoma Mission Inn
Vista
Cal-a-Vie
COLORADO
Beaver Creek
Hyatt Regency
Colorado Springs
Broadmoor
Edwards
Lodge & Spa at Cordillera
Telluride
Peaks
FLORIDA
Miami
Turnberry Isle Resort
Naples
Ritz-Carlton
Palm Beach
Breakers
Four Seasons
GEORGIA
Sea Island
Cloister
HAWAII
Big Island
Four Seasons Hualalai
Hilton Waikoloa Village
Kauai
Hyatt Regency
Princeville
Lanai
Manele Bay

Maui
Four Seasons Wailea
Ritz-Carlton Kapalua
Oahu
JW Marriott Ihilani
MASSACHUSETTS
Lenox
Canyon Rch./Berkshires
NEVADA
Las Vegas
Venetian
NEW JERSEY
Short Hills
Hilton at Short Hills
NEW YORK
New York City
Four Seasons
PENNSYLVANIA
Farmington
Nemacolin Woodlands
PUERTO RICO
San Juan
Ritz-Carlton
TEXAS
Arlington
Greenhouse
Dallas/Ft. Worth
Four Seasons/Las Colinas
VERMONT
Ludlow
Green Mountain/Fox Run
VIRGINIA
Hot Springs
Homestead
WEST VIRGINIA
White Sulphur Springs
Greenbrier
WISCONSIN
Kohler
American Club

All-Inclusive Price

ARIZONA
Catalina
Miraval, Life in Balance
Tucson
Canyon Rch. Health Resort
CALIFORNIA
Escondido
Golden Door
COLORADO
Vail
Sonnenalp
MASSACHUSETTS
Lenox
Canyon Rch./Berkshires

Beauty

ARIZONA
Catalina
Miraval, Life in Balance
Phoenix/Scottsdale
Arizona Biltmore
Boulders
Four Seasons/Troon North
Phoenician
Sedona
Enchantment
Tucson
Canyon Rch. Health Resort
Loews Ventana Canyon
CALIFORNIA
Carmel Area
Lodge at Pebble Beach
Escondido
Golden Door
Los Angeles
Peninsula Bev. Hills
Napa
Meadowood
Villagio Inn & Spa
Palm Springs Area
La Quinta Resort
Marriott's Desert Springs
Ritz-Carlton Rcho Mirage
San Diego Area
Four Seasons Aviara
Santa Barbara
Four Seasons Biltmore
Sonoma
Sonoma Mission Inn
Vista
Cal-a-Vie
COLORADO
Beaver Creek
Hyatt Regency
Colorado Springs
Broadmoor
Edwards
Lodge & Spa at Cordillera
Telluride
Peaks
Vail
Sonnenalp
FLORIDA
Miami
Turnberry Isle Resort
Naples
Ritz-Carlton
Palm Beach
Breakers
Four Seasons

GEORGIA
Sea Island
Cloister
HAWAII
Big Island
Four Seasons Hualalai
Hilton Waikoloa Village
Orchid at Mauna Lani
Kauai
Hyatt Regency
Princeville
Lanai
Manele Bay
Maui
Four Seasons Wailea
Ritz-Carlton Kapalua
Oahu
JW Marriott Ihilani
MASSACHUSETTS
Lenox
Canyon Rch./Berkshires
NEVADA
Las Vegas
Bellagio
Venetian
NEW JERSEY
Short Hills
Hilton at Short Hills
NEW YORK
New York City
Four Seasons
PENNSYLVANIA
Farmington
Nemacolin Woodlands
PUERTO RICO
San Juan
Ritz-Carlton
TEXAS
Arlington
Greenhouse
Dallas/Ft. Worth
Four Seasons/Las Colinas
UTAH
St. George
Green Valley Spa
VIRGINIA
Hot Springs
Homestead
WEST VIRGINIA
White Sulphur Springs
Greenbrier
WISCONSIN
Kohler
American Club

Diet/Nutrition

ARIZONA
Catalina
Miraval, Life in Balance
Phoenix/Scottsdale
Four Seasons/Troon North
Phoenician
Sedona
Enchantment
Tucson
Canyon Rch. Health Resort
Loews Ventana Canyon
CALIFORNIA
Escondido
Golden Door
Napa
Meadowood
Palm Springs Area
La Quinta Resort
San Diego Area
Four Seasons Aviara
Sonoma
Sonoma Mission Inn
Vista
Cal-a-Vie
COLORADO
Colorado Springs
Broadmoor
Edwards
Lodge & Spa at Cordillera
Telluride
Peaks
FLORIDA
Naples
Ritz-Carlton
Palm Beach
Four Seasons
GEORGIA
Sea Island
Cloister
HAWAII
Big Island
Four Seasons Hualalai
Hilton Waikoloa Village
Orchid at Mauna Lani
Kauai
Hyatt Regency
Princeville
Maui
Ritz-Carlton Kapalua
Oahu
JW Marriott Ihilani
MASSACHUSETTS
Lenox
Canyon Rch./Berkshires

NEVADA
Las Vegas
Venetian
PENNSYLVANIA
Farmington
Nemacolin Woodlands
PUERTO RICO
San Juan
Ritz-Carlton
TEXAS
Arlington
Greenhouse
Dallas/Ft. Worth
Four Seasons/Las Colinas
VERMONT
Ludlow
Green Mountain/Fox Run
WEST VIRGINIA
White Sulphur Springs
Greenbrier
WISCONSIN
Kohler
American Club

Dining Excellence

ARIZONA
Catalina
Miraval, Life in Balance
Phoenix/Scottsdale
Arizona Biltmore
Boulders
Four Seasons/Troon North
Phoenician
Sedona
Enchantment
Tucson
Canyon Rch. Health Resort
CALIFORNIA
Big Sur
Post Ranch Inn
Ventana Inn
Escondido
Golden Door
Los Angeles
Peninsula Bev. Hills
Palm Springs Area
Ritz-Carlton Rcho Mirage
San Diego Area
Four Seasons Aviara
COLORADO
Edwards
Lodge & Spa at Cordillera
FLORIDA
Amelia Island
Ritz-Carlton
Naples
Ritz-Carlton

Palm Beach
Four Seasons
HAWAII
Big Island
Four Seasons Hualalai
Kauai
Hyatt Regency
Lanai
Manele Bay
Maui
Four Seasons Wailea
Ritz-Carlton Kapalua
NEVADA
Las Vegas
Bellagio
NEW YORK
New York City
Four Seasons
WEST VIRGINIA
White Sulphur Springs
Greenbrier

Hiking/Walking

ARIZONA
Catalina
Miraval, Life in Balance
Phoenix/Scottsdale
Arizona Biltmore
Boulders
Four Seasons/Troon North
Phoenician
Sedona
Enchantment
Tucson
Canyon Rch. Health Resort
Loews Ventana Canyon
CALIFORNIA
Big Sur
Post Ranch Inn
Ventana Inn
Escondido
Golden Door
Napa
Meadowood
Palm Springs Area
La Quinta Resort
Marriott's Desert Springs
Ritz-Carlton Rcho Mirage
San Diego Area
Four Seasons Aviara
Sonoma
Sonoma Mission Inn
Vista
Cal-a-Vie
COLORADO
Beaver Creek
Hyatt Regency

Colorado Springs
Broadmoor
Edwards
Lodge & Spa at Cordillera
Telluride
Peaks
Vail
Sonnenalp
FLORIDA
Naples
Ritz-Carlton
Palm Beach
Breakers
Four Seasons
GEORGIA
Sea Island
Cloister
HAWAII
Big Island
Four Seasons Hualalai
Hilton Waikoloa Village
Orchid at Mauna Lani
Kauai
Hyatt Regency
Princeville
Lanai
Manele Bay
Maui
Four Seasons Wailea
Ritz-Carlton Kapalua
Oahu
JW Marriott Ihilani
MASSACHUSETTS
Lenox
Canyon Rch./Berkshires
PENNSYLVANIA
Farmington
Nemacolin Woodlands
PUERTO RICO
San Juan
Ritz-Carlton
TEXAS
Dallas/Ft. Worth
Four Seasons/Las Colinas
UTAH
St. George
Green Valley Spa
VERMONT
Ludlow
Green Mountain/Fox Run
VIRGINIA
Hot Springs
Homestead
WEST VIRGINIA
White Sulphur Springs
Greenbrier

WISCONSIN
Kohler
American Club

Hydrotherapy

ARIZONA
Catalina
Miraval, Life in Balance
Phoenix/Scottsdale
Arizona Biltmore
Four Seasons/Troon North
Sedona
Enchantment
Tucson
Canyon Rch. Health Resort
CALIFORNIA
Carmel Area
Lodge at Pebble Beach
Desert Hot Springs
Two Bunch Palms
Escondido
Golden Door
Los Angeles
Peninsula Bev. Hills
Napa
Villagio Inn & Spa
Palm Springs Area
La Quinta Resort
Sonoma
Sonoma Mission Inn
COLORADO
Beaver Creek
Hyatt Regency
Colorado Springs
Broadmoor
Edwards
Lodge & Spa at Cordillera
Telluride
Peaks
FLORIDA
Naples
Ritz-Carlton
GEORGIA
Sea Island
Cloister
HAWAII
Big Island
Hilton Waikoloa Village
Maui
Ritz-Carlton Kapalua
Oahu
JW Marriott Ihilani
MASSACHUSETTS
Lenox
Canyon Rch./Berkshires

NEVADA
Las Vegas
Bellagio
Venetian
NEW MEXICO
Santa Fe
Ten Thousand Waves
PENNSYLVANIA
Farmington
Nemacolin Woodlands
PUERTO RICO
San Juan
Ritz-Carlton
TEXAS
Dallas/Ft. Worth
Four Seasons/Las Colinas
UTAH
St. George
Green Valley Spa
VIRGINIA
Hot Springs
Homestead
WEST VIRGINIA
White Sulphur Springs
Greenbrier
WISCONSIN
Kohler
American Club

Meditation

ARIZONA
Catalina
Miraval, Life in Balance
Phoenix/Scottsdale
Boulders
Phoenician
Sedona
Enchantment
Tucson
Canyon Rch. Health Resort
Loews Ventana Canyon
CALIFORNIA
Big Sur
Ventana Inn
Escondido
Golden Door
Palm Springs Area
La Quinta Resort
Sonoma
Sonoma Mission Inn
COLORADO
Edwards
Lodge & Spa at Cordillera
Telluride
Peaks

FLORIDA
Palm Beach
Four Seasons
GEORGIA
Sea Island
Cloister
HAWAII
Big Island
Four Seasons Hualalai
Hilton Waikoloa Village
Orchid at Mauna Lani
Oahu
JW Marriott Ihilani
MASSACHUSETTS
Lenox
Canyon Rch./Berkshires
NEW JERSEY
Short Hills
Hilton at Short Hills
PENNSYLVANIA
Farmington
Nemacolin Woodlands
WISCONSIN
Kohler
American Club

Mineral Springs

CALIFORNIA
Sonoma
Sonoma Mission Inn
PENNSYLVANIA
Farmington
Nemacolin Woodlands
VIRGINIA
Hot Springs
Homestead
WEST VIRGINIA
White Sulphur Springs
Greenbrier
WISCONSIN
Kohler
American Club

New Age

ARIZONA
Catalina
Miraval, Life in Balance
Sedona
Enchantment
Tucson
Canyon Rch. Health Resort
CALIFORNIA
Palm Springs Area
La Quinta Resort
Sonoma
Sonoma Mission Inn

COLORADO
Edwards
Lodge & Spa at Cordillera
Telluride
Peaks
FLORIDA
Palm Beach
Breakers
Four Seasons
HAWAII
Kauai
Princeville
MASSACHUSETTS
Lenox
Canyon Rch./Berkshires
NEW MEXICO
Santa Fe
Ten Thousand Waves
UTAH
St. George
Green Valley Spa
WISCONSIN
Kohler
American Club

Super Deluxe

ARIZONA
Catalina
Miraval, Life in Balance
Phoenix/Scottsdale
Four Seasons/Troon North
Phoenician
CALIFORNIA
Big Sur
Post Ranch Inn
Escondido
Golden Door
San Diego Area
Four Seasons Aviara
Santa Barbara
Four Seasons Biltmore
FLORIDA
Palm Beach
Four Seasons
HAWAII
Big Island
Four Seasons Hualalai
Lanai
Manele Bay
Maui
Four Seasons Wailea
MASSACHUSETTS
Lenox
Canyon Rch./Berkshires
NEW YORK
New York City
Four Seasons

Alphabetical Page Index

Alphabetical Page Index

Alphabetical Page Index